ESSAYS IN
Modern Stylistics

ESSAYS IN
Modern Stylistics

Edited by
Donald C. Freeman

Methuen London and New York

First published in 1981 by
Methuen & Co. Ltd
11 New Fetter Lane, London EC4P 4EE

Published in the USA by
Methuen & Co.
in association with Methuen, Inc.
733 Third Avenue, New York, NY 10017

This collection © 1981 Methuen & Co. Ltd

Filmset in Hong Kong by Asco Trade Typesetting Ltd
Printed in the United States of America

All rights reserved. No part of this book may be reprinted
or reproduced or utilized in any form or by any electronic,
mechanical or other means, now known or hereafter
invented, including photocopying and recording, or in any
information storage or retrieval system, without permission
in writing from the publishers.

British Library Cataloguing in Publication Data

Essays in modern stylistics.
   1. English literature – History and criticism
   2. English language – Style
  I. Freeman, Donald Cary
   820   PR83   80-41753

ISBN 0-416-74420-6
ISBN 0-416-74430-3 (University paperbacks; 731)

Contents

Acknowledgements	*vii*
I Foreword	**1**
II General theory	**5**
1 The role of linguistics in a theory of poetry *Paul Kiparsky*	9
2 Literary competence *Jonathan Culler*	24
3 Generative grammar and stylistic analysis *J. P. Thorne*	42
4 What is stylistics and why are they saying such terrible things about it? *Stanley E. Fish*	53
III Approaches to poetics	**79**
5 Keats's 'To Autumn': poetry as process and pattern *Donald C. Freeman*	83
6 Wallace Stevens: form and meaning in four poems *Samuel Jay Keyser*	100
7 Syntactic deviation and cohesion *Irene R. Fairley*	123
8 Constraints on syntactic rules and the style of Shelley's 'Adonais': an exercise in stylistic criticism *Timothy R. Austin*	138
9 The self-reflexive artefact: the function of mimesis in an approach to a theory of value for literature *E. L. Epstein*	166
IV Approaches to metrics	**201**
10 The iambic pentameter *Morris Halle and Samuel Jay Keyser*	206
11 Stress, syntax and meter *Paul Kiparsky*	225

12 Towards a formal poetics: metrical patterning in 'The Windhover' *Charles T. Scott*   273
13 A generative metrical analysis of 'Sir Gawain and the Green Knight' *Justine T. Stillings*   290

V Approaches to prose style   **321**

14 Linguistic function and literary style: an inquiry into the language of William Golding's 'The Inheritors' *M. A. K. Halliday*   325
15 Speech, literature and the space between *Richard Ohmann*   361
16 Literary cooperation and implicature *Mary Louise Pratt*   377

   Suggestions for further reading   413

Acknowledgements

The editor and publishers would like to thank the following for permission to reproduce copyright material: Ch. 1: *Daedalus*, Journal of the American Academy of Arts and Sciences, Boston, Mass; summer 1973, *Language as a Human Problem*. Ch. 2: Routledge & Kegan Paul Ltd and Cornell University Press; from *Structuralist Poetics* (1975) by Jonathan Culler. Ch. 3: Penguin Books Ltd; from *New Horizons in Linguistics* (Pelican, 1970) ed. John Lyons. Ch. 4: Columbia University Press; from *Approaches to Poetics* (1973) ed. S. Chatman. Ch. 5: *Language and Style* (1978) XI, 3–17. Ch. 6: National Council of Teachers of English; from *College English* (1976) XXXVII. Ch. 7: *Language and Style* (1973) VI, 216–29. Ch. 8: North-Holland Publishing Company; from *Poetics and Theory of Literature* (1979) 4, 315–43. Ch. 9: *Language and Style*; reprinted in *Style and Structure in Literature* (1975) ed. Roger Fowler (Basil Blackwell and Cornell University Press). Ch. 10: New York University Press; from *Versification: Major Language Types* (1972) ed. W. K. Wimsatt. Ch. 11: Linguistic Society of America; from *Language* (1975) LI, 576–616. Ch. 12: *Language and Style* (1974) VII, 91–101. Ch. 13: *Language and Style* (1976) IX, 219–46. Ch. 14: Oxford University Press, Inc.; from *Literary Style: A Symposium* (1971) ed. S. Chatman. Ch. 15: The Johns Hopkins University Press; from *New Literary History* (1972) IV, 47–64. Ch. 16: Indiana University Press; from *Toward A Speech Act Theory of Literary Discourse* (1977) by Mary Louise Pratt.

Material quoted within chapters: Doubleday & Co., Inc. and Faber & Faber Ltd for 'Dolour' (© 1943 Modern Poetry Association, Inc.); reprinted from *The Collected Poems of Theodore Roethke*. Harcourt Brace Jovanovich, Inc. and Faber & Faber Ltd for extracts from *The Inheritors* by William Golding (© 1955 William Golding). Harcourt Brace Jovanovich, Inc. and Granada Publishing Ltd for 'a like a' (© 1946 E. E. Cummings, renewed 1974 Nancy T. Andrews) and 'me up at does' (© 1963 Marion Morehouse Cummings); reprinted from *Complete Poems 1913–1962* by E. E. Cummings. Liveright Publishing Corporation and Granada Publishing Ltd for 'tumbling hair', 'all in green went my lover riding' and 'when God lets my body be' (© 1923, 1925, renewed 1951, 1953 E. E. Cummings; © 1973, 1976 Nancy T. Andrews; © 1973, 1976 George James Firmage); reprinted from *Tulips and Chimneys* by E. E. Cummings. Alfred A. Knopf, Inc. and Faber & Faber Ltd for 'Anecdote of the Jar', 'The Death of a Soldier', 'The Snow Man' (© 1923, renewed 1951 Wallace Stevens) and 'Poetry is a Destructive Force' (© 1942 Wallace Stevens, renewed 1970 Holly Stevens); reprinted from *The Collected Poems of Wallace Stevens*.

I
Foreword

Foreword

Ten years ago, I brought out a collection of essays, *Linguistics and Literary Style* (New York: Holt, Rinehart, & Winston, 1970), in what was then the new and emerging field of stylistics: the application of linguistics to the study of literature. This volume was, perhaps correctly, criticized by one reviewer as 'old hat', for its aims were modest: to assemble what then seemed to be the major theoretical documents in the field; to represent significant approaches and subject matters, and to include essays indicating promising new directions for further work.

Now, a decade later, the field of stylistics may fairly be said to have come of age. An increasing number of colleges and universities in the United States, Great Britain, and Europe offer courses in stylistics at the undergraduate and graduate levels on a regular basis both in literature and in linguistics departments. Several new journals in the field have been founded, and those which had just been started when *Linguistics and Literary Style* was published have become firmly established. Articles on the relationship of linguistics and literature have begun to appear with some regularity in scholarly journals formerly devoted nearly exclusively to one of the two fields. Professional conferences in both areas hold regular discussion groups and paper sections in stylistics. And the entire question of linguistic approaches to literature has recently become a subject of considerable controversy, a fact reflected in one of the essays reprinted here, and elsewhere in several essays and replies.

The field of stylistics has become so large and diffuse as to defy easy summary, and I shall make no attempt at one here. For my assessment of the state of the art as of 1973, see my 'Literature', in *A Survey of Applied Linguistics*, ed. H. Douglas Brown and Ronald Wardhaugh (Ann Arbor: University of Michigan Press, 1973), pp. 229–49. See also the annual stylistics bibliography in *Style*.

In what follows I have made no attempt to represent this diversity, but have rather reprinted those essays which seem to me to indicate the most promising directions for further practical work, and are of the greatest potential use for students in the field. The linguistic approaches in these essays center for the most part, with one exception, on modern transformational-generative grammar and its ramifications. Except for the section on prose style (an area of the field in which there has, in recent years, been less practical work and more in the way of programmatic and theoretical statement), these essays offer various theoretical frameworks for further practical work in stylistics. What I see as the field's four major divisions – general theory, poetics, metrics, and prose style – is reflected in the organization and selection of the book's table of contents. I have included only the barest minimum of editorial apparatus, being content to let the essays speak for themselves. I have included for convenience a brief summary of the essays in each section. The essays include statements both by major figures in the discipline and by younger scholars; the sole criterion for selection has been what I see as a particular essay's significance for future work in stylistics.

For advice and encouragement, both in the compilation of this book and more generally over the years since the publication of *Linguistics and Literary Style*, to which *Essays in Modern Stylistics* should be viewed as a companion volume, I should like to express my thanks to Margaret H. Freeman, John Robert Ross, Muffy E. A. Siegel, Timothy Austin, Roger Fowler, J. P. Thorne, E. L. Epstein, Terence Hawkes, Bruce Fraser, Samuel Jay Keyser, Roland Posner, Herbert E. Brekle, Francis J. Sullivan, George R. Deaux, and Janice Price of Methuen & Co. Ltd. Special thanks are due to the helpful library staffs of the University of Nottingham and the University of Leicester, and to Timothy Costello of the Department of English at Temple University. I am particularly grateful to Donald and Ann Kanter for providing a haven of English peace in which I could complete the final editing of the manuscript.

D. C. F.
Woodland View
Belton, Rutland
January, 1980

II
General theory

Introduction

The essays in Part II of *Essays in Modern Stylistics* all are concerned with various aspects of general theory in stylistics. Of the essays in this section, the most general and far-reaching is Paul Kiparsky's 'The role of linguistics in a theory of poetry'. Kiparsky argues that the essence of poetic expression is the patterned repetition of linguistic sames, and holds that the key questions for a theory of poetic form are: (1) what patterns are relevant in poetry, and (2) what linguistic sames are relevant in poetry. Modern transformational-generative linguistics has, Kiparsky shows, a key role to play in providing answers to the second of these questions in the areas of syntax and phonology, and provides a rich range of examples in support of his hypothesis.

For Jonathan Culler, in 'Literary competence' (a chapter of his *Structuralist Poetics*), the mind cannot be a *tabula rasa* in approaching a literary work. To the task of literary interpretation we bring a 'literary competence', analogous to what Noam Chomsky calls linguistic competence, an array of linguistic knowledge structured along highly predetermined lines. Without literary competence, Culler argues, the act of interpretation would be meaningless, and for him literary competence consists of a set of interpretive conventions such as significance, metaphorical coherence, poetic tradition, or thematic unity, all of which have been assimilated by the reader before he begins the act of reading. These interpretive conventions create certain effects in the reader for particular poems, and it is the task of structuralist poetics, on Culler's account, to make explicit the system which creates such effects. Reading literature thus becomes a 'rule-governed process of producing meanings', and poetics the process of discovering those rules.

In 'Generative grammar and stylistic analysis', J. P. Thorne argues that modern generative grammar has importance for modern stylistics because both are mentalistic; both are concerned with the same kind of phenomena. Aspects of literary style are related to the structural properties of sentences as they are described by transformational-generative grammar. Most predominantly stylistic judgments, Thorne claims, are related to properties of syntactic deep structure. Thus the task of generative grammar in stylistics in the construction of grammars which formally account for literary interpretation.

Stanley E. Fish's 'What is stylistics and why are they saying such terrible things about it?' is the most trenchant and best argued of the many recent attacks on the enterprise of stylistics. While not all researchers in the field, including the present writer, would agree with many of the claims Fish imputes to stylistics (see Section VI, 'Selections for further reading'), Fish's essay points up several controversial aspects in recent work. Readers may assess the validity of Fish's attacks by reading the essays he discusses, several of which are reprinted in this volume. The reader-independent neutral facts which Fish argues stylistics describes are, for him, only the deposits of a specifically human activity, reading, and it is that activity – and only that activity – which can confer meaning on the data of stylistics.

1
The role of linguistics in a theory of poetry

Paul Kiparsky

Of all art forms, literature, and especially poetry, has the greatest continuity of form in the Western tradition.[1] Since classical antiquity, the visual arts and music have been changed profoundly through the introduction of entirely new forms of expression and organization. Consider, for example, how painting was changed in the Renaissance by the discovery of perspective, or how music was changed by the development of chordal harmony. It is impossible, however, to point to any such spectacular enrichments of technique in poetry. Styles and conventions have shifted, but no truly new forms have emerged. Both of the fundamental stylistic elements of poetry – figurative expression, using, for example, metaphor and metonymy, and schemes of formal organization such as those of parallelism, meter, rhyme, and alliteration – have existed from the beginning.

It is true that their relative importance changes all the time. In particular, the rules governing what must, may, and cannot be obligatory in a piece of verse vary from one age to the next. For example, alliteration was obligatory in Old English poetry a thousand years ago, but cannot be obligatory today, and rhyme, which was never an obligatory formal element in Old English, can and in certain forms of verse must be used now. Many such seemingly radical changes in poetic form are actually more or less automatic responses to linguistic change. Alliteration, for example, seems to be found as an obligatory formal element only in languages where the stress regularly falls on the same syllable in the word, which then must be the alliterating syllable. Old English was such a language, for the stress fell predictably on the root syllable. In modern English, on the other hand, words with the same root can be stressed in many different places (take, for example, *ób li gate*, *ob líg a tor y*, and *ob li gá tion*). When this kind of stress system was established in English, verse forms with fixed alliteration were abandoned. The rhymed verse forms which took their place were made possible, or at least more natural, by the evolution of English, specifically by the fact that English lost most of its inflectional endings. Most richly inflected languages do not use rhyme, and those that do, like Russian, tend to avoid rhymes that depend on grammatical endings.

When a particular element ceases to be obligatory, it remains as an optional element in the poetic repertoire of a language. In fact, optional elements of form in a poem are more significant than obligatory elements, precisely because the poet has chosen to use them. In plain rhymed verse, a pair of rhyming words may or may not be related in meaning.[2] Where rhyme is not obligatory, on the other hand, those words which do rhyme are almost always significantly related, as they are, for example, in the internal rhyme in Hopkins's line,

> And all is seared with trade; bleared, smeared with toil....

Similarly, compare the obligatory and therefore only potentially meaningful repetition of lines in refrains or blues verses, with the free and therefore necessarily significant repetition of the line, in Frost's 'Stopping by Woods',

> And miles to go before I sleep.

In obligatory formulaic parallelism, like that found in the Finnish *Kalevala*, the parallel lines may contrast with or complement each other, but they may also be little more than paraphrases. But where parallelism is used as a free feature, it is always essential to the meaning, as in George Starbuck's 'Of Late',

> 'Stephen Smith, University of Iowa sophomore, burned what he said was his draft card'
> and Norman Morrison, Quaker, of Baltimore Maryland, burned what he said was himself.
> You, Robert McNamara, burned what you said was a concentration of the Enemy Aggressor.
> No news medium troubled to put it in quotes.

As a further example, consider Starbuck's use of rhythm. Because he has not tied himself down to a fixed meter, he can use rhythmic variation to reinforce his meaning. The slow regular dactylic rhythm of the second line breaks down completely when McNamara's lies are cited in the third and fourth lines. The changed rhythm also contributes to the sense by directing an accusing stress onto the second 'you' in the line,

> Yóu, Róbert McNamára, búrned what yóu said wás a cóncentrátion of the Énemy Aggréssor.

In such ways, 'free verse' actually frees verse schemas for significant use; hence it can be a more difficult and a more expressive poetic form than regulated verse.

Perhaps our first impulse is to attribute the fact that the forms of poetic expression have not changed much to the sheer weight of the western literary tradition. However, there are several reasons for believing that we must attribute it, at least in part, to the intrinsic nature of verbal art. In the first place, from the available information it appears that all literary traditions, including those of primitive societies in many of which oral poetry plays an important role, utilize the same elements of form as western poetry, and no exotically different ones. In fact it is not clear that there is any such thing as 'primitive literature'. Furthermore, many of the changes in poetic form, at least in the last 200 years, have been conscious innovations made by poets deliberately breaking with tradition. Yet even this conscious search for new forms has left the basic elements of expression essentially unchanged. Certain schemas have gone from obligatory to free or vice versa, and the grammar of poetic language has changed, for example, in its treatment of inversions. The reason, as I will try to show here, is that a good number of what we think of as traditional and arbitrary conventions are anchored in grammatical form, and seem to be, at bottom, a consequence of how language itself is structured.

The *theory of literature* usually concerns itself with classifying, analyzing, and comparing forms of verbal art which do, in fact, exist. But one could ask what characterizes existing forms of verbal art that differentiates them from forms which have never actually come into existence. Could we develop, in other words, a counterpart in the theory of literature to universal grammar in linguistics?[3] Although certain limits are implicit in traditional esthetics and rhetoric, neither poets nor students of literature have thought much about the intrinsic limits of poetry, any more than football players or spectators think much about gravity. The limits of poetic form are simply psychological givens, just as gravity is a physical given. In trying to define them we will have to make the effort, required wherever man studies his own nature, of not taking the 'natural' for granted.

Our starting point will be the observation that various aspects of form all involve some kind of recurrence of equivalent linguistic elements.[4] They differ only in what linguistic element is repeated. Recurrence of *syntactic* elements is called *parallelism*; recurrence of *stress* and *quantity* (and, in some languages, *tone*), is called *meter*; and various kinds of recurrence of *vocalic* and *consonantal* sounds are called *rhyme, alliteration, assonance,* or *consonance.*

We can therefore conceive of poetic form in terms of certain *patterns,* such as *aa, aab, abab,* which are filled by *linguistic* (syntactic and phonological) *elements.* A pattern which is filled in a particular way may be termed a *schema.* A given pattern therefore underlies many potential schemas. For example, *abab* is a *rhyme schema* if *a* and *b* are units which are phonological sames of the kind we commonly called rhyme. If they are units of stress or quantity it is a *metrical schema.* For example, if *a* is an unstressed syllable, and *b* is a stressed syllable, the pattern *abab* represents iambic dimeter.[5] The same pattern, *abab,* can also be a *schema of syntactic parallelism,* such as that found in the first verse of Shelley's 'Song to the Men of England'.

> Men of England, wherefore plow
> For the lords who lay ye low?
> Wherefore weave with toil and care
> The rich robes your tyrants wear?

Understanding this distinction between the abstract pattern and the linguistic sames that are used to fill it will help us to approach in a more precise way the question of the intrinsic limits of poetic form.

The range of patterns in actual poetic use is small. Surprisingly enough, certain patterns of considerable formal simplicity are never utilized in the construction of verse. For example, one rarely encounters patterns which call for repeating sequences of more than three elements. The pattern *abcdabcd*, for example, is rarely used either as a rhyme schema, or as a pattern of parallelism. The choice of pattern, of course, depends in some measure on what sort of linguistic element is to fill it. For example, the pattern *abcabc* is common in short-term, line-internal recurrence, such as meter, but not so common in cross-line recurrence such as parallelism and rhyme, evidently because it is psychologically easier to keep track of as many as three elements if they recur fairly quickly. However, the fact remains that overriding constraints prevent the use of some potential patterns, regardless of the linguistic elements which might be used to fill them.

The range of linguistic *sames* actually in poetic use is likewise limited. One can easily dream up great numbers of plausible-looking principles of organization which no poet ever uses, and, more importantly, which even the most experimental poet would intuitively recognize as irrelevant were he introduced to a piece of work based on them. (Of course, if he were challenged to do so, he might detect them, by much the same process that a code is cracked.) For example, no one thinks of filling in a stanzaic pattern on the principle that the last words of certain lines must contain the same number of sounds. Nor do we find a type of rhyme in which the last sound or the last *n* sounds must be the same. (We will return to this question in the discussion of slant rhyme below). Naturally not, we might say. But a visiting Martian might find these nonexistent conventions no more peculiar than, for example, the Earthlings' custom of *rhyming*, whereby the last stressed vowel and anything that follows it must be the same.

To answer our Martian's objection would require a theory of poetic form that included a precise answer to the following two questions:

> What patterns are relevant in poetry?
> What linguistic sames are relevant in poetry?

Such a theory does not exist, although we do have certain useful bits and pieces. In what follows I should like to sketch out a partial answer to the second of these questions, in which I will argue that linguistics has a key role to play.

An initial tentative answer is this: *the linguistic sames which are potentially relevant in poetry are just those which are potentially relevant in grammar*. Since one part of the theory of generative grammar is a precise characterization of what sames are relevant in grammar, we can test this hypothesis very specifically. In fact, the hypothesis is so rich that its implications can hardly be grasped yet, let alone fully tested. All we can do here is to explore its consequences in particular areas. By doing so, we can clarify some long-standing questions of poetics as well as some that have thus far gone unasked.

Transformational grammar defines 'grammatically relevant sameness' in terms of syntax by analyzing the constituent structure of sentences. First of all sentences are analyzed according to tree diagrams like this one:

(A)
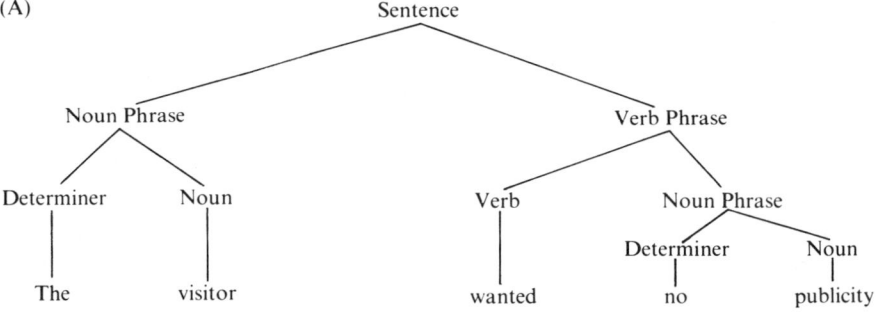

Such a tree structure shows how a sentence can be analyzed on various different levels. For example, depending on which level of the tree one looks at, the above sentence is described as made up of

    Determiner + Noun + Verb + Determiner + Noun

or of

    Noun Phrase + Verb + Noun Phrase

or of

    Noun Phrase + Verb Phrase.

Such trees can be turned into other trees according to *transformational rules*. The tree above is a surface structure and has undergone a number of transformations; it derives directly, for instance, from another tree, shown on the next page, which is one step closer to the original, or *deep structure*, a tree in which the negation marker stands at the beginning of the sentence. The transformational rule moves the negation marker 'not' into the determiner 'any' of tree (B), and the resulting 'not any' becomes 'no' in the phrase 'no publicity' of sentence (A). In this transformation, 'any publicity' is changed at the Determiner + Noun level of the tree. Other transfor-

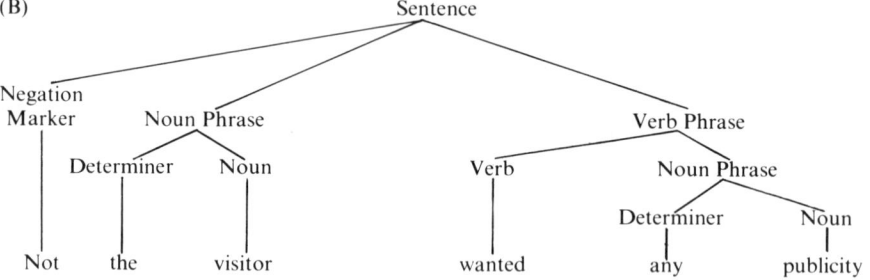

mations, such as the passive transformation, would treat it at the Noun Phrase level.

    A transformational syntax of a language provides a derivation from a deep structure via many intermediate trees to a surface structure for each sentence in the language. These derivations say what elements can and cannot count as the same with respect to syntax: two elements count as the same at a given stage in the transformational derivation if they are labeled alike in the tree for that stage. My hypothesis is that those syntactic elements which are counted as parallel for purpose of verse are, at some point in the derivation, counted as sames according to transformational grammar. Let me now map out existing varieties of syntactic parallelism in poetry, using the syntactic notions of constituent structure and transformational rules.

The poetry of both Walt Whitman and Dylan Thomas abounds in parallelism; this is one reason for the driving, incantatory quality which they have in common. But there is a big difference between the parallelism of the poets, as is clear from these excerpts.

> Where the striped and starred flag is borne at the
>   head of the regiments;
> Approaching Manhattan, up by the long-stretching
>   island,
> Under Niagara, the cataract falling like a veil
>   over my countenance;
> Upon a door-step ... upon the horse-block of hard
>   wood outside,
> Upon the race-course, or enjoying pic-nics or
>   jigs or a good game of base-ball....
>   Whitman, *Leaves of Grass*

> A process in the weather of the heart
> Turns damp to dry; the golden shot
> Storms in the freezing tomb.
> A weather in the quarter of the veins
> Turns night to day; blood in their suns
> Lights up the living worm.
>   Thomas, 'A Process in the
>   Weather of the Heart'

The difference derives from the level of constituent structure for which the parallelism holds. Walt Whitman characteristically uses what we may call *loose* parallelism, in which only the highest syntactic constituents of the tree diagram are the same; although he uses a place adverbial in every line, each one differs from the others in form and complexity. In contrast, Dylan Thomas uses a *strict* parallelism, in which even constituents on the lower levels of the tree diagram are parallel. In other words, Whitman uses larger syntactic blocks to build his parallel structure. Now all form in poetry is potentially functional: this syntactic difference, for example, corresponds directly to the contrast between the 'metonymic' Whitman and the typically 'metaphoric' Thomas.

But parallelism can vary stylistically not only with respect to the level in the tree at which it is determined, but also with respect to the stage in the syntactic derivation from deep to surface structure for which it holds. Aside from actual repetition (as in refrains or blues verses) no syntactic parallelism is ever required to be complete on the level of surface structure. Even the strictest parallelism allows divergence of surface structure according to certain types of transformational rules that delete and reorder constituents. Thus, Dylan Thomas's

> The force that through the green fuse drives the flower
> Drives my green age,

is strictly parallel to

> The force that drives the water through the rocks
> Drives my red blood,

in spite of the fact that the constituents are crossed. Even in the obligatory strict parallelism of Finnish folk poetry, word order may vary freely.

Similar observations may be made about syntactic deletion. In Finnish folk poetry a verb is frequently 'missing' in the second line. In nearly all such cases, the second line is derived from a structural parallel to that of the first by a transformational process (the *Gapping* rule) which calls for the deletion of a repeated verb in the second of two parallel sentences.

So far, we have discussed three variables pertinent to the analysis of poetic form:

1. The choice of abstract pattern: How is the recurrence of linguistic elements organized? For example, do we have symmetry (*abab, aabb*), antisymmetry (*abba*), or closure (*aab, ababcc*)? Is the structure hierarchical (stanzas) or linear (stichic verse)?

The other two variables have to do with how the abstract pattern is matched with linguistic elements.

2. The choice of linguistic elements: What are the syntactic or phonological building blocks which are subject to patterned recurrence? For example, do we have strict parallelism, where identity is maintained down to the smaller constituents of the tree, or loose parallelism, involving only the major constituents?

3. The choice of the derivational stage: Where in the transformational or phonological derivation do we make the match between linguistic elements and abstract patterns? For example, do we define parallel structure before or after the passive transformation has been applied – that is, is an active sentence regarded as parallel in structure to a corresponding passive one?

These three variables are, in principle, independent of each other. Theoretically, either strict or loose parallelism in terms of linguistic elements could hold either at a point in the transformational derivation near the deep structure or closer to surface structure. However, there is in fact a close relationship among the three. The tighter the constraints on the abstract pattern, the stricter the parallelism tends to be, and the closer it holds to surface structure.

There is still a fourth variable, namely the grammar itself. Poetic language differs grammatically from regular speech. Poetry may use stylistic inversions not allowed in prose, as in 'The force that through the green fuse drives....' Such inversions are not imitations of Latin, as is sometimes claimed. Rather they are applications of transformational rules that have only limited existence in standard English prose. The extent to which special rules for poetic language have been acceptable is an important stylistic variable in English poetry. From Gray to Wordsworth, poets sought a more 'natural' poetic diction and a major aspect of their effort was the conscious elimination of inversions. A hundred and fifty years later, however, inversions were brought back with a vengeance by E. E. Cummings, in whose hands they once again became an integral structural device.[6]

Poetic language differs, however, from Standard English in far more than word-order transformations. Perhaps the most striking characteristic of modern poetry is the stretching of grammar. This has led, in recent discussions of poetic language in the framework of generative grammar, to what has at times been a somewhat simplistic reliance on the concept of *ungrammaticality* or *deviance*. Metaphor, in particular, is frequently linked with a certain type of semantic deviance. However, it is clear that nondeviant sentences can have metaphorical interpretations: take, for example, 'He came out smelling like a rose.' In fact, the processes by which we give metaphorical interpretations to deviant sentences are the same as those by which we understand latent meaning in nondeviant sentences. Semantic deviance does not cause metaphorical meaning, but rather brings out what is already latent by blocking out a literal meaning, just as an eclipse of the sun does not 'cause' the moon to shine, but makes its light perceptible by blocking out the sun. In general, then, deviance is a device of *foregrounding*. However, not all grammatical foregrounding involves changing the rules of grammar. Existing rules can also be utilized in new ways. For example, in Starbuck's poem, cited above, the striking phrase 'burned what he said was himself' is not ungrammatical, but it is an unusual construction which may never have been used before.

We turn now from the syntactic to the phonological side of the language, where an examination of patterns has some rather surprising consequences, especially with regard to our habit of thinking of rhyme and alliteration as the simple repetition of sounds. We will find that the same four variables we distinguish in syntax also hold in phonology.

In addition to a set of transformational rules by which the syntax of sentences derives from a deep structure, grammar contains a set of phonological rules[7] by which the phonetic forms of words are derived from more basic underlying forms. The word 'publicity', for example, which could be transcribed phonetically as /pəblísətī/, is derived, by a series of steps, from the more basic form /publik + iti/. The k is the basic form (which we can hear in the related words 'public' and 'publication') is converted to an *s* sound (indicated in the spelling by *c*) before front vowels such as *i*. Other rules place the stress on the third syllable from the end, and weaken all unstressed vowels except the last, which gets lengthened. Thus the *phonological derivation* of 'publicity' is as follows:

/publik + iti/	basic form
publis + iti	change of *k* to *s*
publís + iti	placement of stress
publís + itī	lengthening of final i
pəblís + ətī	weakening of unstressed vowels

Investigation of the way such rules work has become the primary concern of phonologists in recent years, replacing their earlier preoccupation with problems of determining and classifying the phonemes of a language. This research is beginning to make clear that a surprising amount of the system of phonological rules of a language, which one might have thought was a rather arbitrary and unstructured part of its grammar, is actually determined by general principles. Phonological rules ring changes on a fixed repertoire of rules which, though very large in absolute terms, is still only a tiny portion of the huge total which could be imagined. Hence my hypothesis, that the linguistic elements which can count as sames in verse are just those which can count as sames in grammar, can be tested in phonology as well as in syntax. A comparison of the repertoire of phonological rules with the repertoire of metrical and rhyme schemas used in verse does indeed reveal a number of striking homologies.

Consider first this simple example. We know that 'having the same number of sounds' is of no relevance whatever in versification, whereas 'having the same number of syllables' is of fundamental importance. There is no explanation for this fact in the theory of prosody. But the fact has an exact counterpart in phonology. There are no known phonological rules which differentiate among words on the basis of how many sounds they have. The class of words containing exactly three phonemes (for example, 'end', 'shock', 'Anna') is a linguistically irrelevant pseudoclass which plays no role in grammar. But there are, of course, rules which count syllables: in many languages stress falls on the *n*th syllable from the beginning or end of a word, monosyllabic words have special phonological properties, and so on. Therefore, it seems that rules of versification are based on facts which are at bottom linguistic, and that systems of metrics must be explained by phonology.

Consider rhyme and alliteration, which are often defined as involving 'repetition of sounds'. This definition is, in fact, inaccurate. It fails to cover, for example, the type of rhyme known as *slant rhyme*, which is widely used by Dylan Thomas and Sylvia Plath. In slant rhyme, consonants after the last vowel must be the same, but words ending in vowels are considered to rhyme regardless of what the vowels are.

In Sylvia Plath's *Medallion*, which uses terza rima with slant rhyme throughout, we find rhymes like

> wood/dead/crooked/
> him/flame/time
> light/that/trout
> ocher/fire/there

but we also find

> jaw/arrow/eye

where the requirement is satisfied without any 'repetition of sounds'.

Alliteration of consonants, as found for example in the old Germanic languages including Old English, is a mirror image of slant rhyme. In Old English, words alliterate if their stressed syllables begin with the same consonant (with the special proviso that *sp*, *st*, and *sk* behave as if they were single consonants). But words whose stressed syllables begin with vowels alliterate freely with each other (*Atol ȳða geswing*, 'terrible swirl of waves'). Thus the rule for alliteration (and its inverse, slant rhyme) is *not* that syllables must begin (or end) with the same sound, but rather that *if* the syllables begin (or end) with a consonant, then the consonants must be the same. If they begin (or end) with a vowel, they need not repeat the same sound.

How is it possible that certain words rhyme and alliterate without having any sounds in common? This question again has no answer in the theory of prosody. The fact that all vowels alliterate with each other has in fact provoked many ingenious but unsuccessful attempts to conjure up word-initial ghost consonants of some kind to 'carry' the alliteration (which would imply similar ghost consonants at the ends of words to 'carry' slant rhyme). But the problem is not merely that some rhyme and alliteration does not fit the traditional definitions of these concepts, but more importantly, that when the sound in question is a vowel the pattern which one would expect to be normal, that in which the first or last sounds are identical, does not seem to occur at all.

Let us turn to a grammatical analogue of rhyme and alliteration to see if corresponding phenomena are found there. Consider phonological processes of *reduplication*, which copy part of a word for grammatical purposes. It is interesting that we never find among them rules of the form 'reduplicate the first (or last) sound of a word', just as we found no such rules for rhyme and alliteration. Rather, the typical form of reduplication is that of Gothic, where some verbs make their past tense by doubling their initial stem consonant, *if any*, and adding *ai* (pronounce like *e* in *get*):

saltan	'salt'	*sai-salt*	'salted'
haitan	'call'	*hai-hait*	'called'
slepan	'sleep'	*sai-slep*	'slept'
aukan	'increase'	*ai-auk*	'increased'
aikan	'renounce'	*ai-aik*	'renounced'
(ga) staldan	'obtain'	*(ga) stai-stald*	'obtained'

Note that this is very reminiscent of old Germanic alliteration, and even parallels the special treatment of *sk*, *sp*, and *st* as single units. Thus, the reduplication rules of phonology serve as well to circumscribe the kinds of rhyme and alliteration used in poetry.

Again, we have seen how a fact about the structure of verse derives from a fact about the structure of language. The question of how all initial vowels can alliterate with each other is a parallel question to that of how the *ai-* of *ai-auk* can be considered a reduplication of *auk*. Our answer is that language allows certain ways of organizing sounds, and that poetic form must draw on this organization.

More generally, consider how a word can be broken down into parts relevant to verse patterns. We can represent these patterns (or 'analyses') by means of the standard notations used in phonology. For example, letting C stand for *consonant*, V for *vowel*, and ♯ for *word boundary* (indicating whether the sound is an initial or a final sound), we can form the following notations:

♯C   'a word-initial consonant'
♯CV   'a word-initial consonant followed by a vowel'
V♯   'a word-final vowel'
C_0 'any number of consonants'

Each of these expressions defines a class which might be referred to in a phonological rule.

The word 'flash', for example, could pattern, for purposes of rhyme and alliteration, in the following ways:

♯C	f.	⎫
♯C_0	fl.	⎬ alliteration
♯C_0V	fla.	⎭
VC_0♯	.ash	rhyme
V	.a.	assonance
C_0♯ or C♯	.sh	slant rhyme
♯C_0 ... C_0♯	fl.sh	⎫
♯C .... C_0♯	f.sh	⎬ pararhyme (as in Wilfred Owen's poetry)

Now each of these patterns is potentially a pattern in a linguistic rule as well as a rule of versification. The first three represent types of *reduplication* which occur in various languages of the world. The others are found in English in sound symbolism (*phonesthemes*).[8] Thus, an example of a sound symbolism pattern of the form $C\sharp$ is 'fuzz', 'buzz', 'fizz', 'razz', 'jazz'. An example of $VC_0\sharp$ is 'smash', 'crash', 'bash', 'dash'. And $\sharp C \ldots C_0\sharp$ is illustrated by 'pitter', 'patter', 'putter', or 'tick', 'tack', 'tock'.

We have seen that elements are considered to be syntactically parallel even after certain syntactic transformations have reordered or deleted constituents. In other words, to match them exactly we would have to imagine them as they were before they were so transformed. This phenomenon has a counterpart in phonology. It sometimes happens that phonological schemes such as meter and rhyme must be matched to linguistic forms *before* certain phonological rules have been applied to them.

We already made this assumption implicitly in speaking of the slant rhyme of vowel-final words like 'arrow' and 'eye'. While it is true that these words end in a vowel in their basic phonological form, this vowel gets a consonantal glide sound inserted after it by a rule of English phonology, so that 'arrow', as it is actually pronounced, ends with a *w* sound and 'eye' ends with a *y* sound. For purposes of versification, however, we treat these words as if they really ended in vowel sounds – that is, we apply the rhyme schemes to them before the glide insertion rule is applied.

Examples in which poetic form 'looks back' at phonological forms which are not phonetic, can be cited from many languages. In German, most poets rhyme *Mund* 'mouth' and *bunt* 'colorful' (both pronounced with *t*, but different in basic form, since when you add an ending, such as *e*, *Munde* is pronounced with a *d*). Some poets, however, like Stefan George, who strove to achieve unusually pure poetic language, consistently avoid such rhymes. In other words, Stefan George's poetry rhymes according to forms more basic than that in which final stops are unvoiced.

There are cases where a whole block of phonological rules must be peeled away in this fashion before the schema which underlies a given meter is revealed. This is true of the Finnish *Kalevala* as recited by the bards of Ingermanland, and of the *Rigveda* of ancient India. The complexity in these traditions of the interaction between phonological and metrical structure makes them a kind of laser beam with which we can probe into the way language is structured in the mind, via the way it is structured in poetry.[9]

Thus phonological identity in poetry is not a matter of phonetics alone, any more than syntactic identity is a matter of surface structure. In fact, we have arrived at the somewhat surprising conclusion that identity of sound is neither a necessary nor a sufficient condition for rhyme and alliteration.

These observations suggest that at least some constants of poetic form are dependent on the structure of language itself. The intrinsic structure of language, the raw material of poetry, is carried over into poetry. By virtue of the nature of the patterns that are relevant in poetry, the structures involved are primarily those which are universal rather than those which apply only to a particular language. Hence the homologies between grammar and poetry account, at least in part, for the universality of poetic form.

To be sure, that summary of my thesis is rather more sweeping than is justified by the concrete examples analyzed here. I have, after all, dealt only with external form, and hardly touched on such deeper questions as figurative language. Although I believe that it is in these areas that linguistics will make its greatest contribution to literary studies, I have here chosen more tangible aspects of poetic form since the linguistic approach can be more clearly illustrated with them. Furthermore, the linguistic semantics needed to tackle problems such as metaphor is only now beginning to exist. The current work which is being done in this area is highly encouraging, as are many other applications of linguistics to literary problems: Ohmann's syntactically based studies of prose style, for example, and the approach to the structure of narrative initiated in V. Propp's classic work on folktales.[10]

Notes

1 This work was supported in part by grants from the National Institutes of Health (5 TO1 HD00111) and the National Institute of Mental Health (2 PO1 MH13390).
2 On the potential semantic function of rhyme, see W. K. Wimsatt, *The Verbal Icon* (Lexington, Ky.: Kentucky University Press, 1954).
3 An initial attempt, modeled on linguistic theory, is Manfred Bierwisch, 'Poetics and linguistics', *Linguistics and Literary Style*, ed. D. Freeman (New York: Holt, Rinehart & Winston, 1970).
4 This is expressed in Roman Jakobson's famous statement: 'The poetic function projects the principle of equivalence from the axis of selection into the axis of combination.' 'Linguistics and poetics', *Style in Language*, ed. T. Sebeok (Cambridge, Mass.: MIT Press, 1960).
   Note that caesurae (obligatory clause boundaries at a certain point of the line) could be considered either as patterned recurrence of sentence boundaries, or perhaps better as a form of parallelism at the level of sentences. Enjambment may be considered simply as absence of 'caesura' at the end of a line.
5 The distinction between the abstract pattern and its linguistic implementation in the domain of meter has been drawn particularly clearly by M. Halle and S. J. Keyser, 'Chaucer and the study of prosody', *Linguistics and Literary Style*.
6 In her unpublished Harvard dissertation, Irene Fairley shows that Cummings employs several syntactic systems, one of which is quite traditional in the form of its inversion rules. [A revised section is reprinted in this volume, 'Syntactic deviation and cohesion', pp. 123–37.]

7 A detailed analysis of the rules of English phonology is given in N. Chomsky and M. Halle, *The Sound Pattern of English* (New York: Harper & Row, 1968).
8 R. Wellek and A. Warren, *Theory of Literature* (New York: Harcourt, Brace & World, 1961), p. 148.
9 P. Kiparsky, 'Metrics and morphophonemics in the Kalevala', *Linguistics and Literary Style*; 'Metrics and morphophonemics in the Rigveda', *Contributions to Generative Phonology*, ed. M. Brame (Austin: University of Texas Press, 1972); Howard Lasnik, 'Metrics and morphophonemics in Old English verse', (ms.), Stephen Anderson, 'U-Umlaut and Skaldic verse', *Festschrift for Morris Halle*, eds. S. Anderson and P. Kiparsky (New York: Holt, Rinehart & Winston, 1973).
10 R. Ohmann, 'Generative grammars and the concept of literary style', *Word*, XX (1964), 423–39; V. Propp, *Morphology of the Folktale* (Austin: University of Texas Press, 1968). For a new linguistic approach to the question of modes of narrative, such as 'narrated monolog', see S. Y. Kuroda, 'Where epistemology, style and grammar meet', *Festschrift for Morris Halle*.

2
Literary competence

Jonathan Culler

> To understand a sentence means to understand a language. To understand a language means to be master of a technique.
>
> Wittgenstein

When a speaker of a language hears a phonetic sequence, he is able to give it meaning because he brings to the act of communication an amazing repertoire of conscious and unconscious knowledge. Mastery of the phonological, syntactic and semantic systems of his language enables him to convert the sounds into discrete units, to recognize words, and to assign a structural description and interpretation to the resulting sentence, even though it be quite new to him. Without this implicit knowledge, this internalized grammar, the sequence of sounds does not speak to him. We are nevertheless inclined to say that the phonological and grammatical structure and the meaning are *properties* of the utterance, and there is no harm in that way of speaking so long as we remember that they are properties of the utterance only with respect to a particular grammar. Another grammar would assign different properties to the sequence (according to the grammar of a different language, for example, it would be nonsense). To speak of the structure of a sentence is necessarily to imply an internalized grammar that gives it that structure.

We also tend to think of meaning and structure as properties of literary works, and from one point of view this is perfectly correct: when the sequence of words is treated *as a literary work* it has these properties. But that qualification suggests the relevance and importance of the linguistic analogy. The work has structure and meaning because it is read in a particular way, because these potential properties, latent in the object itself, are actualized by the theory of discourse applied in the act of reading. 'How can one discover structure without the help of a methodological model?' asks Barthes (*Critique et vérité*, [Paris: Seuil, 1966] p. 19). To read a text as literature is not to make one's mind a *tabula rasa* and approach it without preconceptions; one must bring to it an implicit understanding of the operations of literary discourse which tells one what to look for.

Anyone lacking this knowledge, anyone wholly unacquainted with literature and unfamiliar with the conventions by which fictions are read, would, for example, be quite baffled if presented with a poem. His knowledge of the language would enable him to understand phrases and sentences, but he would not know, quite literally, what to *make* of this strange concatenation of phrases. He would be unable to read it *as* literature – as we say with emphasis to those who would use literary works for other purposes – because he lacks the complex 'literary competence' which enables others to proceed. He has not internalized the 'grammar' of literature which would permit him to convert linguistic sequences into literary structures and meanings.

If the analogy seems less than exact it is because in the case of language it is much more obvious that understanding depends on mastery of a system. But the time and energy devoted to literary training in schools and universities indicate that the understanding of literature also depends on experience and mastery. Since literature is a second-order semiotic system which has language as its basis, a knowledge of language will take one a certain distance in one's encounter with literary texts, and it may be difficult to specify precisely where understanding comes to depend on one's supplementary knowledge of literature. But the difficulty of drawing a line does not obscure the palpable difference between understanding the language of a poem, in the sense that one could provide a rough translation into another language, and understanding the poem. If one knows French, one can translate Mallarmé's 'Salut', but that translation is not a thematic synthesis – it is not what we would ordinarily call 'understanding the poem' – and in order to identify various levels of coherence and set them in relation to one another under the synoptic heading or theme of the 'literary quest' one must have considerable experience of the conventions for reading poetry.

The easiest way to grasp the importance of these conventions is to take a piece of journalistic prose or a sentence from a novel and set it down on the page as a poem. The properties assigned to the sentence by a grammar of English remain unchanged, and the different meanings which the text acquires cannot therefore be attributed to one's knowledge of the language but must be ascribed to the special conventions for reading poetry which lead one to look at the language in new ways, to make relevant properties of the language which were previously unexploited, to subject the text to a different series of interpretive operations. But one can also show the importance of these conventions by measuring the distance between the language of a poem and its critical interpretation – a distance bridged by the conventions of reading which comprise the institution of poetry.

Anyone who knows English understands the language of Blake's 'Ah! Sun-flower':

> Ah, Sun-flower, weary of time,
> Who countest the steps of the Sun,
> Seeking after that sweet golden clime
> Where the traveller's journey is done:
>
> Where the Youth pined away with desire,
> And the pale Virgin shrouded in snow
> Arise from their graves, and aspire
> Where my Sun-flower wishes to go.

But there is some distance between an understanding of the language and the thematic statement with which a critic concludes his discussion of the poem: 'Blake's dialectical thrust at asceticism is more than adroit. You do not surmount Nature by denying its prime claim of sexuality. Instead you fall utterly into the dull round of its cyclic aspirations.'[1] How does one reach this reading? What are the operations which lead from the text to this representation of understanding? The primary convention is what might be called the rule of significance: read the poem as expressing a significant attitude to some problem concerning man and/or his relation to the universe. The sunflower is therefore given the value of an emblem and the metaphors of 'counting' and 'seeking' are taken not just as figurative indications of the flower's tendency to turn towards the sun but as metaphorical operators which make the sunflower an instance of the human aspirations compassed by these two lines. The conventions of metaphorical coherence – that one should attempt through semantic transformations to produce coherence on the levels of both tenor and vehicle – lead one to oppose time to eternity and to make 'that sweet golden clime' both the sunset which marks the closure of the daily temporal cycle and the eternity of death when 'the traveller's journey is done'. The identification of sunset and death is further justified by the convention which allows one to inscribe the poem in a poetic tradition. More important, however, is the convention of thematic unity, which forces one to give the youth and virgin of the second stanza a role which justifies choosing them as examples of aspiration; and since the semantic feature they share is a repression of sexuality, one must find a way of integrating that with the rest of the poem. The curious syntactic structure, with three clauses each depending on a 'where', provides a way of doing this:

The Youth and the Virgin have denied their sexuality to win the allegorical abode of the conventionally visualized heaven. Arriving there, they arise from their graves to be trapped in the same cruel cycle of longings; they are merely at the sunset and aspire to go where the Sun-flower seeks his rest, which is precisely where they already are.[2]

Such interpretations are not the result of subjective associations. They are public and can be discussed and justified with respect to the conventions of reading poetry – or, as English allows us to say, of *making* sense. Such conventions are the constituents of the institution of literature, and in this perspective one can see that it may well be misleading to speak of poems as harmonious totalities, autonomous natural organisms, complete in themselves and bearing a rich immanent meaning. The semiological approach suggests, rather, that the poem be thought of as an utterance that has meaning only with respect to a system of conventions which the reader has assimilated. If other conventions were operative its range of potential meanings would be different.

Literature, as Genette says, 'like any other activity of the mind, is based on conventions of which, with some exceptions, it is not aware' (*Figures* [Paris: Seuil, 1966], p. 258). One can think of these conventions not simply as the implicit knowledge of the reader but also as the implicit knowledge of authors. To write a poem or a novel is immediately to engage with a literary tradition or at the very least with a certain idea of the poem or the novel. The activity is made possible by the existence of the genre, which the author can write against, certainly, whose conventions he may attempt to subvert, but which is none the less the context within which his activity takes place, as surely as the failure to keep a promise is made possible by the institution of promising. Choices between words, between sentences, between different modes of presentation, will be made on the basis of their effects; and the notion of effect presupposes modes of reading which are not random or haphazard. Even if the author does not think of readers, he is himself a reader of his own work and will not be satisfied with it unless he can read it as producing effects. One would find very strange the notion of a poet saying, 'when I reflect on the sunflower I have a particular feeling, which I shall call 'p' and which I think can be connected with another feeling which I shall call "q",' and then writing 'if p then q' as a poem on the sunflower. This would not be a poem because even the poet himself cannot read the meanings in that series of signs. He can take them as referring to the feelings in question, but that is very much another matter. His text does not explore, evoke or even make use of the feelings, and he will be unable to read it as if it did. To experience any of the satisfactions of having written a poem he must create an order of words which he can read according to the conventions of poetry: he cannot simply assign meaning but must make possible, for himself and for others, the production of meaning.

'Every work', wrote Valéry, 'is the work of many things besides an author', and he proposed that literary history be replaced by a poetics which would study 'the conditions of the existence and development of literature'. Among all the arts, it is 'the one in which convention plays the greatest role', and even those authors who may have thought their works due only to personal inspiration and the application of genius

> had developed, without suspecting it, a whole system of habits and notions which were the fruit of their experience and indispensable to the process of production. However little they might have suspected all the definitions, all the conventions, the logic and the system of combinations that composition presupposes, however much they believed that they owed nothing but to the instant itself, their work necessarily called into play all these procedures and these inevitable operations of the mind.[3]

The conventions of poetry, the logic of symbols, the operations for the production of poetic effects, are not simply the property of readers but the basis of literary forms. However, for a variety of reasons it is easier to study them as the operations performed by readers than as the institutional context taken for granted by authors. The statements authors make about the process of composition are notoriously problematic, and there are few ways of determining what they are taking for granted. Whereas the meanings readers give to literary works and the effects they experience are much more open to observation. Hypotheses about the conventions and operations which produce these effects can therefore be tested not only by their ability to account for the effects in question but by their ability, when applied to other poems, to account for the effects experienced in those cases. Moreover, when one is investigating the process of reading one can make alterations in the language of a text so as to see how this changes literary effects, whereas that kind of experimentation is not possible if one is investigating the conventions assumed by authors, who are not available to give their reactions to the effects of proposed alterations in their texts. As the example of transformational grammar suggests, the best way of producing a formal representation of the implicit knowledge of both speakers and hearers is to present sentences to oneself or to colleagues and then to formulate rules which account for the hearers' judgments about meaning, well-formedness, deviance, constituent structure, and ambiguity.

To speak, therefore, as I shall do, of literary competence as a set of conventions for reading literary texts is in no way to imply that authors are congenital idiots who simply produce strings of sentences, while all the truly creative work is done by readers who have artful ways of processing these sentences. Structuralist discussions may seem to promote such a view by their failure to isolate and praise an author's 'conscious art', but the reason is simply that here, as in most other human activities of any complexity, the line between the conscious and the unconscious is highly variable, impossible to identify, and supremely uninteresting. '*When* do you know how to play chess? All the time? or just while you are making a move? And the *whole* of chess during each move?'[4] When driving a car is it consciously or unconsciously that you keep to the correct side of the road, change gears, apply the brakes, dip the headlights? To ask of what an author is conscious and of what unconscious is as fruitless as to ask which rules of English are consciously employed by speakers and which are followed unconsciously. Mastery may be largely unconscious or it may have reached a stage of highly self-conscious theoretical elaboration, but it is mastery in both cases. Nor does one in any way impugn the author's talent in speaking of his mastery as an ability to construct artefacts which prove extremely rich when subjected to the operations of reading.

The task of a structuralist poetics, as Barthes defines it, would be to make explicit the underlying system which makes literary effects possible. It would not be a 'science of contents' which, in hermeneutic fashion, proposed interpretations for works,

> but a science of the conditions of content, that is to say of forms. What interests it will be the variations of meaning generated and, as it were, capable of being generated by works; it will not interpret symbols but describe their polyvalency. In short, its object will not be the full meanings of the work but on the contrary the empty meaning which supports them all. (*Critique et vérité*, p. 57)

In this sense structuralism effects an important reversal of perspective, granting precedence to the task of formulating a comprehensive theory of literary discourse and assigning a secondary place to the interpretation of individual texts. Whatever the benefits of interpretation to those who engage in it, within the context of poetics it becomes an ancillary activity – a way of using literary works – as opposed to the study of literature itself as an institution. To say that is in no way to condemn interpretation, as the linguistic analogy should make perfectly evident. Most people are more interested in using language to communicate than in studying the complex linguistic system which underlies communication, and they need not feel that their interests are threatened by those who make the study of linguistic competence a coherent and autonomous discipline. Similarly, a structuralist poetics would claim that the study of literature involves only indirectly the critical act of placing a work in situation, reading it as a gesture of a particular kind, and thus giving it a meaning. The task is rather to construct a theory of literary discourse which would account for the possibilities of interpretation, the 'empty meanings' which support a variety of full meanings but which do not permit the work to be given just any meaning.

This would not need to be said if interpretive criticism had not tried to persuade us that the study of literature means the elucidation of individual works. But in this cultural context it is important to reflect on what has been lost or obscured in the practice of an interpretive criticism which treats each work as an autonomous artefact, an organic whole whose parts all contribute to a complex thematic statement. The notion that the task of criticism is to reveal thematic unity is a post-Romantic concept, whose roots in the theory of organic form are, at the very least, ambiguous. The organic unity of a plant is not easily translated into thematic unity, and we are willing to admit that the botanical gaze be allowed to compare one plant with another, isolating similarities and differences, or to dwell on formal organization without immediately invoking some teleological purpose or thematic unity. Nor has discourse on literature always been so imperiously committed to interpretation. It used to be possible, in the days before the poem became pre-eminently the act of an individual and emotion recollected in tranquillity, to study its interaction with norms of rhetoric and genre, the relation of its formal features to those of the tradition, without feeling immediately compelled to produce an interpretation which would demonstrate their thematic relevance. One did not need to move from poem to world but could explore it within the institution of literature, relating it to a tradition and identifying formal continuities and discontinuities. That this should have been possible may tell us something important about literature or at least lead us to reflect on the possibility of loosening interpretation's hold on critical discourse.

Such loosening is important because if the analyst aims at understanding how literature works he must, as Northrop Frye says, set about 'formulating the broad laws of literary experience, and in short writing as though he believed that there is a totally intelligible structure of knowledge attainable about poetry, which is not poetry itself, or the experience of it, but poetics' (*Anatomy of Criticism* [Princeton: Princeton University Press, 1957], p. 14). Few have put the case for poetics more forcefully than Frye, but in his perspective, as this quotation shows, the relationship between poetry, the experience of poetry and poetics remains somewhat obscure, and that obscurity affects his later formulations. His discussions of modes, symbols, myths and genres lead to the production of taxonomies which capture something of the richness of literature, but the status of his taxonomic categories is curiously indeterminate. What is their relation to literary discourse and to the activity of reading? Are the four mythic categories of Spring, Summer, Autumn and Winter devices for classifying literary works or categories on which the experience of literature is based? As soon as one asks why these categories are to be preferred to those of other possible taxonomies it becomes evident that there must be something implicit in Frye's theoretical framework which needs to be made explicit.

The linguistic model provides a slight reorientation which makes apparent what is needed. Study of the linguistic system becomes theoretically coherent when we cease thinking that our goal is to specify the properties of objects in a corpus and concentrate instead on the task of formulating the internalized competence which enables objects to have the properties they do for those who have mastered the system. To discover and characterize structures one must analyse the system which assigns structural descriptions to the objects in question, and thus a literary taxonomy should be grounded on a theory of reading. The relevant categories are those which are required to account for the range of acceptable meanings which works can have for readers of literature.

The notion of literary competence or of a literary system is, of course, anathema to some critics, who see in it an attack on the spontaneous, creative and affective qualities of literature. Moreover, they might argue, the very concept of literary competence, which carries the presumption that we can distinguish between competent and incompetent readers, is objectionable for precisely those reasons which lead one to propose it: the postulation of a norm for 'correct' reading. In other human activities where there are clear criteria for success and failure, such as playing chess or climbing mountains, we can speak of competence and incompetence, but the richness and power of literature depend, precisely, on the fact that it is not an activity of this kind and that appreciation is varied, personal, and not subject to the normative legislation of self-styled experts.

Such arguments, however, would seem to miss the point. None would deny that literary works, like most other objects of human attention, can be enjoyed for reasons that have little do with understanding and mastery – that texts can be quite blatantly misunderstood and still be appreciated for a variety of personal reasons. But to reject the notion of misunderstanding as a legislative imposition is to leave unexplained the common experience of being shown where one went wrong, of grasping a mistake and seeing why it was a mistake. Though acquiescence may occasionally be disgruntled yielding to a higher authority, none would maintain that it was always thus; more often one feels that one has indeed been shown the way to a fuller understanding of literature and a better grasp of the procedures of reading. If the distinction between understanding and misunderstanding were irrelevant, if neither party to a discussion believed in the distinction, there would be little point to discussing and arguing about literary works and still less to writing about them.

Moreover, the claims of schools and universities to offer literary training cannot be lightly dismissed. To believe that the whole institution of literary education is but a gigantic confidence trick, would strain even a determined credulity, for it is, alas, only too clear that knowledge of a language and a certain experience of the world do not suffice to make someone a perceptive and competent reader. That achievement requires acquaintance with a range of literature and in many cases some form of guidance. The time and effort devoted to literary education by generations of students and teachers creates a strong presumption that there is something to be learned, and teachers do not hesitate to judge their pupil's progress towards a general literary competence. Most would claim, no doubt with good reason, that their examinations are designed not simply to determine whether their students have read various set works but to test their acquisition of an ability.

'Everyone who has seriously studied literature', Northrop Frye maintains, 'knows that the mental process involved is as coherent and progressive as the study of science. A precisely similar training of the mind takes place, and a similar sense of the unity of the subject is built up' (ibid., pp. 10–11). If that seems overstated it is no doubt because what is explicit in the teaching of science usually remains implicit in the teaching of literature. But it is clear that study of one poem or novel facilitates the study of the next: one gains not only points of comparison but a sense of how to read. One develops a set of questions which experience shows to be appropriate and productive and criteria for determining whether they are, in a given case, productive; one acquires a sense of the possibilities of literature and how these possibilities may be distinguished. We may speak, if we like, of extrapolating from one work to another, so long as we do not thereby obscure the fact that the process of extrapolation is precisely what requires explanation. To account for extrapolation, to explain what are the formal questions and distinctions whose relevance the student learns, would be to formulate a theory of literary competence. If we are to make any sense at all of the process of literary education and of criticism itself we must, as Frye argues, assume the possibility of 'a coherent and comprehensive theory of literature, logically and scientifically organized, some of which the student unconsciously learns as he goes on, but the main principles of which are as yet unknown to us' (p. 11).

It is easy to see why, from this perspective, linguistics offers an attractive methodological analogy: a grammar, as Chomsky says, 'can be regarded as a theory of a language', and the theory of literature of which Frye speaks can be regarded as the 'grammar' or literary competence which readers have assimilated but of which they may not be consciously aware. To make the implicit explicit is the task of both linguistics and poetics, and generative grammar has placed renewed emphasis on two fundamental requirements for theories of this kind: that they state their rules as formal operations (since what they are investigating is a kind of intelligence they cannot take for granted intelligence used in applying rules but must make them as explicit as possible) and that they be testable (they must reproduce, as it were, attested facts about semiotic competence).

Can this step be taken in literary criticism? The major obstacle would seem to be that of determining what will count as evidence about literary competence. In linguistics it is not difficult to identify facts that an adequate grammar must account for: though one may need to speak of 'degrees of grammaticalness' one can produce lists of sentences which are incontestably well formed and sentences which are unquestionably deviant. Moreover, we have a sufficiently strong intuitive sense of paraphrase relations to be able to say roughly what a sentence means for speakers of a language. In the study of literature, however, the situation is considerably more complex. Notions of 'well-formed' or 'intelligible' literary works are notoriously problematic, and it may be difficult to secure agreement about what should count as a proper 'understanding' of a text. That critics should differ so widely in their interpretations might seem to undermine any notion of a general literary competence.

But in order to overcome this apparent obstacle we have only to ask what we want a theory of literature to account for. We cannot ask it to account for the 'correct' meaning of a work since we manifestly do not believe that for each work there is a single correct reading. We cannot ask it to draw a clear line between the well-formed and the deviant work if we believe that no such line exists. Indeed, the striking facts that do require explanation are how it is that a work can have a variety of meanings but not just any meaning whatsoever or how it is that some works give an impression of strangeness, incoherence, incomprehensibility. The model does not imply that there must be unanimity on any particular count. It suggests only that we must designate a set of facts, of whatever kind, which seem to require explanation and then try to construct a model of literary competence which would account for them.

The facts can be of many kinds: that a given prose sentence has different meanings if set down as a poem, that readers are able to recognize the plot of a novel, that some symbolic interpretations of a poem are more plausible than others, that two characters in a novel contrast with one another, that *The Waste Land* or *Ulysses* once seemed strange and now seems intelligible. Poetics bears, as Barthes says, not so much on the work itself as on its intelligibility (*Critique et vérité*, p. 62) and therefore problematic cases –

the work which some find intelligible and others incoherent, or the work which is read differently in two different periods – furnish the most decisive evidence about the system of operative conventions. Any work can be made intelligible if one invents appropriate conventions: the most obscure poem could be interpreted if there were a convention which permitted us to replace every lexical item by a word beginning with the same letter of the alphabet and chosen according to the ordinary demands of coherence. There are numerous other bizarre conventions which might be operative if the institution of literature were different, and hence the difficulty of interpreting some works provides evidence of the restricted nature of the conventions actually in force in a culture. Moreover, if a difficult work later becomes intelligible it is because new ways of reading have been developed in order to meet what is the fundamental demand of the system: the demand for sense. A comparison of old and new readings will shed light on the change in the institution of literature.

As in linguistics, there is no automatic procedure for obtaining information about competence, but there is no dearth of facts to be explained.[5] To take surveys of the behaviour of readers would serve little purpose, since one is interested not in performance itself but in the tacit knowledge or competence which underlies it. Performance may not be a direct reflection of competence, for behaviour can be influenced by a host of irrelevant factors: I may not have been paying attention at a given moment, may have been led astray by purely personal associations, may have forgotten something important from an earlier part of the text, may have made what I would recognize as a mistake if it were pointed out to me. One's concern is with the tacit knowledge that recognition of a mistake would show rather than with the mistake itself, and so even if one were to take surveys one would still have to judge whether particular reactions were in fact a direct reflection of competence. The question is not what actual readers happen to do but what an ideal reader must know implicitly in order to read and interpret works in ways which we consider acceptable, in accordance with the institution of literature.

The ideal reader is, of course, a theoretical construct, perhaps best thought of as a representation of the central notion of acceptability. Poetics, Barthes writes, 'will describe the logic according to which meanings are engendered in ways that can be *accepted* by man's logic of symbols, just as the sentences of French are *accepted* by the linguistic intuitions of Frenchmen' (*Critique et vérité*, p. 63). Though there is no automatic procedure for determining what is acceptable, that does not matter, for one's proposals will be sufficiently tested by one's readers' acceptance or rejection of them. If readers do not accept the facts one sets out to explain as bearing any relation to their knowledge and experience of literature, then one's theory will be of little interest; and therefore the analyst must convince his readers that meanings or effects which he is attempting to account for are indeed appropriate ones. The meaning of a poem within the institution of literature is not, one might say, the immediate and spontaneous reaction of individual readers but the meanings which they are willing to accept as both plausible and justifiable when they are explained. 'Ask yourself: How does one *lead* anyone to comprehension of a poem or of a theme? The answer to this tells us how meaning is to be explained here'.[6] The paths by which the reader is led to comprehension are precisely those of the logic of literature: the effects must be related to the poem in such a way that the reader sees the connection to be just in terms of his own knowledge of literature.

One cannot therefore emphasize too strongly that every critic, whatever his persuasion, encounters the problems of literary competence as soon as he begins to speak or write about literary works, and that he takes for granted notions of acceptability and common ways of reading. The critic would not write unless he thought he had something new to say about a text, yet he assumes that his reading is not a random and idiosyncratic phenomenon. Unless he thinks that he is merely recounting to others the adventures of his own subjectivity, he claims that his interpretation is related to the text in ways which he presumes his readers will accept once those relations are pointed out: either they will accept his interpretation as an explicit version of what they intuitively felt or they will recognize from their own knowledge of literature the justice of the operations that lead the critic from text to interpretation. Indeed, the possibility of critical argument depends on shared notions of the acceptable and the unacceptable, a common ground which is nothing other than the procedures of reading. The critic must invariably make decisions about what can in fact be taken for granted, what must be explicitly defended, and what constitutes an acceptable defence. He must show his readers that the effects he notices fall within the compass of an implicit logic which they are presumed to accept; and thus he deals in his own practice with the problems which a poetics would hope to make explicit.

William Empson's *Seven Types of Ambiguity* (Harmondsworth: Penguin, 1961; 1st. ed, 1930) is a work from a non-structuralist tradition which shows considerable awareness of the problems of literary competence and illustrates just how close one comes to a structuralist formulation if one begins to reflect on them. Even if Empson were content to present his work as a display of ingenuity in discovering ambiguities, his enterprise would still be governed by conceptions of plausibility. But of course he wants to make broader claims for his analysis and finds that to do so entails a position very like that recommended above:

> I have continually employed a method of analysis which jumps the gap between two ways of thinking; which produces a possible set of alternative meanings with some ingenuity, and then says it is grasped in the preconsciousness of the reader by a native effort of the mind. This must seem very dubious; but then the facts about the apprehension of poetry are in any case very extraordinary. Such an assumption is best judged by the way it works in detail. (p. 239)

Poetry has complex effects which are extremely difficult to explain, and the analyst finds that his best strategy is to assume that the effects he sets out to account for have been conveyed to the reader and then to postulate certain general operations which might explain these effects and analogous effects in other poems. To those who protest against such assumptions one might reply, with Empson, that the test is whether one succeeds in accounting for effects which the reader accepts when they are pointed out to him. The assumption is in no way dangerous, for the analyst 'must convince the reader that he knows what he is talking about' – make him see the appropriateness of the effects in question – and 'must coax the reader into seeing that the cause he names does, in fact, produce the effect which is experienced; otherwise they will not seem to have anything to do with each other' (p. 249). If the reader is brought to accept both the effects in question and the explanation he will have helped to validate what is, in essence, a theory of reading. 'I have claimed to show how a properly qualified mind works when it reads the verses, how those properly qualified minds have worked which have not at all understood their own working' (p. 248). Such claims about literary competence are not to be verified by surveys of readers' reactions to poems but by readers' assent to the effects which the analyst attempts to explain and the efficacy of his explanatory hypotheses in other cases.

It is Empson's self-awareness and outspokenness as much as his brilliance which make his work invaluable to students of poetics; he has little respect for the critical piety that meanings are always implicitly and objectively present in the language of the poem, and thus he can attend to the operations which produce meanings. Discussing the translation of a Chinese fragment,

> Swiftly the years, beyond recall.
> Solemn the stillness of this spring morning.

he notes that

> these lines are what we should normally call poetry only by virtue of their compactness; two statements are made as if they were connected, and the reader is forced to consider their relations for himself. The

reason why these facts should have been selected for a poem is left for him to invent; he will invent a variety of reasons and order them in his own mind. This, I think, is the essential fact about the poetical use of language. (p. 25)

This is indeed an essential fact, and one should hasten to point out what it implies: reading poetry is a rule-governed process of producing meanings; the poem offers a structure which must be filled up and one therefore attempts to invent something, guided by a series of formal rules derived from one's experience of reading poetry, which both make possible invention and impose limits on it. In this case the most obvious feature of literary competence is the intent at totality of the interpretive process: poems are supposed to cohere, and one must therefore discover a semantic level at which the two lines can be related to one another. An obvious point of contact is the contrast between 'swiftly' and 'stillness', and there is thus a primary condition on 'invention': any interpretation should succeed in making thematic capital out of this opposition. Moreover, 'years' in the first sentence and 'this morning' in the second, both located in the dimension of time, provide another opposition and point of contact. The reader might hope to find an interpretation which relates these two pairs of contrasts. If this is indeed what happens it is no doubt because the experience of reading poetry leads to implicit recognition of the importance of binary oppositions as thematic devices: in interpreting a poem one looks for terms which can be placed on a semantic or thematic axis and opposed to one another.

The resulting structure or 'empty meaning' suggests that the reader try to relate the opposition between 'swiftly' and 'stillness' to two ways of thinking about time and draw some kind of thematic conclusion from the tension between the two sentences. It seems eminently possible to produce in this way a reading which is 'acceptable' in terms of poetic logic. On the one hand, taking a large panoramic view, we can think of the human lifespan as a unit of time and of the years as passing swiftly; on the other, taking the moment of consciousness as the unit, we can think of the difficulty of experiencing time except discontinuously, of the stillness of a clock's hand when one looks at it. 'Swiftly the years' implies a vantage point from which one can consider the passage of time, and the swiftness of passage is compensated for by what Empson calls 'the answering stability of self-knowledge' implicit in this view of life (p. 24). 'This morning' implies other mornings – a discontinuity of experience reflected in the ability to separate and name – and hence an instability which makes 'stillness' the more valued. This process of binary structuring, then, can lead one to find tension within each of the lines as well as between the two lines. And since thematic contrasts should be related to opposed values we are led to think about the advantages and disadvantages of these two ways of conceiving of time. A variety of conclusions are of course possible. The claim is not that competent readers would agree on an interpretation but only that certain expectations about poetry and ways of reading guide the interpretive process and impose severe limitations on the set of acceptable or plausible readings.

Empson's example indicates that as soon as one reflects seriously on the status of critical argument and the relation of interpretation to text one approaches the problems which confront poetics, in that one must justify one's reading by locating it within the conventions of plausibility defined by a generalized knowledge of literature. From the point of view of poetics, what requires explanation is not the text itself so much as the possibility of reading and interpreting the text, the possibility of literary effects and literary communication. To account for the notions of acceptability and plausibility on which criticism relies is, as J.-C. Gardin emphasizes, the primary task of the systematic study of literature.

> This is in any case the only sort of objective that a 'science' may set for itself, even if it be a science of literature: the regularities unveiled by natural phenomena correspond, in the literary field, to certain convergences of perception for members of a given culture. ('Semantic analysis procedures in the sciences of man', *Social Science Information* 8:1 [1969], p. 33)

But one should stress that even if the analyst showed little explicit interest in notions of acceptability and merely set out to explain in a systematic way his own reading of literature, the results would be of considerable moment for poetics. If he began by noting his own interpretations and reactions to literary works and succeeded in formulating a set of explicit rules which accounted for the fact that he produced these interpretations and not others, one would then possess the basis of an account of literary competence. Adjustments could be made to include other readings which seemed acceptable and to exclude any readings which seemed wholly personal and idiosyncratic, but there is every reason to expect that other readers would be able to recognize substantial portions of their own tacit knowledge in his account. To be an experienced reader of literature is, after all, to have gained a sense of what can be done with literary works and thus to have assimilated a system which is largely interpersonal. There is little reason to worry initially about the validity of the facts which one sets out to explain; the only risk one runs is that of wasting one's time. The important thing is to start by isolating a set of facts and then to construct a model to account for them, and though structuralists have often failed to do this in their own practice, it is at least implicit in the linguistic model: 'Linguistics can give literature the generative model which is the principle of all science, since it is a matter of making use of certain rules to explain particular results'. (Barthes, *Critique et vérité*, p. 58)

Since poetics is essentially a theory of reading, critics of every persuasion who have tried to be explicit about what they are doing have made some contribution to it and indeed in many cases have more to offer than structuralists themselves. What structuralism does provide is a reversal of critical perspective and a theoretical framework within which the work of other critics can be organized and exploited. Granting precedence to the task of formulating a theory of literary competence and relegating critical interpretation to a secondary role, it leads one to reformulate as conventions of literature and operations of reading what others might think of as facts about various literary texts. Rather than say, for example, that literary texts are fictional, we might cite this as a convention of literary interpretation and say that to read a text as literature is to read it as fiction. Such a reversal may, at first sight, seem trivial, but to restate propositions about poetic or novelistic discourse as procedures of reading is a crucial reorientation for a number of reasons, wherein lie the revitalizing powers of a structuralist poetics.

First of all, to stress literature's dependence on particular modes of reading is a firmer and more honest starting point than is customary in criticism. One need not struggle, as other theorists must, to find some objective property of language which distinguishes the literary from the non-literary but may simply start from the fact that we can read texts as literature and then inquire what operations that involves. The operations will, of course, be different for different genres, and here by the same model we can say that genres are not special varieties of language but sets of expectations which allow sentences of a language to become signs of different kinds in a second-order literary system. The same sentence can have a different meaning depending on the genre in which it appears. Nor is one upset, as a theorist working on the distinctive properties of literary language must be, by the fact that the boundaries between the literary and the non-literary or between one genre and another change from age to age. On the contrary, change in modes of reading offers some of the best evidence about the conventions operative in different periods.

Second, in attempting to make explicit what one does when reading or interpreting a poem one gains considerably in self-awareness and awareness of the nature of literature as an institution. As long as one assumes that what one does is natural it is difficult to gain any understanding of it and thus to define the differences between oneself and one's predecessors or successors. Reading is not an innocent activity. It is charged with artifice, and to refuse to study one's modes of reading is to neglect a principal source of information about literary activity. By seeing literature as something animated by special sets of conventions one can attain more easily a sense of its specificity, its peculiarity, its difference, shall we say, from other modes of discourse about the world. Those differences lie in the work of the literary sign: in the ways in which meaning is produced.

Third, a willingness to think of literature as an institution composed of a variety of interpretive operations makes one more open to the most challenging and innovatory texts, which are precisely those that are difficult to process according to received modes of understanding. An awareness of the assumptions on which one proceeds, an ability to make explicit what one is attempting to do, makes it easier to see where and how the text resists one's attempts to make sense of it and how, by its refusal to comply with one's expectations, it leads to that questioning of the self and of ordinary social modes of understanding which has always been the result of the greatest literature. My readers, says the narrator at the end of *A la recherche du temps perdu*, will become 'les propres lecteurs d'eux-mêmes': in my book they will read themselves and their own limits. How better to facilitate a reading of oneself than by trying to make explicit one's sense of the comprehensible and the incomprehensible, the significant and the insignificant, the ordered and the inchoate. By offering sequences and combinations which escape our accustomed grasp, by subjecting language to a dislocation which fragments the ordinary signs of our world, literature challenges the limits we set to the self as a device or order and allows us, painfully or joyfully, to accede to an expansion of self. But that requires, if it is to be fully accomplished, a measure of awareness of the interpretive models which inform one's culture. Structuralism, because of its interest in the adventures of the sign, has been exceedingly open to the revolutionary work, finding in its resistance to the operations of reading confirmation of the fact that literary effects depend on these conventions and that literary evolution proceeds by displacement of old conventions of reading and the development of new.

And so, finally, structuralism's reversal of perspective can lead to a mode of interpretation based on poetics itself, where the work is read against the conventions of discourse and where one's interpretation is an account of the ways in which the work complies with or undermines our procedures for making sense of things. Though it does not, of course, replace ordinary thematic interpretations, it does avoid premature foreclosure – the unseemly rush from word to world – and stays within the literary system for as long as possible. Insisting that literature is something other than a statement about the world, it establishes, finally, an analogy between the production or reading of signs in literature and in other areas of experience and studies the ways in which the former explores and dramatizes the limitations of the latter. In this kind of interpretation the meaning of the work is what it shows the reader, by the acrobatics in which it involves him, about the problems of his condition as *homo significans*, maker and reader of signs. The notion of literary competence thus comes to serve as the basis of a reflexive interpretation.

Notes

1 Harold Bloom, *The Visionary Company* (New York, 1961), p. 42.
2 ibid.
3 P. Valéry, *Œuvres*, II, pp. 629 and I, pp. 1439–41.
4 Ludwig Wittgenstein, *Philosophical Investigations*, p. 59.
5 See N. Chomsky, *Aspects of the Theory of Syntax*, (Cambridge, Mass.: The MIT Press, 1965); p. 19.
6 L. Wittgenstein, op. cit., p. 144.

3
Generative grammar and stylistic analysis

J. P. Thorne

The name 'stylistics' is given to studies of many different kinds (cf. Bailey and Burton, 1968). About the only thing they all have in common is that they involve in some form or another an analysis of the linguistic structure of texts. One can, of course, comment on the linguistic structure of a text without having a formal knowledge of grammar, but obviously such a knowledge is very useful. Any advance in grammatical studies is, therefore, likely to have some effect on stylistics. The purpose of this chapter is to suggest that there are special reasons for thinking that the introduction into linguistics of the notion 'generative grammar' will have an effect upon stylistics.

To see why this should be so it is necessary first to understand what a generative grammar is intended to be. In constructing a generative grammar of a language the linguist is attempting to construct a model of the native speaker's 'linguistic competence'; that is, of what he knows about the structure of his language. An obvious and important manifestation of linguistic competence is the English speaker's ability to recognize that some word strings, like *The children are asleep*, are well-formed (i.e. 'grammatical') English sentences while others, like *Asleep children the are*, are not. That is to say, anyone who speaks English possesses knowledge which enables him to recognize on hearing the first of these utterances that it has the syntactic structure of an English sentence and, on hearing the second, to recognize that it does not. This, in turn, is connected with the fact that he will understand the first while the second will appear meaningless to him. A generative grammar as described by Chomsky (1965), is organized in such a way that the output of the syntactic component of the grammar is the input to an interpretative semantic component. This aspect of linguistic competence can be accounted for quite naturally, then, by setting up the grammar in such a way that only well-formed sentences are generated (and, therefore, interpreted). But between these extremes of well-formedness occur sentences of varying degrees of grammaticalness (cf. Chomsky, 1965*b*, p. 148–60). For example, a sentence like *The houses are asleep*, while clearly not ungrammatical in the sense in which *Asleep children the are* is ungrammatical, is nevertheless not completely well-formed. These 'semi-sentences' pose a serious problem for the linguist. Their ungrammaticalness is the result, not of their having no syntactic structure, but of their having a syntactic structure that differs from that of any well-formed sentence. By the same token they can be interpreted, even though the interpretation has to be distinguished as 'figurative'. To solve this dilemma Katz (1964) has proposed that the linguist's task should include, not only the construction of a grammar that generates and interprets all and only the well-formed sentences in a language, but also the construction of a 'counter-grammar' that will generate and interpret all the semi-sentences of that language.

Another aspect of linguistic competence to which linguists have paid particular attention is termed 'acceptability' (cf. Ross, 1967). In the sense in which the term is being used here the sentences *An old man came in who suffered with asthma* and *An old man who suffered with asthma came in* are equally acceptable, whereas in the case of the sentence *An old man with asthma came in* and *An old man came in with asthma* the former is more acceptable than the latter. To take some other examples, the sentences *I called most of the girls up* and *I called up most of the girls* are equally acceptable but the sentence *I called up the girls who lived there* is more acceptable than the sentence *I called the girls who lived there up*. These last examples are important because they illustrate very clearly that the crucial factor here is not the mere length of certain elements in these sentences but their syntactic structure. This aspect of linguistic competence is accounted for by specifying output conditions (in the case of the sentences cited above these relate to the domains of certain optional permutation transformations), all sentences generated by the grammar but failing to meet these conditions being unacceptable sentences.

Linguists have tended to be preoccupied by the phenomena of grammaticalness and acceptability. But these are not the only structural phenomena that an adequate grammar should reflect. Another, to which some attention has been paid is illustrated by sentences like *The dog chased the cat that killed the rat that ate the corn* and *The rat the cat the dog chased killed ate the corn*. Both of these contain more than one underlying sentence. These happen to be the same in each case. It is therefore particularly interesting that the second sentence is more difficult to understand than the first. It seems somehow to be more complex. The relevant structural facts are that the first sentence is a right-branching structure while the second is self-embedding. That is to say, the tree-diagram for the first sentence shows that in each case the embedded sentence forms part of the predicate of its matrix sentence, whereas the tree-diagram for the second shows that each embedded sentence forms part of the subject of its matrix sentence. Sentences that have a self-embedding structure always appear more complex than corresponding sentences with right-branching structures. It could be argued that a grammar which failed to specify the structural characteristics of this phenomenon would be open to criticism in exactly the same way as one which failed to specify the structural characteristics of grammaticalness or acceptability.

Generative grammarians are not the first to be interested in the phenomenon of complexity. In fact, traditionally the characterization of a sentence as 'complex' would be accounted a stylistic judgment. The term 'complex' itself forms part of the traditional vocabulary of stylistics. The same is true, in effect, of judgments concerning grammaticalness and acceptability. Both 'ungrammatical' and 'unacceptable' can be related to traditional stylistic terms. The connection between certain kinds of ungrammatical structures and certain kinds of figurative expressions has already been noted. Some of the examples of unacceptable sentences given above could serve in a handbook on style as examples of how not to construct sentences. Conversely, if terms like 'loose', or 'terse', or 'emphatic' (to take other examples from the traditional vocabulary of stylistics) have any significance as descriptions of style – and surely they do – it must be because, like the description 'complex', they relate to certain identifiable structural properties. If this is less obviously the case with other stylistic terms it is only because the relationship is less clear, not because it does not exist. What the impressionistic terms of stylistics are impressions of are types of grammatical structures. The ability to form these judgments is just as much a manifestation of linguistic competence as the ability to form judgments about grammaticality and acceptability.

The main reason, then, for suggesting that generative grammar might prove to have an important influence on stylistic studies is that they are both concerned with essentially the same kind of phenomena. This is because the basic postulates of both studies (generative grammar explicitly, traditional stylistics implicitly) are mentalistic (in the sense of Katz, 1964). In both cases the most important data are responses relating to what is intuitively known about language structure. It can be argued that only a mentalistic grammar can provide an adequate basis for stylistics. It follows from the same argument that the failure of pre-Chomskyan linguistics to provide such a basis can be traced to its extreme anti-mentalist tendencies. This resulted in linguists' attention being restricted almost entirely to those structural facts which can be directly related to what is observable in language. Generative grammar is important to stylistics because, in addition to these 'surface structure' facts, it is concerned with the so-called 'deep structure' aspects of language, that is, those facts about linguistic structure which cannot be directly related to what can be observed. Most stylistic judgments relate to deep structure.

Obviously there is no reason why there should not be quite general studies of a phenomenon like terseness in just the same way as there are quite general studies of a phenomenon like acceptability. But presumably stylistics will continue to be mainly concerned with characterizing the structural properties of particular texts – especially literary texts. In describing the style of a particular text as 'terse' or 'complex' one is, of course, indicating the general impression one receives. Thus a passage which most people would describe as 'terse' usually turns out to contain a majority of – but not necessarily only – sentences which involve deletion rules in their generation. Particularly interesting cases of this kind of overall impression are those which lead us to describe the style of a passage as, say, Shakespearian or Jamesian, or which lead us to ascribe a text to a certain author. The fact that we can recognize successful parodies as being parodies of particular writers emphasizes the fact that it is structural considerations that form the basis for these impressions.

A study of the basis for these kinds of judgments is given in Ohmann (1964). Ohmann shows very clearly how an author's style can be related to his predilection for certain grammatical structures. Among the passages he examines is the following extract from Faulkner's *The Bear* (1942; 255–6):

> the desk and the shelf above it on which rested the letters in which McCaslin recorded the slow outward trickle of food and supplies and equipment which returned each fall as cotton made and ginned and sold (two threads frail as truth and impalpable as equators yet cable-strong to bind for life them who made the cotton to the land their sweat fell on), and the older ledgers clumsy and archaic in size and shape, on the yellowed pages of which were recorded in the faded hand of his father Theophilus and his uncle Amodeus during the two decades before the Civil War, the manumission in title at least of Carothers McCaslin's slaves ....

Ohmann describes the style of this passage as 'complex, highly individual and difficult ... also ... quite typically Faulknerian'. His analysis shows the structural correlates of this style to be a high proportion of (1) relative constructions, particularly those deleting the relative pronoun and the verb *to be*; (2) compound structures formed with the conjunction *and*; (3) comparative constructions. To support his claim that these represent the key structures in Faulkner's writing Ohmann also analyses characteristic passages from three other modern English prose writers showing that none of them reveal Faulkner's preference for this particular combination of structures.

It is probably true that most writers – perhaps all writers – maintain a preference for certain structures throughout the whole of their work. It is also true, of course, that a writer can vary the kinds of structures he employs in order to produce corresponding variations in style. Often a stylistic effect can be produced by just a slight shift in syntactic structure. Take for example the following passage from Raymond Chandler's novel *The Lady in the Lake* (1952, p. 139–40):

> An elegant handwriting, like the elegant hand that wrote it. I pushed it to one side and had another drink, I began to feel a little less savage. I pushed things around on the desk. My hands felt thick and hot and awkward. I ran a finger across the corner of the desk and looked at the streak made by the wiping off of the dust. I looked at the dust on my finger and wiped that off. I looked at my watch. I looked at the wall. I looked at nothing.
>
> I put the liquor bottle away and went over to the washbowl to rinse the glass out. When I had done that I washed my hands and bathed my face in cold water and looked at it. The flush was gone from the left cheek, but it looked a little swollen. Not very much, but enough to make me tighten up again. I brushed my hair and looked at the grey in it. There was getting to be plenty of grey in it. The face under the hair had a sick look. I didn't like the face at all.
>
> I went back to the desk and read Miss Fromsett's note again. I smoothed it out on the glass and sniffed it and smoothed it out some more and folded it and put it in my coat pocket.
>
> I sat very still and listened to the evening grow quiet outside the open windows. And very slowly I grew quiet with it.

The two most frequently occurring words in his passage are *I* and *and*. This superficial observation relates to the fact that most of the sentences have deep structures conforming to the pattern *I Verb Phrase and I Verb Phrase*. The number of underlying sentences joined together in this way being anything up to five. In each case the corresponding surface structure is formed by the deletion of the repeated first person pronoun. In fact, nearly every underlying sentence in this passage repeats some element from a previous sentence. Thus while 'repetitive' is undoubtedly an accurate description of the style of this passage its linguistic basis can be properly established only with reference to the deep structure of the sentences in it, a very general condition of English grammar determining that most of the repeated elements should not appear in their surface structures. This highly repetitive style plays a major part in creating the mood of aimless, nervous agitation the passage conveys. The last sentence stands apart from the rest of the sentences in the passage. Not merely because it announces a change of mood. Grammatically too, it forms an exception. It is the only sentence where the sequence *and I* occurs in a surface structure. This is because this sentence connects to the previous one, not only by repeating the subject (*I*) of its matrix but also by repeating the verb phrase (*grow quiet*) of its underlying constituent sentence. Several sentences repeat the verb phrase of a previous sentence, but this is the only case where a repeated verb does not have the subject *I* in both of its occurrences. Moreover, in its first occurrence the subject is inanimate (*evening*). How effective the resulting zeugma is can be judged by substituting another verb for the second occurrence of *grow quiet* (say, *relaxed*). At least part of its effectiveness comes from the fact that this sentence which announces a change of mood, a change from alienation to reconciliation, connects syntactically with the rest of the sentences in the passage in a different way from that in which they connect with each other.

So far we have been discussing aspects of linguistic structure that are common to both prose and poetry. Stylisticians have always been attracted to the question of whether or not it is possible to identify aspects of linguistic structure which distinguish prose from poetry. The problem is very old and very difficult. For the most part those writers, of any period, who have interested themselves in this problem have looked for features over and above the phonological features of rhythm and rhyme. But some of them have seen these features as providing an essential insight into the way in which the organization of the language of poetry differs from that of prose, claiming that what distinguishes poetry from mere verse is that in the case of the former these phonological regularities are matched or reinforced by grammatical regularities. This view is summarized in Mac Hammond's (1961, p. 482) statement that 'syntax is poetic when grammatically equivalent constituents in connected speech are juxtaposed by coordination or parataxis, or are otherwise prominently accumulated'. The phenomenon of 'parallelism' in poetry has been studied by among others Jakobson (1960, 1966) and Levin (1962). Implicit in some of these studies is the idea that not only with regard to the phonological component of the grammar but with regard also to the syntax and semantics the poet works under the restraint of self-imposed rules; that is, rules which do not form part of the grammar of a natural language. An attempt to restate this view of poetry within the larger context of the view of language structure provided by generative grammar is contained in Thorne (1965). (See also Hendricks, 1969; Fowler, 1969; Thorne, 1969).

The discussion centres around two observations. The first is that ungrammatical sentences tend to occur far more frequently in poetry than in prose. (The proportion tends to vary from the works of one poet to the next and, even more strikingly, from the poetry of one period to the next, but this remark is true, broadly speaking, of the work of all poets and all periods.) Recognition of these deviant sentences forms an essential element in our response to poetry. The second is that although, inevitably, we recognize these deviant sentences as being deviant, it is sometimes also the case that they are felt not to be deviant within the context of the poem. One of the poems studied (Thorne, 1965, p. 59) is Donne's 'A Nocturnal Upon S. Lucies Day'. The first stanza of the poem contains the clause (*mee*) *who am their Epitaph* where the deep structure would be equivalent to that of the sentence *I am their epitaph*. This is a semi-sentence. It breaks selectional rules which specify that noun phrases on either side of the copula *to be* should be marked in the same way for the feature *animacy*, that is either both should be plus animate or both should be minus animate. (Cf. *I am a student,* **I am a desk,* **The desk was a student, His desk was an old oil drum.*) In succeeding stanzas there occur the sentences *I am every dead thing, I ... am the grave of all*, and *I am None*, all of which break this same rule. (One could also add here *I am ... of the first nothing the Elixir grown* which involves a different kind of structure but the same selectional rule being broken.) At the same time the poem also contains the sentences *All these seem to laugh* (where *these* refers back to *the sunne* and *th'hydroptique earth*) and *Yea plants, yea stones detest and love*. In these sentences too, a selectional rule is broken – verbs which demand an animate subject taking here an inanimate subject. In short the poem has sentences which have inanimate nouns where one would usually expect to find animate nouns and animate nouns (or rather the animate first person pronoun) where one would expect to find inanimate nouns. These irregularities are regular in the context of the poem. It seems likely that these linguistic facts underlie the sense of chaos and breakdown of natural order which many literary critics have associated with the poem.

One way of representing these facts is simply to do what has just been done, that is, simply to list those structures in the poem which are deviant, indicating in each case which rules have been broken. Another way involves stating the rules which would actually generate these structures. Most of the rules would form part of the grammar of Standard English (that is, a grammar which would generate only well-formed sentences), but it would be necessary to give special rules for the first person pronoun, which in the language of the poem always selects an inanimate predicate (interestingly enough the sentence which might look as though it is an exception to this rule has a subjunctive copula, *Were I a man* ...) and for verbs like *laugh* and *love*, which in the language of the poem can select inanimate subjects. There is a good reason for preferring the second approach. It suggests a quite interesting hypothesis about what it is poets (or at least some poets) are trying to do when they write poetry and, therefore, also about what it is that distinguishes some kinds of poetry from prose. Behind the idea of constructing what is in effect a grammar for the poem lies the idea that what the poet has done is to create a new language (or dialect) and that the task that faces the reader is in some ways like that of learning a new language (or dialect).

There is room here only for one more example to illustrate this approach to the stylistic analysis of poetry. The poem is by Theodore Roethke (1957, p. 55).

Dolour
I have known the inexorable sadness of pencils,
Neat in their boxes, dolour of pad and paperweight,
All the misery of manila folders and mucilage,
Desolation in immaculate public places,
Lonely reception room, lavatory, switchboard,
The unalterable pathos of basin and pitcher,
Ritual of multigraph, paper-clip, comma,
Endless duplication of lives and objects.
And I have seen dust from the walls of institutions,
Finer than flour, alive, more dangerous than silica,
Sift, almost invisible, through long afternoons of tedium,
Dropping a fine film on nails and delicate eyebrows,
Glazing the pale hair, the duplicate grey standard faces.

From the point of view of this approach the most interesting feature of this poem is the ungrammatical constructions; *the inexorable sadness of pencils, dolour of pad and paperweight, misery of manila folders and mucilage.* These provide a particular problem for the analyst. There is, of course, nothing to stop one constructing a grammar which would assign quite arbitrary analyses to these or any of the constructions in the poem. This would be equivalent to making the claim that they were meaningless. But although they are deviant they are clearly not meaningless. They can be understood. The whole point of constructing a grammar which would generate these constructions is that it provides a way of stating clearly the interpretation that one finds for them.

The grammar that one constructs for a poem must therefore meet one of the conditions for a 'counter-grammar'. Although it contains rules which are not rules of Standard English, they must relate to rules of Standard English (cf. Katz, 1964, p. 412). Now constructions like *the ... sadness of pencils*, etc. are, presumably, nominalizations of underlying sentences of the form *The pencils are sad, The paperweight is dolorous, The manila folders are miserable*. Obviously these are deviant sentences. The problem is that there are at least two ways of accounting for their ungrammaticalness. This is because adjectives like *sad* and *miserable* select either animate nouns like *boy* and *girl* or certain subcategories of abstract nouns like *experience, occasion* and *spectacle*. Thus if one wants to say that nouns like *pencil, paperweight, manila folder*, etc. constitute a special subcategory of nouns in the language of the poem, one then has to decide whether the rule which governs their distribution relates to that governing the distribution of nouns like *boy* and *girl*, etc. or that governing the distribution of nouns like *experience, spectacle*, etc. in Standard English. A decision that is not open to one is to make the distribution of *pencil, paperweight*, etc. coincide with that of both of these subcategories, since this would mean that one had still not indicated the way in which one understood phrases like *the sadness of pencils*; the semantic interpretation of *sad boy* being, of course, different from that of *sad experience*. (Roughly speaking, in the first case the relationship is like that of verb to object, in the second like that of subject to verb.) The problem is typical of the kind of problem one encounters in attempting to construct grammars for poems and to some extent justifies the exercise. In making choices about the grammar one is choosing between readings of the poem.

In discussing the grammars both of the Donne poem and the Roethke poem the rules we have been concerned with have all been deep-structure rules. This is important in view of what it suggests about what it is these poets are trying to achieve, because (in terms of the grammatical model we have adopted) the deep structure of a sentence determines its meaning. For these poets the point of creating a new language, therefore, seems to be that it enables them to say not only things that can be said in Standard English, but in a different way, but also things that cannot be said in Standard English at all – though they can be understood only by someone who understands Standard English. Donne has created a language in which the word *I* is still the animate first person. But to attribute the regular occurrence in the language of the poem of sentences like *I am a grave* (and, by implication, the absence of sentences like *I am a man*) to a difference in the deep grammar of this pronoun is to attribute to it a different meaning (cf. Putnam, 1962, p. 222–3). The words *stone* and *plant* still retain all the features that together make up their ordinary meanings. But if the grammar of the language of the poem is such that *Stones love* is a well-formed sentence in it, then they too have changed their meaning. Similarly, in the language of Roethke's poem *pencil, pad,* etc. are still the names of pieces of stationery, but at the same time they acquire new meanings because they have (under one reading) acquired the selectional range of words like *experience* and *occasion*.

This has a bearing on the declared inability of many people to understand poems like these. It also explains why it is impossible to paraphrase some of the sentences in these poems. We have been concerned exclusively with selectional rules. Deviation from selectional rules seems to have always been the main source of 'witty' writing in English. This is particularly the case for selectional rules involving the features animate, inanimate, concrete, and abstract. There are comparatively few good jokes in English arising from dislocation of rules concerning the features, masculine and feminine. Poets do also invent their own surface-structure rules, of course. But on the whole it seems to be the case that poems in which the grammar differs from that of Standard English only in the surface structure are usually bad poems. Take the following lines of Longfellow:

> Have I dreamed? Or was it real,
>   What I saw as in a vision,
>   When to marches hymeneal
>   In the land of the Ideal
>   Moved my thought o'er Field Elysian?

The superficial strangeness of these lines is associated with the *ad hoc* transformations that have to be postulated for the analysis of the sentences in them. Their basic banality (their prosaicness) is associated with the fact that the deep structure of these sentences would be generated by rules which form part of the grammar of Standard English.

References

Bailey, W. and Burton, M. (1968). *English Stylistics: A Bibliography*. Cambridge, Mass.: MIT Press.
Chomsky, N. (1965a). *Current Issues in Linguistic Theory*. The Hague: Mouton.
Chomsky, N. (1965b). *Aspects of the Theory of Syntax*. Cambridge, Mass.: MIT Press.
Fowler, R. (1969). 'On the interpretation of "nonsense strings".' *Journal of Linguistics* 5, 75–83.
Hammond, M. (1961). 'Poetic syntax'. In Davie, D. *et al.* (eds.), *Poetics: Proceedings of the First International Conference of Work in Progress Devoted to the Problems of Poetics*. The Hague: Mouton.

Hendricks, W. (1969). 'Three models for the description of poetry'. *Journal of Linguistics* 5. 1–22.

Jakobson, R. (1960). 'Linguistics and poetics.' In Sebeok, T. (ed.), *Style in Language*. Cambridge, Mass.: MIT Press.

Jakobson, R. (1966). 'Grammatical parallelism and its Russian facet'. *Language* 42, 399–429.

Katz, J. (1964). 'Semi-sentences'. In Fodor, J. and Katz, J. (eds.) *The Structure of Language*. Englewood Cliffs: Prentice-Hall.

Levin, S. (1962). *Linguistic Structures in Poetry*. (Janua Linguarum; Series Minor, 23). The Hague: Mouton.

Ohmann, R. (1964). 'Generative grammars and the concept of literary style'. *Word*, 20. 423–39.

Putnam, H. (1962) 'Dreaming and "Depth Grammar"'. In Butler, R. J. (ed.), *Analytical Philosophy*. Oxford: Blackwell.

Ross, J. (1967). *Constraints on Variables in Syntax*. Unpublished doctoral dissertation. MIT.

Thorne, J. P. (1965). 'Stylistics and generative grammars'. *Journal of Linguistics* 1. 49–59.

Thorne, J. P. (1969). 'Poetry, stylistics and imaginary grammars'. *Journal of Linguistics* 5. 147–50.

4
What is stylistics and why are they saying such terrible things about it?

Stanley E. Fish

The first of the questions in my title – what is stylistics? – has already been answered by the practitioners of the art. Stylistics was born of a reaction to the subjectivity and imprecision of literary studies. For the appreciative raptures of the impressionistic critic, stylisticians purport to substitute precise and rigorous linguistic descriptions, and to proceed from those descriptions to interpretations for which they can claim a measure of objectivity. Stylistics, in short, is an attempt to put criticism on a scientific basis. Answering my second question – why are they saying such terrible things about it? – will be the business of this essay, and I would like to begin (somewhat obliquely, I admit) by quoting from the *New York Times Book Review* of 23 April 1972. On pages 18 and 19 of that issue we find the publishing firm of Peter Wyden, Inc., proclaiming the merits of a new book by Tom Chetwynd. The book is entitled *How to Interpret Your Own Dreams (In One Minute or Less)*. The title appears on a reproduction of the book jacket and beneath it are the following descriptive claims: 'Your key to 583 Dream Subjects with 1442 Interpretations', 'An Encyclopedic Dictionary'. These claims are supported and extended by a report of the author's researches and by a portion of the index. 'What do *you* dream about?' the reader is asked, 'Angels (see page 171), Babies (page 150), Bells (page 40), Cars, Collisions, Cooking, Death, Dogs, Doors, Exams, Falling, Hands, Hats, Illness, Monsters, Mother, Nudity, Sex, Teeth, Travel....' 'And these', the blurb continues, 'are just a few of the 583 dream subjects covered'. 'To compile this book', we are told, 'the author spent 10 years analyzing the works of Freud, Jung, Adler and other dream authorities. Carefully indexed and cross indexed, each dream subject is rated in four ways: what it most likely means; what it could well mean; what it might mean; and what it might possibly mean.... This remarkable dream dictionary enables you to look up any dream instantly ... find complete clues to its meaning.' Finally, and with typographic aids, the claims underlying these claims are put forward: in italics, *it really works*, and in large white letters against a black bar background, BASED ON SOLID SCIENCE.

However amusing one finds this advertisement, it would be a mistake to underestimate the desire to which it appeals: the desire for an instant and automatic interpretive procedure based on an inventory of fixed relationships between observable data and meanings, meanings which do not vary with context and which can be read out independently of the analyst or observer who need only perform the operations specified by the 'key'. It is a desire as new as information theory and as old as the impulse to escape from the flux and variability of the human situation to the security and stability of a timeless formalism. It is also, I think, the desire behind stylistics, and in the first part of this paper I should like to examine some representative attempts to achieve it.

My first example is taken from the work of Louis Milic, author of *A Quantitative Approach to the Style of Jonathan Swift* and other statistical and computer studies. In an article written for *The Computer & Literary Style*, Milic attempts to isolate the distinctive features of Swift's style.[1] He is particularly interested in the Swiftian habit of piling up words in series and in Swift's preference for certain kinds of connectives. His method is to compare Swift, in these and other respects, with Macauley, Addison, Gibbon, and Johnson, and the results of his researches are presented in the form of tables: 'Word-Class Frequency Distribution of All the Whole Samples of Swift, with Computed Arithmetic Mean', 'Percentage of Initial Connectives in 2000-Sentence Samples of Addison, Johnson, Macauley, and Swift', 'Total Introductory Connectives and Total Introductory Determiners as Percentages of All Introductory Elements', 'Frequency of Occurrence of the Most Common Single Three-Word Pattern as a Percentage of Total Patterns', 'Total Number of Different Patterns per Sample'. It will not be my concern here to scrutinize the data-gathering methods of Milic or the other stylisticians (although some of them are challengeable even on their own terms), for my interest is primarily in what is done with the data after they have been gathered. This is also Milic's interest, and in the final paragraphs of his essay he poses the major question: 'What interpretive inferences can be drawn from the material?' (p. 104). The answer comes in two parts and illustrates the two basic maneuvers executed by the stylisticians. The first is circular: 'The low frequency of initial determiners, taken together with the high frequency of initial connectives, makes [Swift] a writer who likes transitions and made much of connectives' (p. 104). As the reader will no doubt have noticed, the two halves of this sentence present the same information in slightly different terms, even though its rhetoric suggests that something has been explained. Here is an example of what makes some people impatient with stylistics and its baggage. The machinery of categorization and classification merely provides momentary pigeonholes for the constituents of a text, constituents which are then retrieved and reassembled into exactly the form they previously had. There is in short no gain in understanding; the procedure has been executed, but it hasn't gotten you anywhere. Stylisticians, however, are *determined* to get somewhere, and exactly where they are determined to get is indicated by Milic's next sentence. '[Swift's] use of series argues [that is, is a sign of or means] a fertile and well stocked mind.' Here the procedure is not circular but arbitrary. The data are scrutinized and an interpretation is *asserted* for them; asserted rather than proven because there is nothing in the machinery Milic cranks up to authorize the leap (from the data to a specification of their value) he makes. What does authorize it is an unexamined and highly suspect assumption that one can read directly from the description of a text (however derived) to the shape or quality of its author's mind, in this case from the sheer quantity of verbal items to the largeness of the intelligence that produced them.

The counterargument to this assumption is not that it can't be done (Milic, after all, has done it), but that it can be done all too easily, and in any direction one likes. One might conclude, for example, that Swift's use of series argues the presence of the contiguity disorder described by Roman Jakobson in *The Fundamentals of Language*;[2] or that Swift's use of series argues an unwillingness to finish his sentences; or that Swift's use of series argues an anal-retentive personality; or that Swift's use of series argues a nominalist rather than a realist philosophy and is therefore evidence of a mind insufficiently stocked with abstract ideas. These conclusions are neither more nor less defensible than the conclusion Milic reaches, or reaches for (it is the enterprise and not any one of its results that should be challenged), and their availability points to a serious defect in the procedures of stylistics, the absence of any constraint on the way in which one moves from description to interpretation, with the result that any interpretation one puts forward is arbitrary.

Milic, for his part, is not unaware of the problem. In a concluding paragraph, he admits that relating devices of style to personality is 'risky' and 'the chance of error ... great' because 'no personality syntax paradigm is available ... neither syntactic stylistics nor personality theory is yet capable of making the leap' (p. 105). Once again Milic provides a clear example of one of the basic maneuvers in the stylistics game: he acknowledges the dependence of his procedures on an unwarranted assumption, but then salvages both the assumption and the procedures by declaring that time and the collection of more data will give substance to the one and authorize the other. It is a remarkable *non sequitur* in which the suspect nature of his enterprise becomes a reason for continuing in it: a personality syntax paradigm may be currently unavailable or available in too many directions, but this only means that if we persist in our efforts to establish it, it will surely emerge. The more reasonable inference would be that the difficulty lies not with the present state of the art but with the art itself; and this is precisely what I shall finally argue, that the establishment of a syntax-personality or of any other paradigm is an impossible goal, which, because it is also an assumption, invalidates the procedures of the stylisticians before they begin, dooming them to successes that are meaningless because they are so easy.

Milic affords a particularly good perspective on what stylisticians do because his assumptions, along with their difficulties, are displayed so nakedly. A sentence like 'Swift's use of series argues a fertile and well stocked mind' doesn't come along very often. More typically, a stylistician will interpose a formidable apparatus between his descriptive and interpretive acts, thus obscuring the absence of any connection between them. For Richard Ohmann, that apparatus is transformational grammar and in 'Generative grammars and the concept of literary style' he uses it to distinguish between the prose of Faulkner and Hemingway.[3] Ohmann does this by demonstrating that Faulkner's style is no longer recognizable when 'the effects of three generalized transformations' – the relative clause transformation, the conjunction transformation, and the comparative transformation – are reversed. 'Denatured' of these transformations, a passage from 'The Bear', Ohmann says, retains 'virtually no traces of ... Faulkner's style' (p. 142). When the same denaturing is performed on Hemingway, however, 'the reduced passage still sounds very much like Hemingway. Nothing has been changed that seems crucial' (p. 144). From this, Ohmann declares, follow two conclusions: (1) Faulkner 'leans heavily upon a very small amount of grammatical apparatus' (p. 143); and (2) the 'stylistic difference ... between the Faulkner and Hemingway passages can be largely explained on the basis of [the] ... apparatus' (p. 145). To the first of these I would reply that it depends on what is meant by 'leans heavily upon'. Is this a statement about the apparatus or about the actual predilection of the author? (The confusion between the two is a hallmark of stylistic criticism.) To the second conclusion I would object strenuously, if by 'explained' Ohmann means anything more than made formalizable. That is, I am perfectly willing to admit that transformational grammar provides a better means of fingerprinting an author than would a measurement like the percentage of nouns or the mean length of sentences; for since the transformational model is able to deal not only with constituents but with their relationships, it can make distinctions at a structural, as opposed to a merely statistical, level. I am not willing, however, to give those distinctions an independent value, that is, to attach a fixed significance to the devices of the fingerprinting mechanism, any more than I would be willing to read from a man's actual fingerprint to his character or personality.

But this, as it turns out, is exactly what Ohmann wants to do. 'The move from formal description of styles to ... interpretation', he asserts, 'should be the ultimate goal of stylistics', and in the case of Faulkner, 'it seems reasonable to suppose that a writer whose style is so largely based on just these three semantically related transformations demonstrates in that style a certain conceptual orientation, a preferred way of organizing experience' (p. 143). But Faulkner's style can be said to be 'based on' these three transformations only in the sense that the submission of a Faulkner text to the transformational apparatus yields a description in which they dominate. In order to make anything more out of this, that is, in order to turn the description into a statement about Faulkner's conceptual orientation, Ohmann would have to do what Noam Chomsky so pointedly refrains from doing, assign a semantic value to the devices of his descriptive mechanism, so that rather than being neutral between he processes of production and reception, they are made directly to reflect them. In the course of this and other essays, Ohmann does just that, finding, for example, that Lawrence's heavy use of deletion transformations is responsible for the 'driving insistence one feels in reading' him,[4] and that Conrad's structures of chaining reflect his tendency to 'link one thing with another associatively',[5] and that Dylan Thomas's breaking of selectional rules serves his 'vision of things' of 'the world as process, as interacting forces and repeating cycle';[6] in short – and here I quote – 'that these syntactic preferences *correlate* with habits of meaning'.[7]

The distance between all of this and 'Swift's use of series argues a fertile and well stocked mind' is a matter only of methodological sophistication, not of substance, for both critics operate with the same assumptions and nominate the same goal, the establishing of an inventory in which formal items will be linked in a fixed relationship to semantic and psychological values. Like Milic, Ohmann admits that at this point his interpretive conclusions are speculative and tentative; but again, like Milic, he believes that it is only a matter of time before he can proceed more securely on the basis of a firm correlation between syntax and 'conceptual orientation', and the possibility of specifying such correlations, he declares, 'is one of the main justifications for studying style'.⁸ If this is so, then the enterprise is in trouble, not because it will fail, but because it will, in every case, succeed. Ohmann will always be able to assert (although not to prove) a plausible connection between the 'conceptual orientation' he discerns in an author and the formal patterns his descriptive apparatus yields. But since there is no warrant for that connection in the grammar he appropriates, there is no constraint on the manner in which he makes it, and therefore his interpretations will be as arbitrary and unverifiable as those of the most impressionistic of critics.

The point will be clearer, I think, if we turn for a moment to the work of J. P. Thorne, another linguist of the generative persuasion. While Ohmann and Milic are interested in reading from syntax to personality, Thorne would like to move in the other direction, from syntax to either content or effect, but his procedures are similarly illegitimate. Thorne begins in the obligatory way, by deploring the presence in literary studies of 'impressionistic terms'.⁹ Yet, he points out, these terms must be impressions of something, and what they are impressions of, he decides, 'are types of grammatical structures'. It follows from this that the task of stylistics is to construct a typology that would match up grammatical structures with the effects they invariably produce: 'If terms like "loose", or "terse" or "emphatic" have any significance ... – and surely they do – it must be because they relate to certain identifiable structural properties' (pp. 188–9). What follows is a series of analyses in which 'identifiable structural properties' are correlated with impressions and impressionistic terms. Thorne discovers, for example, that in Donne's 'A Nocturnal Upon St Lucie's Day' selectional rules are regularly broken. 'The poem has sentences which have inanimate nouns where one would usually expect to find animate nouns, and animate nouns ... where one would expect to find inanimate nouns.' 'It seems likely', he concludes, 'that these linguistic facts underlie the sense of chaos and the breakdown of order which many literary critics have associated with the poem' (p. 193). This is at once arbitrary and purposeful. The 'breakdown of order' exists only within his grammar's system of rules (and strange rules they are, since there is no penalty for breaking them); it is a formal, not a semantic fact (even though the rules are semantic), and there is no warrant at all for equating it with the 'sense' the poem supposedly conveys. That sense, however, has obviously been preselected by Thorne and the critics he cites, and is, in effect, responsible for its own discovery. In other words, what Thorne has done is scrutinize his data until he discerns a 'structural property' which can be made to fit his preconceptions. The exercise is successful, but it is also circular.¹⁰

It is not my intention flatly to deny any relationship between structure and sense, but to argue that if there is one, it is not to be explained by attributing an independent meaning to the linguistic facts, which will, in any case, mean differently in different circumstances. Indeed these same facts – animate nouns where one expects inanimate and inanimate where one expects animate – characterize much of Wordsworth's poetry, where the sense communicated is one of harmony rather than chaos. Of course, counterexamples of this kind do not prove that a critic is wrong (or right) in a particular case, but that the search for a paradigm of formal significances is a futile one. Those who are determined to pursue it, however, will find in transformational grammar the perfect vehicle; for since its formalisms operate independently of semantic and psychological processes (are neutral between production and reception) they can be assigned any semantic or psychological value one may wish them to carry. Thus Ohmann can determine that in one of Conrad's sentences the deep-structural subject 'secret sharer' appears thirteen times and conclude that the reader who understands the sentence must 'register' what is absent from its surface;[11] while Roderick Jacobs and Peter Rosenbaum can, with equal plausibility, conclude that the presence of relative-clause reduction transformations in a story by John Updike results 'in a very careful suppression of any mention of individual beings' as agents.[12] In one analysis the grammatical machinery is translated into an activity the reader must perform; in the other it prevents him from performing that same activity. This is a game that is just too easy to play.

It is possible, I suppose, to salvage the game, at least temporarily, by making it more sophisticated, by contextualizing it. One could simply write a rule that allows for the different valuings of the same pattern by taking into account the features which surround it in context. But this would only lead to the bringing forward of further counterexamples and the continual and regressive rewriting of the rule. Eventually a point would be reached where a separate rule was required for each and every occurrence; and at that point the assumption that formal features *possess* meaning would no longer be tenable, and the enterprise of the stylisticians – at least as they conceive it – will have been abandoned.[13]

One can be certain, however, that it will not be abandoned, partly because the lure of 'solid science' and the promise of an automatic interpretive procedure is so great, and partly because apparent successes are so easy to come by. For a final and spectacular example I turn to Michael Halliday and an article entitled 'Linguistic function and literary style.'[14] Halliday is the proprietor of what he calls a category-scale grammar, a grammar so complicated that a full explanation would take up more space than I have. Allow me, however, to introduce a few of the basic terms. The number of categories is four: unit, structure, class, and system. Two of these, unit and structure, are categories of chain; that is, they refer to the syntagmatic axis or axis of combination. The category of unit relates the linear constituents of discourse to one another as they combine; representative units are morpheme, word, group, clause, and sentence. The category of structure is concerned with the syntagmatic relationships within units: subject, complements, adjunct, and predicator are elements of structure. The other two categories are categories of choice, of the paradigmatic axis or the axis of selection. The category of class contains those items which can be substituted for one another at certain points in a unit; classes include nouns, verbs, and adjectives. The category of system refers to the systematic relationships between elements of structure, relationships of agreement and difference, such as singular and plural, active and passive. Together, these categories make it possible for the linguist to segment his text either horizontally or vertically; that is, they make possible an exhaustive taxonomy.

This, however, is only part of the story. In addition, Halliday introduces three scales of abstraction which link the categories to each other and to the language data. They are rank, exponence, and delicacy. The scale of rank refers to the operation of units within the structure of another unit: a clause, for example, may operate in the structure of another clause, or of a group, or even of a word, and these would be first, second, and third degree rank shifts, respectively. Exponence is the scale by which the abstractions of the system relate to the data: it allows you to trace your way back from any point in the descriptive act to the actual words of a text. And finally the scale of delicacy is the degree of depth at which the descriptive act is being performed. While in some instances one might be satisfied to specify at the level of a clause or a group, in a more delicate description one would want to describe the constituents and relationships within those units themselves.

If this were all, the apparatus would be formidable enough; but there is more. Halliday also adopts, with some modifications, Karl Bühler's tripartite division of language into three functions – the ideational function or the expression of content; the interpersonal function, the expression of the speaker's attitudes and evaluations, and of the relationships he sets up between himself and the listener; and the textual function, through which language makes links with itself and with the extralinguistic situation.[15] Obviously these functions exist at a different level of abstraction from each other and from the taxonomic machinery of categories and scales, and just as obviously they create a whole new set of possible relationships between the items specified in that taxonomy; for as Halliday himself remarks, in a statement that boggles the mind with its mathematical implications, 'each sentence embodies all functions ... and most constituents of sentences also embody more than one function.'[16]

The result is that while the distinctions one can make with the grammar are minute and infinite, they are also meaningless, for they refer to nothing except the categories of the system that produced them, categories which are themselves unrelated to anything outside their circle except by an arbitrary act of assertion. It follows, then, that when this grammar is used to analyze a text, it can legitimately do nothing more than provide labels for its constituents, which is exactly what Halliday does to a sentence from *Through the Looking Glass:* 'It's a poor sort of memory that only works backwards.' Here is the analysis:

> The word *poor* is a 'modifier', and thus expresses a subclass of its head word *memory* (ideational); while at the same time it is an 'epithet' expressing the Queen's attitude (interpersonal), and the choice of this word in this environment (as opposed to, say, useful) indicates more specifically that the attitude is one of disapproval. The words *it's ... that* have here no reference at all outside the sentence, but they structure the message in a particular way (textual), which represents the Queen's opinion as if it were an 'attribute' (ideational), and defines one class of *memory* as exclusively possessing this undersirable quality (ideational). The lexical repetition in *memory that only works backwards* relates the Queen's remark (textual) to *mine only works one way* in which *mine* refers anaphorically, by ellipsis, to *memory* in the preceding sentence (textual) and also to *I* in Alice's expression of her own judgment *I'm sure* (interpersonal). Thus ideational content and personal interaction are woven together with, and by means of, the textual structure to form a coherent whole. (p. 337)

What, you might ask, is this coherent whole? The answer is, 'It's a poor sort of memory that only works backwards.' But that, you object, is what we had at the beginning. Exactly. When a text is run through Halliday's machine, its parts are first disassembled, then labeled, and finally recombined into their original form. The procedure is a complicated one, and it requires a great many operations, but the critic who performs them has finally done nothing at all.

Halliday, however, is determined to do something, and what he is determined to do is confer a value on the formal distinctions his machine reads out. His text is William Golding's *The Inheritors*, a story of two prehistoric tribes one of which supplants the other. The two tribes – the 'people' and the 'new people', respectively – are distinguished not only by their activities but by their respective languages, and these, in turn, are distinguishable from the language of the reader. Language A, the language of the 'people', is, according to Halliday, dominant for more than nine tenths of the novel. Here is a sample of it:

62 *Essays in Modern Stylistics*

> The man turned sideways in the bushes and looked at Lok along his shoulder. A stick rose upright and there was a lump of bone in the middle. Lok peered at the stick and the lump of bone and the small eyes in the bone things over the face. Suddenly Lok understood that the man was holding the stick out to him but neither he nor Lok could reach across the river. He would have laughed were it not for the echo of screaming in his head. The stick began to grow shorter at both ends. Then it shot out to full length again. The dead tree by Lok's ear acquired a voice. 'Clop.' His ears twitched and he turned to the tree. By his face there had grown a twig. (p. 360)

From this and other samples Halliday proceeds to a description of the people's language, using the full apparatus of his category-scale grammar; but what begins as a description turns very quickly into something else:

> The clauses of passage A ... are mainly clauses of action ... location ... or mental process ... the remainder are attributive.... Almost all of the action clauses ... describe simple movements ... and of these the majority ... are intransitive.... Even such normally transitive verbs as *grab* occur intransitively.... Moreover a high proportion ... of the subjects are not people; they are either parts of the body ... or inanimate objects ... and of the human subjects half again ... are found in clauses which are not clauses of action. Even among the four transitive action clauses ... one has an inanimate subject and one is reflexive. There is a stress set up, a kind of syntactic counterpoint, between verbs of movement in their most active and dynamic form ... and the preference for non-human subjects and the almost total absence of transitive clauses. (pp. 349–50)

Here, of course, is where the sleight of hand begins. To label a verb 'active' is simply to locate it in a system of formal differences and relationships within a grammar; to call it 'dynamic' is to semanticize the label, and even, as we see when the description continues, to moralize it:

> It is particularly the lack of transitive clauses of action with human subjects ... that creates an atmosphere of ineffectual activity; the scene is one of constant movement, but movement which is as much inanimate as human and in which only the mover is affected.... The syntactic tension expresses this combination of activity and helplessness. No doubt this is a fair summary of the life of Neanderthal man. (pp. 349–50)

This paragraph is a progression of illegitimate inferences. Halliday first gives his descriptive terms a value, and then he makes an ideogram of the patterns they yield. Moreover, the content of that ideogram – the Neanderthal mentality – is quite literally a fiction (one wonders where he got his information), and it is therefore impossible that these or any other forms should express it.

What happens next is predictable. The novel receives a Darwinian reading in which the grammatically impoverished 'people' are deservedly supplanted by the 'new people' whose fuller transitivity patterns are closer to our own: 'The transitivity patterns ... are the reflexion of the underlying theme ... the inherent limitations of understanding of Lok and his people and their consequent inability to survive when confronted with beings at a higher stage of development' (p. 350). The remainder of the essay is full of statements like this; the verbal patterns 'reflect' the subject matter, are 'congruent' with it, 'express' it, 'embody' it, 'encode' it, and at one point even 'enshrine' it. The assumption is one we have met before – 'syntactic preferences correlate with habits of meaning' – but here it is put into practice on a much grander scale: 'The "people's" use of transitivity patterns argues a Neanderthal mind.'

In short, when Halliday does something with his apparatus, it is just as arbitrary as what Milic and Ohmann and Thorne do with theirs. But why, one might ask, is he arbitrary in this direction? Given the evidence, at least as he marshals it, the way seems equally open to an Edenic rather than a Darwinian reading of the novel, a reading in which the language of the 'people' reflects (or embodies or enshrines) a lost harmony between man and an animate nature. The triumph of the 'new people' would then be a disaster, the beginning of the end, of a decline into the taxonomic aridity of a mechanistic universe. There are two answers to this question, and the first should not surprise us. Halliday's interpretation precedes his gathering and evaluating of the data, and it, rather than any ability of the syntax to embody a conceptual orientation, is responsible for the way in which the data are read. There is some evidence that the interpretation is not his own (he refers with approval to the 'penetrating critical study' of Mark Kinkead-Weakes and Ian Gregor), but whatever its source – and this is the second answer to my question – its attraction is the opportunity it provides him to make his apparatus the hero of the novel. For in the reading Halliday offers, the deficiencies of the 'people' are measured by the inability of their language to fill out the categories of his grammar. Thus when he remarks that 'in Lok's understanding the complex taxonomic ordering of natural phenomena that is implied by the use of defining modifiers is lacking, or ... rudimentary' (p. 352), we see him sliding from an application of his system to a judgment on the descriptions it yields; and conversely, when the 'new people' win out, they do so in large part because they speak a language that requires for its analysis the full machinery of that system. Not only does Halliday go directly from formal categories to interpretation, but he goes to an interpretation which proclaims the superiority of his formal categories. The survival of the fittest tribe is coincidental with a step toward the emergence of the fittest grammar. Whether Golding knew it or not, it would seem that he was writing an allegory of the ultimate triumph of Neo-Firthian man.

Is there, then, no point to Halliday's exercise? Are the patterns he uncovers without meaning? Not at all. It is just that the explanation for that meaning is not the capacity of a syntax to express it, but the ability of a reader to confer it. Golding, as Halliday notes, prefaces *The Inheritors* with an excerpt from H. G. Wells's discussion of Neanderthal Man. As a result, we enter the story expecting to encounter a people who differ from us in important respects, and we are predisposed to attach that difference to whatever in their behavior calls attention to itself. It is in this way that the language of the 'people' becomes significant, not because it is symbolic, but because it functions in a structure of expectations, and it is in the context of that structure that a reader is moved to assign it a value. The point is one that Halliday almost makes, but he throws it away, on two occasions; first when he remarks that the reader's entrance into the novel requires a 'considerable effort of interpretation' (p. 348), and later when he specifies the nature of that effort: 'the difficulties of understanding are at the level of interpretation – or rather ... of re-interpretation, as when we insist on translating "the stick began to grow shorter at both ends" as "the man drew the bow"' (p. 358). Here I would quarrel only with the phrase 'we insist'; for the decision to reinterpret is not made freely; it is inseparable from the activity of reading (the *text* insists), and the effort expended in the course of that activity becomes the measure and sign of the distance between us and the characters in the novel. In other words, the link between the language and any sense we have of Neanderthal Man is fashioned in response to the demands of the reading experience, it does not exist prior to that experience, and in the experience of another work it will not be fashioned, even if the work were to display the same formal features. In any number of contexts, the sentence 'the stick grew shorter at both ends' would present no difficulty for a reader; it would require no effort of reinterpretation, and therefore it would not take on the meaning which that effort *creates* in *The Inheritors*. Halliday's mistake is not to assert a value for his data but to locate that value in a paradigm and so bypass the context in which it is actually acquired.

This goes to the heart of my quarrel with the stylisticians: in their rush to establish an inventory of fixed significances, they bypass the activity in the course of which significances are, if only momentarily, fixed. I have said before that their procedures are arbitrary, and that they acknowledge no constraint on their interpretations of the data. The shape of the reader's experience is the constraint they decline to acknowledge. Were they to make that shape the focus of their analyses, it would lead them to the value conferred by its events. Instead they proceed in accordance with the rule laid down by Martin Joos: 'Text signals its own structure',[17] treating the deposit of an activity as if it were the activity itself, as if meanings arose independently of human transactions. As a result, they are left with patterns and statistics that have been cut off from their animating source, banks of data that are unattached to anything but their own formal categories, and are therefore, quite literally, meaningless.

In this connection it is useful to turn to a distinction made by John Searle, between institutional facts – facts rooted in a recognition of human purposes, needs, and goals – and brute facts – facts that are merely quantifiable. 'Imagine', says Searle,

> a group of highly trained observers describing a ... football game in statements only of brute facts. What could they say by way of description? Well, within certain areas a good deal could be said, and using statistical techniques certain 'laws' could even be formulated ... we can imagine that after a time our observers would discover the law of periodic clustering: at regular intervals organisms in like colored shirts cluster together in roughly circular fashion.... Furthermore, at equally regular intervals, circular clustering is followed by linear clustering ... and linear clustering is followed by the phenomenon of linear interpenetration.... But no matter how much data of this sort we imagine our observers to collect and no matter how many inductive generalizations we imagine them to make from the data, they still have not described football. What is missing from their description? What is missing are ... concepts such as touchdown, offside, game, points, first down, time out, etc. ... The missing statements are precisely what describes the phenomenon on the field *as a game of football*. The other descriptions, the description of the brute facts can [only] be explained in terms of the institutional facts.[18]

In my argument the institutional facts are the events that are constitutive of the specifically human activity of reading, while the brute facts are the observable formal patterns that can be discerned in the traces or residue of that activity. The stylisticians are thus in the position of trying to do what Searle says cannot be done: explain the brute facts without reference to the institutional facts which give them value. They would specify the meaning of the moves in the game without taking into account the game itself. Paradoxically, however, this gap in their procedures does not hamper but free them; for while it is true, as Hubert Dreyfus has recently observed, that once the data have 'been taken out of context and stripped of all significance, it is not so easy to give it back',[19] the corollary is that it is *very* easy to replace it with whatever significance you wish to bring forward. The result is interpretations that are simultaneously fixed and arbitrary, fixed because they are specified apart from contexts, and arbitrary because they are fixed, because it is in contexts that meaning occurs.

The stylisticians, of course, have an alternative theory of meaning, and it is both the goal of, and the authorization for, their procedures. In that theory, meaning is located in the inventory of relationships they seek to specify, an inventory that exists independently of the activities of producers and consumers, who are reduced either to selecting items from its storehouse of significances or to recognizing the items that have been selected. As a theory, it is distinguished by what it does away with, and what it does away with are human beings, at least insofar as they are responsible for creating rather than simply exchanging meanings. This is why the stylisticians almost to a man identify meaning with either logic or message or information, because these entities are 'pure' and remain uninfluenced by the needs and purposes of those who traffic in them. I have been arguing all along that the goal of the stylisticians is impossible, but my larger objection is that it is unworthy, for it would deny to man the most remarkable of his abilities, the ability to give the world meaning rather than to extract a meaning that is already there.

This, however, is precisely what the stylisticians want to avoid, the protean and various significances which are attached, in context and by human beings, to any number of formal configurations. Behind their theory, which is reflected in their goal which authorizes their procedures, is a desire and a fear: the desire to be relieved of the burden of interpretation by handing it over to an algorithm, and the fear of being left alone with the self-renewing and unquantifiable power of human signifying. So strong is this fear that it rules their procedures even when they appear to be taking into account what I accuse them of ignoring. Michael Riffaterre is a case in point. In every way Mr Riffaterre seems to be on the right side. He criticizes descriptive techniques that fail to distinguish between merely linguistic patterns and patterns a reader could be expected to actualize.[20] He rejects the attempts of other critics to endow 'formal ... categories ... with esthetic and ... ethical values'.[21] He insists that the proper object of analysis is not the poem or message but the 'whole act of communication'.[22] He argues for the necessity of 'following exactly the normal reading process',[23] and it is that process he seeks to describe when he asks readers, or as he calls them, informants, to report on their experiences. Once the process is described, however, Riffaterre does something very curious: he empties it of its content.[24] That is, he discounts everything his readers tell him about what they were doing and retains only the points at which they were compelled to do it. The pattern that emerges, a pattern of contentless stresses and emphases, is then fleshed out by the interpretation he proceeds to educe.

In short, Riffaterre does exactly what the other stylisticians do, but he does it later: he cuts his data off from the source of value and is then free to confer any value he pleases. The explanation for this curious maneuver is to be found in his equation of meaning with message or information; for if the message is the meaning, a reader's activities can only be valued in so far as they contribute to its clear and firm reception; anything else is simply evidence of an unwanted subjectivity and must be discarded. While the reader is admitted into Riffaterre's procedures, there is no real place for him in the theory and he is sent away after he has performed the mechanical task of locating the field of analysis. In the end, Riffaterre is distinguished only by the nature of his diversionary machinery. Like the other stylisticians, he introduces a bulky apparatus which obscures the absence of any connection between his descriptive and interpretive acts; the difference is that his is precisely the apparatus that would supply the connection (it is not taxonomic but explanatory); but after introducing it, he eviscerates it.

Richard Ohmann performs somewhat the same operation on an entire school of philosophy. In his most recent work, Ohmann has proposed literary applications to the Speech Act theory of J. L. Austin (*How to Do Things with Words*) and John Searle,[25] a theory that turns traditional philosophy around by denying the primacy and even the existence of pure or context-free statements, All utterances, argue Austin and Searle, are to be understood as instances of purposeful human actions which happen to require language for their performance. Some of these are promising, ordering, commanding, requesting, questioning, warning, stating, praising, greeting, etc. Even this abbreviated list should be enough to suggest the main contention of this school, which is captured in Searle's declaration that propositional acts do not occur alone.[26] What this means is that every utterance possesses an illocutionary force, an indication of the way it is to be taken (as a promise, threat, warning, etc.) and that no utterance is ever taken purely, without reference to an intention in a context. Thus, for example, the string of words 'I will come' may, in different circumstances, be a promise, a threat, a warning, a prediction; but it will always be one of these, and it will never be just a meaning unattached to a situation. What an older theory would have called the pure semantic value of the utterance is in this theory merely an abstraction, which, although it can be separated out for the sake of analysis, has no separate and independent status. The various illocutionary lives led by 'I will come' are not different handlings of the same meaning, they are different meanings. In Speech Act theory, there is only one semantic level, not two; detached from its illocutionary force, a sentence is just a series of noises. Illocutionary force *is* meaning. (This is obvious in the paradigm instances where the illocutionary force marker is explicit, that is, a part of the utterance, which certainly cannot be detached from itself.)

It is not my intention here to embrace this theory (although I am attracted to it) but to explain some of its terms, terms which Ohmann appropriates. He also distorts them, in two predictable directions. First of all, he takes the slice of the speech act that Searle insists cannot stand alone and gives it an independent status. He calls it the locutionary act – a designation he borrows from Austin – and endows it with a force of its own, the semantic force of logical and grammatical structures.[27] This locutionary act then becomes the basic level of a two-level system of significations. The second, and subsidiary, level is occupied by the inventory of illocutionary forces, which function more or less as a rhetoric of soical conventions and intentions. Illocutionary force is thus dislodged from its primary position and reduced to a kind of *emphasis*, something that is added to a content which is detachable from it and survives its influence. Ohmann, in short, turns the major insight of the speech-act philosophers on its head, precisely undoing what they have so carefully done. It is in a way a remarkable feat: he manages to take a theory rooted in the recognition of human meaning and make it assert the primacy of a meaning that is specifiable apart from human activities. He succeeds, in the face of great odds, in preserving the context-free propositional core that is necessary if there is to be a rationale for the procedures of stylistics,[28] and it is only a measure of his success that he is then able to define literature impossibly as 'discourse without illocutionary force'.[29]

I do not mean to suggest conscious intention on Ohmann's part, any more than I would argue that the stylisticians consciously perform illegitimate acts of interpretation which they then deliberately disguise. Indeed I take the performance of these acts as evidence of the extent to which they are unaware of their assumptions; for if they were true to their covert principles (as are, for example, the structuralists)[30] they would be content with the description of formal patterns and admit that the value-free operation of those patterns has always been their goal. But they are not so content and insist on leaping from those patterns to the human concerns their procedures exclude. The dehumanization of meaning may be the implication, as well as the result, of what they do; but it is not, I think, what they consciously *want* to do.

What we have then, is a confusion between methodology and intention, and it is a confusion that is difficult to discern in the midst of the pseudo-scientific paraphernalia the stylisticians bring to bear. I return to my opening paragraph and to a final paradox While it is the program of stylistics to replace the subjectivity of literary studies with objective techniques of description and interpretation, its practitioners ignore what is *objectively* true – that meaning is not the property of a timeless formalism, but something acquired in the context of an activity – and therefore they are finally more subjective than the critics they would replace. For an open impressionism, they substitute the covert impressionism of anchorless statistics and self-referring categories. In the name of responsible procedures, they offer a methodized irresponsibility, and, as a result, they produce interpretations which are either circular – mechanical reshufflings of the data – or arbitrary – readings of the data that are unconstrained by anything in their machinery.

What makes this picture particularly disturbing is the unlikelihood of its changing; for among the favorite pronouncements of the stylisticians are two that protect them from confronting or even acknowledging the deficiencies of their operations. The first is: 'Stylistic studies are essentially comparative.' Properly understood, this article of faith is a covert admission of the charges I have been making. What the stylisticians compare are the statistics derived from applying their categories to a variety of texts; but since those categories are unattached to anything (are without meaning) the differences revealed by the statistics are purely formal, and the only thing one can legitimately do with them is compare them with each other. The weakness of the exercise is that it is without content, but this is also its strength, since it can be endlessly and satisfyingly repeated without hazarding assertions about meaning or value. It is when such assertions are hazarded that the stylisticians get into trouble, but at this point they are ready with a second article of faith: the apparent unreliability of our procedures is a condition of insufficient data. Thus while Lúbomir Doležel (to cite just one example) is forced to admit that 'there are surprising contradictions in the various interpretations of style characteristics', he manages to escape the implications of his admission by hanging everything on a future hope: 'All conclusions about the properties and nature of style characteristics, about the speaker type and text type, and about stylistic differences, are to be considered hypotheses that will be confirmed or refuted by the accumulation of vast empirical material.'[31] But the accumulation of empirical material will make a difference only if the ability of human beings to confer meaning is finite and circumscribable within a statistical formula; if it is not, then the resulting data will do nothing more than trace out more fully the past performance of that ability, rather than, as Doležel and others hope, make its future performances predictable. In other words, the statistics will never catch up with the phenomenon they seek to circumscribe. But one can avoid this realization simply by forever advancing the date when the availability of more data will make everything all right.[32] The failure of the basic assumption to prove itself is also the mechanism which assures its continuing life, and assures too that stylisticians will never come to terms with the theoretical difficulties of their enterprise.

If the enterprise is so troubled, if, in short, the things people say about stylistics aren't terrible enough, what is the remedy? What is the critic who is interested in verbal analysis to do? The answer to this question would be the substance of another essay, but it has been more than anticipated here, especially in my counteranalysis of *The Inheritors*. I do not, the reader will recall, deny that the formal distinctions Halliday uncovers are meaningful; but where he assumes that they *possess* meaning (as a consequence of a built-in relationship between formal features and cognitive capacities), I would argue that they *acquire* it, and that they acquire it by virtue of their position in a structure of experience. The structure with which the stylisticians are concerned is a structure of observable formal patterns, and while such patterns do exist they are themselves part of a larger pattern the description of which is necessary for a determination of their value. Thus, for example, while it is certainly possible (as Halliday demonstrates) to specify the properties of the languages spoken by the tribes in *The Inheritors*, the significance of those properties is a function of their reception and negotiation by a reader who comes upon them already oriented in the direction of specific concerns and possessed of (or by) certain expectations. These concerns and expectations themselves arise in the course of a consecutive activity engaged in by a finite consciousness; and it is my contention that a characterization of that activity must precede, and by preceding control, the characterization of the formal features which become part of *its* structure. In short, I am calling not for the end of stylistics but for a new stylistics, what I have termed elsewhere an 'affective' stylistics,[33] in which the focus of attention is shifted from the spatial context of a page and its observable regularities to the temporal context of a mind and its experiences.

Does this mean a return to the dreaded impressionism? Quite the reverse. The demand for precision will be even greater because the object of analysis is a process whose shape is continually changing. In order to describe that shape, it will be necessary to make use of all the information that formal characterizations of language can provide, although that information will be viewed from a different perspective. Rather than regarding it as directly translatable into what a word or a pattern *means*, it will be used more exactly to specify what a reader, as he comes upon that word or pattern, is *doing*, what assumptions he is making, what conclusions he is reaching, what expectations he is forming, what attitudes he is entertaining, in short, what acts he is being moved to perform. When Milic observes that in Swift's prose connectives are often redundant and even contradictory – concessives cheek by jowl with causals[34] – we can proceed from what he tells us to an account of what happens when a reader is alternately invited to anticipate a conclusion and asked to qualify it before it appears. When Ohmann declares that the syntactical deviance of Dylan Thomas's 'A Winter's Tale', 'breaks down categorical boundaries and converts juxtaposition into action',[35] the boundaries, if they exist, take the form of a reader's expectations and their breaking down is an action *he* performs, thereby fashioning for himself the 'vision of things' which the critic would attribute to the language. And when Halliday demonstrates that in the language of the 'people' in Golding's *The Inheritors*, agency is given not to human but to inanimate subjects ('the stick grew shorter at both ends'), we can extrapolate from his evidence to the interpretive effort demanded of the reader who must negotiate it. In each case, a statement about the shape of the data is reformulated as a statement about the (necessary) shape of response, and in the kind of analysis I propose, a succession of such shapes would itself be given shape by the needs and concerns and abilities of a consciousness moving and working in time.

Information about language can be turned into information about response even when the formalizations are unattached to specific texts. Searle's analyses of questions, commands, promises, etc., in terms of the roles they involve, the obligations they institute, and the needs they presuppose, allow us, indeed oblige us, to include these things in any account of what a reader of a question or command or promise understands. Thus when Joan Didion begins *Play It As It Lays* with the sentence 'What makes Iago evil?', simply by taking the question in, the reader casts himself in the role of its answerer. Moreover, he is directed by the tense, aspect (frequentative), and semantic content of 'makes' to play that role in the context of a continuing and public literary debate about causality and motivation (how different would it be were the question 'Why is Iago evil?'); and he will respond, or so Miss Didion assumes, with one or more of the many explanations that have been offered for Iago's behavior.[36] That same reader, however, will be made a little less comfortable in his role by the second sentence: 'Some people ask.' The effect of 'some' is to divide the world into two groups, those who seek after reasons and causes and those who don't. The reader, of course, has already accepted the invitation extended by the prose to become a member of the first group, and, moreover, he has accepted it in assumed fellowship with the first-person voice. That fellowship is upset by the third sentence – 'I never ask' – which is also a judgment on what the reader has been (involuntarily) doing.

Reader and narrator are now on different sides of the question originally introduced by the latter, and the tension between them gives point and direction to the experience of what follows.

Little of what I have said about this paragraph would emerge from a formal characterization of its components, but in my description of its experience I have been able to make use of formal characterizations – of a Speech Act analysis of a question, of a logician's analysis of the properties of 'some', of a philosopher's analysis of making something happen – by regarding their content as cues for the reader to engage in activities. What is significant about these activities is that they are interpretive; for this means that a procedure in which their characterization is the first order of business avoids the chief theoretical deficiency of stylistics as it is now practiced. I have repeatedly objected to the absence in the work of the stylisticians of any connection between their descriptive and interpretive acts. In the kind of stylistics I propose, *interpretive acts are what is being described*; they, rather than verbal patterns arranging themselves in space, are the content of the analysis. This is more than a procedural distinction; for at its heart are different notions of what it is to read which are finally different notions of what it is to be human. Implict in what the stylisticians do is the assumption that to read is to put together discrete bits of meaning until they form what a traditional grammar would call a complete thought. In this view, the world, or the world of the text, is already ordered and filled with significances and what the reader is required to do is get them out (hence the question, 'What did you get out of that?'). In short, the reader's job is to extract the meanings that formal patterns possess prior to, and independently of, his activities. In my view, these same activities are constitutive of a structure of concerns which is necessarily prior to any examination of meaningful patterns because it is itself the occasion of their coming into being. The stylisticians proceed as if there were observable facts that could first be described and then interpreted. What I am suggesting is that an interpreting entity, endowed with purposes and concerns, is, by virtue of its very operation, determining what counts as the facts to be observed,[37] and, moreover, that since this determining is not a neutral marking out of a valueless area, but the extension of an already existing field of interests, it *is* an interpretation.

The difference in the two views is enormous, for it amounts to no less than the difference between regarding human beings as passive and disinterested comprehenders of a knowledge external to them (that is, of an *objective* knowledge) and regarding human beings as at every moment creating the experiential spaces into which a personal knowledge flows. It is also a difference in methodological responsibility and rigor, between a procedure which is from the very beginning organizing itself in terms of what

What is stylistics? 73

is significant, and a procedure which has no obligatory point of origin or rest. That is, if one sets out to describe in the absence of that which marks out the field of description, there is no way of deciding either where to begin or where to stop, because there is no way of deciding what counts. In such a situation, one either goes on at random and forever (here we might cite the monumental aridity of Jakobson's analyses of Baudelaire and Shakespeare) or one stops when the accumulated data can be made to fit a preconceived interpretive thesis. It has seemed to many that these are the only alternatives, and that, as Roger Fowler has declared, the choice is between 'mere description' or description performed at the direction of a preformulated literary hunch.[38] I have been arguing for a third way, one which neither begs the question of meaning nor predecides it arbitrarily, but takes as its point of departure the interpretive activity (experience) by virtue of which meanings occur.

This, then, is the way to repair the ruins of stylistics, not by linking the descriptive and interpretive acts, but by making them one.[39] It is hardly necessary to say that this kind of analysis is not without problems, and the problems are for the most part a direct consequence of its assumptions about what it means to be human. It can have no rules in the sense of discovery procedures, since the contextualizing ability that characterizes being human is not circumscribed by its previous performances, performances which, while they constitute the history of that ability, do not constitute its limits. Thus the value a formal feature may acquire in the context of a reader's concerns and expectations is local and temporary; and there is no guarantee that the value-formal feature correlation that obtains once will obtain again (although an awareness that obtains once will obtain again (although an awareness that it has obtained once is not without interest or usefulness). All you have when you begin is a sense of this finite but infinitely flexible ability and a personal knowledge of what it means to have it. You then attempt to project the course that ability would take in its interaction with a specific text, using as the basis of your projection what you know, and at the same time adding to what you know by the very effort to make analytical use of it. There are other things that can help. Formal linguistic characterizations can help, if, as I have said, one views their content as potential cues for the performing acts. Literary history can help, if one views its conventions in the same way; a description of a genre, for example, can and should be seen as a prediction of the shape of response. Other minds can help, because they know what you know, but with the same lack of distance between themselves and their knowledge which makes the effort so difficult. Analyses of perceptual strategy can help,[40] because they acquaint us with the past performances of the ability we are trying to know. (Our trying is itself just such a performance.) Finally, however, you are left only with yourself and with the impossible enterprise of understanding understanding; impossible because it is endless, endless because to have reached an end is to have performed an operation that once again extends it beyond your reach. In short, this way lacks the satisfaction of a closed system of demonstration and is unable ever to prove anything, although, paradoxically, this makes rigor and precision more, not less, necessary; but these very deficiencies are the reverse side of its greatest virtue (in both the modern and Renaissance sense): the recognition that meaning is human.

Notes

1 'Unconscious ordering in the prose of Swift', in *The Computer & Literary Style*, ed. Jacob Leed (Kent, Ohio, 1966), pp. 79–106.
2 Roman Jakobson and Morris Halle, *The Fundamentals of Language* (The Hague, 1955), pp. 69–96.
3 'Generative grammars and concept of literary style', in *Contemporary Essays on Style*, ed. Glen A. Love and Michael Payne (Glenview, Ill., 1969), pp. 133–48. This essay originally appeared in *Word*, XX (December, 1964), 423–39.
4 ibid., p. 148.
5 'Literature as sentences', in *Contemporary Essays on Style*, p. 154. This essay originally appeared in *College English*, XXVII (January, 1966), 261–7.
6 ibid., p. 156.
7 ibid., p. 154.
8 'Generative grammars and the concept of literary style', p. 143.
9 J. P. Thorne, 'Generative grammar and stylistic analysis', in *New Horizons in Linguistics*, ed. John Lyons (Baltimore, 1970), p. 188. [Reprinted in this volume, pp. 42–52.]
10 For other examples of Thorne's work, see 'Stylistics and generative grammars', *Journal of Linguistics*, I (1965), 49–59; 'Poetry, stylistics and imaginary grammars', *Journal of Linguistics*, V (1969), 147–50.
11 'Literature as sentences', pp. 152–3.
12 Roderick A. Jacobs and Peter S. Rosenbaum, *Transformations, Style and Meaning* (Waltham, Mass., 1971), pp. 103–6.
13 My argument here has affinities with Hubert Dreyfus's explanation (in *What Computers Can't Do* [New York, 1972]) of the impasse at which programmers of artificial intelligence find themselves. 'The programmer must either claim that some features are intrinsically relevant and have a fixed meaning regardless of content ... or the programmer will be faced with an infinite regress of contexts' (p. 133). Dreyfus's conclusion anticipates the proposal I will offer at the end of this essay for the reform of stylistics. 'Human beings seem to embody a third possibility which would offer a way out of this dilemma. Instead of a hierarchy of contexts, the present situation is recognized as a continuation or modification of the present one. Thus we carry over from the immediate past a set of anticipations based on what was relevant and important a moment ago. This carry-over gives us certain predispositions as to what is worth noticing' (p. 134).
14 'Linguistic function and literary style', in *Literary Style: A Symposium*, ed. Seymour Chatman (New York, 1971), pp. 330–65. [Reprinted in this volume,

pp. 325–60.] See also Halliday, 'Categories of the theory of grammar', *Word*, XVII (1961), 241–92; 'The linguistic study of literary texts', in *Proceedings of the Ninth International Congress of Linguists*, ed. H. Lunt (The Hague, 1964), pp. 302–7; 'Descriptive linguistics in literary studies', in *Linguistics and Literary Style*, ed. Donald C. Freeman (New York, 1970), pp. 57–72; 'Notes on transitivity and theme in English', *Journal of Linguistics*, III (1967), 37–81, 199–244, and *Journal of Linguistics*, IV (1968, 179–215; 'Language structure and language function', in *New Horizons in Linguistics*, ed. John Lyons (Baltimore, 1970), pp. 140–65. For an exposition of Halliday's grammar and its application to literary analysis, see John Spencer and Michael J. Gregory, 'An approach to the study of style', in *Linguistics and Literary Style* (London, 1964), pp. 59–105. For a critique of the tradition in which Halliday works, see D. T. Langendoen, *The London School of Linguistics* (Cambridge, Mass., 1968).
15 'Linguistic function and literary style', p. 339.
16 ibid., p. 334.
17 Martin Joos, 'Linguistic prospects in the United States', in *Trends in European and American Linguistics* (Utrecht, 1961), p. 18.
18 John Searle, *Speech Acts: An Essay in the Philosophy of Language* (Cambridge, 1969), p. 52.
19 *What Computers Can't Do*, p. 200.
20 'Criteria for style analysis', *Word*, XV (1959), 164.
21 'Describing poetic structures', in *Structuralism*, ed. Jacques Ehrmann (New York, 1970), p. 197. This volume was originally published in 1966 as numbers 36 and 37 of *Yale French Studies*.
22 ibid., p. 202.
23 ibid., p. 203.
24 ibid., See also 'Criteria for Style Analysis', p. 164.
25 See, in addition to Ohmann, 'Literature as act', in *Approaches to Poetics*, ed. Seymour Chatman (New York, 1973), pp. 81–108; 'Speech acts and the definition of literature', *Philosophy and Rhetoric*, IV (Winter, 1971), 1–19; 'Speech, action and style', in *Literary Style: A Symposium*, ed. Seymour Chatman (New York, 1971), pp. 241–59; 'Speech, literature, and the space between', *New Literary History*, IV (Autumn, 1972), 47–64 [reprinted in this volume, pp. 361–76]; 'Instrumental style: notes on the theory of speech as action', in *Current Trends in Stylistics*, ed. Braj B. Kachru (Edmonton, 1972).
26 *Speech Acts*, p. 25.
27 See 'Speech, action, and style', pp. 249–50.
28 That is to say, stylistics requires that there be two separate systems – one of content or message, the other of everything else – which it is the stylistician's job to match up or correlate. Otherwise, they complain, there would be nothing for them to do. Ohmann is consistent in his dualism from his earliest writings – when his grammar was structural – to his 'middle period' – when the deep-surface distinction of Transformational Grammar seemed to give new authorization to the form-content split – to the present day – when the illocutionary force-propositional content distinction serves the same need. See 'Instrumental style' (MS paging): '[In] the distinction between the unactivated meaning and the fully launched illocutionary act we have the kind of split required for style to exist' (4).
29 'Speech acts and the definition of literature', p. 13. The definition is impossible because discourse without illocutionary force would be discourse unrelated to

the conventions of everyday speech and therefore discourse that was unintelligible (just a series of noises). To put it another way, the language of literature would be wholly discontinuous with the language we ordinarily speak, and in order to read it one would have to learn it from scratch. (Of course there *are* special poetic vocabularies, for example, silver-age Latin, but these are always precisely parallel to, that is, parasitic on, everyday usage.) Ohmann seems aware of this difficulty in his definition, since he modifies it on the very next page, admitting that a literary work has illocutionary force, but declaring that it is 'mimetic'. These mimetic speech acts, however, turn out to be just like real ones, and it seems that this strange class has been instituted only to remedy the deficiency of the original definition.

30 That is, like the stylisticians, the structuralists dislodge man from his privileged position as the originator of meanings, and locate meaning instead in the self-sufficient operation of a timeless formalism. The difference is that they do consciously what the stylisticians do inadvertently; they deliberately raise the implied antihumanism of other formalist methodologies to a principle. The parallel holds too in the matter of interpretation. Since the structuralists' goal is the system of signifiers – intelligibility rather than what is made intelligible – they either decline interpretation or perform it in such a way as to make its arbitrary contingent nature inescapable (for example, Roland Barthes in *S/Z*). Again the similarity with what the stylisticians do is less important than the self-consciousness with which it is done. One may disagree with the assumptions impelling the structuralists' enterprise, but one cannot accuse them of being unaware of those assumptions.

31 'A framework for the statistical analysis of style', in *Statistics and Style*, ed. Lúbomir Doležel and Richard W. Bailey (New York, 1969), p. 22.

32 Indeed the stylisticians often make incredibly damaging admissions and then walk away from them as if their entire program were still intact. Two examples from the work of Manfred Bierwisch will have to suffice. In an article entitled 'Semantics' written for *New Horizons in Linguistics* (ed. John Lyons), Bierwisch points out that a semantic theory will have to be able 'to explain how one of the several meanings associated with a particular word or sentence is selected in accordance with a particular universe of discourse' (p. 183). He then admits that at the present time there seems no way precisely to formalize (i.e., make predictable) the process by which, for example, the various meanings of the word 'group' are selected; but he can still conclude (with no warrant whatsoever) that 'although little progress has yet been made in the systematic treatment of these problems, they do not seem to pose difficulties of principle' (p. 184). In another of his articles, the problem is not an unsupported conclusion but a conclusion he fails to make. The article is 'Poetics and linguistics' (in *Linguistics and Literary Style*, ed. Donald C. Freeman), and at the close of it Bierwisch points out that references in poems to other poems or to other universes of discourse (e.g., art history) 'can never be expressed in an exhaustive linguistic semantics and ... thus mark ... the boundaries of a complete theory of poetic effect and style' (p. 112). The conclusion that he doesn't reach (although it seems inescapable) is that a theory with those limitations is of questionable value.

33 See 'Literature in the reader: affective stylistics', *New Literary History*, II (Autumn, 1970), 123–62. See also *Self-Consuming Artifacts* (Berkeley and Los Angeles, 1972) and *Surprised by Sin: The Reader in Paradise Lost* (New York and London, 1967).

34 Louis Milic, 'Connectives in Swift's prose style', in *Linguistics and Literary Style*, ed. Donald C. Freeman, pp. 243–57.
35 'Literature as sentences', p. 156.
36 Let me take the opportunity this example offers to clarify what I mean by *the* reader or, as I have elsewhere termed him, the 'informed' reader. There are at least four potential readers of this sentence: (1) the reader for whom the name Iago means nothing; (2) the reader who knows that Iago is a character in a play by Shakespeare; (3) the reader who has read the play; (4) the reader who is aware that the question has its own history, that everyone has had a whack at answering it, and that it has become a paradigm question for the philosophical-moral problem of motivation. Now each of these readers will assume the role of answerer because each of them (presumably) is a native speaker of English who knows what is involved in a felicitous question. (His knowledge is the content of Searle's formalizations.) But the precision with which that role is played will be a function of the reader's particular knowledge of Iago. That is, the reader who is a member of my fourth class will not only recognize that he is being asked to perform the activity of answering but will perform it in a very specific direction (and consequently the speaker's withdrawal from that direction will be felt by him all the more sharply). He will be my informed reader and I would want to say that his experience of the sentence will be not only different from, but better than, his less-informed fellows. Note that this is not a distinction between real and ideal readers; all the readers are real, as are all their experiences. Nor do I assume a uniformity of attitude and opinion among informed readers. Some readers may believe that Iago is motivated by jealousy, others that he is motiveless, still others that he is not evil but heroic. It is the ability of the reader to have an opinion (or even to know that having an opinion is what is called for), and not the opinion he has, which makes him informed in my sense; for then, no matter what opinion he has, he will have committed himself to considering the issues of motivation and agency. That commitment will be the *content* of his experience and it will not be the content of the experience of readers less informed than he.
37 Again my argument intersects with that of Dreyfus in *What Computers Can't Do*: 'There must be some way of avoiding the self-contradictory regress of contexts, or the incomprehensible notion of recognizing an ultimate context, as the only way of giving significance to independent, neutral facts. The only way out seems to be to deny the separation of fact and situation ... to give up the independence of the facts and understand them as a product of the situation. This would amount to arguing that only in terms of situationally determined relevance are there any facts at all' (p. 136).
38 Roger Fowler, *The Languages of Literature: Some Linguistic Contributions to Criticism* (London, 1971), pp. 38–9.
39 The resulting 'single-shot' procedure also spells the end of another distinction, the distinction between style and meaning. This distinction depends on the primacy of propositional content (that which it is the reader's job to extract), but in an analysis which has as its object the structure of the reader's experience, the achieving of propositional clarity is only one among many activities, and there is no warrant for making it the privileged center in relation to which all other activities are either appendages or excrescences. Rather than the traditional dichotomy between process and product (the how and the what), everything becomes process and nothing is granted the stability that would lead to its being

designated 'content'. Thus there is only style, or, if you prefer, there is only meaning, and what the philosophers have traditionally called meaning becomes an abstraction from the total meaning experience. Describing that experience becomes the goal of analysis and the resulting shape is both the form and the content of the description. (This is a 'monism' not open to the usual objection that it leaves you with nothing to do.)

40 I am thinking, for example, of the work of T. G. Bever. See 'Perceptions, thought, and language', in *Language Comprehension and the Acquisition of Knowledge*, ed. Roy O. Freedle and John B. Carroll (New York, 1972), pp. 99–112.

III
Approaches to poetics

Introduction

The essays which follow all are concerned with the contributions of poetic syntax to poetic form. All are exercises in practical criticism, and all, to a greater or lesser extent, use the transformational-generative model of modern linguistics.

My 'Keats's "To Autumn": poetry as pattern and process', argues that analysis of the causative, inchoative, transitivity, and instrumental patterns in the poem's syntax shows it to be a poem about Autumn as the ultimate causer of natural process, and, further, about that process as emblematic of the imaginative act. The essay makes a claim for poetic syntax as iconic, embodying in its form, and the mental processes which are required to experience that form, much of the poem's content.

Essentially the same claim is made by Samuel Jay Keyser's 'Wallace Stevens: form and meaning in four poems', written at about the same time. He shows, in Stevens's 'Death of a Soldier', a suppression of agency through choice of nonprogressive verbs, and a law-like timelessness in the poem's actions arising from the poet's use of the untypical (for English) simple present tense. Keyser traces phonological, syntactic, and thematic chiasmus as they work together to create a reading of 'Poetry is a Destructive Force'. Phonology and semantics interact in 'Anecdote of the Jar' to yield, on Keyser's account, an interpretation of the poem in which the jar is the poetic form imposing order on the wilderness of language. Finally, in an extended analysis of 'The Snow Man', Keyser shows that the poem's syntax requires a constant reanalysis consistent with the poem's major theme: that we must constantly reanalyze 'our perception of the world in order to perceive the truth of the world's reality'.

In 'Syntactic deviation and cohesion', Irene R. Fairley suggests that E. E. Cummings provides a sense of patterning in his poems through the device of deviation from the syntactic norm, in contrast to the 'foregrounding' function usually associated with deviation of this sort. Her analytical method is to assume that a complete, grammatical sentence is recoverable from a particular syntactically deviant structure, and to recover that sentence as poetic theme by postulating the transformations which must have taken place in order to produce the deviant structure. This analytical method is applied to 'a like a', 'Tumbling-hair', 'Me up at does', 'All in green went my love riding', and 'when god lets my body be'. For the last poem, she shows Cummings's changes in the direction of cohesion by deviance in comparing earlier drafts of the final poem.

Timothy R. Austin's 'Constraints on syntactic rules and the style of Shelley's "Adonais"' is a complexly argued analysis of Shelley's violation for stylistic effect of what have been held to be universal movement constraints on English syntax. He locates the violations of these constraints in the poem's first part, where they 'correspond to the poet's concern in these same stanzas with mankind's confused and inadequate comprehension of the fact of death itself'. Austin concludes with a discussion of stylistic criticism in the context of other critical theories and the recent controversy which has arisen over the role of linguistics in literary theory (see 'Suggestions for further reading', Part VI of the present volume).

E. L. Epstein argues strongly for 'formal mimesis of content as part of a criterion for literature' in 'The self-reflexive artefact: the function of mimesis in an approach to a theory of value for literature'. He distinguishes mimetic from non-mimetic relationships of form to content, and claims the former to be more highly valued. Mimesis is, for Epstein, 'the presence of analogous schemata in the lexical level and one or both of the lower levels of syntax or phonology (or graphemics)', and he demonstrates this mimesis in examples from Pope, Milton, Renaissance French poetry, Jonson, Valery, and, in an extended analysis, Blake's 'The Tyger'.

5

Keats's 'To Autumn': poetry as process and pattern

Donald C. Freeman

We read fine things but never feel them to the full until we have gone the same steps as the Author.
John Keats, Letter to John Hamilton Reynolds, 3 May 1818

[A] poem is an act, the symbolic act of the poet who made it – an act of such a nature that, in surviving as a structure or object, it enables us as readers to re-enact it.
Kenneth Burke, *A Grammar of Motives*

This study proceeds on two hypotheses: that poetic form is embedded in poetic syntax, and that our experience of that form is, first, the process of internalizing and decoding the complex web of relationships which its syntax embodies, and, second, the perception of pattern arising from that process. Syntax is an element of design available to the poet, just as are imagery, lexis, rhyme, and meter, and syntactic strategy is equally subject to the 'esemplastic power' which Samuel Taylor Coleridge attributed to the act of poetic creation.

The aim of the present work is to show how Keats's syntactic strategy functions to help create poetic form and statement in one of his richest short poems, 'To Autumn'. What emerges from this analysis is not any revolutionary new reading of the poem. Rather, the result is to show how Keats's syntactic choices themselves create an important part of the poem's central statement: to epitomize the act of imaginative creation. I am going to argue that in 'To Autumn' we have a poem ostensibly about autumn that is really a poem about the poetic imagination; that, further, the poetic imagination is for Keats a reciprocal force between poet and reader located in the poem's syntax; that, finally, in the idealized act of reading the poem – that is, of internalizing its syntactic patterns – we resynthesize the imaginative act which created it.

To Autumn

I

Season of mists and mellow fruitfulness,
    Close bosom-friend of the maturing sun;
Conspiring with him how to load and bless
    With fruit the vines that round the thatch-eves run;
To bend with apples the moss'd cottage-trees,
    And fill all fruit with ripeness to the core;
        To swell the gourd, and plump the hazel shells
With a sweet kernel; to set budding more,
And still more, later flowers for the bees,
Until they think warm days will never cease,
    For Summer has o'er-brimm'd their clammy cells.

II

Who hath not seen thee oft amid thy store?
    Sometimes whoever seeks abroad may find
Thee sitting careless on a granary floor,
    Thy hair soft-lifted by the winnowing wind;
Or on a half-reap'd furrow sound asleep,
    Drows'd with the fume of poppies, while thy hook
        Spares the next swath and all its twined flowers:
And sometimes like a gleaner thou dost keep
    Steady thy laden head across a brook;
    Or by a cyder-press, with patient look,
        Thou watchest the last oozing hours by hours.

III

Where are the songs of Spring? Ay, where are they?
    Think not of them, thou hast thy music too, –
While barred clouds bloom the soft-dying day,
    And touch the stubble-plains with rosy hue;
Then in wailful choir the small gnats mourn
    Among the river sallows, borne aloft
        Or sinking as the light wind lives or dies;
And full-grown lambs loud bleat from hilly bourn;
    Hedge-crickets sing; and now with treble soft
    The red-breast whistles from a garden-croft;
        And gathering swallows twitter in the skies.

We are immediately struck, in our initial experience of the poem, by a constellation of syntactically complex and semantically rich verb phrases:

(1) to load and bless with fruit the vines that round the thatch-eves run
(2) to bend with apples the moss'd cottage-trees
(3) [to] fill all fruit with ripeness to the core
(4) to swell the gourd
(5) [to] plump the hazel shells with a sweet kernel

All of these verb phrases have strongly parallel surface syntactic structure:[1]

(6)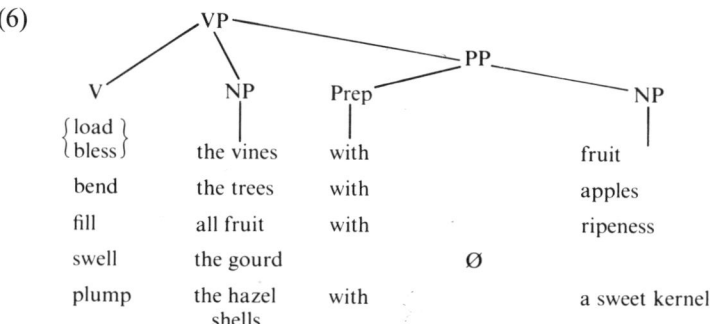

They also appear at the same circled point in the deep-structure representation of the Noun Phrase which constitutes the ode's entire first stanza:[2]

(7)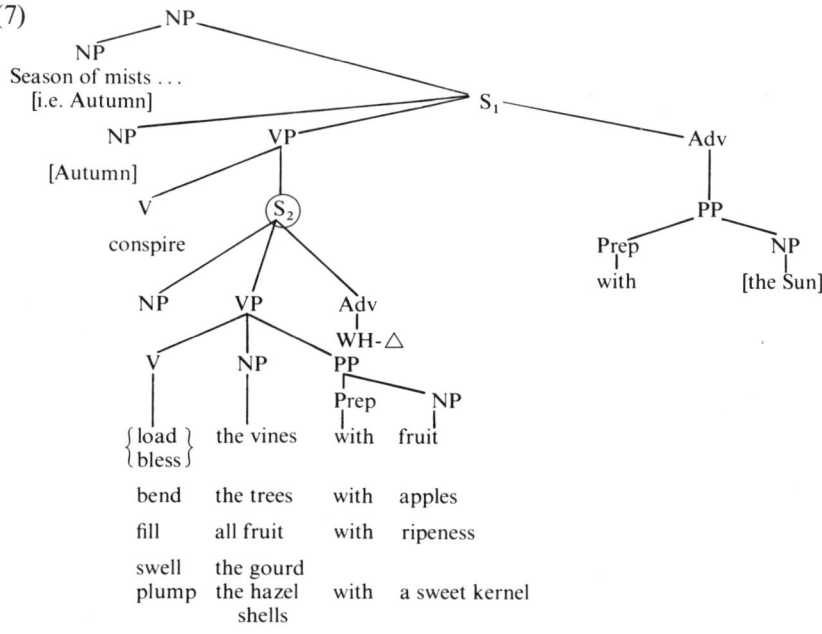

The verb phrases 'to load and bless', 'to bend with apples', '[to] fill all fruit with ripeness to the core', etc., thus strongly satisfy Kiparsky's definition of poetic form as 'some kind of recurrence of equivalent linguistic elements':[3] their surface syntactic structure is virtually identical, and they occur at identical points in the larger syntax of the stanza.[4]

All of these verb phrases are to some extent *causative*, with Autumn as the agent. We may 'translate' – that is, semantically interpret – them as Autumn (and the Sun – but Autumn is clearly the more important partner, as we shall see) *causing* something to happen: the vines to become laden and blessed with fruit; the trees to become bent with apples; the fruit to fill with ripeness to the core; the gourd to swell; the hazel shells to become plump with a sweet kernel. This observation leads to two others. First, in the surface structure of these verb phrases, all of the verbs are transitive, with expressed direct objects, whereas in their underlying, non-derived forms, two of them, *plump* and *swell*, must be intransitive; one, *fill*, has an intransitive reading; and the remaining three, *load*, *bless*, and *bend*, can (I shall argue) have underlying intransitive readings. Second, our 'semantic translation' of most of these verb phrases involves the pattern N *become* Adj. This pattern is the mark of the inchoative[5] verbs which denote some state which is in the process of coming about. The paradigm includes *redden* (i.e., *come to be red*), *ripen*, *darken*, *thicken*, *lighten*, etc., all of which are intransitive in their root forms.

It is not immediately obvious that the verbs under discussion here are in fact inchoative. Yet if we give them the *-en* suffix of *redden* and *thicken*, their inchoative nature becomes clearer. Just as *the sauce thickened* in some sense underlies *John thickened the sauce*, so does *the hazel shells plump[en]* underlie *to plump the hazel shells*. So, too, the swelling of the gourd – we would want to say *the gourd swell[ens]*, but for a similar lexical gap; the same observation holds for *the trees bend[en] with apples* (i.e., come to be bent), which in its intransitive sense as proposed here is strikingly close to the requisite *OED* definition (8b): 'To curve over from the erect position (usually said of things that recover their position when the bending force is withdrawn).' The case is clearer with 'all fruit fills' – i.e., becomes full – 'with ripeness to the core', strengthening the intransitive and inchoative paradigms.[6]

The most difficult and at the same time most interesting argument to make for the underlyingly intransitive and inchoative nature of these verbs is that for *load* and *bless*. *Load* seems clear enough: the analogous sentence is

(8) The ferry is loading (i.e., load[en]ing) at the pier.[7]

Bless is embedded in a seeming violation of grammaticality. The class of instruments one might use to *bless* would include perhaps *holy water*, *pràyer*, etc., but not *fruit*, except as part of a metaphor: *fruit* is the instrument of conferring blessedness (but not the agent – we shall come to that) in a natural universe, and as the trees *load*[*en*] with fruit, so at the same time do they *bless*[*en*].

Part of the richness with which Keats imbues this passage of 'To Autumn' stems from his fusion into transitive structures of the causative and inchoative forces of the poem – from

(9) a. Autumn CAUSES vines to load and bless with fruit
    b. Autumn CAUSES trees to bend with apples
    c. Autumn CAUSES all fruit to fill with ripeness to the core
    d. Autumn CAUSES the gourd to swell
    e. Autumn CAUSES the hazel shell to plump

to

(10) a. Autumn loads and blesses the vines with fruit
     b. Autumn bends the trees with apples
     c. Autumn fills all fruit with ripeness to the core
     d. Autumn swell[s] the gourd
     e. Autumn plump[s] the hazel shell with a sweet kernel

Keats's choice of a transitive pattern here has the effect of making the *subjects* of these natural processes – the vines (which load), the trees (which bend), the fruit (which fills with ripeness), the gourd (which swells), and the hazel shells (which plump) – into *objects* of Autumn's all-powerful agency.[8] All of the verb phrases of the first stanza reflect the transformation of natural *states* (ladenness, blessedness, bentness, fullness, swollenness, and plumpness) into active dynamic *processes* fundamental to the poem's structure.[9] The verbs in this passage also share an important semantic property: they all have to do with a kind of repleteness – getting fatter, heavier, riper. This strong semantic parallelism interacts with other syntactic properties of the passage, as we shall see.

Another strong linguistic equivalence of all but one of these verb phrases ('To swell the gourd') is what appear to be instrumentals – the *with*-phrases. These display some highly idiosyncratic – and at times seemingly contradictory – semantic and syntactic properties.[10]

Ordinarily, *with*-phrases of this sort are not true instrumentals.

(11) *The window was broken with a hammer*

implies that someone broke the window;

(12) *the streets were filled with people*

does not imply that someone filled the streets. In (11) a *hammer* is a vehicle, an instrument for the agent to use. In (12) *with people* can be seen as a result of the action of filling. The resultative *with*-phrase under discussion here will take a 'stative' reading (*the basket is filled with apples*); true instrumental *with*-phrases will not (**the window is broken with a hammer*). These resultative *with*-phrases can occur with a true instrumental in the same sentence (*the truck was loaded with apples with a forklift*), whereas two true instrumentals cannot co-occur in the same sentence (**the window was broken with a hammer with a chisel*). Whereas true instrumentals are preposable (*with a hammer, John broke the window*), resultative *with*-phrases are not (**with apples, Autumn loaded the vines*).

These facts follow naturally from a deep-structure analysis of these resultative *with*-phrases as VP-adverbs rather than S-adverbs, as indicated in (7): That is, they are dominated by the category Verb Phrase rather than the category Sentence, and their properties are consistent with membership in the VP category. But as a consequence of the transitivization from the pattern of (9) – 'Autumn CAUSES trees to bend with apples' – to that of (10) – 'Autumn bends the trees with apples' – these *with*-phrases appear to pass a semantic paraphrase test for instrumentals:

(13) a. Autumn USES fruit to load and bless the vines
 b. Autumn USES apples to bend the trees
 c. Autumn USES ripeness to fill all fruit to the core
 d. Autumn USES a sweet kernel to plump the hazel shells

This transitivization, then, can be seen as a kind of syntactic pun, allowing us to reinterpret the resultative *with*-phrase as a real instrumental phrase, again reinforcing a structural pattern in the poem's language which makes *processes* (with both agents and instruments) out of *states*.

These phrases share another semantic peculiarity. All of these resultatives become part of their objects as the result of this process of which each has become the instrument. The fruit becomes part of the vines, the apples part of the trees, the ripeness part of the fruit, and the kernel part of the hazel shells, all as a consequence of the semantic 'burgeoning' of the verbs with which they occur. This phenomenon recurs in two other similar uses of 'with' in the second and third stanzas. The spirit of Autumn is 'drows'd with the fume of poppies'. This line echoes the first stanza in other structural properties: 'something CAUSES Autumn to BECOME drows'd with the fume of poppies.' Here again the poem's syntax makes the resultative 'fume of poppies' into the instrument of making (Autumn) drowsy, and it becomes a part of, literally inhaled into, its object. In the final stanza, when the 'barred clouds ... touch the stubble-plains with rosy hue', the 'rosy hue' remains as part of the stubble-plains (again the same resultative *with*-phrase occurs). Notice, too, that the other set of patterns we have discussed occurs again at just this point: 'barred clouds bloom the soft-dying day', which we may 'translate' as 'barred clouds CAUSE the soft-dying day to bloom[en]'. An intransitive state (that of being in bloom) is transformed into a transitive, active, dynamic process, and the verbs which reflect that process (*drowse*, *bloom*) share the qualities of repleteness and inchoativeness noticed in the verbs of the first stanza (see note 12). Once again, the poem's syntax and its semantics interact perfectly.

So far we have made the following observations about the five verb phrases in the first stanza of 'To Autumn':
(i) Their internal surface syntactic relationships are virtually identical.
(ii) Their external syntactic relationships are identical – that is, they appear at the same point in the syntactic organization of the noun phrase which constitutes the stanza.
(iii) The semantic interpretation of each verb phrase contains a causative, an inchoative, and (except for *to swell the gourd*) a resultative *with*-phrase semantically interpretable as an instrument.
(iv) The surface syntactic structure of the verb phrases is such that the *subject* of a natural process becomes the *object* of Autumn's agency – a static, intransitive state is transformed into a dynamic, active process (but see note 9).
(v) The instrumental of each verb phrase becomes semantically a part of its object as a consequence of that natural process.
(vi) The verbs embodying natural process share the semantic property of repleteness, or 'burgeoning'.
(vii) The semantic and syntactic properties observed in (iii), (iv), and (v) are echoed in the second and third stanzas.

If we now examine the opening lines of the poem, we see figured in small the patterns which unite the strongly equivalent verb phrases just analyzed. *Conspire* is a syntactically intransitive, but semantically transitive, verb; yet Keats chooses a syntactic framework within which to portray the conspiracy between Autumn and the Sun, which seems transitive, even though in fact 'how to load and bless ..., to bend ...', etc., is a complement, not a direct object, of *conspire*.[11] The effect of this sleight-of-hand is once again to stress Autumn's agency and power, and to make the conspiracy an active, dynamic natural process, in the same manner as the 'transitivization' of the five verb phrases which follow.

The modifying participle *maturing* shares the properties of *load*, *bless*, *bend*, *fill*, *swell*, and *plump*: in its underlying form it is intransitive and inchoative (*the maturing sun* < *the sun matures* [i.e., comes to be mature, grows older, wanes, as in autumn]). But in a derived form it is transitive and causative (*the maturing sun* < *the sun matures things* [i.e., causes things to become mature]), and has the 'burgeoning' quality noticed elsewhere in the poem. The irony of the autumn season rests upon just this ambiguity:

Autumn produces the lush fullness of the harvest at the same time that it presages the onset of winter.

This ambiguity is immediately connected to another, less obvious one. 'Conspiring with him how to load and bless ...' can, and probably should, be read as 'plotting along with him'. But Keats has already sensitized us, with 'maturing', to a kind of syntactic counterpoint which will dominate this poem in the transitivization which is to come. Another reading for 'conspiring with him' can be 'conspiring to *use* him (i.e., the sun) to load and bless the vines ...' *etc.* – that is to say, precisely the instrumental reading, involving a *with*-phrase, that Keats's strategy of transitivization invites us to infer in the next few lines for *fruit, apples, ripeness*, and *kernel*. Keats only implies this reading here, but he is directly creating a template for the design of the poem's syntactic patterns: V (with NP) (NP). The implied instrumental sense of 'with him' (the sun) carries with it the same semantic property of becoming part of its object: fruit matures and loads vines; apples grow and bend trees; fruit fills with ripeness; the gourd swells; hazel shells become plump; and later flowers bud, all as a direct, physical consequence of the sun, whose light and heat become part of the natural objects which it matures, or, better, *causes* to *become* mature.[12]

We may now summarize the rather explicit set of parallels between the syntax and semantics of the poem's opening lines and that of the remainder of the first stanza and isolated instances elsewhere.

(i) *Maturing*, on one reading, contains a causative and an inchoative, and displays the semantic quality of 'burgeoning'.

(ii) *Conspiring with him*, on one reading, contains an instrumental, and, while itself an intransitive verb, is couched in a pseudo-transitive surface structure. *How to load and bless* ... appears to be an included clause as NP direct object; only on closer analysis is it revealed to be a complement.

(iii) On the instrumental reading of *Conspiring with him*, the instrument (the sun = him) becomes a part of the objects upon which it is employed (the fruit, the apples, the ripeness, the sweet kernel), just as they in turn become, as a consequence of the process of transitivization noted earlier, a part of the objects upon which they are employed as instruments (the vines, the trees, the fruit, the hazel shells).

(iv) This passage shares with several of the verb phrases which follow it an idiosyncratic stylistic transformation – the intraposition of the (on one reading) instrumental *with*-phrase from its normal, clause-final position (normal word-order for instrumentals is 'he broke the window with a hammer', not 'he broke with a hammer the window'). Keats appears to be enforcing a deliberately artificial parallelism in the sequence 'Conspiring with him ... to load and bless with fruit ... to bend with apples the moss'd cottage-trees'. 'With him' is just faintly instrumental, but this faint syntactic paronomasia sets us up for the larger, crucial syntactic pun which is to follow.

On this reading, the sun can be seen, in the poem's grammar, as a meta-instrument for Autumn, the ultimate agent of all the natural forces in the poem. Keats at first asks us to experience the poem in a deliberately ambiguous way – indeed, with Negative Capability[13] ('the maturing sun') – and then makes the shadowy instrumental relationship of Sun and Autumn the embracing design of the poem: as the sun is a natural instrument which remains as a part of the objects upon which it is used, so do the natural 'instruments' of fruit, apples, ripeness, kernel, fume of poppies, and rosy hue remain a part of the objects they are used upon. The verbs embodying that usage – all of which, in the first stanza, occur at the same point in the syntactic tree – all share the semantic property of 'burgeoning' (indeed, one might go further to say that they are all special cases of 'maturing') and the poem's syntax moves from the ultimate causer to the proximate causers of natural process, making the growing, maturing (in the non-causative sense) entities of the poem thrice objects: objects of autumn's agency, objects of the sun's maturing, and objects of the natural entities – apples, fruit, kernel – that actually perform the actions central to the poem.

A broader reading of this crucial first stanza and its relationships to the poem's larger structure makes clear that 'To Autumn' is written to more than autumn. Its syntactic patterns, in my view, epitomize Keats's theory of the imagination.

'To Autumn' 's first stanza is at great pains, as the previous analysis suggests, to establish the *agency* of an *abstraction*. The 'bendings' of natural-language syntax so important to the stanza's (and the poem's) structure operate here without exception to reinforce the autonomy and power of Autumn as avatar of the imagination. Autumn controls and impels the process of fruition; transient natural states are made permanent processes in Art by the agency of Autumn *qua* Imagination (a theme also crucial to 'Ode on a Grecian Urn' – 'For ever wilt thou love, and she be fair!'). The stanza's syntactic patterns are mimetic of this autonomy and agency: they create instruments from non-instruments (thus implying an agent using those instruments), processes from states (implying a causer of those processes), and transitivity from inchoativeness (implying an actor upon natural entities made into objects of action). The vision of this stanza is likewise abstract and generalized: the vines, the cottage trees, the fruit (significantly, 'all fruit'), the gourd, the hazel shells, the flowers, are all generic objects or classes of objects upon which Autumn's all-powerful agency works at several removes. The generality and abstractness of the stanza are heightened by the fact that nothing is directly predicated of Autumn: the stanza is one large complex Noun Phrase.

In the second stanza Keats gives us a more particularized, less abstract vision of Autumn personified, but not the strongly active, powerful Autumn we have seen. This Autumn has that 'wise passiveness' which Wordsworth saw as essential to the poetic mind: she (and only now can we identify Autumn as 'she') is object, patient, acted upon by the forces she has herself set in motion. Keats surrounds nearly every mention of Autumn here with past participles, which are reduced passives ('soft-lifted', 'half-reap'd', 'drows'd,', 'twined', 'laden'). Even the transitive verbs predicated of Autumn are strangely inactive ('spares', 'keep stead', 'watchest'). The sentence patterns also are more particular – a rhetorical question and three conjoined but fully elaborated sentences. It is as if, having established the autonomy of the imagination, Keats now wished to show its dialectical relationship with the natural universe which inspires the very poetic powers by which it is controlled and ordered.

The personified vision fades, and with it the last vestiges of the strong agency and transitivity which Keats is so insistent upon establishing in the poem's opening stanza, and which are strongly implied in the passivity of the second. After a syntactic allusion to the patterns of the first stanza (see p. 89), the poem ends in a series of short conjoined sentences all of which have intransitive verbs which focus on minute and precise detail, and which, with the dying of the light, leave us with only sound – the unaffected, utterly spontaneous and natural end of another 'diurnal course' in a wholly ordered and harmonious natural universe.[14]

The language of 'To Autumn' thus moves in a direct line from establishing the primacy of the imaginative powers over natural objects to a final vision – indeed, a *non*-vision, a symphony – of those powers perfectly fused in natural objects themselves. This movement is a steady diminution of transitivity, agency, and causation: by the last lines of the poem, natural processes occur self-caused, autonomously.

This grand pattern is an epitome of the Keatsian poetic process. 'I am certain of nothing', he wrote to Benjamin Bailey,[15] 'but of the holiness of the Heart's affections and the truth of Imagination – What the imagination seizes as Beauty must be truth – whether it existed before or not – for I have the same idea of all our Passions as of Love they are all in their sublime, creative of essential Beauty'. The primacy and the powers of the Imagination were crucial for Keats – yet less than a year later he wrote to John Taylor that 'if Poetry comes not as naturally as the Leaves to a tree it had better not come at all.'[16] Keats's linking of poetry to natural process is no accident: poetry must be unforced, unaffected, natural; the Imagination must animate all of the objects of art. 'A Poet is the most unpoetical of any thing in existence; because he has no Identity – he is continually [informing][17] and filling some other body – the Sun, the Moon, the Sea....'[18]

Ultimately, for Keats, the poet is no poet at all; he refines himself out of existence in the process of the artistic act: 'that which is creative must create itself.'[19]

'To Autumn' encapsulates just such an act of self-creation. Autumn, external to natural process at the outset of the poem, controls it, is informed by it, and at poem's end is one which it. That movement is precisely mirrored in the poem's syntax: from strong transitivization and causation through passivity to the simple autonomy of intransitivity. 'To Autumn' is not only a poem about poetry. It is a poem about Poetry.

I want to conclude with some general remarks on poetic form. 'To Autumn' seems to me to be a striking example of what I shall call syntactic mimesis,[20] imitation by the poem's syntactic patterns of its subject matter. The syntax of 'To Autumn' is mimetic in two ways. First, the poem's syntax controls the pattern of its imagery so that in its grammatical relationships we recreate the natural relationships constituting the world of the poem. Second, the syntax of 'To Autumn' controls the process of the poem; it forces us to perceive the poem in an order which causes us to recreate for ourselves Keats's central statement: Autumn is first the impeller of natural states into natural processes, working all-powerfully at several removes; she is then acted upon by those processes, and is made one with natural objects now self-animated as the end-products of the imaginative act.

If this view of the larger form of 'To Autumn' is correct – that its syntax makes us recreate for ourselves its central statement[21] – then this way of looking at poetic form taking as its structural units the underlying syntactic and semantic relationships of poetic language, surface linguistic form, and the processes which relate them, may be a start, at least, at characterizing that process of making critical and aesthetic *subject* out of poetic and linguistic *object* which hermeneutic critics saw as crucial to the poetic experience (and which they criticized structuralists for ignoring).[22]

To experience poetic form is to make it a part of ourselves by a process which we may, initially at least, be entirely unable to describe explicitly. So, too, with language; the processes of producing and understanding utterances are not, to quote an old saw in linguistics, easily available to introspection. Modern linguistics has taken as its task the making explicit of the implicit 'knowledge' we have when we say we 'know' a language. I take one task of literary criticism to be the making explicit of our intuitions about poetic form, of the 'knowledge' we have when we say we 'know' – possess, understand, are reached by – a poem.

To approach poetry along the lines proposed here is to make the subject of literary criticism the union of two very abstract processes: natural-language syntax and poetic design. If it makes any sense at all to say that language is the medium of poetic art, it is in that union that this

94 *Essays in Modern Stylistics*

relationship must begin. This poem is a particularly clear case, in a work of literature whose language is not highly deviant, of a mimetic relationship between a poem's syntax and its subject.

There are, obviously, limitations in the approach to poetics proposed here. Research in syntactic theory is very far from a definitive account of the analyses of underlying structure and transformational process relied upon in the foregoing discussion. Such a state of affairs has dictated caution, but it should not be disabling. Future work in English syntax may disconfirm some of the analysis put forward here. The question of artistic design brings with it the question of artistic intention. Do we as readers actually perceive the ambiguities, causatives, inchoatives, instrumentals, reduced passives, intransitives, etc., of this poem's language, or does linguistic analysis merely supply them after the fact? Can a poet in any serious sense 'intend' these syntactic patterns?

Whatever the answers to these questions, the merit of this approach to poetics will depend upon its ability to illuminate poetic form and its bases in patterns of language. The foregoing discussion has sought to show that the experience of a poem's syntax is a part of that 'process of successive abstraction' that Norman N. Holland sees as central to the 'fusion or merger of self and book'[23] which is the experience of literature. The thesis of the present work is complementary to Holland's. To experience a poem's syntax is to recreate the poem, and to begin the process of making it wholly ours.[24]

Notes

1 A minor stylistic transformation of Intraposition shifts the *with*-phrases inside the Verb Phrase. This syntactic choice has consequences for the poem's larger patterns as well (see p. 90).
2 I have conflated the *load and bless, bend ..., etc.* paradigm under one S node for the sake of simplicity. In fact a more nearly full representation would represent S_2 as:

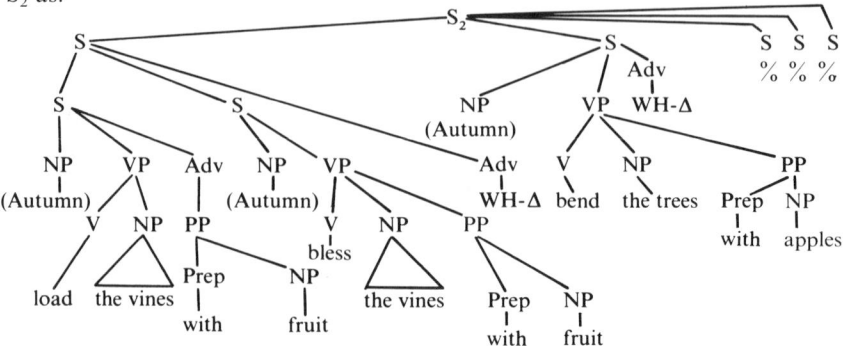

Where % means 'repeat the structure of the sister S node, inserting appropriate lexical items from (7).'

3 Paul Kiparsky, 'The role of linguistics in a theory of poetry', *Daedalus*, CII (1973), 233. [Reprinted in this volume, pp. 9–23]. This way of looking at poetic form was of course originated, as was so much else in poetics, by Roman Jakobson. Kiparsky's restatement of this Jakobsonian principle is a particularly felicitous one, embedded in an exceptionally rich study of this general question.
4 There is more to the underlying syntactic structure of these verb phrases than is represented in (7), because constructions of this sort are at the heart of a major controversy in linguistic theory. Whether these constructions are analyzed in terms of interpretive or generative semantics is immaterial to the points at issue. What is important for our purposes here is to notice the very intricate parallelisms among the underlying grammatical relationships in each of the verb phrases in question.
5 The best treatment of inchoatives known to me is George Lakoff. *Irregularity in Syntax* (New York: Holt, Rinehart & Winston, 1970), pp. 32–43.
6 A parallel poetic usage is Robert Frost's 'To watch his woods fill up with snow' 'Stopping by Woods on a Snowy Evening'). John Robert Ross has pointed out to me an increasing 'adjectivity' in this crucial series of verbs. Two tests for 'adjectivity' in verbs, he suggests, are to put *very* or *seems* before a particular verb's past participle.

(i) Those vines $\begin{Bmatrix} \text{seem} \\ \text{are very} \end{Bmatrix}$ loaded. (iv) That gourd $\begin{Bmatrix} \text{seems} \\ \text{is very} \end{Bmatrix}$ swollen.

(ii) Those trees $\begin{Bmatrix} \text{seem} \\ \text{are very} \end{Bmatrix}$ bent. (v) Those hazel shells $\begin{Bmatrix} \text{seem} \\ \text{are very} \end{Bmatrix}$ plumped.

(iii) That fruit $\begin{Bmatrix} \text{seems} \\ \text{is very} \end{Bmatrix}$ filled.

There is a more or less steady 'improvement' in grammaticality from (i) through (v); hence, Ross would argue, an increase in adjectivity. If the foregoing syntactic analysis is right, this steadily increasing 'adjectivity' from 'pure' verbs to verbs that are just about adjectives (and in fact are derived in a rather jarring way from adjectives) is a consequence of a steadily increasing effort to make processes (i.e., verbs) out of states (i.e., adjectives); more important, it reinforces a reading of the poem's larger structure, in which Keats builds up to a strong statement of agency in the first stanza, and then progressively infuses that agency into every object of the natural universe (see p. 92).
7 *OED* in fact cites an obsolete *loaden* in just this sense, with examples from 1586 to 1889.
8 This aspect of the paradigm continues at the end of the stanza: 'For Summer has o'erbrimm'd their clammy cells'. Underlying this transitive structure with *clammy cells* as object is an intransitive, causative, inchoative structure with *clammy cells* as subject: Summer CAUSES their clammy cells to o'erbrim.
9 A tempting characterization of this strategy is to consider in terms of a straightforward transformational relationship the making of what are *subjects* of natural processes into *objects* under the agency of Autumn. If underlying the verb phrase 'to bend with apples the moss'd cottage-trees' (and similarly for the other verb phrases of this passage) is in part a tree of the form

(i)

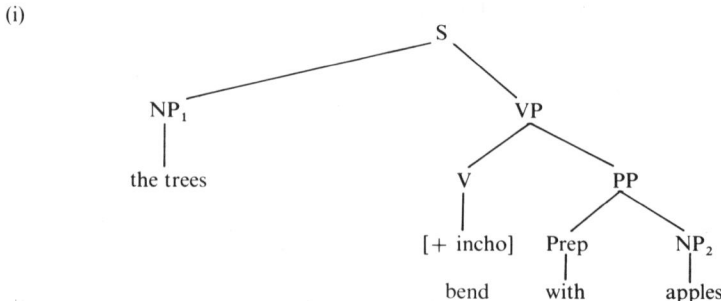

we can perceive two alternative syntactic strategies. One is a kind of 'activization transformation analogous to the 'passivization' transformation of natural-language syntax. It works in just the opposite way: it makes the NP of the oblique prepositional phrase the subject (passivization makes the subject into an oblique prepositional phrase), deletes the preposition, and makes the underlying subject the derived direct object (passivization makes the underlying direct object the derived subject):

(ii)

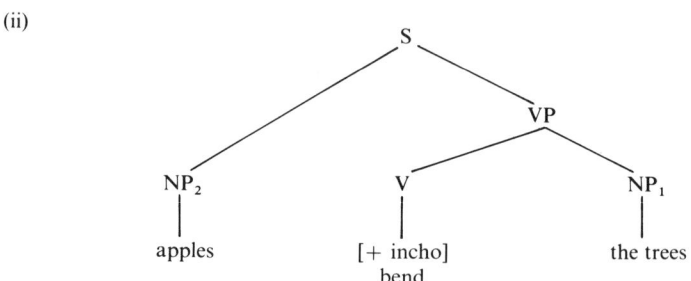

Another – which, on this analysis, Keats chooses over that of (ii), is one which 'creates a vacancy' in the subject position, makes the underlying subject the direct object, and preserves intact the remaining grammatical relations:

(iii)

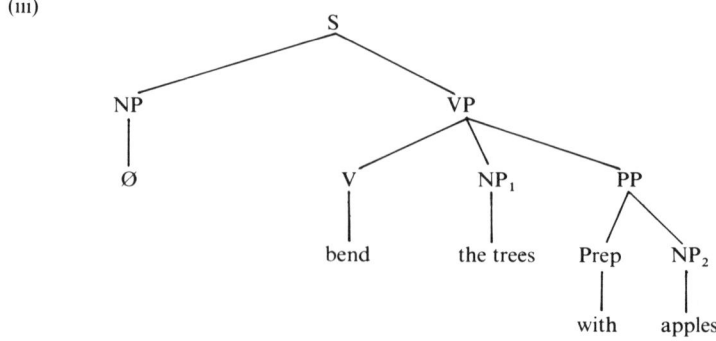

Keats's 'To Autumn' 97

For every base structure, then, there would be two choices, as in the following table:

(iv)

Base Structures	Possible Derived Structures
a. The vines load with fruit	(1) fruit loads with vines (2) load the vines with fruit
a'. The vines bless with fruit	(1) fruit blesses the vines (2) bless the vines with fruit
b. Trees bend with apples	(1) apples bend the trees (2) bend the trees with apples
c. All fruit fills with ripeness	(1) ripeness fills all fruit (2) fill all fruit with ripeness
d. The gourd swells (with Δ)	(1) Δ swells the gourd (2) swell the gourd (with Δ)
e. The hazel shell plumps with a sweet kernel	(1) a sweet kernel plumps the hazel shell (2) plump the hazel shell with a sweet kernel

In each case Keats chooses the (2) alternative. When these derived direct objects, formerly subjects of a 'pure' inchoative, are created by a strategy which leaves the subject position vacant, as can be seen in (v), the subject supplied must be the agent of a causative structure:

(v) The fruit ripened → —————————— ripened the fruit

Presumably on the next transformational cycle a rule would operate inserting *Autumn* from its place in a higher sentence into the subject position at this point. It is possible to compose a 'Mock-Autumn' using strategy (1) instead of strategy (2):

(vi) Season of mists and mellow fruitfulness;
Conspiring with thy close bosom-friend the Sun,
That fruit loads and blesses the vines
That round the thatch-eves run,
Apples bend the moss'd cottage-trees,
And ripeness fills all fruit to the core.
—————————— swells the gourd,
And a sweet kernel plumps the hazel shells ...

The effect of this exercise in desecration – choosing to make the agents the subjects of these verbs rather than, as Keats does, making the subjects of the natural processes embodied in the verbs into objects, shows the consequences of Keats's syntactic road not taken: an aesthetic or naive impressionism, mere parataxis.

Unfortunately, this enterprise founders. Linguists disagree on whether (i) underlies (iii) or vice versa, or whether a third structure underlies them both, and the general form of the argument takes us deep into the generative-interpretive semantics debate, one which I am neither equipped nor disposed to join. Nevertheless, I am convinced that the inchoative-causative pattern in 'To Autumn' reflects stylistic preference, and therefore, following Ohmann, cognitive (or, for my purposes, aesthetic) preference. Preference over what is a question whose precise answer awaits further work in the theory of syntax.

10 I am indebted to Paul Kiparsky (personal communication) for clarifying a number of points and supplying several of the examples in what follows.

11 One test in transformational syntax for whether a particular structure is a Noun Phrase is to see whether it will undergo the so-called Pseudo-Clefting transformation, from

(i) Sue likes ice cream

to

(ii) What Sue likes is ice cream.

So *the claim that the world is flat* is at some level of analysis an NP because it behaves in the same manner as *ice cream* in (i) and (ii) when the sentence *John believed the claim that the world is flat* is 'pseudo-clefted' to *What John believed was the claim that the world is flat*. But *to marry John* is not an NP in *Jane condescended to marry John* because **What Jane condescended was to marry John* is ungrammatical. We know that *how to load and bless* ... is a complement (and hence of itself not an NP), not a direct object (which would be an NP), because under Pseudo-Clefting **What Autumn conspired with the Sun was how to load and bless with fruit the vines* ... is ungrammatical as well. At first glance this line looks to be parallel and part of a pattern. In a display of syntactic *trompe-l'oeil* similar to that of the resultatives, Keats shows us a pattern which on close analysis is very different from what it first appears to be.

12 The same relationship can be observed between the sun and a natural object in the poem's final stanza: 'barred clouds bloom the soft-dying day.' *Bloom* is an inchoative, causative, intransitive verb: the sun USES barred clouds to CAUSE the soft-dying day to bloom, and the sun's light becomes a part of its object, the clouds, just as they become part of a sunset.

13 '... that is, when a man is capable of being in uncertainties, mysteries, doubts, without any irritable reaching after fact and reason ...', letter to George and Thomas Keats, 21 December 1817.

14 Geoffrey H. Hartman's brilliant study of 'To Autumn' perfectly expresses this naturalness and harmony at the poem's end: 'Here, at the consummate point of Keats's art, in-feeling achieves its subtlest act. Keats conspires with autumn to fill even the air. Air becomes a granary of sounds, a continuation of the harvest, or *spätlese*. In this last and softest stanza, the ear of the ear is ripened.' ('Poem and Ideology: A Study of Keats's "To Autumn",' in *Literary Theory and Structure*, ed. Frank Brady, John Palmer, and Martin Price (New Haven: Yale Univ. Press, 1973), p. 313).

15 22 November 1817.

16 Letter to John Taylor, 27 February 1818.

17 I accept G. Beaumont's emendation from MS. 'In for –.' *TLS*, 27 February and 1 May 1930.

18 Letter to Richard Woodhouse, 27 October 1818.

19 Letter to James Augustus Hessay, 9 October 1818.

20 The term is new; the observation is not. See Freeman, 'The Strategy of Fusion: Dylan Thomas's Syntax', in *Style and Structure in Literature: Essays in the New Stylistics*, ed. Roger Fowler (Oxford: Blackwell, 1975), pp. 19–39, and Samuel

Jay Keyser, 'Wallace Stevens: Form and Meaning in Four Poems', *College English*, XXXVII (1976), 578–98 [reprinted in this volume, pp. 100–22].

21 This statement is not a claim about the reading process. Such a claim could be made, but I do not believe it could be either supported or refuted, given the present state of our knowledge about language perception. An ambitious and in my view promising start at tackling this problem for readings of poetry is Irene R. Fairley, 'Reader responses to poems as empirical data', unpub. ms. (Northeastern University, 1976). The claims in the present essay are (a) that these patterns exist in the poem's syntax, (b) that they match up to a remarkable extent with the process of artistic creation which is an important part of the poem's subject, and (c) that a significant proportion of the medium in which the poem's statement is made is the patterns of (a). The syntax of 'To Autumn', in short, is in large part iconic.

22 I rely here on the excellent account of this controversy in Robert Scholes, *Structuralism in Literature* (New Haven: Yale Univ. Press, 1974), pp. 7–12.

23 Holland, *The Dynamics of Literary Response* (New York: Oxford Univ. Press, 1968), pp. 6, 67.

24 This essay is part of a longer study of syntax and form in Romantic poetry which I began during a recent sabbatical leave from the University of Massachusetts, Amherst. Together with some work in progress (an essay on 'Ode to Psyche' and 'Ode on a Grecian Urn', Timothy Austin's University of Massachusetts doctoral dissertation on the poetics of the major Romantic poets, and a working paper on iconic syntax in Blake) and already published (see the references in note 20), it is a tentative and beginning step toward a general theory of poetic form from the point of view of modern linguistics. I have profited greatly from discussions with audiences at University College, Cardiff; the University of East Anglia; the University of Missouri-Columbia, and the State University of New York at Stony Brook, and from a study visit in December, 1974, to the Technische Universität, Berlin, sponsored by the Deutscher Akademischer Austauschdienst and the University of Massachusetts Research Council, whose assistance is gratefully acknowledged. I am particularly grateful for helpful comments and criticisms to Muffy Siegel, Paul Kiparsky, Richard Ohmann, John Robert Ross, Michael Egan, Norman N. Holland, Timothy Austin, Irene R. Fairley, Terence Hawkes, Samuel Jay Keyser, George R. Deaux, and Margaret H. Freeman.

6

Wallace Stevens: form and meaning in four poems

Samuel Jay Keyser

Introduction

It is a commonplace of literary criticism to observe that form and content in a poem are closely related. It is less common, however, to encounter explicit analyses of particular poems which support this commonplace. The analyses which follow will attempt to do this. Four poems by Wallace Stevens will be analyzed from a formal standpoint. Then an attempt will be made to show how the formal analysis is closely related to what the poem is about.[1]

The Death of a Soldier

Let us look first at a poem which appeared in the 1923 collection called *Harmonium*. The poem is one which Yvor Winters (1937, p. 70) includes in a list of poems which according to him rank Stevens as being '... probably the greatest poet of his generation'. The text of the poem follows:

> *The Death of a Soldier*
>
> Life contracts and death is expected,
> As in a season of autumn.
> The soldier falls.
>
> He does not become a three-days personage,
> Imposing his separation,
> Calling for pomp.

> Death is absolute and without memorial,
> As in a season of autumn,
> When the wind stops.
>
> When the wind stops and, over the heavens,
> The clouds go, nevertheless,
> In their direction.

The verbs in the poem can be divided into two distinct types, finite verbs and nonfinite verbs. Finite verbs are those which take endings that agree with their subjects in number. For example, in *He works.* the ending *-s* is determined by the third person singular subject, *be*. Nonfinite verbs show no such agreement. We list these verbs with their corresponding subjects, expressed or otherwise, in (1) and (2) below:

finite verbs	*nonfinite verbs*
(1) Life contracts	(2) (who) imposing his separation
death is expected (by someone)	(who) calling for pomp
soldier falls	
he does not become a three-days personage	
Death is absolute and without memorial	
the wind stops	
the clouds go	

A notion which plays a role in the semantic and syntactic structure of many languages, including English, is agency. The agent of a verb is normally but not necessarily the animate instigator of whatever action the verb describes. For example,

(3) a. John opened the door with a key.
   b. The door opened.
   c. The door was opened by John.
   d. The door was opened.

In (3a) *John* is interpreted as the instigator of the action of door-opening in marked contrast to (3b) where the subject *the door* is clearly the recipient of the action of the verb *open*. In such sentences we normally understand that *John* is capable of exercising voluntary control over the action of the verb. It is for this reason that agents are left to be animate.[2] If we look at these two sentences, however, we see that not every subject of a verb can be interpreted as the agent. Moreover, the agent of an action may appear in a position other than subject position. This is illustrated in (3c) where the passive construction has the agent as object of the preposition *by* and the recipient of the action as subject of the sentence. From (3d) we see that it is possible to suppress an agent altogether.

Armed with the notion of agent we return to the verbs in (1)–(2) and recategorize them in terms of whether or not an agent is present. These judgments are by no means automatic and require some critical appraisal, but the recategorization that appears in (4)–(5) will hopefully do:

finite verbs

(4) A VERBS WITH AGENT

(none)

B VERBS WITHOUT AGENT
life contracts
death is expected
soldier falls
he does not become
Death is absolute
wind stops
clouds go

nonfinite verbs

(5) A VERBS WITH AGENT
(who) imposing his separation
(who) calling for pomp

B VERBS WITHOUT AGENT
(none)

The obvious feature of this categorization is a systematic asymmetry. All the finite verbs in the poem have subjects which are not understood as agents, while all the nonfinite verbs have subjects which are. Before we consider the significance of this asymmetry, let us focus attention on the reasons for the categorization in (4) and (5). Beginning with (4) we note that these verbs can be further subdivided into verbs which can never take an agent because of their inherent meaning and verbs which can but do not in this poem:

finite verbs

(6) A CAN NEVER TAKE AN AGENT

is
become
fall

B CAN TAKE AN AGENT BUT DO NOT IN THIS POEM

contract
is expected
stop
go

Recall that agency requires an action verb. Since *is* does not describe an action, its subject cannot be an agent. Similarly, *become* describes a state. One becomes something but *become* itself is not an action. Its subject too can never be understood as an agent. The verb *fall* in the line *the soldier falls* describes an action that has happened to the subject but not an action which the subject can bring about through his own instigation. *Fall* is like *die* or *live* in this respect and its subject can not be its agent.

The verbs in (6B) can take agents in other contexts in English, though it is clear from inspection of the contexts in the poem that the subjects are not agents. Compare

(7) a. life contracts
b. the wind stops
c. the clouds go

with

(8) a. God contracts life.
b. God stopped the wind.
c. God goes everywhere.

In the examples in (7a–c) the verbs, like *fall* above, describe actions which have happened to the subject but not actions which the subject has instigated.These contrast with (8a–c) where the subject is simultaneously the instigator. In the poem *contract*, *stop* and *go* have happened to *life*, *wind* and *clouds* but there is no indication of any agency for these events.

A word needs to be said about *is expected*. In the line *death is expected*, *death* is the goal of *is expected*, not the agent. It is in other words, the grammatical subject of the sentence but the semantic object. The semantic subject of the verb has been suppressed from the line, and left vague. Therefore *is expected* is categorized as not taking an agent.[3]

We turn now to the nonfinite verbs in (5). These are *imposing* and *calling for* and they occur in sentences related syntactically to sentences like:

(9) The three-days personage imposes his separation.

and

(10) The three-days personage calls for pomp.

In (9) the role of the subject, i.e. *three-days personage* as agent of *imposes*, is clear and requires no comment. The second of these has *three-days personage* as subject of the verb *call for*. Now *call for* has two meanings which are possible here. The first is the meaning 'order, demand' and in this meaning *three-days personage* is also an agent, paralleling (9). The second meaning is 'require, need' and in this reading *three-days personage* cannot be an agent. The parallel with *impose* suggests the agentive reading and we assume that *impose* and *call for* are agentive verbs.

Having made the judgments outlined above, we return to the asymmetry observed earlier; namely, that finite verbs in *Death of a Soldier* occur with grammatical subjects which are not agents while the nonfinite verbs do take agentive subjects. There is, however, a peculiarity of the nonfinite verbs. These verbs appear in syntactic constructions in which the agents have been deleted; that is, they do not occur on the actual surface of the poem. This enables us to make a generalization about the poem. In selecting phrases from the infinite number of possible phrases available to him to make this particular poem, Stevens has done three distinct things, namely:

(11) 1. He has selected verbs which can under no circumstances take agents.
2. He has selected the nonagentive sense of verbs which can but need not take agents.
3. In the two instances where he has selected the agentive sense of a verb, i.e. *impose* and *call for*, he has displayed the verbs in a syntactic construction which requires that the agent be deleted from the surface of the poem.

What all three items in (11) have in common, of course, is to remove from the poem's surface any agentive phrase. If we accept this intention as part of the poet's design – conscious or otherwise – we are essentially saying that the second stanza of *Death of a Soldier* is consistent with the poem as a whole in a way in which the following stanza would not be:

(12) He does not become a three-day personage,
Who imposes his separation,
Who calls for pomp.

Note, in particular, that the hypothetical stanza (12) is metrically virtually identical to the corresponding one in the poem. In fact, in any other terms, save deletion of surface agents, the two stanzas seem identical. At this point we ask whether there is a relationship between the suppression of surface agency and the meaning of the poem? In the world of the poem the death of a soldier in particular and of anyone, for the matter, is a natural event which is not to be associated with an initiator any more than one looks for an initiator in the death of a leaf that falls from a tree in autumn. In this world where things happen without the intervention of an initiator, the apparent paradox of the last stanza disappears:

(13) When the wind stops and, over the heavens
The clouds go, nevertheless,
In their direction.

This would be a surprise only if one supposed the wind was the agent of the clouds' motion. But in the world in which the *soldier falls*, it is not.[4] The manipulation of syntax and semantics to remove all vestiges of an agent from the surface of this poem corresponds to the world of the poem in which there are no initiators.

Once this is established, however, we can understand yet another aspect of the poem. The most obvious feature of the poem's tense system is that all of the verbs are in the simple present. Were it not the case that all agents are also suppressed, this would be a peculiar feature of the poem, even a bizarre one. Recall that agents presuppose actions and that actions develop through time. In English the means of expressing action developing through time is not the present tense but rather the present progressive tense. For example, if there is a knock at the door, one would say, 'Someone is knocking.' and not 'Someone knocks.' The latter has an archaic tone which is absent from the poem. As a consequence, the line *The soldier falls.* does not describe an ongoing action. The absence of agents in the poem, therefore, is consistent with the absence of the progressive aspect of the verbal system.

There is a morphological contrast in this connection employed by Stevens which is worth noting. The *-ing* forms *imposing* and *calling for* resemble present progressive forms; e.g. 'The king is imposing his will at this very moment.' Stevens could have chosen another construction at this point; for example, the infinitival *to impose* or *to call for* which might appear in the hypothetical 'He does not become a three-days personage/come to impose his separation/to call for pomp.' Rather he has chosen that construction which resembles the present progressive and which, by its presence in the poem, calls attention to the present progressive's absence. This use of the design possibilities inherent in the syntax of English is even more apparent in what follows.

Having established the rationale for the absence of the present progressive tense in the poem, let us consider the function of the tense which does appear in the poem, namely, the simple present. The first line of the second stanza *He does not become a three-days personage* introduces a notion of transitoriness. This is emphasized by the brief time span explicit in the phrase *three-days personage* who engages in the transitory actions of *imposing separation* and *calling for pomp*, and by the nonfinite verbs themselves, whose forms resemble the transitory present progressive tense. This stanza contrasts with all the others in focussing on persons and actions which take place in time. In contrast to this, the present tense in the first line of the third stanza, *Death is absolute*, expresses a truth which is outside of time. The use of the present tense here is like that in such sentences as 'Two and two is four.' or 'The set of all prime numbers is infinite.' This use of the simple present expresses general truths which, because they are always so, are timeless. The simple present adds this force to all of the verbs in the

106 *Essays in Modern Stylistics*

poem, imparting to each the sense that its action is lawlike rather than transitory.

Two independent syntactic and semantic features converge in the poem. First, agency is suppressed. This requires a nonprogressive form of all verbs. Second, consistent with this requirement, the simple present tense is chosen. This imparts timelessness to the actions described in the poem. Both syntactico-semantic choices delimit a special world; namely, a timeless world without agency, a world in which events are inevitable and human agency is absent. Such a world is, from a human standpoint, absolute. It is both free from and impervious to human intervention. Death is like this world and Stevens has ordered the syntactic and semantic parameters described above so as to make the form of his poem reflect its content, which is, ultimately, that death is inevitable and timeless; in a word, absolute.

Poetry is a Destructive Force

Poetry Is a Destructive Force

That's what misery is,
Nothing to have at heart.
It is to have or nothing.

It is a thing to have,
A lion, an ox in his breast,
To feel it breathing there.

Corazon, stout dog,
Young ox, bow-legged bear,
He tastes its blood, not spit.

He is like a man
In the body of a violent beast.
Its muscles are his own ...

The lion sleeps in the sun.
Its nose is on its paws.
It can kill a man.

In this rather strange poem the syntactic chiasmus or reversal of the second, third and forth lines stands out quite clearly. We can represent it diagramatically as follows:

```
Nothing to have (at heart)
      to have (or)        nothing
            (It is a)       thing to have
```

In other words, using the words *nothing* and *have* he constructs these lines so that the second is a reversal of the first and the third is a reversal of the second.

What is perhaps not so obvious is that this same device of reversal, albeit on a phonological scale, appears much later in the poem. Consider the first line of the fourth stanza and the last line of the fifth stanza:

>He is like a man
>It can kill a man.

The fact that *like* and *kill* are phonological reverses (1-k, k-1) is no accident and is merely the device of reversal seen in the first two stanzas, though now worked at a different level.

We shall assume that the principal formal device which characterizes this poem is chiasmus at the morphological and phonological levels. Now let us turn to the meaning of the poem.

The first two lines state that misery is to have nothing at heart. The third line of the first stanza expands this definition of misery, saying that it is both to have and it is nothing. The logic of the first two sentences is one of reversal, matching the formal chiasmus.

The next two stanzas appear to continue this consistency with respect to form and meaning. The first line of the second stanza continues the device of chiasmus, reversing the pattern of the last line of the first stanza and repeating, in particular, that misery is a thing to have. The poem then goes on to characterize this thing. It is to have a lion and, by extrapolation from the first stanza, it is to have a lion in one's heart. If the phrase *ox in his breast* is taken in parallel with *lion* and if, further, *his* refers to an unnamed poet implied through the title of the poem, then the second stanza may be paraphrased as follows:

>Misery for the poet is to have a thing at heart,
>For example, to have a lion in his heart or an ox in his breast
>And to feel it breathing there.

Given this paraphrase, the series of names that follows in the third stanza, *corazon*, *stout dog*, *young ox*, *bow-legged bear*, are all appropriate epithets for someone with a thing in his heart. That is, they are all names that might be given to someone to represent that the person so named has within him the spirit of the animal or object contained in the name. The next line states that he (the poet) tastes the blood of the animal contained in his breast and not spit. The implication of this is that the poet is someone possessed by something violent in his breast and therefore tastes its blood as opposed to the unpossessed person who tastes spit.

Up to this point, then, the poem seems to be saying that the poet is like someone with a beast inside him. When we come to the next stanza, however, we find that this image is dramatically reversed so that now we are told that a poet with a beast inside him is like a man inside a violent beast. This sudden reversal of the dramatic image that has been developed up to this point corresponds in an obvious fashion to the devices of reversal seen in the chiasmus linking the first two stanzas and in the phonological chiasmus of *like* and *kill* linking the last two stanzas.

The final stanza is now clear. The lion is presented as a destructive force outside of the poet who can kill a man (and a poet, of course). Simultaneously, it symbolizes the destructive force inside the poet which makes him a poet, and, of course, it represents the poet himself. Thus phonological, morphological, and imagistic chiasmus all converge relating form and content in an integral fashion.

Anecdote of the Jar

Anecdote of the Jar

I placed a jar in Tennessee,
And round it was, upon a hill.
It made the slovenly wilderness
Surround that hill.

The wilderness rose up to it,
And sprawled around, no longer wild.
The jar was round upon the ground
And tall and of a port in air.

It took dominion everywhere.
The jar was gray and bare.
It did not give of bird or bush,
Like nothing else in Tennessee.

The immediate impression one receives upon reading this poem is that it is akin in some way to a painting. The juxtaposition of objects in an incongruous and unexpected way and the ways in which the juxtaposed objects influence one another is common to much surrealistic art and to this poem. It would be useful to see if there is some deeper reason for this impression.

The most obvious feature of the poem is the unnatural word order of the first line. Were it to be paraphrased naturally the first sentence would be:

I placed a jar upon a hill
In Tennessee, and it was round.

or perhaps:

>   I placed a jar, and it was round,
>   Upon a hill in Tennessee.

By inverting the order as he has done, Stevens has constructed a second line of the form:

>   And round it was, upon a hill

And this line is paralleled by the fourth line of the first stanza:

>   Surround that hill

where the obvious repetition of the nouns and verbs appears, though with the variation of the prefix *sur*-added to the verb

```
           round it was, upon a hill
   (sur)round    that        hill
```

The second line of the second stanza continues the variation on *round* by prefixing *a*- to it:

```
              round it was, upon a hill
      (sur)round    that        hill
sprawled  (a)round  no longer   wild
```

And the third line of the stanza completes the variation by returning to *round* itself but this time with internal rhyme:

```
              round it was, upon a hill
      (sur)round    that        hill
sprawled  (a)round  no longer   wild
The jar was     round
  upon the   (g)round
```

Thus one formal device made use of in this poem through the first two stanzas is simple variation on the syllable *round*.

Between the second and third stanzas the introduction of rhyme words takes over where variation on *round* stops so that the last line of the second stanza ending in *air* rhymes with *everywhere* and *bare* of the first two lines of the last stanza. Then, in the third line of the last stanza, alliteration picks up where rhyme ends off. This appears in the alliteration of /b/ in *bird* and *bush*. Finally, in the last line a repetition of the ending of the very first line, *in Tennessee*, concludes the poem.

There is, then, a nonoverlapping succession of rhyming devices which appear in a serial fashion in this poem beginning with variations on -*round*, moving to end-rhyme, then to alliteration and terminating with identical rhyme between the first and last lines. This by no means exhausts the devices in the poem, for example, the heavy repetition of liquid and nasal consonants, but these devices are certainly the central ones.

In Winters (1937) the poem is explicated in a way which takes issue with certain previous explications. For Winters the central point of the poem is that the juxtaposition of a jar in a wilderness makes the wilderness slovenly in the poet's eyes, and, taking dominion everywhere, dominates the wilderness to its detriment. The jar is described as gray and bare, a barren object. Being barren, then, it is like nothing else in Tennessee. It is lifeless and therefore objectionable. The clash of the artificial in the jar and the natural in the wilderness to the detriment of the latter is the point of the anecdote.

Winters presents this explanation to counter an opposing interpretation whereby the placing of the jar acts not to the detriment of the wilderness but to its benefit. According to this view, the jar lends an order to the wilderness which it did not possess before.

In favor of Winters's view is the sense it makes of the phrase *sprawled around*. The notion of *sprawling* is, according to Winters, best viewed as a negative attribute imposed on the wilderness by the jar. Moreover, any interpretation which treats the placing of the jar as beneficial to the wilderness must be embarrassed not only by the phrase *sprawled around*, but also by the obviously negative properties of the jar cited later; namely, *The jar was gray and bare*. On the other hand, Winters's own interpretation requires a special view of the phrase *slovenly wilderness* which appears in the first stanza. Thus he wants to argue that the jar makes the wilderness slovenly; however, the use of slovenly as an adjective implies that it was already slovenly prior to the placing of the jar. This is certainly the most natural reading of the first stanza, and any other reading requires a special dispensation on the part of the reader.

Neither reading; (1) that which views the jar as beneficial to the wilderness, or (2) that which views the jar as detrimental to the wilderness is without difficulty. If, however, there exists a relationship between form and meaning in this poem, it should be possible for us to find an interpretation congenial to the structure that we have already established for *Anecdote of the Jar*, i.e. the successive nonoverlapping series of rhyming devices.

There is no apparent relationship between either reading and the structure we have discerned. There is, however, a third interpretation of the poem. This interpretation avoids viewing the placing of the jar as detrimental or beneficial. Rather it takes a more distant view and notes that the placing of the jar in Tennessee changes the perception of the wilderness. That is to say prior to the introduction of the jar, there was a wilderness. After the introduction of the jar, there was a new object: namely, a wilderness containing a jar. It is quite literally as if Stevens were creating a still-life painting in words (cf. Buttel 1967, p. 166).

This still life is seen in terms of the properties of the new element introduced. The jar possesses three properties which are germane: (1) it is round; (2) it is tall and of a port in air, i.e. imposing; (3) it is gray and bare, i.e. barren. These properties have a specific effect on the environment in which they are introduced. Consider the property round. Placing the jar on the hill causes several things to happen. The jar makes the wilderness, already slovenly according to the poem, appear to surround the hill on which the jar is placed. Further, the jar makes the wilderness sprawl around, where here the word *around* is meant in its directional sense; i.e. the wilderness literally sprawled circularly around the hill on which the jar stands, whereas before, without the focal point of the jar, it simply sprawled without direction. Now it sprawls *no longer wild.*

Notice that the apparent contradiction between slovenly wilderness in the first stanza and sprawling wilderness in the second stanza now disappears. In both stanzas the wilderness is slovenly and sprawling; moreover, in both stanzas the placing of the jar on the hill has had the same effect, i.e. it has given direction to the slovenly and sprawling wilderness by making it seem to surround and sprawl around the hill. The jar has tamed the wilderness by imposing upon it a certain order.

The second property of the jar is described in the phrase *tall and of a port in air*. This means that the jar is of an imposing bearing. The wilderness appears to be diminished since, because of this property, the jar *takes dominion everywhere*. The final property, described in the phrase *gray and bare*, contrasts with the wilderness. The jar appears as a barren object that does not offer life, that does *not give of bird or bush*. In this respect the jar is like nothing else in Tennessee.

In summary, then, the poem is structured in a very simple fashion. A property of the jar is mentioned and the relationship of the property to the environment is specified. With respect to the property round, the jar made the wilderness surround the hill. With respect to the property tall and of a port in air, the jar dominated the wilderness. With respect to the property gray and bare, the jar contrasted its own barrenness to the implied life of the wilderness.

We can now relate the structural properties of the poem to the semantic properties just discussed in an attempt to integrate form and content. We have seen that the first structural device of the poem concerns the syllable *round*. The poem begins with variations of this syllable, starting with *surround*, moving through *around* and *round* to *ground*. The actual phonological shape of the property of the jar which, in English, takes the form of the word *round* imposes an order on the poem just as the semantic property 'round', which the jar possesses, imposes an order on the wilderness. Using the shape of the word *round* to impose an order on the poem parallels using the actual shape of the object to impose an order on the wilderness.

This relationship exists with respect to the second property, namely *tall and of a port in air*. Once again the physical shape of a word used to describe the property, i.e. *air*, imposes a new rhyming order on the poem (*air*: *everywhere*: *bare*) and this parallels the imposition of a new perception on the wilderness by the semantic content of the phrase of which the word is part, i.e. *tall and of a port in air* takes dominion everywhere.

Finally, a new property appears, *gray and bare*. This property contains the word *bare* which begins with the sound /b/ and it is this sound which participates in the alliteration of the following line. (Indeed, the assumption that the physical shape of the word imposes order explains why the alliteration in the next line is on /b/ and not some other sound.) In this case too the physical shape of a word imposes an order on the poem just as the meaning of the property which takes that physical shape imposes an order on the wilderness. That is, the jar imparts a sense of contrast between its barren self and the life of the wilderness. And the closing line, *like nothing else in Tennessee*, indicates the uniqueness of the object described, the wilderness with jar.

The apparent order of this poem is consistent with its affinity to a still-life painting. The latter is a highly ordered form of visual art with great emphasis placed on the structure of conjoined objects in a single field. Indeed, the apparent framing of this poem between the repeated phrases *in Tennessee* which appear in the opening and the closing line of the poem provides a verbal counterpart of a frame to the still life in words.[5] However, there appears to be yet another level of meaning which can be imposed on this poem, especially in view of the analysis which has gone before.

It is possible to view the poem as follows. Placing a jar in a wilderness becomes, like juxtaposing objects in a still life, an artistic act. The chief characteristic of this act is that it imposes an order where none was before. The poem, then, becomes an allegory of what it is about. The wilderness is language. The jar is the poetic form which orders that wilderness. The placing of the jar in the wilderness is the act of poetic creation which imposes form on disorder. The poem is an allegory because Stevens has constructed *Anecdote* so that as each property imposes order on the wilderness, it also imposes an order on the form of the poem. The poem is in form what it is about in content.

The Snow Man

The final poem to be analyzed in this discussion is also from *Harmonium*. This poem is considered to be not only one of Stevens's best, but one of the best short poems of the twentieth century.

The Snow Man

(14)   One must have a mind of winter
To regard the frost and the boughs
Of the pine-trees crusted with snow;

And have been cold a long time
To behold the junipers shagged with ice,
The spruces rough in the distant glitter

Of the January sun; and not to think
Of any misery in the sound of the wind,
In the sound of a few leaves;

Which is the sound of the land
Full of the same wind
That is blowing in the same bare place

For the listener, who listens in the snow,
And, nothing himself, beholds
Nothing that is not there and the nothing that is.

The opening stanza constitutes what appears at first sight to be a complete sentence and, for all intents and purposes, simply the first of a series of coordinate statements which make up the poem. If we were to diagram its syntax, we would obtain the following schematic representation (where S means that the sequence of words connected to S by lines forms a sentence):

(15)

S

One must have a mind of winter
To regard the frost and the boughs
Of the pine-trees crusted with snow;

What is rather striking about this stanza, however, is that while it at first glance appears to stand alone as a complete syntactic structure, the beginning of the next stanza requires that the reader reassess the syntactic analysis in a very special way. The beginning of the next stanza indicates that an ellipsis has occurred and that the sentence which apparently terminated at the end of the first stanza is, in fact, the first member of a coordinate sentence. The ellipsis is with the phrase 'one must' and reinserting it, we represent in (16) the diagram of the first stanza and the new

114   *Essays in Modern Stylistics*

syntactic material which extends over the second stanza and ends at the semicolon in the middle of the first line of the third stanza:

(16)
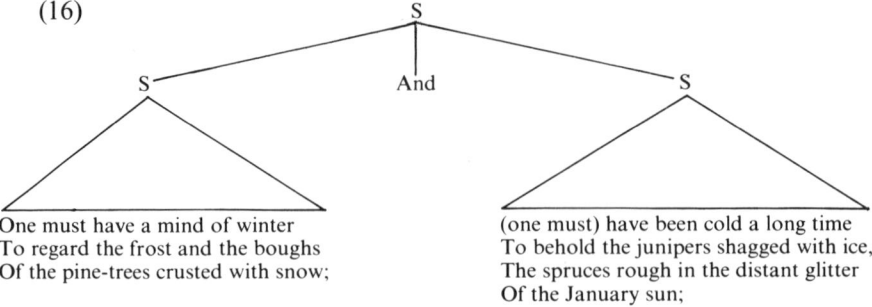

One must have a mind of winter
To regard the frost and the boughs
Of the pine-trees crusted with snow;

(one must) have been cold a long time
To behold the junipers shagged with ice,
The spruces rough in the distant glitter
Of the January sun;

At this point the almost perfect symmetry between each member of the coordinate pair which spans stanzas one and two becomes apparent. In (15) there is a main clause *one must have a mind of winter* and a subordinate clause introduced by the truncated subordinate conjunction (*in order*) *to*. The subordinate clause is *to regard the frost and the boughs of the pine-trees crusted with snow*. Notice that it contains a verb *regard* and a compound object; namely, *frost and the boughs*.... When we come to the second member of the coordinate sentence, we find that it is structured in precisely the same way. There is a main clause (*one must*) *have been cold a long time*, a subordinate clause introduced by the same subordinate conjunction (*in order*) *to*, the subordinate clause contains a verb *behold* and a compound object; namely, *junipers* (*and*) *spruces rough*....

This near perfect symmetry cannot but reassure the reader of the correctness of the reanalysis occasioned by the ellipsis at the beginning of the second stanza. It is for this reason that the ellipsis which appears in the middle of the first line of the third stanza is especially striking. For this new ellipsis shows that once again we have been mistaken in our syntactic analysis, and we must now go back and reanalyze.

The occurrence of *and* before the phrase *not to think* indicates that we have to do with yet another coordinate phrase and if we backtrack, we find that it must be taken as coordinate with *behold* syntactically and semantically. We find, then, that to reanalyze the structure through the third stanza, we have the schematic representation, shown by the diagram in (17) on page 115.

The results of our analysis up to (17) have been as follows. The second stanza proved to be the second conjunct of two coordinate sentences which are, in addition, perfectly symmetrical. However, the third stanza proved to be precisely the same thing, namely the second conjunct of two coordinate sentences which are perfectly parallel, only at a deeper level of embedding

(17)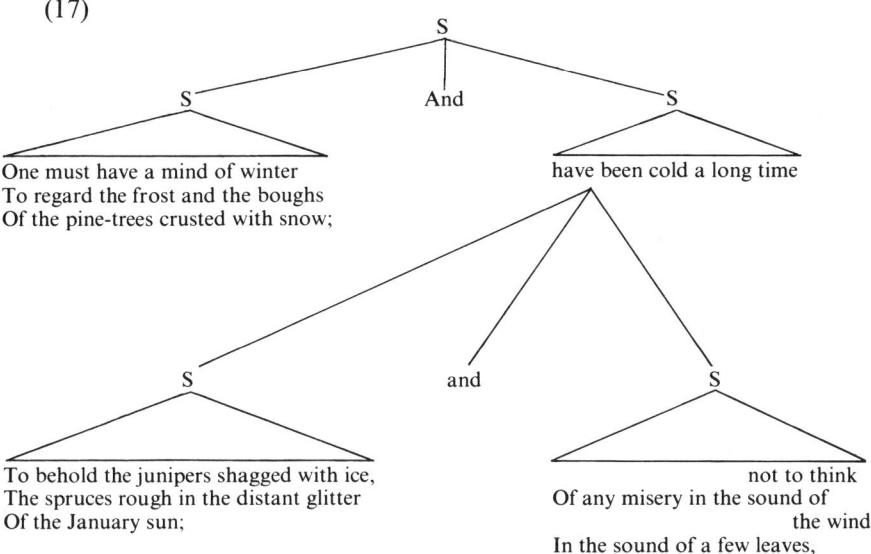

than the first and the second stanzas. This literal syntactic design is possible only because the second stanza, in particular the phrase:

(18)   To behold the junipers shagged with ice,
       The spruces rough in the distant glitter
       Of the January sun;

plays a double role. It mirrors the structure of the phrase beginning *to regard* ... in the first stanza and is itself mirrored in the third stanza in the phrase beginning *and not to think*....

This maintenance of syntactic parallelism while deepening the level of embedding and at the same time requiring the reader to take an active part in determining through reassessment the syntactic structure of the poem constitutes something of a virtuoso performance in manipulation of syntactic form. We shall see below that this formal structure is closely related to its semantic content. At this point we must continue to explore the formal structure itself.

The fourth stanza of the poem consists of a deepening of levels of embedding. The diagram in (17) contains in its rightmost S the noun phrase (NP) *the sound of a few leaves*, which we schematically represent as:

(19)

116   *Essays in Modern Stylistics*

Picking up the syntax at this point we find we must extend the diagram in (17) by adding a series of relative clauses attached to the NP in (19) which is, itself, part of the overall diagram in (17). We do this as follows:

(20)

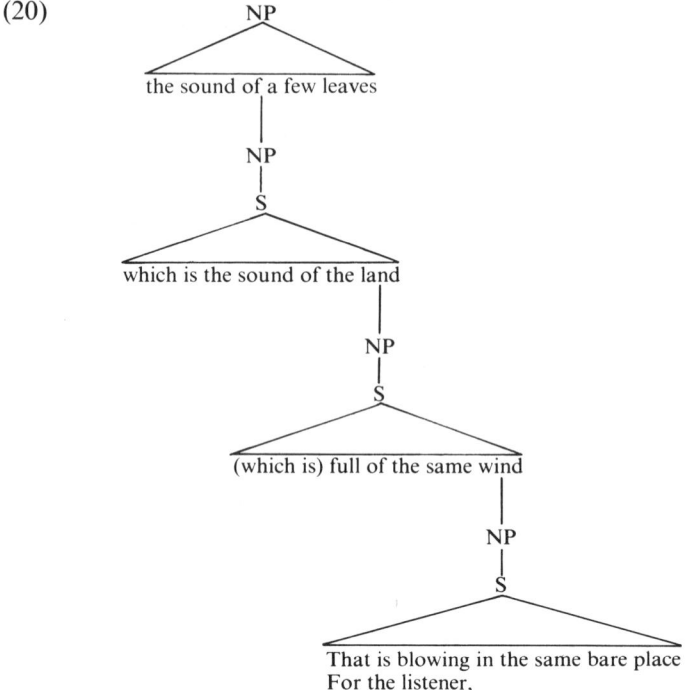

The three relative clauses descending from the NP *the sound of a few leaves* comprise the fourth stanza of the poem. Syntactically this stanza consists of a repetition of the same syntactic structure, a relative clause, three times. This recalls the earlier repetition of the same syntactic structure, conjunction, which also occurs three times [cf. (17) above].

Along with this repetition there is the obvious repetition of certain words. Thus, in the second line of the third stanza *sound* and *wind* appear in a noun phrase. The next line echoes the word *sound*. The same word appears in the relative clause which begins the fourth stanza. The second relative clause contains the word *wind* repeated from the third stanza. It also contains the word *same* and this is repeated in the third relative clause in the phrase *same bare place*. Finally, on the even narrower level of alliteration, it is noteworthy that from the noun phrase *in the sound of the wind* in the third stanza all the way through each relative clause to the last (i.e. to *For the listener*) alliteration of *s*-occurs. Since the subject of this entire construct is the sound of the wind, /s/ alliteration is undoubtedly sound symbolic.

The mark of a great poet is his ability to juggle many interesting balls at once. The brief passage we have been analyzing illustrates Stevens's ability to perform syntactic, lexical, and phonological repetitions simultaneously, and in part this virtuosity has been perceived by the critics and praised by them.

We now come to what is perhaps the most striking syntactic manipulation of all. The third relative clause represented in (20) ends with the phrase *For the listener*. It is followed by these lines:

(21)   who listens in the snow,
      And, nothing himself, beholds
      Nothing that is not there and the nothing that is.

The most obvious aspect of (21) is that it, too, is a relative clause. It begins with the relative pronoun *who* and it obviously modifies the NP *the listener*. The structure of this stanza is represented in the diagram (22) without attempting to relate it to the previous diagrams.

(22)

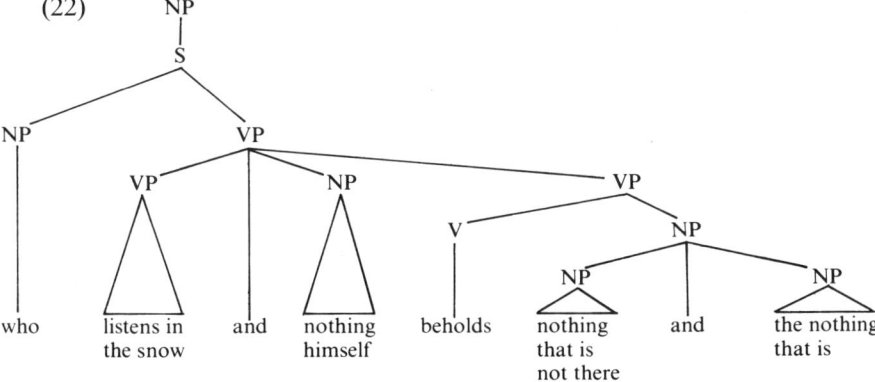

Note: In the above diagram the symbol VP abbreviates *verb phrase* and V abbreviates *verb*. The symbols NP (*noun phrase*) and S (*sentence*) have appeared earlier.

The most obvious fact about the structure in (22) is that it contains all of the properties which we have seen earlier in the poem. Thus (22) contains a compound VP just as (17) contains a compound S. Moreover, the second conjunct of the compound VP contains a compound NP just as the second conjunct of the compound S in (17) itself contains a compound S. Thus (22) is very close to being a structural repetition of all of the structure that has gone before.

There are two possible ways to relate (22) to the structure elaborated thus far. The first is simply to treat (22) as yet another relative clause atached to the NP *the listener*. In other words, the diagram in (20) would have one more relative clause extending downward; namely, the relative clause in (22).

There is, however, an alternative proposal. It has long been observed that there is a similarity between nonrestrictive relative clauses and coordinate clauses. The following paraphrases of one another are illustrative:

(23) a. John will come, and he is certainly trustworthy.
b. John – and he is certainly trustworthy – will come.
c. John, who is certainly trustworthy, will come.

Assuming the validity of treating nonrestrictives as being derived from conjoined clauses, we are now able to provide another analysis for the structure in (22). (Notice that Stevens himself punctuates the lines in question as a nonrestrictive relative clause.) In particular, we may now view (22) as yet another conjunct of a conjoined sentence. With its introduction in the last stanza, we find ourselves once again required to reanalyze the syntactic structure of the poem just as we were required to do upon encountering the syntactic material in the second and third stanzas. If we accept this analysis, the fact that the syntactic structure of (22) parallels the preceding structure is nothing more than the same device used by Stevens earlier, though now in a slightly different disguise. Thus, whereas the second stanza paralleled the first and the third paralleled the second, each time within a conjoined sentence, we now find that the last stanza parallels the first four, itself in a conjoined sentence. The syntactic unity that this analysis of (22) provides is represented in (24), once again very schematically:

(24)

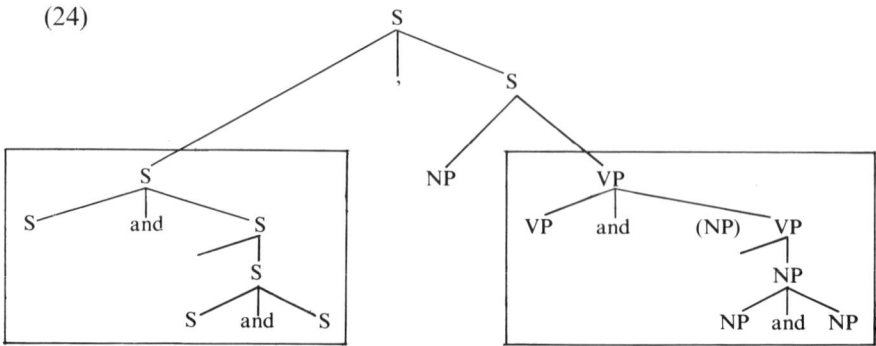

Note: The sections of this schematic tree which are parallel are enclosed in the superimposed boxes. The diagram has been simplified to emphasize the structural parallel between the first part of the poem and the last stanza. In particular, the parenthetical NP *nothing himself* has been placed in parentheses in (24). The comma extending below the highest S indicates the use of the nonrestrictive relative clause in its conjunctional sense.

The reason for adopting the analysis in (24) is precisely that the resultant structure is consistent with a poem requiring reanalysis at several key points in the reader's progress through the poem. The poem demands that we analyze and then reanalyze yet again as we pass linearly and in time from one point to another in the structure.

At this point let us look at the relationship between the formal device described above and the meaning of the poem. Frank Kermode talks, in part, of its meaning as follows:

> Out of 'The Snow Man' grows the recurring metaphor of winter as a pure abstracted reality, a bare icy outline purged clean of all the accretions brought by the human mind to make it possible for us to conceive of reality and live our lives. So purged, reality has no human meaning, nor has a man; he is
>
> ... the listener, who listens in the snow,
> And, nothing himself, beholds
> Nothing that is not there and the nothing that is.
>
> In winter, things are seen as they are. (1960, 34)

In contrast to Kermode's interpretation of *The Snow Man* we have Wallace Stevens's own explanation which he gives in a letter to Hi Simons, dated 18 April 1944: 'I shall explain the Snow Man as an example of the necessity of identifying oneself with reality in order to understand it and enjoy it.' Now while the interpretations differ in the value assigned to having a mind of winter (i.e. Stevens speaks of it as being a state in which to enjoy reality while Kermode speaks of it as a state in which enjoyment is absent, indeed in which no human meaning is present), there is a clear common core of meaning. Both Kermode and Stevens speak of the need to perceive reality in a clear fashion.

Now if we return for a moment to the development of the poem, we find that in the implied regimen needed to move toward a clear perception of reality there is a constant change of perspective. Thus Stevens observes that to begin with one must have a mind of winter, i.e. a particular state of mind in order to regard the frost. However, this state of mind is not in itself reliable for one must have had it for a long time in order to behold the junipers shagged with ice and not think of misery. In other words, a mind of winter will enable perception of winter but will not separate the perception of winter from the misery it entails. However, if one has a mind of winter for a long time, one will be able to see the winter without thinking of the misery.

At this point one becomes, according to the poem, a listener who is now able to behold nothing that is not there and the nothing that is. In this ultimate state of mind one sees clearly, i.e. one sees no thing that is not there and in seeing only those things which are there one will finally perceive the nothing that is really there. This final change of perspective is one in which the ultimate realization is that in seeing what is really there one sees that what is really there is nothing. It is this perception which is underscored by describing the listener as being nothing himself and presumably able to perceive nothing.

It seems quite reasonable then to view the semantic thrust of the poem as the need to constantly change perspective in order to achieve a real understanding of reality. But now let us return to the formal structure of the poem. We saw that in an extremely intricate fashion the poem consists of a syntactic pattern whose main characteristic is that its structure at any one time seems clear but which, at the next moment, requires a complete reanalysis. What seemed clear earlier turns out to be an illusion. This designed need to change syntactic perspective cannot more closely parallel the sense of the poem which is to change one's outward perspective in order to more accurately understand reality. The poem is in its structure precisely what it talks about in its content. It demands of readers that they reanalyze in order to see the truth of its syntax and this is what Stevens claims one must do with respect to one's perception of the world in order to perceive the truth of the world's reality. There can be no more direct relationship between a poem's form and its content than that exhibited by *The Snow Man*. Indeed, making the poem's syntax a virtual allegory of its content constitutes a brilliant poetic achievement.[6]

Conclusion

In each of the four poems analyzed above a formal structural feature was isolated. An attempt was then made to show how this feature is related to what the poem is about; in a word, how form and content correlate. Since it is logically possible for the formal structure encountered in a poem to bear no relation to that poem's content, it seems significant that in these four poems such a correlation can be drawn. The question immediately arises, to what extent can similar correlations be found in other poems and other poets? An attractive and obvious conclusion that one might ultimately wish to draw is that the aesthetic worth of a poem in part depends on the existence of such correlations. The worth of this conclusion must await a much more comprehensive body of studies of which the present study is, hopefully, one.[7]

Notes

1 I would like to acknowledge the debt I owe those students who participated in a poetry seminar in the spring of 1971 at Brandeis University whose insights

contributed significantly to this essay: Louise Arthur, Janet Stojak Kaplan, Ann Reed, Kim Weeks, Suzanne Spadola and Julia Waldman. In addition, I would like to thank Noam Chomsky, Morris Halle, and Eleanor Young for their insightful comments on an earlier version of this paper, as well as Mr Dan Wallace for his valuable suggestions for presenting this material schematically. An earlier version of this article appeared in French translation in *Change 16–17*, Seghers/Laffont, Paris, 1974. This work was in part sponsored by NSF Grant No. GS 3179 to Brandeis University and in part by a NSF Grant No. GS 35283 to the University of Massachusetts at Amherst.

2 Sentences like:
   a. The robot washed the dishes.
   b. The wind opened the door.

suggest that some other category beside that of agent, or perhaps in addition to agent, is required (cf. Huddleston 1970). In particular, it may be that a category like Causer must be set up and subdivided into agentive Causer, like *John* in (3a,c) and nonagentive Causer like *robot* and *wind* above. But even so the point to be made below will still go through though with the category Causer, animate or otherwise, substituted for agency.

3 That *expect* can be considered as a verb which can take an agent is based upon some observations in Huddleston (1970, 508):
   i. Don't expect any mercy from John.
   ii. Expect me when you see me.

These sentences involve clear commands and commands are limited to actions which the hearer is assumed to have some control over. This sense of *expect* does not appear in the poem. But notice that even if one supposed that it did, the agent of the action of *expect* would still be suppressed from the surface. And this, as will be seen, is what is really crucial to the analysis.

4 The separation of *wind* (the causer) from *clouds go* (the effect) is underlined by the phrase *in their direction*. That is to say, the clouds have a direction that they are going in and they continue in that direction irrespective of the wind.

5 For a discussion of the relationship between poetry and painting in the work of William Blake, Henri Rousseau and Paul Klee see Jakobson (1970).

6 It is noteworthy that the last line of the poem contains within itself precisely the kind of syntactic change of perspective which characterizes everything that has gone before. Thus, in the line *Nothing that is not there and the nothing that is*, the first occurrence of *nothing* constitutes a noun phrase composed of a determiner and a noun and can be represented as:

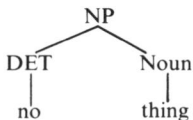

The second occurrence, however, contains *nothing* now as a noun within the noun phrase *the nothing* and can be represented as:

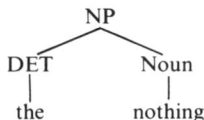

Thus, the syntactic shift from *nothing* to *the nothing* parallels the shift whereby the listener, beholding what is there beholds the nothing there.

It has been pointed out to me by Morris Halle that the shifting of syntactic perspective in *The Snow Man* is quite parallel to the building of several perspectives into a single plane in the work of the Cubists. This parallel between a poetic device in Stevens and a painter's device in say Picasso or Braque is quite striking and has not gone unnoticed: 'In a more serious vein, "Metaphors of a Magnifico" (1918), Stevens seems to have the Cubists' ability to see different perspectives of an object simultaneously.... On must assimilate the multiplicity here just as the viewer of Duchamp's painting must assimilate the fragmentation and multiplicity of the nude descending the staircase' (Buttel, 1967, pp. 165–6).

For a discussion of the relationship between poetic and visual forms see Jakobson (1970).

7 Two recent studies which attempt to draw the same kinds of correlation between form and content are Freeman (1975 and 1978).

References

Buttell, R. *Wallace Stevens: The Making of Harmonium*. Princeton. N.J.: Princeton Univ. Press, 1967.

Freeman, D. C. 'The strategy of fusion: Dylan Thomas's syntax'. *Style and Structure in Literature*, ed. R. Fowler. Oxford: Blackwells, 1975.

Freeman, D. C. 'Keats's "To Autumn": poetry as pattern and process.' [Reprinted in this volume, pp. 83–99].

Huddleston, R. 'Some remarks on case grammar', *Linguistic Inquiry*, 1.4 (1970), 501–11.

Jakobson, R. 'The verbal art of William Blake and other poet painters', *Linguistic Inquiry* 1.1 (1970), 1–23.

Kermode, F. *Wallace Stevens*. London: Oliver Boyd, 1960.

Stevens, H. *The Letters of Wallace Stevens*. London: Faber & Faber, 1965.

Stevens, W. *The Collected Poems of Wallace Stevens*. London: Faber & Faber, 1955.

Winters, Y. *In Defense of Reason*. Denver: Univ. of Denver Press, 1937.

7
Syntactic deviation and cohesion
Irene R. Fairley

In 1963, in a class on English Structure at MIT, Professor Noam Chomsky introduced examples of word-order violations from a poem written by E. E. Cummings, entitled 'Me up at does' – it had appeared in *The New Yorker* that week. Professor Chomsky called our attention to the poem as containing sequences that are not permissible in standard English. His examples led me to study Cummings's syntactic deviations; they are of interest to linguists curious about rule violations. Cummings's counter-grammatical devices have drawn considerable attention because of the boldness of the deviations.

There is another just as interesting, but, I believe, overlooked, facet of Cummings's irregular syntax – the function of syntactic deviation as a device of structural cohesion. Cummings's cohesive deviation is an aspect of his style to be recognized as equally important and innovative as his idiosyncratic use of specific syntactic deviations.[1]

There are, to be sure, instances of Cummings using syntactic deviation conventionally as a device of foregrounding, so that the deviations do not pattern or appreciably alter the statement of a poem. In such instances deviation provides relief and contrast within a context of otherwise parallel and regular constructions.

In the single occurrence (inter-sententially), deviation creates tension and may reduce the redundancy of a statement, but when repeated intrasententially it can reinforce understanding. Cummings often sustains deviation to provide through its repetition a level of patterning within a poem. Instances, or tokens of a particular type of deviation, thus form a set of equatable items. For example, functional shifts pervade the sonnet 'true lovers in each happening of their hearts', preparing the reader for the final instance: 'their eyes would never miss a yes.' Deviant compounds such as 'dream-send', 'moan-loll', 'moon-cease', correspond in the poem 'riverly is a flower'. Violations of cooccurrence restrictions pattern in the poem beginning 'the hours rise up putting off stars and it is.' In Cummings's poems, repetition of a type of deviation becomes another source of motif.

More subtle and innovative, though, is Cummings's use of syntactic deviation to relate levels within the organization of the poem. 'a like a', a brief poem, illustrates this principle.

> a like a
> grey
> rock wanderin
>
> g
> through
> pasture
> wom
>
> an creature whom
> than
> earth hers
>
> elf
> could
> silent more no
> be

Although syntactically the poem is a fragment, an expanded noun phrase lacking a main verb or predicate, the nominalization is functional, since the poem conveys an Imagist description rather than an action or predication. Theme and form are joined in Cummings's selected deviations.

A common method of dealing with fragments is to assume that a complete sentence is recoverable, and to seek the nearest equivalent grammatical statement. Constituents in this poem suggest to me three underlying sentences and a derivation that is in harmony with the expression of the poem.[2] Setting aside inversions, the sequence could be derived as follows: from two simple sentences, 'a woman creature is like a grey rock', 'she (or it) is wandering through pasture', which can be combined by relative-clause embedding to form a matrix sentence, and one complex sentence, 'earth herself could not be more silent than her', which in turn can be embedded into the matrix. The entire sentence can be subsequently nominalized and the main verb *be* deleted, to provide the sequence of the poem. Relative clauses identify and describe and are therefore a suitable vehicle, given Cummings's statement, while reduction and nominalization allow for compression. Because *be* has a high probability frequency and is readily reinserted, its omission is minimally disruptive. Deletion of *be* when if functions as a 'neutral' copulative is a device used to increase the imagistic effect of descriptions, and has been favored by twentieth-century poets.[3]

The major ambiguity (attributable to relative-clause reduction) furthers an identification of woman and rock. Is the woman creature or the grey rock wandering through pasture? It is difficult to determine. Since the participle is placed between the two noun phrases, like a squinting modifier, it may apply to either. 'Wander' calls for an animate subject, but the placement of the participle makes 'rock' also a possible head noun. Both selections involve deviance, one conflicting features, the other impermissible word order. The ambiguity suggests indistinctness perhaps due to distance. 'Silence' indicates distance as well, and only slight movement. Cummings's typographical concentration defines a limited movement, and even the semantic value of the participle 'wandering' is countered by association with a 'grey rock'. The total effect is of stasis.

Cummings skilfully selects and manipulates verbs so as to minimize the expression of action. The main verb *be* has been deleted, and functioning within the subordinate clause, 'be' is dislocated so that it closes the poem. That single final token stresses the descriptive mode, recalling all the deleted (or suppressed) instances of *be* (in accordance with the suggested derivation) while avoiding surface repetition.

Several levels in the poem are integrated by the impermissible shift of the 'like' modifier to a position before the noun; a visual and syntactic axis is established. 'Woman creature' is postponed and centered, her position – possibly a location in the field – is supported typographically and lexically by an equal distribution of words and lines, and at the phonological level: 'wom/an creature whom'.[4] Syntactically, the shift permits 'woman creature' to be both preceded and followed by descriptive comparative clauses, giving an impression of balance to an entirely left-branching sequence. Centering of the noun phrase contributes to the overall impression of quiescence and equilibrium.

All of the ungrammatical features of 'a like a', the deletions and dislocations, function to relate syntactic, semantic, and visual levels into a consistent whole. They are not incidental, but are crucial to the structure of the poem and to its rendering of the image of woman in field preserved at an instant in time.

126   *Essays in Modern Stylistics*

<pre>
             Tumbling-hair
                      picker of buttercups
                                     violets
         dandelions
         And the big bullying daisies
                            through the field wonderful
           with eyes a little sorry
         Another comes
                    also picking flowers
</pre>

A similar cohesion can be found in 'Tumbling-hair', The poem is organized as a pair of contrastive images, or characterizations, hinged by the phrase 'throught the field wonderful', which can be syntactically attributed to either unit and divides them about equally in terms of word count and visual grouping. The first unit, a fragment, depicts spontaneity, exuberance; the second sentence, grammatically regular, a person sad or conventional, perhaps engrossed in thought. The contrast is expressed through a network of synonymous and antonymous typographical, semantic, and syntactic elements.[5]

With hair tumbling, the first person gathers flowers, identified by concrete nouns as violets, daisies and dandelions, scattered typographically as in a field. 'Wonderful' ambiguously describes both the person's involvement in the activity and the field.[6] The syntax is incomplete, abbreviated, but not confusing. What has been deleted can be easily reconstructed in context on the basis of remaining constituents. Also, possible replacements occur in the paired grammatical sentence. A missing verb of motion pointed to by the typography, the activity designated by 'picker', and the predicate complement 'through the field', is reinforced by 'comes' in the second description. From the phrase 'with eyes a little sorry' we might borrow 'with' for the opening: 'with Tumbling-hair'.[7] These insertions would further the already partial parallelism, indicated by 'another', and 'also picking flowers'.

The parallelism is, of course, deliberately incomplete. 'Wonderful' provides a hinge with ironic overtones, for, typographically represented, the movement of 'Another' is confined, in keeping with the activity abstractly and flatly designated as 'picking flowers', and corresponding to the syntax that is conventional, unimaginative. The 'Tumbling-hair picker' is characterized by a syntax that is free, unconventional in its deviation. Syntactical form thus characterizes the two persons.

At least three levels correlate to form the composition. Visually, the typography suggests first broad and spontaneous, secondly circumscribed movement. Lexically, we find a contrast between colorfully concrete and flatly abstract descriptions. And syntactically, the composition alternates from imaginative and deviant to conventional expression.

'Me up at does' is still another poem in which syntactic deviation is cohesive. The burden of relating structure and statement rests more obviously upon the syntactic component in this poem.

>Me up at does
>
>out of the floor
>quietly Stare
>
>a poisoned mouse
>still who alive
>
>is asking What
>have i done that
>
>You wouldn't have

The speaker is startled, his confusion communicated by jumbled speech. It is, curiously, what we might expect of a poisoned mouse, but the imagined speech of the mouse is in standard order, straightforward and concise. The irony of the situation, the emotional reversal, is conveyed by impermissible word order. Inversion of the prepositional object ('Me up at') and the adverbial inversion ('still who alive') are errors that belie agitation. The auxiliary 'does' is also dislocated, so that it functions ambiguously, expressing at once emphasis, 'a poisoned mouse *does* quietly stare', and disbelief, 'does a poisoned mouse quietly stare?'

In 'Me up at' and 'still who alive' Cummings preserves the constituent unit while disturbing the internal sequence. More disruptive dislocations of the entire indirect object ('Me up at'), place adverbial ('out of the floor'), and finite verb ('does') within the sentence, serve to postpone the matrix subject, 'a poisoned mouse'. The noun phrase is emphatically centered (visually as well) so that modification precedes and follows, a pattern Cummings favors. Because it is delayed, 'a poisoned mouse' surprises the reader, as well as the speaker in the poem.

As in the two previous poems, organization and meaning depend upon syntactic deviation to the extent that correction of the deviant sequences would irreparably alter formal relations, causing a collapse of both unity and rhythm. In each of the poems Cummings has included deviation as an element of poetic structure.

Cummings did not limit a supportive role for deviant syntax to his brief poems. In longer poems he combines repetition of deviation with a cohesive function in patterning that secures the unity of the poem. 'All in green went my love riding' has a complex sequence of stanzas, with alternately repeated patterns incorporating constituent dislocations. The syntactic level of the poem is a pervasive parallelism based on syntactic deviation.[8]

All in green went my love riding
on a great horse of gold
into the silver dawn.

four lean hounds crouched low and smiling
the merry deer ran before.

Fleeter be they than dappled dreams
the swift sweet deer
the red rare deer.

Four red roebuck at a white water
the cruel bugle sang before.

Horn at hip went my love riding
riding the echo down
into the silver dawn.

four lean hounds crouched low and smiling
the level meadows ran before.

Softer be they than slippered sleep
the lean lithe deer
the fleet flown deer.

Four fleet does at a gold valley
the famished arrow sang before.

Bow at belt went my love riding
riding the mountain down
into the silver dawn.

four lean hounds crouched low and smiling
the sheer peaks ran before.

Paler be they than daunting death
the sleek slim deer
the tall tense deer.

Four tall stags at a green mountain
the lucky hunter sang before.

All in green went my love riding
on a great horse of gold
into the silver dawn.

four lean hounds crouched low and smiling
my heart fell dead before.

Four distinct stanza patterns are formed by the surface interlacing of semantic and syntactic features. Stanza 1 clearly groups with 5, 9 and 13, stanzas 1 and 13 being identical. Stanza 5 varies the pattern by changing lexically and syntactically two modifying phrases while preserving the larger syntactic pattern (adverbial phrase, finite verb, subject noun phrase, gerund, two adverbial complements). Stanza 9 echoes the modifications of 5, with additional lexical variation.

An even stronger congruence exists among the set of stanzas 3, 7, and 11, which, excepting substitutions for some lexical items, does not vary in grammatical structure (adjectival predicate, finite verb, subject pronoun, predicate complement, two appositive noun phrases).

The second stanza links with 6, 10, and 14, the major variation being lexical, a change in subject noun phrase in each repetition of the pattern (predicate noun phrase as object, subject noun phrase, finite verb, preposition). The noticeable variant is the final substitution: 'my heart fell dead before', in which noun phrase and verb are marked semantically as well as syntactically.

The fourth set, stanzas 4, 8, and 12, contains more variation, but limited entirely to lexical items within the subject and object noun phrases. The grammatical structure remains stable (predicate noun phrase as object, subject noun phrase, finite verb, preposition). The lexical substitutions in all four sets are synonymic and metonymic, supporting while varying the network of correspondences like the incremental repetition of ballads.

This quaternary stanzaic system based on syntactic and semantic correspondence represents only part of the structure of the poem. Another axis of organization follows a binary principle, complementing the semantic opposition of the lovers' struggle as hunter ('my love') and prey (the speaker's heart). Each lover has a dual identity, one as four hounds, the other as four deer. There are two systems of correspondence – one quaternary and one binary, observed as well in the distribution of grammatical features.

Stanzas pair, advancing the descriptive level, then the narrative. But they also alternate regarding focus. Triplets (stanzas 1, 3, 5, 7, 9, 11, 13) describe first the pursuer, then the pursued. Likewise, couplets (stanzas 2, 4, 6, 8, 10, 12, 14), designating relative positions during the hunt, alternately focus on hounds and deer. The topic of a triplet is introduced in the first line and functions as sentence subject. The topic of the couplet, also introduced in the first line, reflects the focus of the previous triplet, but functions as an object thus introducing another feature of grammatical alternation. The grammatical subject of the couplet on the second line, serves as a transition to the next triplet.

Glancing at stanza 3, we can see how this alternation works. The subject 'they', referring back to the 'merry deer' of the previous couplet, is echoed in the appositive noun phrases that conclude the triplet, and then referred to again in the topic of the following couplet: 'Four red roebuck'. But the syntactic subject of the couplet does not occur until the second line: 'the cruel bugle', and it, in turn, is echoed in the subject of the following triplet: 'Horn at hip went my love'.

It is also interesting to note how Cummings augments a sense of action by reversing constituents in couplets. He misleads us into thinking that the first NP VP is the main NP VP. We are likely to read the first line as a sentence with a finite verb, until we come to 'and smiling', which forces us to re-evaluate, reading the entire first line as a noun phrase with a reduced relative-clause modifier, and as object of the preposition 'before'. Dislocation, then, results in a dual reading of the lines, as a series of actions and a statement of spatial relationships. But because the device is repeated and stylized, only the first instance is disruptive.

Even syntactic deviation is made to conform with the extravagantly regular patterning that characterizes this poem. A very general correspondence of deviation holds among odd stanzas and among even stanzas. Triplets are characterized by verb/subject inversion, a predicate complement in initial position, and paired phrasal modifiers in terminal position. In couplets constituents are reversed, with the object of the preposition in initial position. Postponement of the subject noun phrase is common to all stanzas, triplets, and couplets, but triplets have additionally inversion of the subject and verb. In respect to deviation the duple rhythm of the poem could be presented as two counts alternating with one. Couplets show inversion ($a.\beta \to \beta.a$), triplets both inversion and discontinuity.[9] Syntactic deviation is integral to the pervasive parallelism and to the binary organization of the poem. Repetition and intricate linking of features, including features of deviation, contribute importantly to the textual coherence of the poem.

Consider still another, and final, poem. Formal structure (English sonnet) and syntactic divisions are less obvious, and deviation, as dislocation, is incorporated more subtly. Unifying devices and interrelationships are much less conspicuous in 'when god lets my body be'.[10]

    when god lets my body be

    From each brave eye shall sprout a tree
    fruit that dangles therefrom

    the purpled world will dance upon
    Between my lips which did sing

    a rose shall beget the spring
    that maidens whom passion wastes

> will lay between their little breasts
> My strong fingers beneath the snow
>
> Into strenuous birds shall go
> my love walking in the grass
>
> their wings will touch with her face
> and all the while shall my heart be
>
> With the bulge and nuzzle of the sea

While there is lexical repetition, it is not prominent. The auxiliaries 'shall' and 'will' alternate, and prepositions repeat but in differing sentence positions. Quatrains are semantically parallel, having synonymous images, each quatrain presenting an image of death and regeneration, each including a 'shall' sentence that predicts regeneration from the dead body and a 'will' sentence that describes response from the living. A couplet concludes the poem, climaxing the series of images in the identification of 'heart' and 'sea'.

The closing reveals in 'the bulge and nuzzle of the sea' the underlying rhythm of the poem and the key to its composition. Lines pair contrary to rhyme, sentence, and quatrain units, but in doing so emphasize syntactic dislocations within each sentence. This oppositional pairing approximates the motion of the sea, to and fro and overlapping. Undulating movement is represented graphically, lines corresponding to crests, the spaces between them to troughs, the poem, then, beginning and ending with the peak of a crest. Determining wave units from crest to crest, as it is customarily measured and illustrated in geology texts, accounts for the rhyme scheme across paired lines. In Cummings's poem the initial and final crests figuratively join – simultaneous with the completion and renewal of the cycle of life and death.

He must have had in mind the oscillating movement that defines waves – particles of water move circularly returning to a point close to origin. Syntactically, the poem can be considered a single sentence with an introductory dependent clause: 'when god lets my body be'. Since a final period is lacking, the sentence is potentially circular. The closing line returns us to the opening, rhyme concurring in the completed wave. The elimination of punctuation is as appropriate as the selected deviation, which is dislocation. Cummings's sea image effectively ends the poem as it aligns the semantic with other structural levels. All levels of the poem converge in an elaborate metaphor.

The strongest syntactic congruence is found, not at the surface level, but at the level of syntactic deviation (somewhat below the surface of the wave). Corresponding dislocations link the first and second quatrains – the first sentence of each pairing by two features, topicalization (shift to an initial position, before subject and verb, of an adverb or an item that has the sense of predicate object or complement) and verb/subject inversion; the second sentence by topicalization. (It is an alternation similar to that of 'All in green went my love riding'.) In the third quatrain internal parallelism holds, with complement/verb inversion common to both sentences. The pattern of topicalization and verb/subject inversion reiterates in the couplet:

lines	
1	when god lets my body be
2	From each brave eye shall sprout a tree
	3 2 1
5	Between my lips which did sing
6	a rose shall beget the spring
	3 2 1
	3
3	fruit that dangles therefrom
4	the purpled world will dance upon
	1 2
	3 1
7	that maidens whom passion wastes
8	will lay between their little breasts
	2
	1
9	My strong fingers beneath the snow
10	Into strenuous birds shall go
	3 2
	1
11	my love walking in the grass
12	their wings will touch with her face
	3 2

The rhythmic effect of these dislocations can be ascertained by reading the deviant sequences in normal order. Topicalization, especially, complements the central metaphor in creating an impression of overlapping, and all the dislocations are emphasized by Cummings's seemingly perverse distribution of couplets. But the semantically shifting relationships between subjects and objects and the introduction of new pairs with each image assures a progressive thrust.

Given the matrix of dislocations, the third quatrain is certainly marked – foregrounded – as only those two sentences begin conventionally with subject noun phrases: 'My strong fingers' and 'my love'. It is amusing – and characteristic of Cummings – to have redefined the relationship of deviation to regularity in the context of the poem. The change to verb phrase inversion maintains a form of correspondence (within the quatrain) but varies the overall rhythm of the poem. In this respect and in the apportionment of correspondence generally (phonologically, lexically and grammatically) 'when god lets my body be' is less symmetrical than 'All in green went my love riding', which may be too lyrical for contemporary taste.

1

When God lets my body be from each brave eye shall sprout a tree;
Fruit that dangles therefrom the purpled world shall dance upon.
Between my lips that did sing a flower shall beget spring;

2

When God lets my body be,	7
From each brave eye shall sprout a tree,	8
Fruit that dangles therefrom	6
will	
The purple world shall dance upon.	8
did	
Between my lips that no more sing	7
A flower shall beget (the) spring,	7
That maidens whom passion wastes	7
Will	
Shall lay between their little breasts.	8
My strong fingers beneath the snow	7
strenuous	
Into slender birds shall go,	8
My love walking in the grass	7
will touch on her face.	
Their wings shall seek e'er they pass.	7
And all the while shall my heart be	8
With the bulge and nuzzle of the sea.	9

3

When god lets my body be from each brave eye shall
sprout a tree;
Fruit that dangles therefrom the purpled world will
dance upon.

> Between my lips which did sing a rose shall beget
> the spring,
> That maidens whom passion wastes will lay between
> their little breasts.
> My strong fingers beneath the snow into strenuous
> birds shall go.
> My love moving in the grass their wings will brush
> on her face.
> And all the while shall my heart be with the bulge
> and nuzzle of the sea.

A comparison of earlier versions of the sonnet reveals some of Cummings's deliberate refinements.[11] Three of the drafts (for which no order is specified in manuscript) show a relatively conventional and static distribution, although the syntactic dislocations are already present and dominate structurally. In a fourth version we perceive Cummings working toward the subtle scheme of the poem, bringing the rhyme scheme, line divisions, and typographical distribution of lines into a complex relationship with syntactic units. In the fourth version, I believe, the metaphor of the poem is established.

> 4
>
> When God lets my body be
>
> from each brave eye shall sprout a tree,
> fruit that dangles therefrom
>
> the purpled world will dance upon.
> Between my lips which did sing
> a rose shall beget the spring,
> that maidens whom passion wastes
>
> will lay between their little breasts.
> My strong fingers beneath the snow
>
> into strenuous birds shall go
> my love walking in the grass
> their wings will touch with her face.
> And all the while shall my heart be
>
> With the bulge and nuzzle of the sea.

'All in green went my love riding' and 'when god lets my body be' prove an innovative bonding of syntactic deviation and parallelism, the last a recognized major element of verse. In all of the poems considered – varying in theme and verse form – syntactic deviation functions as a source of correspondence, of integration and structural cohesion. In short, Cummings indicates that deviation may be structurally supportive, may function much like lexical, grammatical, and phonological features, to unify a poem.

The range of devices from overt repetitions to subtle and intricate patterns is interesting as a factor of Cummings's individual style, and I hope that this analysis reveals his selections of deviation as being carefully calculated rather than anarchic or frivolous, as some critics supposed. Cummings may use deviations more frequently than most poets and may have a wider range of options, but he also appears to use them in unique contexts. In those contexts, and given their cohesive functions, Cummings's deviations may indeed be original uses of irregular syntax. But while original, they are not without ties to literary tradition. Cummings's deviations are manipulations of possibilities inherent in English syntax, and I would expect a diachronic study to show that his innovations follow guidelines long in existence in English poetry.[1 2]

Notes

1 Earlier versions of this paper were presented at the New England Linguistic Society Meeting, October 1971, McGill University, and at the Linguistics and Literature Section of the April, 1972, meeting of the Northeast Modern Language Association at Skidmore College.

The analyses that follow are directed to Cummings's special use of irregular syntax; they are not intended as complete studies of individual poems. The poems by Cummings are from *Poems 1923–1954* (New York, 1954), with the exception of 'Me up at does,' which is included in *73 Poems* (New York, 1963).

2 The derivation is not intended to represent Cummings's creative process. Unfortunately, manuscripts are not available for this poem.

3 The verb *be* is optionally deleted in certain standard English constructions; poets have always extended the options. For a discussion of fragmentary style see William E. Baker, *Syntax in English Poetry, 1870–1930* (Berkeley, 1967).

4 In his commentary on the free verse stanza of the poem, Norman Friedman, *e e cummings, The Art of His Poetry* (Baltimore, 1960) p. 99, notes the series of puns, remarking on 'wom/an creature' and 'hers/elf.' He identifies the poem as a description of a New Hampshire country wife.

5 During the discussion at NEMLA Richard Kennedy, of Temple University, suggested that the poem with its original title, "Epitaph', as it appeared in *Eight Harvard Poets* (Cambridge, 1917), referred to the rape of the mythical Persephone. Following that interpretation, the contrast can be seen as one figure spontaneously gathering flowers, while another, Hades, closes in with more direct movement, picking flowers to cover his purpose. Cummings dropped the title, including the poem under TULIPS, as V in the group of 'Chansons

Innocentes' in *Tulips and Chimneys* (New York, 1923), and subsequently as III of that same group in *Poems 1923/1954*. Title removed, a more broad interpretation is possible.

6 'through the field wonderful' is multiply ambiguous in regard to both the function of the entire adverbial phrase and of the single modifier 'wonderful'. This kind of productive ambiguity that allows for complementary interpretations is characteristic of Cummings's poems.

7 Disregarding the parallelism there would be other options. For example, adding the definite article would result in a type of impermissible adjectival modification that Cummings frequently employs: 'the Tumbling-hair picker'.

8 Two interpretations of this poem have appeared. Barry Sanders in *The Explicator*, 25 (November 1966), 23, describes the speaker as an unrequited lover whose heart is captured by the classical goddess, the huntress Diana, and mentions a cyclical, seasonal structure. Will C. Jumper in *The Explicator*, 26 (September, 1967), 6, has taken issue with Sanders's interpretation, insisting that the gender of the speaker is female, that the speaker recounts in courtly fashion the tale of her lover's fatal hunt. He argues that 'the structure of the poem is not 'cyclic' but is merely a sophisticated improvisation on the ballad pattern with repetition and repetition with variation throughout.' Personally, I agree with Sanders and hold to a male speaker and a figurative hunt (green is the color traditionally associated with feminine riding habit), but the identification of gender is not crucial to my analysis. It is necessary, however, to recognize the play of a sexual or binary opposition. Also, both observations regarding the structure of the poem would seem to have some validity, and are, I believe, supported by the following discussion of two related stanzaic systems and the structural complexity of the poem.

To the reader who wishes to pursue the structure of 'All in green went my love riding', I recommend also an essay by Philip J. West, 'Medieval style and the concerns of modern criticism', in *College English*, 34 (March, 1973), which presents an analysis of the poem from oral-formulaic premises.

9 These terms are used after the manner of Dolores M. Burton in her essay on Shakespeare's syntax, 'Toward a theory of deviant word order', *Proceedings – 1968 ACM National Conference*, 801–5. Two of the dislocations observed in this poem – complements to initial position and verb/subject inversion – recur frequently in Cummings's poems. These and other dislocations are treated at length in my dissertation, 'Syntactic deviance in the poetry of E. E. Cummings: a stylistic investigation', Harvard University, 1971. In concluding Chapter V, I outline three rearrangement rules, conceived as late stylistic adjustments in a generative grammar of English, that derive Cummings's major constituent dislocations. The rules are presented in rough form and at best represent the kind of formalization which may eventually be possible in stylistics. They resemble options in English, both diachronic and synchronic; not surprising, since Cummings is innovating within the context of English syntax. Rule (1), topicalization, moves items (noun phrase, adverb, predicate phrase) in main and subordinate clauses. Rule (2), V/S inversion, shifts the finite verb. A third rule, O/V inversion, reorders within the verb phrase. To return to the analysis of 'All in green went my love riding', it is of interest that the dislocations when accounted in terms of these rules, as reiterative and alternating rule application (rules 1 + 2 in triplets, rule 1 in couplets), confirm the binary principle of organization.

10 Robert E. Wegner, in *The Poetry and Prose of E. E. Cummings* (New York, 1965), p. 57, mentions this poem as one of a group reflecting Cummings's belief in reintegration. Wegner states that in Cummings's view 'dying is an extension of life, for the individual who responds with love to the phenomena of his existence.'
11 Cummings's manuscripts and poems are included by permission of the Harvard College Library and the estate of Marion Morehouse Cummings.
12 Many of Cummings's inversions echo devices of Milton, Shakespeare, Keats, and Hopkins, and the pattern 'adverb-verb-subject' is one that even Hemingway uses (as in the narration of 'Big Two-Hearted River'). There are clearly predilections in English which are reflected in conventional devices and in their various extensions. The problem of defining style, or of identifying idiosyncratic devices, involves comparisons at many levels, but those comparisons still elude us. Morton W. Bloomfield, 'Generative grammar and the theory of literature', *Proceedings of the Tenth International Congress of Linguists* (Bucharest, 1970), argues in support of a complex comparative matrix, essential to both a theory of literature and of style. Other references I have found helpful to my approach are Bloomfield's 'The syncategorematic in poetry: from semantics to syntactics', in *To Honor Roman Jakobson, Essays On The Occasion Of His Seventieth Birthday* (The Hague, 1967); Roman Jakobson, 'Grammatical parallelism and its Russian facet', *Language*, 42 (1966), 399–429; George M. Landon, 'The grammatical description of poetic word-order in English verse', *Language and Style*, 1 (1968), 194–200; and Samuel R. Levin, 'The analysis of compression in poetry', *Foundations of Language*, 7 (1971), 38–55.

8

Constraints on syntactic rules and the style of Shelley's 'Adonais': an exercise in stylistic criticism

Timothy R. Austin

More often than not it is hard to suggest any legitimate motive for attempting to delineate a movement or school within a given discipline. While particular directions and emphases of contemporary study may individually be worthy of attention, the precise categorization of each scholar as the member of some group oversimplifies what is of importance and obscures valuable distinctions. Such a situation can only be exacerbated by those who further devise and apply to a school or movement attractive but essentially contentless titles, thereby furthering the often specious impression of close methodological agreement between its members, and encouraging the scholarly equivalent of name-calling. Thus, for example, Roger Fowler's excellent collection of recent contributions to stylistic scholarship (1975a) would have forfeited little by the omission of the term 'The New Stylistics', (title and p. 3) and much of the invective of Barbara Herrnstein Smith's riposte (1977) might consequently have been avoided.

In the present paper we shall investigate both practical and theoretical aspects of stylistic criticism. We shall first consider in some detail one particular feature of P. B. Shelley's style in his poem 'Adonais', and its relation to that poem's overall aesthetic form. Thereafter, we shall rely on the conclusions of that individual analysis to provide the basis for a discussion of the general aims and the methodology of stylistic criticism. In doing so, we shall hope both to exemplify some of the significant technical refinements achieved in recent papers in this area and to clarify to some extent those respects in which the allegiances and beliefs of their authors have been most subject to misconstruction. In effect, the paper will seek to provide a sound argument in favor of stylistic research without being drawn into the unproductive dispute over nomenclature.

Our initial analysis of Shelley's poem will proceed in three stages whose relevance to broader theoretical issues will become clear in the closing section of the paper.

Three consecutive stanzas of Shelley's elegy for John Keats, 'Adonais', contain lines whose form is intuitively not of a kind expected in contemporary everyday speech.[1] The following are the three relevant citations:[2]

  (i) *Stanza V.*
  'And happier they their happiness who knew,'
  (CWS, II, 390:39)

  (ii) *Stanza IV.*
  'He died [...]
  [...] when his country's pride
  The priest, the slave, and the liberticide
  Trampled and mocked with many a loathed rite
  Of lust and blood.'
  (CWS, II, 390: 29, 31–34).

  (iii) *Stanza VI.*
  'The extreme hope, the loveliest and the last,
  The bloom, whose petals nipt before they blew
  Died on the promise of the fruit, is waste,'
  (CWS, II, 390, 51–53).

In the initial section of this study, we shall consider these passages individually, attempting, with the aid of concepts developed by modern linguistic theorists, to isolate the precise source of the intuitive 'abnormality' of each case.

Almost certainly the most significant contribution to linguistic science made by early proponents of the transformational generative (TG) theory of language was the recognition of precise, formally statable relationships between pairs of sentences such as those shown in (1) and (2).

  (1) a. Leopold ate the clams.
      b. The clams were eaten by Leopold.
  (2) a. Geraldine took four large apples out of the closet.
      b. Out of the closet, Geraldine took four large apples.

In each of these cases, the (b) sentence may be viewed as a transformational variant of the corresponding (a) sentence, with certain material from the (a) sentence having been permuted, in a fully predictable fashion, in order to derive an acceptable variant form. The recognition of such relations between sentences, and the promulgation of formally precise transformational rules to capture their inherent regularities, occupied the bulk of the attention of theoretical linguists for several years following the groundbreaking publication of Chomsky's *Syntactic Structures* (1957).

Transformations remain central to generative linguistic theory to this day. However, as was soon recognized by syntacticians working within Chomsky's system, some of the most characteristic features of human language are not in fact capturable by means of a simple transformational model alone. In particular, straightforward transformational rules, formulated to account for correspondences such as those shown in (1) and (2), are in themselves hopelessly over powerful. They falsely predict, for example, that precisely as the (a) sentences in (3) and (5) below can be transformed into the corresponding (b) sentences, so the same should also be true for the very similar sentence pairs in (4) and (6).

(3) a. I believe [that fellow to have a lean and hungry look].
 b. That fellow is believed by me [to have a lean and hungry look].
(4) a. I believe [that fellow has a lean and hungry look].
 b. *That fellow is believed by me [has a lean and hungry look].
(5) a. I believed] my aunt to have taken her poodles and a cane into the garden].
 b. Into the garden I believed [my aunt to have taken her poodles and a cane-].
(6) a. I asked my aunt [why she had taken her poodles and a cane into the garden].
 b. *Into the garden, I asked my aunt [why she had taken her poodles and a cane-].

The manifest unacceptability of (4b) and (6b) as sentences of English conflicts with the predictions of two otherwise apparently straightforward transformational rules, and early attempts to adjust the relevant rules themselves to account for such cases developed rapidly into complex exercises in formal notation.[3]

For the early transformationalists, however, all was not yet lost, for those cases in which various transformational rules derived intuitively unacceptable sentences themselves appeared to conform to certain fairly general patterns. These sub-regularities in the language could thus be formally captured by means of a set of 'constraints' or 'conditions' which would act to rule out, on a principled basis, the bad sentences generated by the transformational rules of the grammar. In particular, as we shall see immediately below, sentences (4b) and (6b) could be correctly ruled unacceptable by this method. Since J.R. Ross (1967) first directed linguists' attention to them, therefore, the form, method of application and role within the grammar of such syntactic constraints have been at the heart of advanced research in syntactic theory (cf. for example Bresnan [1972; 1976]; Chomsky [1973; 1976]; Kuno [1974]; Horn [1974]; Stillings [1977]). It is with three such constraints on transformations that we shall be concerned in the present discussion.

We may now return briefly to sentences (3) and (6). It was observed in the preceding discussion that no explanation of both the acceptability of sentences (3b) and (5b) and the unacceptability of the apparently analogous (4b) and (6b) appeared to be possible (without numerous and complex *ad hoc* adjustments) within a grammar whose only syntactic tool was the simple transformational rule. By utilizing a single constraint on syntactic rules, by contrast, it is possible to account straightforwardly for all of the relevant judgments, even though two distinct syntactic processes (*Passive* and *Prepositional Phrase* (*PP*) *Movement*) are involved.

The requisite constraint, which was originally proposed by Chomsky (1973), and has since then been clarified and revised both by him (Chomsky, 1976) and by Justine Stillings (1977), is based on a simple observation about the particular kind of subordinate clause involved in transformationally related sentence pairs such as those in (3) to (6). Chomsky noted that, where the embedded clause was infinitival, transformational rules could move material out of them (or into them) freely, as in examples (3) and (5). Where, however, the embedded clause contained a finite verb, the same movement resulted in unacceptable sentences such as (4b) and (6b). He therefore proposed to capture this fact by stating formally (Chomsky, 1973, p. 238) that

No rule can involve X, Y in the structure
$\ldots X \ldots [a \ldots Y \ldots] \ldots$
where a is a tensed sentence.

To see how this constraint, termed by Chomsky the *Tensed S Condition*, would apply to block an ungrammatical sentence such as (4b), it is only necessary to observe that the Passive rule, in applying to the underlying (4a), would have to move the Noun Phrase (NP), [*that fellow*], out of the sentence (S), [*that fellow has a lean and hungry look*], and that that sentence contains a tensed Verb (V), [*has*].

(4) *[NP *That fellow*] is believed by me [S ⎯⎯ [V has] a lean and hungry look].

We may now reexamine the line from Shelley's 'Adonais' cited in (i) above. The reader of this line is aware that *know* is a transitive verb in English.[4] Clearly, furthermore, the object of *knew* in this particular case must be [NP *their happiness*], and this NP would, in most cases, be expected to appear to the immediate right of the verb. That NP has however been moved in this instance, as shown in (7) below.

(7)   And happier they [NP *their happiness*] [S who knew ___].

Formally, substituting [NP *their happiness*] for '*X*', S for '*a*', and the site from which the object NP was moved for '*Y*', it is a simple matter to show that Shelley's (i) can only have been derived by violating Chomsky's Tensed S Condition. Alternatively, for those unhappy with such formalism, it is equally satisfactory merely to note the 'surface' parallelism between Shelley's (i) and the unacceptable English non-sentence (4b). For the moment, we are concerned only with pinpointing linguistically the intuitive infelicity of Shelley's syntactic style in these lines. We shall return in due course to a consideration of the literary significance of Shelley's employment of such demonstrably ungrammatical linguistic forms as (i). Before doing so, we shall examine the different but related syntactic problems associated with the other citations from 'Adonais' given in (ii) and (iii) above.

G. L. Dillon, in a paper which analyzes those transformations most favored by literary artists (Dillon, 1975), mentions one transformation whose function is to prepose an object NP into a position between its verb and the sentence subject. This transformation (*Object Movement*) thus derives, for example, sentence (9) from the underlying (8) as shown below:

(8)   Harry bought [NP the tickets].
(9)   Harry [NP *the tickets*] bought ___ .

Dillon rightly observes that, although application of this transformation generally results in a somewhat 'literary' derived sentence, its employment in English poetry has been sufficiently common to justify a formal statement of the rule.

At the same time, in both literary and non-literary usage, we also find sentences such as (10) is also derived from (8), but by means of a different syntactic rule known as *Topicalization*. Here, the moved NP is preposed past the subject and into sentence-initial position, as shown.

(10)   [NP *The tickets*], Harry bought ___ .

Both (9) and (10), therefore, are acceptable transformational variants of (8).

Neither of these derived sentences, it should be noted, exemplifies the NP-V-NP sequence upon which the native speaker of English relies for the syntactic establishment of 'grammatical relations' in simple sentences. Whereas such a standard order in the underlying sentence (8) may be simply matched with the equally standard grammatical relations orientation, Subject — (Verb) — Object, the NP-NP-V sequence exemplified in (9) and (10) has no such automatic counterpart in grammatical relation format: the first of the preverbal NP's may as easily be the subject as the object of the main verb (cf. [9] and [10] respectively).

In this specific instance, of course, the lack of clear syntactic evidence with regard to grammatical relations is not a hindrance to communication. The native speaker of English is well aware that, semantically, the verb *buy* requires a human subject NP and (usually) a non-human object NP. Thus, whatever the syntactic order the preverbal NP's appear in, semantic considerations alone will ensure that *Harry* is interpreted as subject, and *the tickets* as object of *bought*. Consider now, however, sentence (11).

(11) Harry the robber watched ___.

Both of the preverbal NPs in (11) are, semantically, potential subjects of *watch*; both are also potential objects. In consequence, the sentence itself is, out of context, completely ambiguous. It may have been derived from (12) by Object Movement, or from (13) by Topicalization.

(12) Harry ↑ watched [*the robber*].

(13) ↑ The robber watched [*Harry*].

It has been observed by Ann Banfield (1973), following a hint from Chomsky, that, in general, sentences such as (11) are avoided in the language:

> stylistic inversion [...] is tolerated up to ambiguity – that is, up to the point where a structure is produced that might have been generated independently by [other] grammatical rules. (1973, p. 134–5).

In the present context we may beg the question of what is 'stylistic' inversion, and merely note as a particular case of Banfield's proposed restriction, that the English language appears unwilling to tolerate NP-NP-V sequences whose semantic interpretation is ambivalent, since such configurations, as we have seen, do not provide the hearer (or the reader) with the purely syntactic evidence necessary to establish the grammatical relations obtaining in the sentence.[5]

A brief glance at the syntactic structure of Shelley's lines from Stanza IV

144 *Essays in Modern Stylistics*

of 'Adonais' given in (ii) show that they in fact contain an NP-NP-V sequence, which, if we allow for the possibility of poetic personification, could be ambiguously interpreted.

(14) He died [...]
[...] when [NP$_1$ his country's pride,]
[NP$_2$ The priest, the slave, and the liberticide,]
Trampled and mocked ⎯⎯ with many a loathed rite
Of lust and blood.

A background knowledge of Shelley's enduring hatred of the Established Church and of the complacent British populace will, of course, enable a sophisticated reader to interpret passage (14) correctly. On these *semantic* grounds he will be able to tell that NP$_2$ is the subject, NP$_1$ the object of the conjoined verbs *trampled* and *mocked*, and that (14) is in fact derived via Topicalization from (15).

(15) [...] the priest, the slave and the liberticide trampled
and mocked [NP *his country's pride*] with [...]

The *syntactic* form of Shelley's lines, however, does not carry any indication that this is the intended interpretation, and the application of Topicalization here thus violates Banfield's proposed restriction on the permissibility of syntactic ambiguity, which we shall hereinafter refer to as the *Up-to-Ambiguity Constraint*. Again, we shall return to a full discussion of the broader significance of our findings below.

In this section, we have so far considered two constraints on rules of the English language, the Tensed S Condition and the Up-to-Ambiguity Constraint, demonstrating in each case that these constraints are violated by Shelley in the text of 'Adonais'. A third restriction on English syntax derives from linguistic theoreticians' application to their own field of some basic facts about human cognitive abilities. We may note first that, in general, syntactic structures may be of three distinct kinds, as shown in (16) to (18) below.

(16) Left-Branching.
[[[[[[Bill's] aunt's] chauffeur's] mistress's] domineering father] mistook Bill for the chauffeur and broke his jaw.]

(17) Right-Branching.
[Grumpy mumbled [that Dozy had murmured [that it was Snow White's opinion [that the Wicked Queen knew [that they were all living in the forest]]]]].

(18) Center-Embedded.
[S_1 The woman [S_2 whom the spider [S_3 whose web broke S_3] startled S_2] screamed S_1].

Whereas, in both (16) and (17), syntactic subordination occurs consistently at one end of each construction, we find in (18) that S_3, [*whose web broke*], is embedded in the *center* of S_2, [*whom the spider (...) startled*], and that S_2 itself occurs in the center of the 'matrix' sentence S_1, [*the woman (...) screamed*].

In the course of an extremely complex technical discussion of the formal devices needed in linguistic theory to account for users' 'human limitations', Miller and Chomsky (1963) observed an important feature of the structure types given in (16) and (18) above. They showed that center-embedded structures such as (18) placed a far higher load on humans' notoriously limited short-term memory capacity than did either left- or right-branching structures such as (16) and (17) respectively. To put it in simple terms, this is due to the fact that the hearer of sentence (18) is faced with the task of processing and retaining in memory three separate and incomplete syntactic units ([*the woman (...)*], [*whom the spider (...)*] and [*whose web (...)*]), which must then be retrieved, – and retrieved in reverse order, – to be related respectively to the corresponding predicates [... *broke*], [(...) *startled*] and [(...) *screamed*]. Beyond a certain point, Miller and Chomsky noted, the decoding of such center-embedded structures 'exceed[s] the perceptual capacities [...] of the native speakers of the language', and, as a result, such structures generally 'simply are not used'. To establish the 'certain point' beyond which syntactic processing of center-embedded structures is virtually impossible, it is necessary only to compare the highly complex but interpretable sentence (18) in which three-deep center-embedding has occurred, with a structure such as (19) below, where the addition of one further layer of center-embedded structure virtually forces the hearer/reader to resort to pencil and paper to facilitate interpretation.

(19) I'll introduce the woman who when the spider whose web broke startled her screamed to my aunt tomorrow.

Although many aspects of actual language processing are still very insufficiently understood, it would appear to be indisputable that the constraint prohibiting excessive center-embedding anticipated by Miller and Chomsky is one which refers to surface-structure configurations. It has been similarly treated by Kuno (1973; 1974) and Grosu (1974), and has also played an important role in stylistic criticism in the work of Freeman (1975). Discussing Dylan Thomas's poem 'A Refusal to Mourn the Death, by Fire, of a Child in London', Freeman notes that poet's strategic challenging of limits on the reader's capacity 'to hold in storage syntactic structures which have not yet been resolved'. He argues that in that particular instance, Thomas's syntax comes close to being unacceptable, but that Thomas avoids actual incomprehensibility by including in the text syntactic 'clues', which enable the reader to establish, albeit with some effort, which parts of the various constructions 'belong together'. Freeman thus concludes that the aesthetic consequence of center-embedding for Thomas's poem is rather the creation of syntactic 'tension' than any appearance of 'obfuscation'. Clearly, however, literary usage of structures which approximate multiple center-embedded sentences runs the risk of outright incomprehensibility if its flouting of perceptual capabilities is not balanced by the inclusion of disambiguating syntactic pointers.

In the light of the preceding discussion, we may now turn to the third of our citations from Shelley's poem, which was given above as (iii). We repeat the lines below with appropriate syntactic bracketing.

(20) [S_1 The extreme hope, the loveliest and the last,
The bloom, [S_2 whose petals [S_3 nipt [S_4 before they blew]]
Died on the promise of the fruit] is waste.]

As our initial premise in the development of this section of the paper, we proposed that the above lines were, like the lines cited in (i) and (ii), intuitively awkward or unusual as a sample of the English language. By comparing (20) with sentences (18) and (19), we may now assert that in this case, the perceived awkwardness stems, in linguistic terms, from the fact that Shelley's sentence displays a classically center-embedded syntactic structure. As we have already shown, such structures do indeed place an inordinate and intuitively perceptible strain on language-processing capabilities.

We have thus discovered that three passages from consecutive stanzas of 'Adonais' are characterized by their violation of three different linguistic constraints. Citation (i) involves movement in contravention of the Tensed S Condition; passage (ii) creates a potential for ambiguity by its reliance on an NP-NP-V syntactic surface structure; and the center-embedded form of (iii) clearly defies natural languages' understandable avoidance of memory-challenging structural configurations.

We must, of course, take care not to give the impression that the three syntactic restrictions involved are too closely related, either in their formal characteristics or indeed in the degree of their acceptance by syntactic theorists. For example, while the Tensed S Condition, a formal constraint on the application of syntactic rules, is a widely accepted and frequently discussed aspect of linguistic theory, Banfield's Up-to-Ambiguity Constraint has never been formally stated, and relies heavily on the somewhat disputed concept of a 'stylistic rule'.

At the same time, there are important similarities. All three conditions were originally devised as means for ruling out certainly supposedly non-ocurring or unacceptable sentences in the language; all are the subject of current theoretical debate; and, most significantly, all have been related, explicitly or implicitly, to language's need to achieve maximum ease of comprehension.[6] Hence it may be with some surprise that the linguist finds himself forced to acknowledge that violations of all three constraints occur within three consecutive stanzas of 'Adonais', which is, by any standards, amongst the most effective and moving poetic works in the English language.

Before considering more carefully the way in which the occurrence of these violations should be treated, and in order to provide a contrast of techniques, we shall digress slightly, and compare examples (i) to (iii) from 'Adonais' with a series of similar cases taken from Shelley's early draft for his major composition *The Revolt of Islam*, which was entitled *Laon and Cythna* and dates from some four years prior to the composition of 'Adonais.'

It would be tedious, and would in no way enhance the argument of this paper, to analyze individually the many passages from *Laon and Cythna* in which attested structures violate the three syntactic constraints discussed in the preceding pages. In the present section, we shall rather study in detail only a few of the more exceptional, linguistically significant examples, referring the reader in footnotes to the many more routinely constraint-violating passages throughout the work. We shall then consider the overall impact on the poem's style of the high density of constructions which violate restrictions on the standard grammar of the language, and conclude by observing an important distinction between *Laon and Cythna* and 'Adonais' with regard to this stylistic feature.

Violations of the Tensed S Condition are common in *Laon and Cythna*, with both PP's and NP's being extracted freely from tensed sentences. Thus we find, for example, the citations (iv) and (v).[7]

(iv) 'The Tartar steed, who, [PP *from his ebon mane*,]
 [S Soon as the clinging slumbers he had shaken ⟵— ,]
 Bent his thin head,' (CWS, I, 340; 380–82).

(v) '[...] and Tartar horse
 Paused, and I saw the shape [NP *its might*][S which swayed ⟵—]'
 (CWS, I, 333; 176–7).

Examples (iv) and (v) constitute clear violations of the Tensed S Condition, as comparison with our earlier example sentences (4b) and (7) above will

148 *Essays in Modern Stylistics*

demonstrate. However, the semantics of the sentences involved here leave no uncertainty about the correct interpretation of the moved phrase. Although awkward, in effect, these constructions cause the reader little more than momentary hesitation.

Such is not the case with the lines cited below in (vi):

(vi) 'And the swift boat the little waves which bore
Were cut by its keen keel,'   (cws, I, 298; 300–301).

We may begin our analysis of this passage by reconstructing the sentence which presumably underlies the surface form of (vi) as shown in (21):

(21) [S$_1$ [NP$_1$ The little waves [S$_2$ which bore [NP$_2$ the swift boat]]] were cut by its keen keel.]

The derivation of the surface form (vi) from the underlying (21) involves the preposing of NP$_4$, [*the swift boat*]; as usual, however, what is of primary interest in the context of the present discussion is not the mere fact of movement, but the freedom from syntactic constraint with which movement has here been permitted to function.

In view of the fact that we have already noted several instances of a lack of regard on Shelley's part for the formal stipulations of the Tensed S Condition, it would scarcely be surprising if we were to find that movement of NP$_2$ had resulted in the constraint-violating derived form (22).

(22) [S$_1$ [NP$_1$ The little waves [NP$_2$ *the swift boat*] [S$_2$ which bore ⎯⎯]
were cut by its keen keel.]

Such, however, is not in fact the case. The actually attested form involves complexity considerably greater than would have been occasioned by sentence (22), for, in the text Shelley published, the moved object NP appears not merely to the left of the relative clause within which it originated, but to the left of the head NP to which that clause itself is attached. We may represent this situation as in diagram (23) below:

(23)
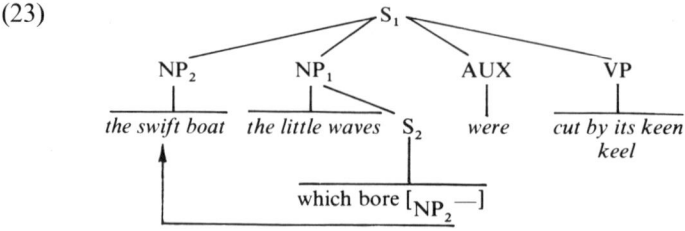

The problems with structure (23) are both formal and pragmatic. On the one hand, if we are indeed correct in assigning to (vi) the syntactic structure

(23), then derivation of that surface linguistic form involves violation not only of the Tensed S Condition, but also of another formal syntactic constraint originally proposed by Ross (1968), the *Complex Noun Phrase Constraint*.[8] In essence this constraint is designed to prohibit all movement out of relative clauses whose heads are lexical items, as shown in (24):

(24)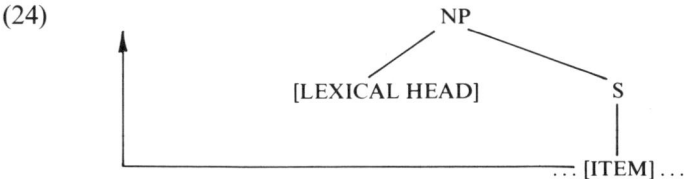

Clearly the movement shown in (23) to have taken place in the derivation of Shelley's (vi) violates this syntactic restriction as well as the Tensed Sentence Condition.

On the other hand, we may also consider in pragmatic terms the succession of steps that must be undertaken by a reader who encounters passage (vi) for the first time, if he wishes to achieve a completely coherent interpretation of these lines. Such a reader will initially be misled by the linear order of the constituents of the sentence into assuming that NP_2, [*the swift boat*], as the first NP in S_1, is the subject of that sentence. On the basis of this erroneous assumption, he will next attempt to relate that NP to the auxiliary verb of S_1, *were*, but will encounter in the process a total mismatch in terms of number agreement between *boat*, a singular noun, and *were*, an auxiliary which is marked for a plural subject. Our putative reader is thus alerted to the need for a reanalysis of the structure of the sentence, since his initial assumptions have led him to a syntactic *impasse*.

In order to complete such a reanalysis successfully, however, and identify the function of NP_2 correctly as the object of S_2, he must realize that Shelley has used language in a way which, for two distinct reasons (the two syntactic constraints noted above) would normally be believed to be impossible. We may thus begin to appreciate the major cognitive problems posed by passages such as (vi), – problems, which, as we shall see shortly, are fatal to the potential impressiveness of the work in which they occur.

Before pursuing this line of argument, however, we may turn briefly to a consideration of sentences from *Laon and Cythna* in which Shelley employs NP-NP-V sequences. Such syntactic configurations, as was seen in the preceding section, deprive the reader of anticipated syntactic information as to the grammatical functions of the preverbal NPs in the sentence. In particular, we may recall our previous observation that NP-NP-V sequences may be derived either by an application of Topicalization as shown in (25), or by an application of Object Movement as in (26).[9]

(25) [NP Subject] Verb [NP Object] – [NP Object][NP Subject] Verb

(26) [NP Subject] Verb [NP Object] – [NP Subject][NP Object] Verb

The deficiency of *syntactic* information determining grammatical relations in the case of sentences containing two preverbal NPs may, as was seen in connection with sentences (9) and (10) above, be compensated for by unambiguous *semantic* interpretive clues. By the same token, in view of the finite nature of any corpus of specifically literary data, ambiguity might also be pragmatically avoided for a given work or group of works, if it would be shown that NP-NP-V sequences within that corpus were derived only by Object Movement, or, conversely, only by Topicalization. If, in other words, a reader were to encounter in Shelley's poems repeated NP-NP-V sequences, *all* of which, as with (ii) above, were the result of Topicalization, he would, despite the technical syntactic ambiguity involved, still be able to interpret every such case on the basis of an *ad hoc* assumption that the first NP would always be the moved object NP.

When, however, we examine closely the NP-NP-V sequences which occur in the text of *Laon and Cythna*, neither the semantic nor the *ad hoc* syntactic means of evading the potential for ambiguity appear to have been adopted by Shelley. Consider, for example, the following representative cases:

(NP_1: Object; NP_2: Subject)
(vii) 'For my light head was hollowed in his lap,
And [NP_1 my bare limbs][NP_2 his mantle] did enwrap,'
(CWS, I, 297; 274–5).

(viii) 'Like light and rest at morn and even is sought,
That wild bird was to me, till [NP_1 madness][NP_2 misery] brought,'
(CWS, I, 348; 125–6).

(NP_1: Subject; NP_2: Object)
(ix) '[...] [NP_1 the lonely man's despair]
[NP_2 Hunger] then overcame, and of his state
Forgetful, on the dust as in a trance he sate [sic],'
(CWS, I, 316; 268–70).

(x) 'Their hourly occupations, were possesst
By hopes which I had armed to overnumber
Those hosts of meaner cares, [NP_1 which][NP_2 life's strong wings] encumber,'
(CWS, I, 367; 79–81).

Examples derived by applications of Topicalization (e.g., [vii] and [viii]) are just as common as those derived by Object Movement (such as [iv] and [x]); and semantic criteria, especially in the cases of examples (vii) and (ix) are scarcely, if at all, capable of resolving the consequent interpretational uncertainty. As a result of such frequent violations of the spirit, as well as the letter, of the Up-to-Ambiguity Constraint, otherwise straightforward sentences become interpretational puzzles and the reader, deprived of virtually all the semantic/syntactic redundancy anticipated in human language, finds himself frequently rereading passages whose basic grammatical configurations have eluded him.[10]

Before moving to a general discussion of the literary significance of the Tensed S Condition and Up-to-Ambiguity Constraint violations to the style of *Laon and Cythna*, we may, finally, note that that poem also contains several passages whose structure, upon close examination, shows itself to be just as complexly center-embedded as was the passage cited from 'Adonais' in (iii) above. Thus, for instance, we might cite the following lines whose neatly center-embedded structure corresponds point-by-point with the 'textbook' sample case (18):[11]

(xi) '[S_1 From that lone ruin, [S_2 when the steed [S_3 that panted]
Paused,] might be heard the murmur of the motion
Of waters,]'

(CWS, I, 334; 200–202).

As we noted in previous discussion, such structures, by relying heavily on short-term memory capacity, dramatically increase the demands placed upon the reader's concentration. Especially when taken in conjunction with the similarly 'disorienting' effects of the extensive violations of the Tensed S Condition and of the Up-to-Ambiguity Constraint noted above and in various footnotes, such challenges to the reader's natural assumptions and expectations about language might reasonably be expected by the linguist to result in a style whose complexity serves only, in Freeman's words, to 'obfuscate' and to distract.

It is not surprising, therefore, to discover that Shelley's mature poetic style has often been attacked by literary critics for its excessive contortedness and unclarity. A contemporary reviewer of the dramatic poem *Prometheus Unbound* in the *Quarterly Review* declared that work 'absolutely and intrinsically unintelligible', laying particular emphasis on the work's syntax, an area in which, he affirmed, 'both the ear and the understanding are disgusted, [...] by awkward and intricate construction of sentences'. More recently and with a broader application Baker (1948, p. 14) has discussed Shelley's 'syntactic disorders', and Rosenfelt (1972, p. 127), in an extremely insightful doctoral dissertation, has drawn particular attention to the damaging effects of center-embedding, a practice which, she notes, creates passages 'full of lengthy interruptions in the main line of the sentence'.[12] Thus the linguist's predictions in this area would appear initially to be confirmed by the intuitive judgments of several sensitive literary critics.

In the case of *Laon and Cythna*, furthermore, there is little reason to dispute the generally critical tone of their observations. One may, with Desmond King-Hele, attribute some portion of the damage incurred by the poem from the complexity of its style to Shelley's refusal to take quite seriously enough the 'craftsmanship' of poetic composition (cf. King-Hele [1960, p. 293]; cp., Stovall [1970, p. 233]). But however explicable its origins, the stylistic awkwardness of this particular poem, which we have traced to Shelley's *repeated and consistent* disregard for syntactic conventions, appears to be devoid of any redeeming feature. We are forced to concede that *Laon and Cythna* is indeed a poem in which Shelley's syntactic style serves only to detract from the general effectiveness of his composition.

We may now turn once more to our discussion of 'Adonais'. In that poem, precisely as in *Laon and Cythna*, violations of syntactic constraints may be easily detected (cf. citations [i] to [iii]), and we might expect to find that literary evaluations of the styles of the two works would be equally damning. Yet critical opinion accords virtually unanimous approval to 'Adonais'. Shelley himself referred to it as 'the least imperfect of my compositions', (an opinion endorsed by King-Hele [1960, p. 311]), and Stovall (1970, p. 253) concurs, asserting that

> Shelley was right in judging *Adonais* [sic] to be technically the most perfect and artistically the most polished of his poems.

The clue which will lead us to an understanding of this surprising discrepancy in critical evaluations of apparently similar poetic styles is the observation that, while constraint violations do indeed occur in 'Adonais', we cannot say of that poem, as we did of *Laon and Cythna*, that it is characterized by '*repeated and consistent*' violations of constraints. In the later poem, as we shall see, a marked concentration of syntactically deviant structures may be detected, and it is to that peculiar aspect of the style of 'Adonais' that we shall turn in the next section of this paper.

When first introducing the constraint-violating passages (i) to (iii), we noted that these citations were excerpted from consecutive stanzas of 'Adonais'. It would certainly be consistent with such an observation merely to remark on the amazing density of such unusual stylistic effects in Shelley's poetry. However, we shall in this section of the paper be more interested in a different aspect of the situation – the fact that, although densely packed where they do occur, 'syntactic disorders' characterize only the first twenty stanzas of this fifty-five stanza poem.¹³ In the other thirty-five stanzas we find only straightforward syntactic structure, devoid of all obstructions to simple semantic interpretation. Such an extreme contrast of styles within a single work naturally prompts us to seek an explanation for its presence.

As an initial step, we may briefly consider the broad thematic form of 'Adonais'. In this poem Shelley approaches what Freeman has called 'the conventional paradox of the elegy – a poem whose occasion is to mark and mourn a passing, explicitly refuses to mourn, and finds an eternal life in death' (1975, p. 30) from the standpoint of his belief in the capacity of the poet to transcend the very limited (and limiting) comprehension of mankind. In grossly oversimplified terms, Shelley relies on his own visionary powers as a poet, and on his resulting sympathy with fellow artist Keats, to reject the finality and pessimism associated with everyday reactions to mortality.

This general theme is realized in the work itself in terms of a development in three stages of approximately equal length. In the opening stanzas, a series of key phrases emphasizes the absoluteness and irrevocability of death, in the course of a conventional lament for the late poet:

(xii) 'I weep for Adonais – he is dead!'
(CWS, II, 389; 1).

(xiii) 'Lost Echo sits amid the voiceless mountains, [. . .]
And will no more reply to winds or fountains,
Or amorous birds perched on the young green spray,'
(CWS, II, 393; 127, 129–30).

(xiv) '*He* will awake no more, oh, never more!'
(CWS, II, 395; 190: emphasis, PBS).

The second section of the poem, however, revolves around the posing of the following rhetorical question, which tentatively challenges the assumptions of the opening lines of the poem:

(xv) 'Nought we know, dies. Shall that alone which knows
Be as a sword consumed before the sheath
By sightless lightning?'
(CWS, II, 395; 177–9).

Shelley finds himself unable to accept that a creative artist should be strictly subject in death to the laws of a natural world he could so easily transcend in life.

The third and final section of the poem, therefore, consists of Shelley's firm negative response to the question he had himself posed in (xv). The poet vigorously affirms his belief that there is a kind of existence above and beyond what we call death, and thus that the conventional assumptions of the opening stanzas totally misrepresented Keats's fate. In a carefully matched set of lines, he systematically refutes the pessimistic negativism of the early statements (xii) to (xiv):

(xvi) 'Mourn not for Adonais,'
(CWS, II, 401; 362).

(xvii) 'He is made one with Nature: there is heard
His voice in all her music, from the moan
Of thunder, to the song of night's sweet bird,'
(CWS, II, 401; 370–72).

(xviii) 'He hath awakened from the dream of life,'
(CWS, II, 400; 344).

Thus, at the conclusion of the poem, the reader is brought to appreciate the *general* theme of the inadequacy of human understanding when unaugmented by poetic vision, as well as to accept the *particular* assurance of Keats's immortality.

The theme of the unsatisfactoriness of mere human sensibilities which we may trace in 'Adonais' is, of course, not unique to that poem, but may also be found in various of Shelley's prose writings. Consider, for example, his own explanation in a letter to Peacock (7 November 1818) of his constant yearing to escape the tyranny of the five senses:

You know I always seek in what I see the manifestation of something beyond the present and tangible object.

Similarly, just as it is one of the functions of 'Adonais' to show mere mortals that

'Tis we, who lost in stormy visions, keep
With phantoms an unprofitable strife,
(CWS, II, 400; 345–6),

so also, in his theoretical treatise *A Defense of Poetry*, Shelley describes poetry as a force which alone enables us to

[defeat] the curse which binds us to be subjected to the accident of surrounding impressions, . . . [and] makes us the inhabitants of a world to which the familiar world is a chaos, (CWS, VII, p. 137).

Now, at last, we are in a position to propose a solution to the apparent conundrum posed by critics' overwhelmingly positive evaluation of a poem whose style, at least in one section, involves syntactic contortion and interpretive complexity. To do so, we need only juxtapose on the one hand our observation of the uneven distribution of such syntactic complexity in 'Adonais', and on the other our hypothesis about that poem's more general thematic structure. It is surely not coincidental that the imperfections, complexities and contortions of language employed by Shelley in 'Adonais' should cluster precisely within the bounds of that portion of the poem which describes the 'stormy visions' of an ugly world untransmuted by poetic vision – a world which, as he suggests in the *Defense*, 'is a chaos', For it is only in those opening stanzas, and particularly when discussing the peculiarly 'temporal' topics of politics (Stanza IV – see example [i]), ambition (Stanza V – see example [iii]) and human grief unrelieved by a broader vision (Stanza VI – see example [ii]), that Shelley indulges in violations of linguistic norms. As the poem progresses, and as Shelley's own escape from the limitations of the commonplace perspective becomes inevitable, so the style of the poetry can be seen to disentangle itself, avoiding the interrelated problems of syntactic contortion and semantic ambiguity.

We may thus point to an important difference between the two poems from the Shelleyan corpus that have been subjected to close analysis in this paper. A single stylistic technique, which, as we suggested above, creates in *Laon and Cythna* nothing but confusion and obfuscation, becomes in 'Adonais' a potent poetic weapon, by virtue principally of its selective employment as an expository aid.

The resulting contrast between one section of the poem which challenges the reader to observe its linguistic awkwardness, and the other sections which, by comparison, flow easily, emphasizes the crucial thematic structure of the whole work, and even, in what has been termed as 'iconic' (Freeman, 1976) or 'mimetic' (Epstein, 1975) sense, suggests the way in which the respective sections are thematically related. Our confusion and incomprehension in the face of Shelley's abrogation of specific linguistic constraints in the first part of the poem correspond to the poet's concern in these same stanzas with mankind's confused and inadequate comprehension of the fact of death itself.

Our analysis of poetic style in both 'Adonais' and *Laon and Cythna* exemplifies, more or less adequately, a mode of stylistic literary criticism whose legitimacy has recently been hotly debated in the literature.[14] While the analysis itself will stand or fall on its own merits, therefore, it may also serve as the basis for a general discussion of the characteristics of this type of critical approach, and for a consideration of some common misapprehensions about the claims and methods of its devotees.

Stylistic criticism, according to many contemporary practitioners, is the study of the relation that holds in a literary artefact between its linguistic form and, in the broadest possible sense, its complete aesthetic form. In most cases, we are safe in assuming further that the former is in fact subsumable within the latter, so that linguistic form may be said to 'contribute' in a certain manner to a work's overall aesthetic impact upon its reader. Stylistic criticism seeks to specify more narrowly the nature of that contribution.

Implicitly, if not explicitly, a stylistic critical analysis will involve three components: a linguistic analysis; a statement about the general aesthetic nature of the work under discussion; and an hypothesis, more or less fully supported by detailed argument, about the connection obtaining between the two. Thus we might tentatively represent the form of the stylist's art as in (27):

(27)

We shall consider first the stylist's method of arriving at a linguistic analysis. We shall then digress briefly to observe a particular means of refining that analysis – the isolation within a given work of aspects of the language which receive stylistic emphasis. And finally, we shall discuss the crucial step of integrating the linguistic analysis with a critical judgment about the work scrutinized.

The most important point to bear in mind when considering the stylist's development of his linguistic analysis is that no reasonable theory of stylistic criticism will restrict its practitioners *a priori* to a particular formal linguistic theory (or even theories). In this connection, we may note the first of several misapprehensions about stylistic criticism at the present time – that contemporary theory is inseparably tied to TG approaches to language. This erroneous assumption is easily made by those who have not understood the function of linguistic analysis as merely one component of stylistic criticism (see [27]). From such a standpoint, it is simple to confuse the part with the whole, and to interpret comments about the post-Structuralist character of modern stylistics in general, as if they referred to permissible frameworks for linguistic analysis also.

There are indeed a number of respects in which post-Structuralist stylistic critics have adopted certain general methodological assumptions which closely parallel the innovations of TG grammarians in the field of language study, a fact which further aids the confusion. In both disciplines, for example, there has been a new (or a renewed) interest in the development of an internally consistent, often somewhat abstract, predictive theory.[15] In both areas emancipation from the restrictive literalism of taxonomic Structuralism has permitted consideration of potentially useful 'contacts with [...] other humane disciplines: [...] philosophy, psychology, sociology, mathematics' (Fowler, 1975b, p. 4). It does not follow, however, from the fact that these two disciplines have developed side by side, that the specific techniques of each are uniquely and ideally suited in all cases to realizing the aims of the other. Thus it should not be surprising to find some contemporary studies in stylistic analysis in which the author is not explicitly committed to post-Chomskyan TG theory.

As an interesting example, we may consider Roger Fowler's excellent analysis of Shakespeare's Sonnet 73 (Fowler, 1975c). That discussion draws heavily on observations about the poem's linguistic form; it concentrates on the linear order of presentation of formal linguistic elements to the reader in a manner untypical of much Structuralist commentary; and, where detailed discussion of anaphora is called for, Fowler occasionally invokes the terminology of TG grammar (though he also often employs 'neutral' or even Structuralist terms). These features of the paper lend Fowler's argument a modern flavor by comparison with more traditional papers in the field. Yet the entire paper contains not one substantive assertion that might not have been equally happily made by a critic whose formal linguistic training did not include transformational generative theory. The paper's value – in a sense totally distinct from the present paper, or, for instance, Freeman (1975), lies in the stylistic insights permitted when a literary work is viewed as a linear, 'kinetic' experience, and definitely not in any deductions from a particular analysis within a particular linguistic framework. In sum, therefore, we may suggest that, in conducting his linguistic analysis of a given work, the contemporary stylistic critic adopts whatever formal framework best enables him to present the linguistic facts he wishes to discuss. Where the resulting analysis is counter-intuitive (i.e., violates commonsense judgments) his overall argument will suffer proportionately. However, it is important to distinguish in this respect between substantive objections to a blatantly implausible analysis, and mere quibbles about linguistic formalism. The former constitutes a legitimate challenge to any stylistic case; the latter completely misses the primary thrust of stylistic study – the correlation of a linguistic analysis with more general aesthetic observations.

Having stated this position at some length, we must immediately proceed to qualify it in two important respects. In the first place, it must be noted that there are significant advantages to be gained from an awareness, at least, of contemporary linguistic techniques. At the simplest level, such an awareness makes available to the practitioner a wider variety of sensitivities to language. Consider an example from an earlier section of this paper. A stylistic critic trained exclusively in the Structuralist linguistic tradition, if confronted with the sentences cited in (i) to (iii), would be able to say little about them. Whether or not he accepted them as grammatical sentences of English – and it is not clear how such a judgment was meaningful for Structuralists – his analysis of their syntactic form could do little to define (linguistically) the source of their 'awkwardness'. Even a critic who was aware of early versions of TG theory would find it hard to explain the lines' unacceptability, since, as we saw previously, each of those sentences appears to be fully generable within a theory which employs only phrase-structure and unconstrained transformational rules. It is, in fact, only in the light of very recent developments in linguistic theory, and particularly in light of the notion of the syntactic constraint, that we can understand the formal reasons for our reactions to such constructions. Only such a principled account of those reactions, it should be noted, permitted us to proceed to the critical evaluation which represented the major goal of that analysis. In this very limited sense, therefore, it is indeed true that 'no criticism can go beyond its linguistics' (Whitehall, 1951, p. 713); the stylist can only gain by staying abreast of current advances in linguistic theory.

Secondly, there is a very particular advantage to be gained from a reliance in stylistic discussion on a formal theory of language which, like TG theory, claims a direct link with psychologically 'real' concepts such as ambiguity, or specifically endorses the consideration of language use as a mental process (e.g. by incorporating the structural definition of unprocessable center-embedding noted above as a structural constraint). As we shall see in discussing the 'relational' component of stylistic criticism, a stylistic analysis which includes a linguistic description with demonstrable psychological or cognitive implications has already covered much of the ground to be considered within that section of its argumentation. Before elaborating this point, however, we shall digress to take note of an important, but by no means obligatory, intermediate step between the development of a linguistic analysis and its literary application.

We may begin our discussion by noting an important difference between our previous studies of Shelley's two major poems. In our close analysis of *Laon and Cythna*, we moved directly from discussion of a linguistic feature of the work's style (persistent violation of syntactic constraints) to a statement about the consequences of this stylistic emphasis for the poem as a whole. In considering 'Adonais' by contrast, we saw that appreciation of the aesthetic function of the same stylistic feature in that poem was impossible until the uneven distribution of instances of its invocation had been carefully observed. In both cases, the overall analysis involved an implicit acceptance of the notion of stylistic 'foregrounding'; in the case of the later poem, however, foregrounding within the work as a whole supplemented the more standard kind of foregrounding for which 'the standard language is the background' (Mukařovský, 1970). We may at this point devote some space to a discussion of the rôle of foregrounding in stylistic criticism.

Kintgen (1977), in a thoroughly well-researched paper on the importance of the reader as a factor in stylistic analysis, draws attention to the continuing debate over 'the problem of relevance, of differentiating between stylistically significant facts and linguistic ones'. He cites as discussants of this topic such distinguished stylists as Saporta, Wellek, Halliday and Riffaterre, to which list we might add the names of Freeman and Fowler. It is, however, to Jan Mukařovský, and to his coinage of the term 'foregrounding' that we owe the conceptual basis for the following discussion.

Undirected linguistic analysis of a literary artefact, whatever its formal allegiances, will, almost by definition, result in a mass of assorted data, much of which will be indistinguishable from data derived from the analysis of any random sample of the language in which the work itself was written. Yet the contemporary stylist will not, in all probability, wish to claim stylistic relevance for all of this analytical data. Rather, some aspects of his analysis will be advanced as important to his overall discussion of the work's style, while others will be dismissed as stylistically insignificant. Mukařovský (1970) suggested that it was those areas in which the literary data diverged from the data for the 'standard language' that would constitute the areas which might reasonably be expected to have stylistic implications.

In general, we may endorse Mukařovský's position, but it is most important to extend his concept of foregrounding in two respects. Firstly, we must insist that a foregrounded stylistic feature may not in fact violate any specific *rule* of the standard grammar. It is indeed true that in the present paper, foregrounding has been the result of such outright violations of linguistic norms. However, it is easy to conceive of alternative means of foregrounding. Since, for example, the standard language is essentially random, in that it does not, except coincidentally, achieve symmetries or patterns of syntactic categories, a poet may foreground certain elements by arranging them into such an 'artificial ' linguistic pattern. If he wishes to, he may then reinforce this pattern by deliberately selecting from the broad inventory of sounds in the language those that will mirror his syntactic arrangement, or he may utilize the orthographical format of poetry in verse lines and stanzas to emphasize crucial elements of the organization.[16] Such a use of language is indeed *non-normative*, and thus foregrounded, but it in no way violates our notions of what is 'acceptable'.[17]

Secondly, we must also insist on the possibility of foregrounding as a process internal to a given work. Such 'distributional' foregrounding often acts as a secondary means of contrast, as when Shelley's *selective* use of constraint-violating structures in 'Adonais' is superimposed upon his use of such constructions at all, itself a foregrounded stylistic feature. In a study of S.T. Coleridge's poetry (see fn. 16) I make an analogous case for that poet's deliberately *targeted* use of mirror-image syntactic and semantic patterns being viewed as intentional heightening of the already foregrounded practice of poetic pattern-building.

What therefore, are we to say in general about the role of foregrounding in a stylistic analysis? Clearly it may constitute a part of, and may even to some extent direct the development of, a formal linguistic account of a given work. Yet we shall not necessarily wish to consider it a subcomponent of the analysis of linguistic form, since it is connected not only with such formal linguistic concepts as 'ungrammaticality', but also with such aesthetic, inherently non-linguistic notions as 'pattern' and 'symmetry'. It can also be shown (see fn. 17) that our best hope for improving our understanding of its operation may be to pay close attention to readers' responses to stylistic variation, an area which, for the present, is unrepresented in our conceptual picture of stylistic criticism (27). We shall return immediately below to the search for a satisfactory description of the place of foregrounding which is capable of accounting fully for all of these, apparently conflicting characteristics.

As has been pointed out by Steinberg (1976), there is no *a priori* objection to a study of a given work which completes a formal linguistic analysis, highlighting where appropriate the linguistically remarkable features, but which makes no attempt to define the aesthetic function of any aspect of that analysis. To confine one's investigations, in effect, to the 'LINGUISTIC ANALYSIS' box of (27) is neither more nor less appealing than to restrict onself to any other subfield of critical discussion, such as imagery or genre, without considering the possible broader implications of one's findings. However, as Steinberg also observes, the term 'stylistic criticism' is generally assumed to refer to studies which go beyond mere linguistic analysis to a discussion of the contribution of style to the overall aesthetic form of the poem. This has been particularly true, furthermore, of the post-Structuralist phase of stylistics. It is therefore to that aspect of stylistic study that we may now turn our attention, moving with particular care, since it is in this area that the greatest number of misunderstandings have seemed to arise in the course of general discussion.

The account of the general 'AESTHETIC FORM' of a work with which the stylist attempts to correlate his linguistic observations (see [27] above) may be his own, or it may derive in part from general critical analyses of the same work by other, non-stylistic critics. A glance at the bibliography to this paper will demonstrate the extent to which, in the present instance, independent corroboration of critical opinion has been sought to support this particular aspect of our discussion of Shelley's style. In many cases, however, the stylist will strike out on his own, discussing but ultimately rejecting other critical theories. This course, adopted by Fowler (1975b), earned him a strongly-worded rebuke from Herrnstein Smith (1977) who accused him of advancing his own analysis of Shakespeare's 73rd Sonnet over that of critical predecessors in the field as being, in some sense, *the* correct account of the poem. It seems clear to this reader that Herrnstein Smith's particular target is very ill-chosen; as we shall see below, Fowler is extremely cautious about the extent of his claims. Her general point however – that the stylist's analysis of a literary artefact is, at bottom, 'simply another reading', and is to be judged as such – is well taken. Indeed, the same notion is also implicit in Freeman's assertion that 'analysis of a poet's [...] manipulation of [...] syntactic processes can lay bare the deep form of particular poems – the form controlling metaphor, theme, tone, imagery and diction' (Freeman, 1975, p. 39). Only a deliberately perverse reading of this statement would deduce from it that a full appreciation of the 'deep form" of a work might not be achieved through analysis of any of the other aspects of poetic style that Freeman mentions. The stylist, in essence, seeks parity with, and not dominance over, critics of alternative methodological allegiances.

The misapprehension that the stylist is proposing as his account of 'AESTHETIC FORM' something apart from that developed by any literary critic stems in part from a mistaken belief that the 'arrow' included in (27) is, in the stylist's own eyes, unidirectional. There are actually two manifestations of this erroneous assumption, and both deserve careful discussion. The first error often committed by critics of stylistic criticism is that they suspect (27), with a single-headed arrow leading from 'LINGUISTIC ANALYSIS' to 'AESTHETIC FORM', of representing the stylist's *pragmatic means* for developing a reading of the work. In this case, every stylist would have to be willing to assert that a full linguistic analysis was a strict prerequisite for a persuasive account of aesthetic form. As I have argued above, few stylists would think of endorsing such an absurd proposition. At most they might claim that, where argumentation in support of a particular reading relied heavily on statements about the work's language, formal analysis in accord with linguistic theory would be advisable.

Even, however, if we admit the misrepresentation involved in considering the unidirectional version of (27) as the stylist's own view of the genesis of all valid critical readings, there are still many who accuse the contemporary stylist of treating the arrow as single-headed when constructing, *ex post facto*, their *arguments* in support of a critical analysis. Herrnstein Smith, for instance, attributes to several of the contributors to Fowler's anthology

(Fowler, 1975a), as the basis for their development of a critical argument, the 'formula: $S(R) X \to X$', which she interprets as follows:

> something in a literary work that is [...] manifest or 'surface', S, bears some relation, R, to something else that is [...] obscure [...] or 'deep', X; therefore, by analyzing S, one may discover X (1977, p. 153).

The unidirectionality of Herrnstein Smith's own arrow betrays her misunderstanding of the nature of the stylistic arguments she attempts to formalize. Her account of the way in which these stylistic arguments work should be contrasted with Fowler's own assertions at the end of his paper (1975c, p. 120):

> I have made it clear [...] that linguistic analysis is not at all the same thing as critical description; and that there cannot be a 'linguistic criticism' in the naive sense [...][of a] mechanical discovery procedure for poetic structure.

Indeed, Herrnstein Smith's accusation that Fowler claims for his critical account 'that it is uniquely [...] controlled' by the 'verbal structure of the poem', conflicts not only with Fowler's stated position, but also with her own observation elsewhere that 'R, the relational term [in her formula, TRA] is a word or a phrase of exceptional vagueness. E.g. S 'might suggest' X [...] S "embraces" X.'

What stylists assert of their own work is that it involves the specification and characterization of a particular correlation of aspects of linguistic analysis on the one hand with aspects of aesthetic form on the other. In our discussion of Shelley's style in 'Adonais' for example, an observation about the distribution of certain kinds of linguistic structures was seen to coincide rather neatly with a common critical assumption about internal divisions within that poem based on its thematic development. There was, in that case, no question of arguing *from* linguistic analysis *to* aesthetic evaluation (or vice-versa), and no belief in the inevitability of the significance of the correlation, once it had been observed, at least in the mind of the author.

In characterizing the significance of the link that he postulates in a given work, in fact, the stylistic critic is neither more nor less immune from 'exceptional vagueness' than the critic whose starting point is imagery, metaphor, or tone. In some cases, and especially where, as we noted above, he is able to make appeal to widely accepted psychological or cognitive implications of specific aspects of his linguistic-analysis, the stylist may hope to base some part of his account on relatively objective arguments. Our discussion of the very real interpretive chaos caused by Shelley's use of constraint-violating constructions is a case in point. In general, however, the delineation of how a work's aesthetic form interacts with (or affects, or is affected by) its linguistic form is, as we stated initially, the conceptual 'core' of stylistics, and is as subject to dispute on grounds of standard critical plausibility as any other critical method.

Two comments should be made in conclusion. Returning briefly to our apparent *impasse* with regard to the rôle of foregrounding in stylistic criticism, we may now understand more clearly its function as a component of the relational aspect of the overall argument. In ways as yet imprecisely understood, both reader and critic are aware of their capacity to identify aspects of both the linguistic *and* the aesthetic forms of a work between which some critical relation is particularly likely to obtain. From such a conceptualization of its place in the system, the optionality of foregrounding as a component of any given stylistic argument, as well as its close relation to both linguistic and aesthetic phenomena, falls out naturally.

Finally, we may note that it is in the area of establishing broad constraints on the *possible kinds of relation* that may obtain between linguistic and aesthetic forms in literary artefacts that the future of a 'theory of style' looks most promising.[18] Some will become impatient with the numerous close individual studies on the basis of which a satisfactorily precise characterization of the general parameters can alone be based. Yet a careful survey of the recent literature displays a growing awareness of some of the major classifications of 'relation-types', and an encouraging willingness on the part of stylists to propose strong and suggestive working hypotheses (see fn. 18). From such approximations, and with a careful avoidance of serious misconstructions of the nature of stylistic study itself, a fully rounded theory of literary style can eventually be developed.

Notes

1 The following discussion of Shelley's style in 'Adonais' is taken in large part from Chapter 4 of my dissertation (1977). My thanks for their help in its refinement are due to Robert P. Creed, Donald C. Freeman, S. Jay Keyser and Stephen G. Lapointe.
2 Citations from Shelley's works are taken from *The Complete Works of Shelley*, R. Ingpen and W. Peck, eds., 1965, New York: Gordian Press (hereinafter 'CWS'). In referencing passages, volume and page numbers will be followed by line numbers of material cited. All emphases are my own unless noted to the contrary.
3 Still more importantly, as we shall see immediately below, tinkering with individual rules fails to isolate the 'true' generalization which is crucially rule-independent.
4 That is to say that the subcategorization of *know* – the fact that it requires an object – is part of the reader's 'linguistic competence', (Chomsky, 1965). Clearly to say that he is aware' of such a feature of his grammar does not imply conscious objective consideration on his part.

5 This is, in fact, a language-particular case of a more general claim made by Thomas Wasow (1973), that *all* natural languages make constant use of some unambiguous means for conveying information about grammatical relations.
6 For the Up-to-Ambiguity Constraint, this link is implicit in Banfield's informal statement of the condition; the general cognitive principles involved in prohibiting center-embedding have already been mentioned above. With respect to more formal syntactic constraints such as the Tensed S Condition, see Bach (1976, p. 16).
7 For other examples, see CWS, I: 292; 133–4: 306; 251: 330; 89–90: 380; 173–4: 401; 153.
8 For a recasting of this constraint see Horn (1974).
9 For more 'concrete' examples, see (12) and (13) above.
10 These violations of Banfield's constraint appear to parallel closely more complex examples of interpretational unclarity in *Laon and Cythna*. Space does not permit a full discussion at this point; the reader is therefore referred to Austin (1977: 125–9; 136–8).
11 For another 'classic' example, see CWS, I, 326; 582–6.
12 Rosenfelt's discussion, which involves an excellent non-linguistic discussion of the contrast between Shelley's style and that of John Keats, prompted my own more technical study of center-embedding.
13 For a full demonstration, see Austin (1977).
14 See references in the introductory paragraph of this paper.
15 For extensive discussion of the arguments in this section of the paper, I am indebted to Stephen G. Lapointe and to Edwin S. Williams.
16 For a discussion of such a case in some detail, see Austin (1977: Chap. 2).
17 It seems to me that a fuller enumeration of various potential means of foregrounding, their relative importance and effect upon the reader, is the implied (but certainly not explicit) aim of the program of research into reader responses proposed by Kintgen (1977).
18 For discussions along these lines, see Epstein (1975), Dillon (1975) and Austin (1977).

References

Austin, Timothy R., 1977. *A Linguistic Approach to the Style of the English Early Romantic Poets*. Unpublished doctoral dissertation, University of Massachusetts, Amherst.

Bach, Emmon, 1976. 'Comments on N. Chomsky's paper for Irvine Conference on Formal Syntax'. Mimeo, University of Massachusetts, Amherst.

Baker, Carlos, 1948. *Shelley's Major Poetry: The Fabric of a Vision*. (Princeton: Princeton UP).

Banfield, Ann M., 1973. *Stylistic Transformations: A Study Based on the Syntax of 'Paradise Lost'*. Unpublished doctoral dissertation, University of Wisconsin.

Bresnan, Joan W., 1972. *Theory of Complementation in English Syntax*. Unpublished doctoral dissertation, Massachusetts Institute of Technology.

——, 1976. 'Evidence for a theory of unbounded transformations', *Linguistic Analysis*, 2:4.

Chomsky, Noam, 1957. *Syntactic Structures* (The Hague: Mouton).

——, 1965. *Aspects of the Theory of Syntax* (Cambridge, Mass.: MIT Press).
——, 1973. 'Conditions on transformations', in: Anderson, S., and Kiparsky, P., eds., *A Festschrift for Morris Halle* (New York: Holt, Rinehart & Winston).
——, 1976. 'Conditions on rules of grammar', *Linguistic Analysis*, 2:4.
Dillon, G. L., 1975. 'Inversions and deletions in English poetry', *Language and Style*, 8:3.
Epstein, E. L., 1975. 'The self-reflexive artefact: the function of mimesis in an approach to a theory of value for literature', in: Fowler, 1975a.
Fowler, R., ed., 1975a. *Style and Structure in Literature: Essays in the New Stylistics* (Ithaca: Cornell UP).
——, 1975b. 'The New Stylistics', in: Fowler, 1975a.
——, 1975c. 'Language and the reader: Shakespeare's Sonnet 73', in: Fowler, 1975a.
Freeman, Donald C., 1975. 'The strategy of fusion: Dylan Thomas's syntax', in: Fowler, 1975a.
——, 1976. 'Iconic syntax in poetry: a note on Blake's "Ah! Sun-Flower"', in: J. Stillings, ed., *U/Mass Occasional Papers in Linguistics*, II.
Grosu, A., 1974. 'On the complexity of centre-embeddings', Unpublished mimeo.
Herrnstein Smith, B., 1977. 'Surfacing from the deep', *PTL* 2.
Horn, George M., 1974. *The Noun Phrase Constraint*. Unpublished doctoral dissertation, University of Massachusetts, Amherst.
King-Hele, Desmond, 1960. *Shelley: The Man and the Poet* (New York: Thomas Yoseloff).
Kintgen, Eugene R., 1977. 'Reader response and stylistics', *Style*, 11:1.
Kuno, Susumu, 1973. 'Constraints on internal clauses and sentential subjects', *Linguistic Inquiry*, 4:3.
——, 1974. 'The position of relative clauses and conjunctions', *Linguistic Inquiry*, 5:1.
Miller, George and Noam Chomsky, 1963. 'Finitary models of language users', in: R. D. Luce, R. R. Bush and E. Galanter, eds., *Handbook of Mathematical Psychology*, II (New York: John Wiley & Sons, Inc.).
Mukařovský, Jan, 1970 'Standard language and poetic language', in: Freeman, D. C., ed., *Linguistics and Literary Style* (New York: Holt, Rinehart & Winston).
Rosenfelt, Deborah Silverton, 1972. *Keats and Shelley: A Comparative Study of their Ideas about Poetic Language and some Patterns of Language Use in their Poetry*. Unpublished doctoral dissertation, University of California, Los Angeles.
Ross, John Robert, 1968. *Constraints on Variables in Syntax*. Unpublished doctoral dissertation, Massachusetts Institute of Technology. Available through the Indiana University Linguistics Club, Bloomington, Indiana.
Steinberg, E. R., 1976. 'Stylistics as a humanistic discipline', *Style*, 10:1.
Stillings, Justine T., 1977. *Remarks on Core Grammar*. Unpublished doctoral dissertation, University of Massachusetts, Amherst.
Stovall, Floyd, 1970. *Desire and Restraint in Shelley* (New York: Haskell House).
Wasow, Thomas, 1973. 'The innateness hypothesis and grammatical relations', *Synthese*, 26:1.
Whitehall, H., 1951. 'From linguistics to criticism', *Kenyon Review*, 13.

9

The self-reflexive artefact: the function of mimesis in an approach to a theory of value for literature

E. L. Epstein

The two pillars upon which a theory of criticism must rest are an account of value and an account of communication.
I. A. Richards, *Principles of Literary Criticism*[1]

It will, I imagine, seem ridiculous that things are made manifest through imitations in letters and syllables; nevertheless it cannot be otherwise.
Plato, *Cratylus* 425d[2]

Introduction

Judgments of poetic value are made, at different times, for different reasons. In many times and places there was a high value placed upon conventional forms, repeated from poem to poem with no more regard for content than a recognition that epic content required epic form, pastoral or lyric content required forms in those genres, and so on. It is true that there were other factors determining *high* value – onomatopoeia, for one – but a poem could be regarded as a craftsmanlike piece simply by adhering to traditional forms.

Consider, for example, the great craftsmanlike complexity of medieval verse-forms – the Welsh forms, the Irish forms (mainly the *Rannaigecht Mor*, the Great Quatrain), and the Old Norse Skaldic forms (primarily the *drottkvaett*). Their complexity is enormous; anyone writing in these forms was accorded credit as a poet, even if his sentiments and themes were conventional and unoriginal – as indeed they almost always were, and had to be.* Consider an example from perhaps the best of the medieval Welsh

---

*For a concise treatment of world verse-forms, see Wimsatt, W. K. (ed.), *Versification: Major Language Types – Sixteen Essays* (New York: Modern Language Association New York University Press, 1972).

poets, Dafydd ap Gwilym, his apostrophe to the seagull (fourteenth century):

> Yr wylan deg ar lanw dioer,
> Unlliw ag eiry neu wénlloer,
> Dilwch yw dy degwch dí,
> Darn fel haul, dyrnfol héli.

> (Fair seagull on the certain tide,
> of color like snow or the bright moon,
> Spotless is your beauty,
> A patch like sunlight, gauntlet of the sea.)

The form is extremely complex:

(1) it rhymes masculine-feminine, in an aabb pattern (dioer-wénlloer, dí-héli).
(2) there are eight syllables in the first two lines, and seven syllables in the last two.
(3) there is a caesura approximately in the middle of each line.
(4) there is *cynghanedd* (alliterative-rhyming harmony) in each line
   a. yR wyLaN Deg/aR LaNw Dioer
      R   L N D / R L N D
    exact repetition over the caesura of consonants (with the exception of the last).
   b. uNLLiw ag eiry/New wehLLoer
      NLL   /N   LL
    repetition of part of the consonantal pattern over the caesura
   c. *dilwch* yw dy *degwch* dí

    dilwch rhymes with *degwch*, and *degwch* alliterates with *dí*
   d. DaRN FeL Haul/DyRNFoL Heli.
      D RN F L H   /D RNF L H
    Exact repetition, over the caesura, of consonants.

And this form is by no means the most complex of the Welsh forms. The *englyn* is written with the above constraints, and a number of others. In fact, some of the Welsh forms, as codified in the fifteenth century, are so complex that it is doubtful that any poems were ever written in those forms, except as examples in bardic schools.

The same is true of the other Celtic forms, and, indeed, of most world poetry. The classic Japanese, Greek, Latin, Uralic, Persian, Arabic, Hebrew, Chinese, Vietnamese, Thai, Malayan forms proceed from the highly ordered to the extremely complex, in the same way as the Welsh (though using different means). It seems almost as if complexity were a universal of world poetry, one that determines value of verse. By these standards, poetry would be mainly valued by its craftsmanlike finish, its exemplification of traditional conventions.

In none of these traditions is there value placed upon close 'fit' of content and form, outside of general rules of genre decorum (an epic topic for an epic form, a lyric topic for a lyric form). A poem can be a valued poem if its form is generally suited to its topic, and if its form is perfect in itself. To be sure, the highest value is often reserved for poetry that fulfills these conditions and goes beyond them, in which we hear a personal voice crying out from a conventional form in response to a specific occasion. Yet in pre-Romantic times such poetry is not seen to be a different sort of poetry, merely a type of poetry like other poetry, which 'somehow' has a deeper effect.

This aesthetic of verse today prevails over much of the world, but in the West the power of the traditional craftsman of verse has waned (except in the atelier of the greeting-card manufacturer). It is a historical truism that traditional forms began to break up in Western poetry with the advent of Romanticism and the entry upon the scene of the self-conscious individual. The content of poetry in Western countries began increasingly to become the expression of private landscapes, and the generalized forms of poetry began to seem less and less satisfactory for the expression of these private contents. Strict form took on ironic function. Forms were borrowed from folk-poetry and nursery rhymes, not so much for the intrinsic value of these forms as for their ironic value: in these poems non-traditional forms expressed dignified contents. They were, in fact, stalking-horses for individualized expression, since they were neutral forms, forms without commitment to the other aesthetic of craftsman's forms. This device was transitional to the modern practice of individualized forms for inevitably individual content, where traditional forms, if used at all, are used entirely ironically, or (as in Eliot) to express intense emotion.

This essay will attempt to construct a general frame of value by which both traditional forms and romantic and post-Romantic Western forms will be assigned relative values from the modern Western point of view. The highest values will be assigned to those works in which form (strictly and microscopically described) conveys and reinforces content.

In appreciating these works, the modern reader 'decodes' a double message, one from content and one from form. In the most highly valued poems, the message will be the same.

Form can be distinguished from content by modern linguistic means. The two lines below mean the same things; that is, they convey the same content.

a. The geese flew overhead honking.
b. Honking overhead flew the geese.

They 'convey the same content' because they co-imply each other; that is, they 'mean the same thing' because their truth-values are always and necessarily the same. If on one occasion it is true that 'the geese flew overhead honking', then it is necessarily true that on that occasion 'honking overhead flew the geese'; conversely, if it is true on one occasion that 'honking overhead flew the geese', then it is necessarily true that on that occasion 'the geese flew overhead honking'. And the relation holds for falseness as well; if *a* is false, then *b* is necessarily false; and if *b* is false, then *a* is necessarily false. This test of 'meaning', as preservation under changing forms of truth-value, provides a clear demonstration that form can with care be distinguished from content. (The principle in one version of transformational-generative grammar that syntactic transformations do not change 'meaning' is based upon a similar principle).

If this is true, that different forms may cloak exactly the same 'meanings', then the question arises, why choose one form over another? Poets do choose one expression over its possible cousins for a number of reasons; most of these reasons reduce to exigencies of form, but some have a more dramatic purpose.

A. E. Housman begins a poem (poem XXXVI of *A Shropshire Lad*)

White in the moon the long road lies.

This line 'means the same thing' as 'The long road lies white in the moon' that is, they always have the same truth-value though the syntactic forms are different. If reading by a traditional aesthetic, the critic may say that Housman chose the form of his line over other forms for metrical reasons;

White ín the moón the long road lies

is more compatible with the loose hymn-meter in which the poem is couched than

The long road lies white in the moon

because 'The long road lies white' with its four strong stresses obscures the basic pulse of the poem. However, a post-Romantic critic would see another reason for the change. Adherence to a conventional meter is an abstract idea that would apply to all traditional verse. Here the specific occasion seems to be conveyed more strongly by the form the lines take than by any truth-preserving alternative. 'White in the moon' conveys the precise way the perception of the landscape takes place; it is not immediately apparent that the road *is* a road, to a night viewer. There is first an impression of 'whiteness', then an identification of the source of the whiteness, 'the moon', and only then is the object identified that is 'white in the moon', the long road, which is then mentally perceived as 'lying'. The form of the lines expresses an act of raw perception leading to mental conclusion – 'White' to 'moon' to 'road' to 'lies' – whose form is iconic or mimetic of the acts of perception and conclusion. The internal, personal act of ascertaining the objects of a hypothetical outside world by phenomenological clues is here mimed in syntactic form. 'The long road lies white in the moon' would give the conclusion first and the clues second, which would falsify the experience conveyed.

So here we have a double decoding, the first decoding performed at the same time as the second. The content is 'understood' more vividly than in a prose form (in which form is not characteristically chosen with such *arrière-pensée*) because it is reinforced by the second code, that of form. The second coding is, then, iconic of the occasion that (presumably) was the source of the poem. Here the reader has received two types of information: *one*, about a road in the moonlight, and *two*, about the poet and his power to recreate vividly his own internal sensations and cognitive processes by which he recreates the world and makes sense of it.

By this and other examples we can see how form is distinguishable from content, and how form can reinforce content. In a Romantic and post-Romantic poetic aesthetic, however, this is not just an option, as it is in previous ages, but an obligation. Wallace Stevens says in a letter, 'A poem must contain a peculiarity, as if it were the momentarily complete idiom of that which prompts it.' Because of the nature of the 'reality' conveyed, an internal, personal reality, an iconic matching of form and content *must* take place, because the reader and the poet are inherently separate and individual sensibilities. The 'content' of one sensibility is not the same as that of another, since each person occupies a unique position in space and time. Any content that is derived from experience is radically ambiguous, that is, it is always going to be different from one person to another. Therefore, 'content' as a component of one memory can never be the same for one person as for another; one person's road in the moonlight can never be another's. However, one person's English syntax *is* (maximally) the same as any other English-speaker's, so a second coding of the road in the moonlight in syntactic terms is received with great exactness. The internal experience of viewing a moonlit landscape and assigning properties and qualities to it is mimed by the syntax, by which means the reader finally receives the double message.

Value for modern Western poetry is based upon this secondary coding, since, as we have seen, the content of any serious poetry is inherently uncommunicable, except loosely and vaguely. A syntactic recoding of the message ensures a high degree of communicability for an otherwise incommunicable message. In the model of language-production that is assumed for the purposes of this paper, a speaker or writer first constructs a lexical constellation which mimes a state of affairs symbolically; this constellation is then realized in linear and segmental form syntactically, and then either phonologically or graphemically. This realization may be produced automatically, that is, with no principle of selection operating among its linear elements other than the style of the speaker or writer (and that style operating outside of awareness), in which case the final speech-act is casual prose. On the other hand, there may be conscious or quasi-conscious selection and arrangement of syntactic and phonological linear elements of form, in which case a poetic function is operating.

In this paper, this poetic type of speech-act will be closely examined and analysed, to observe the relationship or lack of relationship between the principles of selection and arrangement operating on the elements of form. We can therefore see whether they are determined or not determined by the particular state of affairs conveyed by the lexical constellation chosen, and we may also suggest that formal mimesis of content is part of a criterion of value for certain styles of poetry.

The relation of content to form in poetry is one of the perennial issues of criticism. Some critics deny the existence of the problem; 'meaning' for them is a term describing the global and indivisible effect of a work of verbal art. Others, like Roman Jakobson, find in the 'poetic function' of language a degree of organization of form that in casual discourse usually operates only in the choice of expressions of content. However, even among these critics, descriptions of relationships between content and form in poetry are rare.

The clearest description of a possible reflection of content in form is to be found in Donald Davie's *Articulate Energy* (1955). Davie describes five types of organization of syntax in poetry, four of which bear a direct positive relationship to content: (1) *subjective*, whose 'function is to please us by the fidelity with which it follows the "form of thought" in the poet's mind'; (2) *dramatic*, whose 'function is to please us by the fidelity with which it follows the "form of thought" in some mind other than the poet's, which the poet imagines'; (3) *objective*, whose 'function is to please us by the fidelity with which it follows a form of action, a movement not through any mind, but in the world at large'; (4) '*syntax like music*', whose 'function is to please us by the fidelity with which it follows a "form of thought" through the poet's mind but without defining that thought'; (5) '*syntax like mathematics*', when its function is to please us in and for itself.'[3]

Davie recognizes that his 'mathematical syntax' is unlike the other four:

'it differs from other kinds of syntax only in this – that the pleasure it gives has nothing to do with mimesis' (94). This difference, however, should be given greater weight in his scale of effects than he gives it. I would suggest that there are basically only two types of formal relationship to content – *mimetic* and *non-minetic*, in Davie's terms. With this scheme it is possible to describe other sorts of reflection of content besides syntactic – there is the whole subtle problem of lexical mimesis, and the confused problem of sound-symbolism, the phonological contribution to the mimicking of content.

Non-mimetic forms of expression

Logically there are only two types of non-mimetic forms of expression – one type in which no recognizable schemata of formal organization can be discerned (and hence no mimetic forms), and another type in which recognizable forms exist but do not reflect any principle of organization from any level higher than the syntactic.

I The first type, taken in its purest form, would lack any lexical ordering and hence would lack all informative power. There are few utterances of which this is true – even enigmatic grunts usually signal the presence of the grunter. It is doubtful whether such a type exists. A less pure form would acknowledge the mimetic function of lexis, but would only contain the most neutral possible syntactic and intonational structures. (In classical transformational terms, one utterance is more 'neutral' than another if it is derivable with fewer transformations.) There would indeed be mimesis between forms of syntax and such elements of organization of the non-linguistic universe as contiguity in time and space, and psychological processes of perception. Also, the sounds of such utterances could be shown to resemble sound-patterns other than those of speech. However, since these subordinate patterns are 'automatized' in presentation and reception, they do not reflect the non-automatic mimesis of the reality presented by the lexis of the utterance. This type of utterance entirely lacks the 'poetic function' of language, and besides gives rise to certain communicative difficulties even as casual prose. The description of such difficulties also helps to establish the necessity of mimetic subordinate forms within the utterance.

II The second type would include utterances displaying Davie's 'syntax as mathematics', as well as phonological organization such as rhyme, meter, and alliteration, and various rhetorical figures – antithesis, isocolon, phonological chiasmus, and the like. These figures would not reflect lexical content, or might even actively contradict it.

Examples of this second type are easy to find, not only in 'older poetry' and especially in poetry of the English Augustan age, as Davie suggests (94), but among any poetry deriving from an aesthetic in which content may be indefinitely subordinated to form. English Augustan poetry, though it does generally conform to style of content-decorum, contains many examples of organization of form independent of content or contradictory of it. For example, Pope in his early pastoral poetry often displays this non-mimetic degree of organization.

> But see, the Shepherds shun the Noon-day Heat,
> The lowing Herds to murm'ring Brooks retreat,
> To closer Shades the panting Flocks remove,
> Ye Gods! and is there no Relief for Love
> (*Summer: The Second Pastoral*, 11. 85–8)

The syntactic chiasmus in the two middle lines is entirely gratuitous (unless the herds go one way and the flocks another!)

> Where-e'er you walk, cool Gales shall fan the Glade,
> Trees, where you sit, shall crowd into a Shade,
> Where-e'er you tread, the blushing Flow'rs shall rise,
> And all things flourish where you turn your eyes.
> (*Summer: The Second Pastoral*, 11. 73–6)

The peregrinations of the adverbial of place, from initial position to internal position to initial position to final position,[4] do not mime any such wandering on the part of the beloved. If they did, it would suggest she didn't know just where she was going. The motive for the dispersal of the adverbials is, of course, entirely decorative or 'mathematical'; the original version of these lines was all too symmetrical:

> Winds, where you walk, shall gently fan the Glade,
> Trees, where you sit, shall crowd into a Shade,
> Flow'rs, where you tread, in painted Pride shall rise,
> And all things flourish where you turn your Eyes!

There is a psychological value, however, to the final patterning of these adverbials. In the last line the adverbial is in 'normal' position – that is, according to most phrase-structure rules, the place for adverbials is at the end of utterances. By putting the adverbial first at the beginning of the utterance, then by moving it into the utterance (second line), then returning it to initial position (third line), and finally allowing it to appear in its canonical final position, Pope teases the reader at first and finally satisfies him. This effect is entirely dependent upon syntactic placement and has no

174 *Essays in Modern Stylistics*

lexical-mimetic value – the 'teasing' is inappropriate both to the tone of the passage and to the situation expressed by it.

> Lo Earth receives him from the bending Skies!
> Sink down ye Mountains, and ye Vallies rise:
> With Heads declin'd, ye Cedars, Homage pay;
> Be smooth ye Rocks, ye rapid Floods give way!
> The Savior comes! by ancient Bards foretold:
> Hear him ye Deaf, and all ye Blind behold!
> (*Messiah*, 11. 33–8)

There is a mechanically operating pattern of chiastic syntax in this passage – every even line exhibits syntactic chiasmus. There is no reason for this elaborate symmetry in the situation expressed.

> Adieu ye Vales, ye Mountains, Streams and Groves,
> Adieu ye Shepherd's rural Lays and Loves,
> Adieu my Flocks, farewell ye Sylvan Crew,
> Daphne farewell, and all the World adieu!
> (*Winter: The Fourth Pastoral*, 11. 89–92)

There is a double grade of chiasmus expressed in the third and fourth lines syntactically, and a (related) grade of phonological chiasmus.

1. The *Adieu* Clauses are in chiasmus:
   Exclamation – Nominal : *Nominal – Exclamation*
   Adieu   my flocks : all the   Adieu
                           world
2. The *farewell* clauses are in chiasmus:
   Exclamation – Nominal : *Nominal – Exclamation*
   farewell   ye Sylvan : Daphne   farewell
                 Crew
3. The repetition of sounds is chiastic:
   Adieu   farewell   farewell   Adieu

Thus a double syntactic chiasmus is enclosed within a phonological chiasmus. This elegance of patterning, however, mimes no aspect of the situation expressed. It seems to be motivated rather by a formal aspect of the *Pastorals* themselves; Pope seems to feel the need for a 'decorative' ending to provide a formal climax to his structure – these lines end the last *Pastoral*. It could perhaps be said that the complexity of these lines mimes a craftsman's impulse in the poet, and therefore it is, in Davie's terms an example of 'subjective' mimesis. Davie's term 'form of thought' would certainly comprehend conscious acts of formal construction as well as more emotional impulses; when a reader feels that a creator has risen to an occasion, when the poet seems to acknowledge his own understanding of his creation, by 'decorating' important structural points either mimetically or non-mimetically, there is a certain degree of dramatic excitement engendered as a result. This could be illustrated from the works of so diverse a selection of writers as Homer, Milton, Dante, James Joyce, and Henry James.

The last example of non-mimetic verse shows a case of missed opportunity by the poet.

> Then sings by turns, by turns the Muses sing,
> Now Hawthorn blossom, now the Daisies spring,
> Now Leaves the Trees, and Flow'rs adorn the Ground;
> Begin, the Vales shall ev'ry Note rebound.
> (*Spring: The First Pastoral*, 11. 41–4)

The chiasmus in the first line represents an attempt to mime the notion of alternate singing – an example of Davie's 'objective' mimesis – but curiously it fails: alternate singing is chiastic only when the second voice provides a mirror-strophe to the first voice's strophe. As we see from the song actually produced, each strophe is very like every other strophe. The odd fact about this situation is that the poem that Pope is imitating in this passage, Virgil's *Third Eclogue*, achieves an authentic example of objective mimesis:

> Dicite, quandoquidem in molli consedimus herba,
> et nunc omnis ager, nunc omnis parturit arbos,
> nunc frondent silvae, nunc formonsissimus annus.
> Incipe Damoeta, tu deinde sequere, Menalca;
> alterna dicetis; amant alterna Camenae.
> (11. 55–9)

The notion of 'alterna' in the Virgil passage is expressed in lines 56 and 57, before the word actually appears. In these lines the position of the governing verb does indeed alternate:

> nunc omnis ager, nunc omnis *parturit* arbos,
> nunc *frondent* silvae, nunc formonsissimus annus.

Then when the chiasmus within line 59 occurs (*alterna*-Verb: Verb-*alterna*), it includes within itself the notion of alternation established in the previous lines, and is not simply a mirror-repetition, as it is in Pope. For some reason, a chiasmus *between* lines seems to convey alternation, whereas chiasmus *within* a line conveys only mirror-repetition. (C. Day Lewis in his translation of this eclogue also achieves only a single-line chiasmus: 'You begin, Damoetas, and you, Menalcas, follow.')

The presence in utterances of non-mimetic symmetrical or counter-symmetrical syntactic or phonological schemata does not seem to indicate a high degree of poetic value, at least in a post-Romantic age. Traditional craftsmanship as such is not the most highly valued element in an age which has come to expect a perceptible degree of emotional involvement of the writer in his work. If, therefore, the schemata in the utterances that make up the work are lower-level regularities without reference to the lexical level of the work, the judgment of the age is that the work exhibits only a low degree of value. Indeed, such low-level regularities are characteristic more of comic or ironic poetry than of more highly valued forms. The comic or ironic rhymes and rhythms of Eliot, for example, exhibit this preference of modern readers. The metrical perfection of Prufrock's 'I do not think that they will sing to me' contrasts ironically with its completely flat tone, to provide a moment of ironic anticlimax. Therefore, in modern poetry, non-mimetic forms are either automatized, or 'foregrounded' for comic or ironic effect.

Grades of mimesis

Davie provides four types of mimetic syntax (he does not discuss phonology), but the possibility of a ranking of value within these types is only suggested. I would like to propose such a possible ranking.

First, however, I would like to dispose of Davie's 'syntax as music', his fourth type of syntax. It seems to me that here Davie is not describing a mode of regarding syntax distinct from his other three types, but rather a modulation of attention which may be present during the reception of the other types. It would be to the other types of schemata as, for example, amplitude is to pitch in acoustics. The 'morphology' of an emotion, when the emotion itself cannot be named, could be recognized whether the mimesis is that of the writer himself, or of a *persona*, or even (within limits) of an objective situation described by the writer (or indeed described by a *persona*), with emotion or the absence of emotion substituted for the emotion of the human author or his humanoid *persona*. Indeed, Davie's examples of 'syntax as music' clearly seem to provide mimesis of psychological processes, or perceptions of objective processes in the world outside the consciousness, and therefore his musical syntax is reducible either to 'subjective/dramatic' mimesis, or 'objective' mimesis.

The word *mimesis* would here be reserved for the presence of analogous schemata in the lexical level and one or both of the lower levels of syntax or phonology (or graphemics). However I believe that while Davie correctly distinguishes mimesis of entities other than human consciousnesses from mimesis of human consciousnesses (in his description of 'objective' syntax), I am not sure that his distinction between 'subjective' and 'dramatic' mimesis is of the same sort. A *persona* is not an object with an existence independent of the writer; its existence is entirely contingent upon his. I would rather class Davie's dramatic mimesis as a grade of subjective mimesis than as a class of its own. The creation of *personae* has traditionally formed part of the equipment for the expression of the writer's personality. A *persona* has one property that distinguishes it clearly from an objective phenomenon but which does not distinguish it from subjective portraits: neither the description of a fictional *persona* nor the description of the writer's *persona* can be debated, for completeness or for accuracy, with the describer of it. Although no observer ever sees exactly the same object or process as another, from precisely the same point in space and time, relative coincidence of point of view may be achieved for an objective phenomenon. However, points of view on subjective phenomena cannot even begin to be similar. Of course, as Davie remarks (79), even objective phenomena are not observed directly: each observer describes an imago of the object or process, not the phenomenon itself. However, subjective phenomena have, in addition to this 'automatic' criterion of subjectivity, a quite personal subjectivity which cancels the possibility of debate from the beginning.

Therefore I would suggest a schema for the determination of value in Romantic and post Romantic Western poetry as follows:

I. Non-mimetic forms
   a. absolutely non-mimetic (not even lexical mimesis) [possibly non-existent]
   b. relatively non-mimetic (automatic lexical mimesis)
      1. non-mimetic phonological schemata
      2. non-mimetic syntactic schemata
      3. related combined but non-mimetic phonological and syntactic schemata

II. Mimetic forms
   a. objective mimesis of lexis
      1. by phonological schemata
      2. by syntactic schemata
      3. by related combined phonological and syntactic schemata
   b. subjective mimesis of lexis
      1. dramatic mimesis (mimesis of *personae*)
         a. phonological
         b. syntactic
         c. combined
      2. self-reflexive mimesis (mimesis of *imago* of self)
         a. phonological
         b. syntactic
         c. combined

(Graphemic mimesis is graded the same as the corresponding phonological class.) The farther down in the schema is the appropriate designation, the higher the 'value' of the utterance. The assignment of value is made on the principle that the more personal (and therefore the less informative) is the lexical constellation underlying the utterance, the more assistance it requires from mimetic forms of expression to be apprehended, and the more valuable it becomes when it *is* apprehended. Mimetic phonological and syntactic forms, therefore, provide a metaphor for lexis in the more highly valued forms. I assume that in this stage of history the communication of an intensely personal expressive constellation bears the highest value in a verbal work of art.

Of course, 'secondary' phenomena such as comic or ironic effects, or effects created by 'collage' techniques, pose special problems and would perhaps need to be graded on two scales – one, the scale above applied precisely, and two, the (presumed) gap between lexis and expression then re-evaluated as self-reflexive mimesis of the highest grade. Thus, for example, we can evaluate the self-mocking, Pierrotesque writing of Laforgue or Beckett or Donald Barthelme as mirroring the broken *persona* the writer perceives in himself, and the collage techniques of Joyce would first be graded as employing combined techniques for objective and dramatic mimesis of lexis, and would then be re-evaluated as the highest grade of value, a portrait of the artist 'writing the mystery of himself in furniture', the 'zoantholitic furniture' of the 'hueful panepiphanal world' (*Finnegans Wake*, p. 184, lines 9–10; p. 611, lines 13–14).

1. Objective mimesis of lexis

The 'objective' phenomena to be mimed in literary discourse can be divided into objects and processes, but it seems clear that there is an inherent difficulty in miming objects in the linear stream of speech or writing, except as interruptions in flow (like a stone in a stream). This would tend to limit objective mimesis to imitations of processes; and indeed most examples of objective mimesis are of processes in time, psychological processes involved in the apprehension of phenomena external to the consciousness of the observer, as well as the linearly successive phenomena themselves – the flowing of water, waves, echoes, the ripening of vegetation, and the stream of speech itself.

Pope provides many examples of mimesis of objective phenomena. Echo-effects abound in his pastorals.

> Go gentle Gales, and bear my Sighs away!
> Come, Delia, come; ah why this long Delay?

The self-reflexive artefact 179

> Thro' Rocks and Caves the name of *Delia* sounds,
> *Delia*, each Cave and ecchoing Rock rebounds.
>   (*Autumn: The Third Pastoral*, 11. 47–50)
> .... *Delia* sounds,
> *Delia*, ...

The echoing effect is, of course, deliberate; the name of the beloved originally was *Thyrsis*, but was altered to *Delia* to chime with *Delay* (as well as avoiding the suggestion of homosexuality in the Virgilian original). In addition to the repetitions of *Delia* and the chime with *Delay*, there are other repeated sounds – *Go Gales*, *my-Signs*, *Gales-away*, *Come-come*, *Rocks-Caves-Cave-Rock* (this last perhaps not mimetic because chiastic – echoes do not repeat in reverse.)

> In hollow Caves sweet *Echo* silent lies,
> Silent, or only to her name replies,
> Her name with Pleasure once she taught the Shore,
> Now Daphne's dead, and Pleasure is no more.
>   (*Winter: The Fourth Pastoral*, 11. 41–4)

There is much exact echoing: *silent-silent*, *her name-her name*, *pleasure-pleasure*. There is also sound-echoing: *silent-lies*, *taught-shore*, *Daphne's-dead*. There may be syntactic echoing between lines 41 and 42.

Natural processes are mimed syntactically in the first line of a couplet from *Messiah*, Pope's version of Virgil's *Fourth Eclogue*, but falsified in the second:

> To leaf-less Shrubs the flow'ring Palms succeed,
> And od'rous Myrtle to the noisome Weed.
>   (11. 75–6)

The syntactic inversion which places the two nominals together in 1. 75, thus miming the change of vegetation from one state to a succeeding state ('leaf-less' 'flow'ring'), is reversed in 1. 76, becoming countermimetic, and consequently the two lines of the couplet would be of different values.

In a famous passage from *An Essay on Criticism*, 11. 337–73, Pope achieves a pyrotechnical display of mimetic ingenuity. All sixteen mimetic lines in this passage (11. 345, 346, 347, 350, 351, 352, 353, 357, 365, 367, 368, 369, 370, 371, 372, 373) exhibit highly interesting linguistic features, mimetic of content.[5] However, they all derive their mimetic effect from phonological or syntactic structures (often semi-grammatical), or both. Line 347, for example, derives its mimetic effect from a combination of syntax and phonology.

> And ten low Words oft creep in one dull Line.

Pope does indeed attempt to avoid lines composed entirely of monosyllabic words, But the mimetic effect of the line is only partly dependent upon the absence of polysyllabic words, with their 'normal transition' between syllables. One bisyllabic word in line 347, for example, would not by itself speed up the line appreciably. The effect depends partly upon the syntactic nature of the words in the line, and partly upon phonological transition-effects. Eight of the ten syllabic positions in the line are occupied by items from major syntactic classes – nouns, non-equational verbs, adjectives, numerals, adverbials – each demanding a major phonological stress. Only two of the syllables are occupied by members of minor classes – 'and' and 'in'. In this sense, the 'Words' are not 'low', they are all too 'high' for a normal blank-verse matrix.

This stiffness of intonation forbids even the highly limited amount of transitional slurring between syllables (haplology) permitted in the performance of poetry. There are seven points out of the nine points of transition in the line where slurring would occur in casual speech, and where it now may not. This frustration of performance slows the performance of this line to a creep, which objectively mimes the 'lowness' and 'dullness' of a line so constituted.

1. *And-ten*; ordinarily (in casual conversation) a final alveolar plosive (/d/) would haplologize with an initial alveolar plosive (/t/). This is here avoided by an actual pause, a cessation of phonation.
2. *ten-low*; ordinarily an alveolar nasal (/n/) would move too quickly into an alveolar glide (/l/) for the preservation of the plus-juncture which prevents the sequence /ten + lʌw/) from becoming one bisyllabic word.
3. *low-words*; ordinarily the low glide (/w/) in low would be omitted before the initial consonantal /w/ in the following syllable.
4. *oft-creep*; in such a multi-consonantal environment the final alveolar plosive /t/ would be haplologized by an initial velar plosive /k/ in the following syllable.
5. *creep-in*; I find in my reading of these syllables a temptation towards the liaison of the final /p/ in *creep* with the initial vowel of *in*, which here is resisted by introducing a cessation of phonation.
6. *one-dull*; it is too easy to produce an initial alveolar plosive /d/ merely by releasing the previous final alveolar nasal /n/; this, like *ten-low*, would produce an unacceptable bisyllabic word, instead of two separate syllables, each of them entitled to a major stress.
7. *dull-line*; the final /l/ of *dull* must not be haplologized with the initial /l/ of line.

Since objective mimesis is effected by a combination of syntactic and phonological structures, the line would be entitled to a high grade of value.

The rest of Pope's mimetic lines would be entitled to lower or equal grades on a first approximation. However, there is a question about the nature of the mimesis effected. Each of the seventeen lines, in whole or in part, mimes an objective linear phenomenon – the performance of a line of verse – and therefore is entitled to a score reflecting some grade of objective mimesis. However, the lines do not all mime the same objective phenomenon, strictly regarded and viewed in context. The lines of verse they mime are all from forms different from that of the poem in which they are embedded. An *ars poetica*, which is the genre of *An Essay on Criticism*, need not contain imitative effects to be an *ars poetica*; though it usually contains examples of verse, the examples are usually clearly distinguished from the text, not embedded in the commentary. Therefore, these lines are not reflexive or mimetic of the work in which they appear. I would suggest that they must be judged as secondary comic or ironic phenomena, and achieve a value as a whole distinct from and higher than the values of the lines themselves. Here they achieve a high grade of value, since they are reflexive of the self-image of the creator, Pope himself, who takes obvious pleasure in his own virtuosity.

Milton also provides examples of mimesis of various sorts. An especially interesting example occurs in *Lycidas*, 11. 165–7:

> Weep no more, woful Shepherds, weep no more,
> For Lycidas your sorrow is not dead,
> Sunk though he be beneath the watry floar...

Line 167 accomplishes a remarkable degree of objective mimesis through a combination of syntactic and phonological structures. The movements of the tongue and lower jaw to accomplish the stressed vowels of this line mime a motion from mid central to high front to back:

Sunk though   he be beneath the   watry floar
/ sʌŋk + ðʌw + hi + biː | biniːθ + ðə + wɔtri + flɔr
mid central   high front   back

The motion mimes the relationship low-high-low expressed in the lexis – the body of Edward King on the sea floor (low) and the surface of the sea (high). The high front vowels mime the notion 'the watery floor' far beneath which King has sunk. The unusual number of high front vowels – four in a row – flanked by mid or back vowels suggest that this phonological mimesis is deliberate. In this structure lexical 'high' and 'low' is expressed by phonological 'high-front' and 'low-back'. Note also that the mimetic pattern influences the line *as a whole*; 'beneath' is represented as part of the 'high' area, even though semantically it is 'low'; the reverse is true for 'watry floar'.

The vocalic mimesis is reinforced by the structure of stresses. Of the eight words in the line, only three are from major syntactic classes. The syntactic structure of the line could be represented as follows:

Perf Part – Subordinate Conjunction – Pers Pron – Copula –
Prep – Art – *Adj* (*Modifier*) – *Noun*

(The major word classes are italicized.) Only representatives of major word-classes inherently receive major stress, all things being equal, and in this case the words receiving major lexical stress are also (with one exception – 'be') those words centring around mid or back vowels. *Low* and *high* in this line, therefore, are mimed by a *stressed-mid-back – unstressed-high-front* polarization.

It hardly needs saying that the lexical situation is primary in the appreciation of the line and is reinforced by phonological and syntactic mimesis; if there were no polar situation to express, the phonology and syntax structures would be non-mimetic, and the value of the line would be low.

Interesting aspects of objective mimesis are revealed by an examination of French verse. A fragment from the work of the seventeenth-century poet Jean-François Sarasin (1604–54) demonstrates mimesis of an effect found often in poetry of the time, the periodic flow of water:

> Comme avec un grand bruit le Rhône plein de rage,
> Soulevé par les vents, ou grossi par l'orage,
> Vient et traine avec soi milles flots courroucés;
> L'onde flotte après l'onde, et de l'onde est suivie,
> Ainsi passe la vie.
> Ainsi coulent nos ans l'un sur l'autre entassés.[6]

The objective mimesis of periodic flow of water in the fourth line is effected phonologically by the repetition of '*l'onde*'. However, the simple phonological pattern contradicts lexis at an important point. Whereas the three repetitions of *l'onde* mime three successive wave-swells, in a 1-2-3 sound pattern, the actual pattern of the swells of the Rhône, in context, is 2-1-3: the first *onde* mentioned is actually preceded in time by the second, and is succeeded by the third, in the objective situation described. The complexity of the relationship between expression and form here is further complicated by a possible third arrangement, a graphemic one: the three appearances of *l'onde* on the page seem to me to suggest a 3-2-1 pattern – that is, the rightmost swell seems to be the earliest. (This may be conditioned by my right-handedness; perhaps a left-handed person would perceive the reverse.)

Miming of flowing water was often attempted in the seventeenth century, both in France and in England. For example, there is the *Plainte sur la mort de Sylvie* of Saint-Amant (1594–1661):

> Ruisseau qui cours après toi-meme,
> Et qui te fuis toi-même aussi,
> Arrête un peu ton onde ici.[7]

Note that the effect remains when the pro-form 'toi-même' is substituted for the repeating nominal element, 'Ruisseau'. Martial Dumas de Brives (?–1656) accomplishes almost a 'metaphysical' effect within his mimesis (expressed by the word *coule*), in his *Paraphrase sur le Cantique; Benedicite omnis opera Domini Domino*:

> Clairs amas des mers précieuses
> Qui pendant sur le Firmament,
> Et coulant sans écoulement
> Semblent être judicieuses....[8]

Jean-Baptiste Chassignet (1571?–1635?) achieves an impressive effect in much the same way as Sarasin, in his Fifth Sonnet:

> Assieds-toi sur le bord d'une ondante rivière,
> Tu la verras fluer d'un perpetuel cours,
> Et flots sur flots roulant en mille et mille tours
> Decharger par les prés son humide carriere.
>
> Mais tu ne verras rien de cette onde première
> Qui naguère coulait, l'eau change tous les jours,
> Tous les jours elle passe, et la nommons toujours
> Même fleuve et même eau, d'une même manière....[9]

In this verse the effect of flowing water is achieved by the repetition of words only the first pair of which is lexically related to water: flots/flots. The other pairs mime the successive swells by mere repetition: mille/mille, tous les jours/tous les jours/toujours, même/même/même. This phenomenon demonstrates the mimesis to be truly phonological: once the lexis is mimed by sound-repetition in *flots,* any sound-repetition thereafter reinforces the mimesis.

Ben Jonson, during the same period, accomplishes a remarkably successful mimesis of flowing water in his line

> Slow, slow, fresh fount, keep time with my salt tears.

This line mimes the slow welling of the speaker's tears both phonologically and syntactically, in ways similar to Pope's slowing of line 347 from *An Essay on Criticism*.

(a) Phonologically, every syllable (with the exception of the seventh –

'with') contains either a consonant cluster or a 'long vowel', a complex vocalic nucleus. Four syllables have both: /slʌw/, /slʌw/, /fæwnt/, and /tiːrz/. There is, therefore, a great deal of phonic material to get through relative to the number of syllables. In addition, there is the obstructive final t of '*salt*' and the initial of '*tears*' to be pronounced carefully and separately.

(b) Syntactically, there are eight representatives from major syntactic classes out of ten. (The exceptions are the preposition with and the possessive pronoun my.) Eight out of ten syllables, therefore, are entitled to major stresses. In addition, however, each of the 'slow's' is in effect a sentence; in transformational terms each could be the reduced surface-representative of a structure dominated by ♯S♯. These 'imperative quasi-adverbials', as they may be called, are entitled to sentence intonation – that is, each may be followed by a major transitional juncture. These junctures slow the line still further.

The adjectival 'fresh fount' is succeeded by a major transition also, since it is in apposition to both of the imperative quasi-adverbials. This introduces another sentence-ending transition. Three 'sentences' intonationally, and four sentence-ending junctures, in a line of only ten syllables is unusual, and the movement of the performed line is correspondingly unusual.

A modern poet, Paul Valéry, imitates the action of water magnificently in the final section of *La Jeune Parque* (1917):

> Si l'âme intense souffle, et renfle furibonde
> L'onde abrupte sur l'onde abbatue, et si l'onde
> Au cap tonne, immolant un monstre de candeur ...

The mimesis here, perhaps imitated from the Sarasin lines above,[10] is of a sea-swell breaking on a rocky coast. *L'onde* is not wave, in the normal English sense of the word; both for Valery and for Sarasin the word *vague* expressed the normal physical meaning of *wave*. *L'onde* is here the sea itself, by synecdoche (as in 'England rules the wave'). Therefore, the three appearances of *l'onde*, both in Valery and in Sarasin, do not mark the lexical recognition of three separate waves but of three manifestations of the same phenomenon or process. Thus it is the perception of three moments in time which is mimed, three stages in the continuous process of the sea breaking on the shore, or the Rhône flowing to the sea.

The modifiers of *l'onde* in the Valéry also mime the action, syntactically. *Abrupte*, while still retaining some of the force of the Latin participial form from which it was derived, is a 'true' adjective and represents a continuing attribute of the swell, while *abbatue* is a perfect participle and represents completed action. The passage from an attributive adjective to a true participle mimes the passage of time from the first perceived state of the swell, now simply a static attribute, to the second, still an active force. The third stage is represented by a finite verb (*tonne*); the complete action is mimed by a movement from static attribution through participial completed actions to dynamic verbal action.

Objective mimesis always has a tendency to seem trivial, a trick or, at any rate, a not particularly necessary part of poetic technique. Even when skillfully done, as it often is – by Pope, Jonson, and Valéry, for example – there is always a suggestion of a trick about it, an act of conscious craftsmanship. I would suggest that this impression is the result of the basically unnecessary nature of the act itself – the reader knows what slowly flowing tears, echoes, waves, and similar phenomena look, feel, or sound like without the assistance of sub-lexical mimetic techniques. Perhaps the true necessity of *subjective* mimesis conveys a factitious value to other types of mimesis.

2. *Subjective mimesis*

The subtlest, most valuable, and most difficult to achieve grades of mimesis are those that include imitation of personal sequences of emotion. The imitation is not that of the mind apprehending some external process or even of its own procedure in the gradual apprehension of some external phenomenon; it is rather an imitation of the observation of its own proper action. This is the act of the mind in observing the most private recesses of a private mind, its own (where there is no distinguishable *persona*), one in which individual conformations of character are so strong that communication of this component is under a severe inherent handicap. If, therefore, communication of this private component is assisted by elements in the message which mime these privacies by schemata of public syntactic or phonological codes of language, the resulting construct is of the highest value.

When this subjective reality is the content of a work of art to be conveyed, mimesis is extremely important. Here the reader and the author share no common knowledge, unlike the situation in objective mimesis. Both reader and author know what echoes, flowing water, the rhythms of speech, are like, but only the individual really knows what his own configurations of personality and memory are like.

For the purposes of this analysis, I propose to analyse a work universally acknowledged as great, in which the element that is mimed in the work is derived from the self-image of a personalized creator – Blake's *Tyger*. The effect of the poem has been clear to generations of readers. The emotional situation mimed is extremely complex; it seems to me to be compounded of fear and awe, combined with an overall feeling of universal comprehension, of *noesis*, a grasp of the secret of the energy of the universe. Close analysis of the syntax of the poem reveals complex iconic schemata which reinforce and convey this subjective state to the reader.

The Tyger

Tyger Tyger, burning bright,
In the forests of the night:
What immortal hand or eye,
Could frame thy fearful symmetry?

In what distant deeps or skies,
Burnt the fire of thine eyes!
On what wings dare he aspire?
What the hand, dare seize the fire?

And what shoulder, and what art,
Could twist the sinews of thy heart?
And when thy heart began to beat,
What dread hand? and what dread feet?

What the hammer? what the chain,
In what furnace was thy brain?
What the anvil? what dread grasp,
Dare its deadly terrors clasp!

When the stars threw down their spears
And water'd heaven with their tears:
Did he smile his work to see?
Did he who made the Lamb make thee?

Tyger Tyger burning bright,
In the forests of the night:
What immortal hand or eye,
Dare frame thy fearful symmetry?

(Text from Blake, *Songs of Experience*, 1794)

What is here analysed is not a 'first reading' of *Tyger*, in the sense of a first scanning. Rather, it is the experience of a reader who encounters and understands *Tyger* completely for the first time, even though he may have scanned it before. After his 'first complete reading', as it could be called, all further readings contribute nothing new and become increasingly automatized scannings of a familiar linear pattern. In a certain sense, of course, a symbolic poem can never be exhausted of its meaning or completely linearized, and therefore can never have a 'complete' reading. However, in this analysis, a reader has experienced his 'first complete reading' when he realizes all the elements of mimesis in the poem.

There is a considerable amount of phonological structuring in *Tyger*, but it is all non-mimetic. For example, in each stanza there are three lines that exhibit alliteration and one that does not. (In lines two, six, and twenty-two, the alliteration is vocalic, in my idiolect: /farısts/ /naıt/: /faır/ /aız/: /farısts/ /naıt/.) There is also phonological chiasmus in the first line: /taıgər/ /bərnıŋ/ /braıt/. These regularities mime no objective or subjective entity mentioned or suggested in the poem. The commonplace metrical and rhyme schemes are certainly non-mimetic; they are those of 'Twinkle, Twinkle, Little Star.' Indeed, so automatized is the phonology that it seriously interferes with the correct intonation of the syntactic patterning, especially in the first and second lines, where syntactic subtleties are overridden by the insensitivity of the meter. Nor is there objective mimesis in *Tyger*, nothing that corresponds to claws, stripes, fire, roars, teeth, ferocity.

What Blake achieves in *Tyger* is a subjective mimesis, based on syntax, for a very high degree of value. It seems obvious from the poem that what Blake is conveying is his own awe at perceiving the energy that drives the universe and the poet, a force here symbolized as a tiger, a power beyond good and evil.[11]

Energy, action, exuberance, excess, are for Blake the highest values in life and in art: 'All that is not action is not worth reading';[12] 'Energy is the only life and is from the Body and Reason is the Bound or outward circumference of Energy' (*Marriage of Heaven and Hell*). *Tyger* seems to record a moment of illumination, the moment when the nature of the fundamental energy of the universe become clear. There are, therefore, two aspects of this experience – memory of the sensation of mystic illumination, and awe before the object of perception. Both of these aspects are reflected in syntactic structures in *Tyger* that communicate this moment with great power to the reader. (Bertrand Russell is said to have fainted when he first heard *Tyger*, at Cambridge.)

In one way, *Tyger* is unusual in the works of Blake, and in another way it is unusual as compared to the works of any author. It is the only poem Blake ever wrote in which the first stanza is repeated as the last stanza (with one word changed). In addition, it is composed entirely of unanswered questions; the only comparable stretch of questioning in literature occurs in the Book of Job, undoubtedly one of Blake's sources. It is by these two departures, from his own practice and from almost anyone's, that he communicates the two highly unusual psychological aspects of the content of *The Tyger*.

Major frame

The clarity of his mystic perception is conveyed by a movement from ambiguity of syntactic structure to single structures, from the first stanza to the last. There are at least eight different syntactic structures that can be derived from the first two lines of the first stanza – that is, the first two lines contain three points at which two different syntactic structures can be discerned.

1. *'burning bright'*

(a) This expression may be a combination of a present participle and a 'Quasi-predicative', i.e., a phrase like 'the moon was *shining bright*' or the 'candle was *burning blue*', or 'He tried *jumping clear* of the ship'.[13] In this reading, a reading which many readers automatically adopt, it is the Tyger that is 'burning', and it is becoming 'bright' only because of the burning. Hence the main activity of the Tyger is 'burning', and the brightness is ancillary and entirely dependent upon the burning. Another, related, syntactic interpretation would have 'bright' an adverb, even though it is adjectival in form; adverbial forms in Old English and later were frequently adjectival. In this interpretation again it would be the Tyger which is burning, but it would be the *burning* which is bright; this interpretation would require tolerance of a form which by our time, and perhaps by Blake's, would be regarded as dialectal and sub-standard. This interpretation would make 'burning bright' equivalent in meaning to 'burning brightly'.

(b) The expression may have the structure 'Intensifier (Vb) – Adjective subjunct' – that is, it could be an expression like 'boiling hot', and related to forms like 'stony cold', and 'ashy pale'.[14] The Intensifier may take a number of forms; in 'boiling hot', 'shocking bad', and 'burning bright' the forms are verbal, and have the significance respectively of 'very hot, hot enough to boil my hand, were I to put it in', 'very bad, bad enough to shock me,' 'very bright, bright enough to burn my eyes.' This form has the curious property of defining the intensity of the adjective-subjunct it modifies by reference to some perception of an observer. In the case of 'burning bright', it is the Tyger which is bright, and the observer's eyes which are burning – quite a different interpretation from the interpretations in (a) above, which are entirely limited to attributes of the Tyger.

Therefore, the two main syntactic interpretations of the first ambiguous expression could be diagrammed as follows (the brackets indicate a choice; either the top alternative or the bottom must be chosen):

$$\text{The Tyger is} \begin{Bmatrix} \text{burning} \\ or \\ \text{very bright} \end{Bmatrix}$$

2. The second point of syntactic ambiguity occurs after 'bright'. Is the Tyger burning (or bright) *against* the background of 'the forests of the night', or is he merely *within* 'the forests of the night'? In other words, is 'burning bright, / In the forests of the night' one compound adjectival appositive to 'Tyger', or two separate ones? Blake's punctuation suggests the second interpretation, but his punctuation is a risky guide, especially at line endings (every line in the poem ends with a mark of punctuation, with the exception of line seventeen, where there should be one). This second point of ambiguity may be diagrammed as follows:

$$\text{The Tyger is} \begin{Bmatrix} \text{burning} \\ \text{or} \\ \text{very bright} \end{Bmatrix} + \begin{Bmatrix} \text{, and is in the forests of the night} \\ \text{or} \\ \text{within the forests of the night} \end{Bmatrix}$$

3. The third point of syntactic ambiguity comes with the phrase 'the forests of the night'. This expression turns upon the preposition 'of', notoriously one of the most ambiguous particles in the English language, inheriting as it does the combined functions of an Old English preposition and the French genitive *de* (itself the heir of a complex situation from Latin). Here the problem is not to find ambiguities but to weed out the unlikeliest ones.

(a) The possessive interpretation of 'of' gives the expression the meaning 'the night possesses forests' – this would seem to mean that the night is of a forest-like thickness. 'The forests of the night' would then be equivalent to 'thick, tangled night.'

(b) On the other hand, it could be the characterizing 'of' which is employed, as in 'the knight of the woeful countenance', 'the house of the seven gables', or 'the inn of the sword'. This form is much more French than the first, i.e., 'Rue de la Goutte-d'Or', 'Place de la Concorde', and so on. It is more or less equivalent to 'with', and therefore 'the forests of the night' would mean 'the forests with (or characterized by) night', that is, 'dark forests'.

With a phrase turning on 'of', it is difficult to be able to decide which part of the phrase is metaphorical. (Indeed, the whole phrase may be a metaphor for a third entity.)[15] The semantic structure of the first stanza is no help, since the Tyger could just as easily be in forests or (since he is, after all, a cosmic symbol) interstellar night.[16] This situation can be diagrammed as follows:

$$\text{The Tyger is in} \begin{Bmatrix} \text{thick night} \\ \text{or} \\ \text{dark forests} \end{Bmatrix}$$

The complete diagram of this octuply ambiguous expression is as follows:

The Tyger is
$$\begin{Bmatrix} \text{burning} \\ \text{or} \\ \text{very bright} \end{Bmatrix} + \begin{Bmatrix} \text{, and is in} \\ \text{or} \\ \text{against the} \\ (\text{or} \\ \text{within the}) \end{Bmatrix} + \begin{Bmatrix} \text{thick night} \\ \text{or} \\ \text{dark forests} \end{Bmatrix}$$

The reader may not realize consciously that these ambiguities are present in his reading, but in fact the suspension of closure in these lines is a functional element of the first importance in the reading of the poem.

This complex set of ambiguities is resolved by the time the stanza is repeated at the end of *Tyger*, and the resolution provides the major formal frame for the poem. In the second, third, and fourth stanzas it is made clear that the Tyger has been forged in a cosmic smithy, or perhaps in a cannon-foundry, one of Blake's dark, Satanic mills.[17] This information immediately resolves the first point of ambiguity, and leads to the resolution of the other two. Artefacts in the process of being forged by a smith or a founder are often extremely 'bright' as they come from the furnace or smithy fire, but although flames sometimes flicker along the edges of red-hot or white-hot metal, it cannot really be said that they are normally 'burning'. Therefore, the Tyger is not burning but rather is 'very bright'. Since 'brightness' requires contrast more strongly than does 'burning', the Tyger is *within* or *against* 'the forests of the night'. Then finally the more 'English' of the two possibilities for 'the forests of the night', the one employing the possessive 'of', is also the more semantically likely. Hence, the syntactic structure of the last stanza is different from that of the first in being completely unambiguous. The first two lines of this stanza are also unambiguous (syntactically); they can be paraphrased

> The Tyger is very bright, burning to the beholder's eye, against thick tangled darkness.

Although the resolution is effected by semantic means, the effect is gained by the reduction of syntactic possibilities.*

The movement from eightfold syntactic ambiguity to single structure provides syntactic mimesis for the feeling of universal understanding with which the reader finishes the poem, and also reveals the structural reason for the repetition, unique in Blake's poetry, of the first stanza at the last. Beethoven, Blake's almost exact contemporary, accomplishes the same

---

* Lexical ambiguity is never in question here except as deriving entirely from syntactic ambiguity; there are a great many different possible meanings for 'Tyger', or for 'forests', or 'night'. Exploration of these lexical ambiguities, on top of the syntactic ones, would expand the interpretation of the poem to immense lengths, and would not ever be resolvable to the same degree of explicitness as its syntactic complexities.

effect in some of his late sonatas and quartets, in which a simple melody is explored through all its manifestations until all of its structural elements are expanded and developed and its meaning and nature thoroughly understood by the listener, at which point the melody is brought back again in its simple form to be fully appreciated in all its parts. It could be said that the only alteration in Blake's repeated stanza, from 'could frame' to 'dare frame', a move from a neutral auxiliary to a more intense verbal particle, is an acknowledgement of the movement from confusion to clarity, from a multiple vision of the energy of the universe to a clear, more awed view of the same phenomenon.

This movement of understanding provides the large frame for the poem, a frame of revelation. Within this major frame there is a minor frame, one which provides a much more moderate degree of enlightenment, less of a definitive revelation. The question-forms in *Tyger* move from peculiar forms of 'what'-questions which, as we will see, cannot even begin to be answered, to 'yes/no' questions, in the penultimate stanza, which one can at least begin to answer, confident that the answer to them will be either 'yes' or 'no'.

There are, then, two frames of revelation in 'The Tyger':

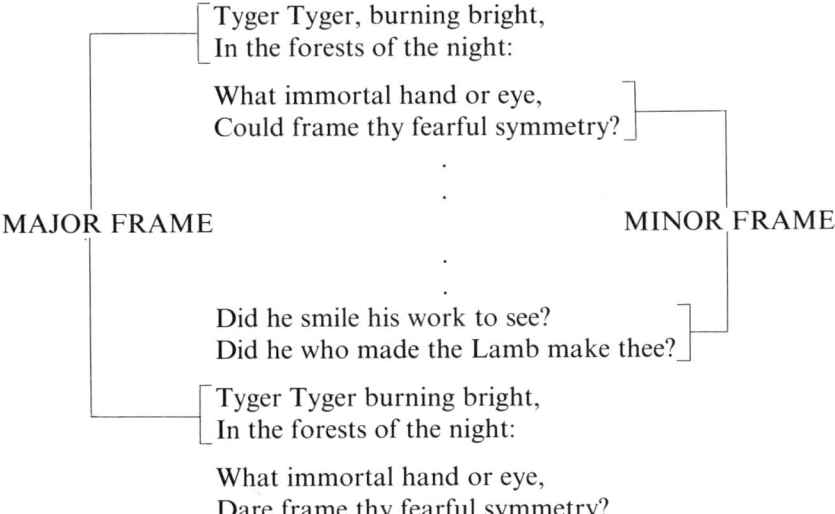

Minor frame

The form of the 'what-questions' in the poem contribute the second psychological effect of the poem – the awe unmixed with ignorance before the phenomenon of the Tyger. The fact that the form of the questions reinforces a feeling of awe with remarkable subtlety helps to clarify the apparent paradox of an act of mystic revelation expressed partly by questions – forms usually associated with lack of knowledge, not with complete understanding.

In two ways, Blake weakens the illocutionary force of his 'questions' by reducing what could be called the 'ignorance motive' normally operative in the creation of questions.[18] First of all, the fact that the questions in *Tyger* are written questions weakens them considerably as questions. All written questions, with the exception of those in printed plays, personal letters, and government forms, are 'rhetorical' questions, or as Robinson calls them, 'exclamatory' questions.[19] They are exclamatory questions in the sense that no answer is required, since no answer is possible in such a form. (In a trivial sense, of course, no answer can be expected from a tiger, not even a cosmic one, and especially no answers about his own process of manufacture.) Blake employs graphemic/discoursal expectations to keep part of the illocutionary force of questioning without the *substance* of it – the confession of ignorance that a true question-situation almost inevitably reveals.

The second reason, more complex but also more powerfully effective, why Blake's questions in stanzas one through four of the poem are only the husks of questions, is that they are questions of a highly unusual type. There are two sorts of questions in English. First, there are 'yes/no' questions, characterized by word-order inverted from that of the normal indicative sentence, and answerable, at least in theory, by a simple assent or negation. (There are some more complex forms of this type of question, but they play no part in the poem.) Second, there are what Jespersen calls 'x-questions', questions to which the answer cannot be 'yes' or 'no' but which must be a phrase, a substitute for an interrogative pronominal, and whose syntactic class is strictly governed by the choice of interrogative pronominal.[20] For example, in a 'where'-question the only non-evasive or non-irrelevant answer would be in the form of an adverbial of place; a 'when'-question is answerable only by an adverbial of time; and so on. In English the interrogatives 'where', 'when', 'why', 'who' only possess a *simple* form in questions – that is, nothing but a verbal auxiliary may appear immediately after the interrogative in a question: 'Where *did* you go?' 'When *could* he go?' (the only apparent exception to this rule is the so-called 'echo-question' – 'Why a horse? Why not a cow?') Other interrogatives – 'how' and 'what' – may appear either in *simple* or *complex* form – either 'How *do* you feel? and 'What *do* you want?' or 'How *long* did it take?' and 'What *man* did you want to see?' In these complex forms the interrogative pronoun may be followed by adjectives, or nouns, or both. 'Which' and 'whose' may appear only in *complex* forms – 'Which *button* do I press?' or

The self-reflexive artefact 193

'Whose *hat* is missing?' This last is true, unless the following nominal has been deleted, either because it has just been mentioned in some previous sentence or because it has been indicated in some non-verbal manner:

Man A: Look at the row of buttons.
Man B: Which do I press?

Or Man B may simply point to the array of buttons without waiting for Man A to introduce them to him, and say, pointing, 'Which do I press?' This does not alter the rule that 'Which'-and 'Whose'-questions must be either explicitly or implicitly complex in form.

With this situation in mind, for the language as a whole, let us examine the Blake questions. All but four of Blake's x-questions are complex in form; they either begin with 'What + Noun' or 'What + Modifer + Noun'. (One of them begins with a preposition, 'in', a situation which does not alter the analysis.)

There are rules, as yet unformulated, for the use of complex interrogatives in discourse that Blake subtly infringes. The emotional effect of this infringement is a reinforcement of the awe of the lexical level; the 'ignorance-factor', which is one of the 'constitutive conditions' of an utterance with the complete illocutionary force of a question, is hereby reduced, without affecting other emotive factors concomitant with the asking of questions.

A tentative approach to the description of these rules can be made by considering why 'which' and 'whose' are always complex interrogatives (subject to the reservations above). We then may be able to ascertain why 'what' is more flexible, in that it can appear in both simple and complex form. A man who asks another man, 'Which button do I press?' seems to have 'ordered' his immediate situation, i.e. before a panel of buttons the dimensions and characteristics of which are well known to him. The use of 'which' is, therefore, a sign of an advanced comprehension of a situation, and the question-form is based upon this understanding. Hence the nominal which by rule follows 'which'; attention has already been focused on the entity expressed by the nominal, an array of buttons, one of which is to be pressed. The same description would apply for 'whose'; the situation is clear enough to the questioner to allow him to ask for an assignment of possession of an entity already sufficiently analysed to deserve such an 'advanced' interrogative. In simple 'what'-questions, however, the questioner's attention has *not* been so focused, and the perception of the situation is far less advanced than in the 'which' and 'whose' situations. An ordering of the situation still remains to be done, and this is accomplished by a discourse pattern commencing with a simple 'what'-question and proceeding to more and more complex ones, each complex 'what'-question demanding a further modifier of the nominal until the situation is sufficiently ordered:

Q. 1:	What do I press?	(*Primary question*)
A. 1:	The button.	(*Primary answer*)
Q. 2:	What button?	(*Secondary question*)
A. 2:	The red button.	(*Secondary answer*)
Q. 3:	What red button?	(*Tertiary question*)
A. 3:	The red button marked 'Start'.	(*Tertiary answer*)

And so on; there is no reason why there should not be complex questioning of a higher order than tertiary. It will be noted, first, that while the primary question elicits a nominal answer, the secondary and higher grades of question elicit the primary nominal qualified by the appropriate number of modifiers, and second, that every grade of question and answer higher than the first, in a 'normal' discourse-frame such as the above, is characterized by contrastive stress and pitch patterning, on the secondary and tertiary interrogatives and on the modifiers supplied. If the process is abbreviated – that is, if the first question in a discourse is tertiary in form, i.e. Q: 'What red button marked "Start" do I press?', or if the answer to a primary question, 'What do I press?' is tertiary, 'The red button marked "Start"', the situation for contrastive stress is not present, since either the questioner or the answerer has already advanced beyond the point of confronting an unordered situation. The canonical ordering of questions as demonstrated above has as its purpose the ordering of a situation such as the 'which' or 'whose'-questioner has already ordered.

Blake violates this rule of question-precedence in *Tyger*. All of his questions in the poem that begin with 'what' are, with four exceptions, either secondary or tertiary questions, none of them preceded by the appropriate primary question. The effect of this violation is to rob the questions of the power to elicit information of which the questioner is ignorant – that is, these 'questions' are semi-grammatical, not really questions at all, but disguised exclamations. Blake's situation, it is implied by this practice, is not really unordered, and his information is therefore much more complete than his questioning pose would suggest. Therefore, while his utterances look like questions and sound like questions, they lack the illocutionary force of questions. In cognitive terms they are awed exclamations – 'awed' because of the question-flavour still clinging to these husks, but 'exclamations' rather than questions because of the high degree of information that Blake cannot conceal he possesses.[21]

This highly skilful and unprecedented violation of norms of syntax in discourse (see Appendix) provides the right tone for the core of the poem: the reader is uneasily aware that exclamations are disguised as questions which cannot even begin to be answered, since their form in discourse is incorrect and the syntactic form of the answer expected is not clear. When the 'yes/no' questions in stanza five appear, they come as a great relief, since they are in perfect canonical form, and the construction of an answer can at least begin for them. Thus the 'true' questions in stanza five act to release tension previously created by the asking of questions subtly false in form. This movement from high tension to much lower tension provides the dynamic for the minor frame of the poem. A similar structure is to be found in music, of a slightly later period, in Schumann's song 'Im Wunderschönen Monat Mai'. In this song, famous in the history of harmony, the ending is a dominant seventh chord in one of the main keys of the song. A dominant seventh ordinarily demands resolution to the tonic in imperious terms, but the hearer of this song is content with the unresolved dominant seventh, since the body of the song is so chromatic and its modulations so volatile that a reference to a main key, even in the form of a dominant seventh, is accepted almost with composure. The 'composure' is not complete, because the dominant seventh still keeps a fragment of its restless power even in this context, just as the 'questions' in *Tyger* retain enough of their illocutionary force as questions to produce the requisite feeling of awe, but are robbed of their power of demanding cognitive resolution, and do not interfere with the main psychological mood of complete understanding provided by the major frame.

In the description of some structures in *Tyger* we have seen how two subtle, complex, and apparently contradictory emotional states, complete knowledge and questioning awe, are mimed, reinforced, and finally reconciled by the satisfaction and frustration of syntactic expectations in the reader. Not only does this entitle the poem to a very high grade of value; it actually makes the poem possible. It is difficult to see how just this highly subjective proportion of differing elements, awe and illumination, could otherwise have been conveyed.

Conclusion

The procedure of critical analysis employed in this paper relies upon linguistic techniques of description. Applied with some caution, this approach has the virtue of accounting for certain judgments of value, now made on an intuitive basis, of literary artefacts by a comparatively objective procedure.

However, the comments in this paper on sub-lexical mimesis as an indicator of value are obviously incomplete in a number of respects. For one thing, it should be clear from the examples chosen to illustrate the thesis that this standard of value applies mainly to varieties of Renaissance

196 *Essays in Modern Stylistics*

and post-Renaissance poetry from the technologically advanced countries of Western Europe and America. Other sorts of poetry would be measured by other standards. For example, classical Welsh and Irish poetry, skaldic verse, and similar medieval forms seem to derive their value from their approximation to abstract phonological schemata, not from their degrees of mimetic approximation to their content. It is an open question whether the need for mimesis of an increasingly heterogeneous lexical situation from medieval periods to our own caused the abandonment of the medieval scale of valued schemata in favour of our own more loose schemes of metrical and rhyming alliterative patterns, or whether the most highly valued forms of poetry were *always* those that demonstrated mimesis beneath the lexical level, and that it was the gradual realization of this that caused the general abstract paradigms of verse-making to crumble.

Another question to be explored involves judgment of a work in which there exist several grades of value as measured by sub-lexical mimesis. Is the work *as a whole* to receive a value related to the value of its parts, and if so, what value should it receive? Or perhaps the assignment of value to a work of literature is ultimately an assignment of value to the (putative) author of it, so the rule for assignment of value for a whole work might be that it receives the value as a whole which is equal to the highest value *any part* of it displays; the author has demonstrated an ability to 'rise to the occasion' which is the mark of an outstanding craftsman. Then the further question arises, is a work by one author in which the highest grade of value is assigned to one of its parts only half as valuable (in some other sense) than a work by another author in which the highest grade of value is assigned to *two* of its parts? Can a *whole work* be mimetic on several levels? How is 'part of a work' to be defined?

These and other questions remain to be answered. However, investigations along this line eventually might enable us to answer the ultimate critical questions, 'What are works of art, and why are they *necessary*?'

Appendix

Secondary and tertiary questions, prepared or unprepared, are comparatively rare in most types of literature. For example, there are none in the Book of Job, one of Blake's major sources for *The Tyger*, and not very many in the King James Bible as a whole; there are a number of 'What + Noun' and 'What + Adjective' questions, mostly in the books of Genesis and I Kings, and a fair number of archaic 'What manner + of + Noun' questions. There are only two 'What + Modifier + Noun' questions, both unprepared and both obviously 'exclamatory':

And what one nation in the earth is like thy people ...?
(II Samuel 8:23 I Chr. 17:21)
What further need was there ...? (Hebrews 1:11)

In all of the works of another of Blake's primary sources, Shakespeare, except for an archaic use of 'what time' as a substitute for the relative pronoun 'when', there is only one secondary question and no tertiary ones:

What news on the Rialto? (*M Ven* 1.3.39)

Even this secondary question is archaic; a modern version would not be in secondary form: 'What is the news on the Rialto?'

They are rather more common in the works of another of Blake's primary influences, Milton, who may have provided Blake a model for the use of these sentences. In the table below there is tabulated the primary, secondary, and tertiary questions, all of them 'unprepared', in the poetry in English of Milton, in *Tyger* and all the other writings of Blake, and in the poetry and plays of a modern poet much influenced by Blake, W. B. Yeats, this last as a 'control'.

Table 9.1 *What-questions in the works of Blake, Milton, and Yeats*

	Primary (*incl. archaic 'What + the + Noun' forms, and forms intro. by a preposition*)	Secondary (*incl. forms intro. by a preposition*)	Tertiary (*incl. forms intro. by a preposition*)
BLAKE			
Tyger	3	1	5
Other	106	17	4
Total	109	18	9
MILTON			
Poetry in English	104	58	15
YEATS complete poems and plays	92	24	10
AVERAGE	102	34	12

It seems clear that the unprepared tertiary form is statistically unusual in written utterances, at least in those examined by me, and that they all seem to be reserved for the purpose Blake employs them for in *the Tyger* – as pseudo-questions, exclamations of awe.

Another source besides Milton is possible for the use of these forms – the preachings and meditations of Hervey and Augustus Toplady, in which these exclamatory questions are very common. Blake knew the works of these popular preachers very well; he even did a water-colour illustration for Hervey's *Meditations*; see David Erdman, *Blake: Prophet against Empire* (rev. ed. 1969), p. 113.

One of the Yeats examples of an unprepared tertiary questions seems to show a link, not only to Blake but specifically to *The Tyger*. As the table above shows, there are more tertiary questions in *Tyger* than in all the rest of Blake. (What the table does not show is that there are actually more tertiary questions in *Tyger* than in any single work of Milton; there are only three in all of *Paradise Lost* and only three in *Samson Agonistes*.)

> The darkness drops again: but now I know
> That twenty centuries of stony sleep
> Were vexed to nightmare by a rocking cradle,
> And what rough beast, its hour come round at last,
> Slouches towards Bethlehem to be born?
>
> ('The Second Coming')

It is tempting to find in the Yeats poem a great coincidence of syntax, theme, and mood with that of *The Tyger*; may we not answer Yeats's unanswerable question, 'What rough beast ...?' with 'The Tyger'? (However, see A. M. Gibbs, 'The "rough beasts" of Yeats and Shakespeare', *Notes and Queries* N.S. 17:2 (February 1950), 48–9, for a Shakespearian source for the 'rough beast'.)

Notes

1 I. A. Richards, *Principles of Literary Criticism*, 2nd ed. (London: Routledge & Kegan Paul, 1926), p. 25.
2 Plato, *Cratylus* 425d, trans. H. N. Fowler, Loeb Classical Lib. Ed., Vol. VI (London: Heinemann, and Cambridge, Mass.: Harvard U.P., 1953).
3 Donald Davie, *Articulate Energy: an Inquiry into the Syntax of English Poetry* (London: Routledge and Kegan Paul, 1955), pp. 68, 76, 79, 86, 92.
4 See Winifred Nowottny, *The Language Poets Use* (London: Athlone Press, 1962), pp. 11–12.
5 See E. L. Epstein, 'The imitative effects in Pope's "An Essay on Criticism"' (forthcoming).
6 Text from Andre Blanchard, ed., *Tresor de la poesie baroque et precieuse* (Paris: Seghers, 1969), pp. 155–6.
7 Blanchard, p. 124.
8 Blanchard, p. 119.
9 Blanchard, pp. 79–80.
10 Blanchard, pp. 16–17.

11 See Warren Stevenson, 'The Tyger as Artefact', *Blake Studies* 2:11 (Fall, 1969), 5–19. The suggestion by H. Bloom in *The Oxford Anthology of English Literature*, eds. Kermode and Hollander (London and New York: Oxford University Press, 1973), Vol. II, p. 28 n., that the *persona* in the poem is not that of Blake himself but that of a limited perceiver of reality resembling Cowper, one overwhelmed by an essentially incomplete perception of reality, seems to me to be unlikely. I find no difficulty in seeing the poem as a direct reflection of Blake's own growing perception of the energy of the universe and its potentialities for good and evil.

12 David V. Erdman, ed., *The Poetry and Prose of William Blake* (New York: Doubleday, 1965), p. 594.

13 Otto Jespersen. *A Modern English Grammar on Historical Principles* (Copenhagen: Ejnar Munksgaard, 1927), Vol. II, 17–17.3.

14 Jespersen, op. cit., 15.21.

15 See Christine Brooke-Rose, *A Grammar of Metaphor* (London: Secker, 1958), pp. 93 ff.

16 Blake could have imagined the Tyger as a constellation; he had been apprenticed to the engraver for the Royal Society, who provided diagrams for the astronomical reports of Herschel; see William S. Doxey, 'William Blake and William Herschel: the poet, the astronomer, and THE TYGER', *Blake Studies* 2:2 (Spring, 1970), 5–13.

17 David V. Erdman, *Blake: Prophet against Empire*, rev. ed. (Princeton, N.J.: Princeton U.P., 1969), p. 203.

18 For a description of the question of illocutionary force, see J. L. Austin, *How to Do Things with Words* (Oxford: Clarendon Press, 1962); William P. Alston, *Philosophy of Language* (Englewood Cliffs, N.J.: Prentice-Hall, 1964); John R. Searle, *Speech Acts* (London, Cambridge University Press, 1969). However, Richard Ohmann believes that illocutionary forces normally associated with utterances are lost, except as mimesis, in all literary works; see Monroe Beardsley's discussion of this point in 'The concept of literature', in *Literary Theory and Structure*, eds. Brady, Palmer, and Price (New Haven, Conn.: Yale Univ. Press, 1973), pp. 30 ff. In my opinion, whatever the merit of Ohmann's argument, utterances that would otherwise possess illocutionary force may lose it by other means than by being included in a literary artefact – by, for example, being subtly incorrect in form, as in the analysis above – and this loss is different in kind from the inherent literary loss of illocutionary force, and logically precedent to it.

19 Fred Robinson, 'Verb tense in Blake's "The Tyger",' *PMLA*, 79: 5(1964), 666–9. Bloom (see note 9 above) refers to the 'increasingly rhetorical questions' in the poem without really describing how the rhetoricity of the Tyger questions 'increases'. See also Eli Pfefferkorn, 'The Question of the Leviathan and the Tiger', *Blake Studies*, 3:1 (Fall, 1970), 53–60, for an interpretation of the poem based upon the 'rhetorical' nature of the questions. None of the above, however, pursues the problem of what a rhetorical question is, or how we can tell one from a non-rhetorical question.

20 Otto Jespersen, *A Modern English Grammar on Historical Principles* (Copenhagen: Ejnar Munksgaard, 1940), Vol. IV, 480–1.

21 See Robinson, p. 669, and E. Kruisinga, *A Handbook of Present-Day English*, 5th ed. (Groningen: P. Noordhoff, 1932), pt. 3, pp. 319–20.

IV
Approaches to metrics

Introduction

The essays which follow, all of which are contributions to the theory of meter within the framework of modern transformational-generative linguistics, are somewhat technical, and require some familiarity with the formal notation and methods of argument and illustration in generative phonology as exemplified in such works as Noam Chomsky and Morris Halle, *The Sound Pattern of English* (New York: Harper & Row, 1968). All provide analytical systems for statements about metrical style in poetry ranging from Middle to Modern English. For discussion of a similar system for Old English poetry, see Morris Halle and Samuel Jay Keyser, *English Stress: Its Form, Its Growth, and Its Role in Verse* (New York: Harper & Row, 1971), pp. 147–64, and references in Section VI, 'Suggestions for further reading', of the present volume.

The theoretical approach of Morris Halle and Samuel Jay Keyser's 'The iambic pentameter' may fairly be said to have revolutionized the linguistic study of poetic meter. In this essay, Halle and Keyser abandon the traditional notion of the foot as the prime unit in favor of the ten-position metrical line, whose positions can be filled by phonetic material in accordance with specific abstract correspondence rules. Meter, for Halle and Keyser, thus is proscriptive rather than prescriptive; it is not that the iambic pentameter line must contain five iambic feet, but that it must not contain a fully stressed syllable flanked by unstressed syllables. This principle arises from the fact that 'deviations' from strict iambic pentameter in one 'foot' are not independent from deviations in another. The traditional 'exceptions' to strict iambic pentameter are exhaustively captured within the Halle-Keyser framework. Finally, the authors propose an ordered series of correspondence rules between abstract metrical pattern and actualization in phonetic form which, because each subsumes the generalizations of an earlier role, provide an index of metrical tension, a concept which is crucial to all studies of poetic meter.

In 'Stress, syntax and meter', Paul Kiparsky argues that the Halle-Keyser theory of meter, in insisting that the Stress Maximum (a stressed syllable flanked by unstressed syllables) can be only the greatest stress above zero in each word, returns to the traditional binary-stress problem in traditional meter, in which a two-stress system is imposed upon the phonetic material of English, which has more than two levels of linguistically assigned stress. The most important constraints on meter, Kiparsky suggests, do not involve stress, but the grammatical structure of the verse. Kiparsky thus abandons the Stress Maximum principle, and arrays the abstract metrical pattern of each line as a stressed-unstressed sequence of (for iambic pentameter) 4141414141, together with a metrical tension index for the phonetic material filling each position. This scheme, he argues, enables us to account, where the Halle-Keyser system cannot, for particular occurrences of otherwise unmetrical compounds, phrasal stress, trisyllabic compounds, and other problematic areas. In particular, initially stressed bisyllabic nouns do not normally begin in odd metrical positions in a line of iambic poetry, a fact uncapturable in the Halle-Keyser framework. The Kiparsky system also makes more precise earlier studies of metrical style, and is extended to a wide range of literary periods and metrical forms in English.

Charles T. Scott, in 'Towards a formal poetics: metrical patterning in "The Windhover"', proposes that although there are some similarities between the formal metrical properties of Gerard Manley Hopkins's 'The Windhover' and those of Old English isochronous alliterative verse, the Old English principles do not govern the poem's meter. Under the Halle-Keyser theory, the poem can be shown to be underlyingly iambic in metrical form. There is, Scott argues, a second 'shape of presentation' in the poem based on rhyme as well as meter, showing it to consist, together with its title and dedication, of an iambic tetrameter octave and a sestet. He shows that the breakdown in the poem's iambic meter is mirrored in the poem's structure, on the word 'fall'; 'Towards a formal poetics' thus is in part an attempt to relate metrical and thematic structure in poetry.

The problematic question of the meter of the Middle English *Sir Gawain and the Green Knight* is approached by Justine T. Stillings, who shows that modern theories of meter are unable to explain *Sir Gawain*. Stillings proposes a new theory of meter in which permutations of metrical patterns are specified before, rather than after, correspondence rules between these patterns and the lexical materials that fill them. These permutations are analogous to the phrase-structure rules of transformational syntax, on Stillings's account. Each poet, for Stillings, has a unique set of metrical base rules. She asserts, contrary to Halle and Keyser, the importance of the foot in a theory of meter, and proposes and illustrates the working of the metrical base rules, together with a complexity measure and a scansion principle, for the iambic lines of *Sir Gawain*. For the long alliterative lines of the poem, Stillings argues for an interplay of the Old English tonic and the modern English syllabotonic metrical traditions. She accounts for these lines as anapestic, using, with only minor additions, the same metrical base rules as those accounting for the iambic portions of the poem.

10

The iambic pentameter

Morris Halle and Samuel Jay Keyser

> What, then, exactly is Prosody? Our English word is not carried over from the Greek word with its uncertain and various meanings, but it must have come with the French word through the scholastic Latin; and like the French term it primarily denotes the rules for the treatment of syllables in verse, whether they are to be considered as long or short, accented or unaccented, elideable or not, etc., etc. The syllables, which are the units of rhythmic speech, are by nature of so indefinite a quality and capable of such different vocal expression, that apart from the desire which every artist must feel to have his work consistent in itself, his appeal to an audience would convince him that there is no chance of his elaborate rhythms being rightly interpreted unless his treatment of syllables is understood. Rules must, therefore, arise and be agreed upon for the treatment of syllables, and this is the first indispensable office of Prosody.
>
> Robert Bridges 'A Letter to a Musician on English Prosody'

When a poet composes metrical verse, he imposes certain constraints upon his choice of words and phrases that ordinary language does not normally obey.[1] The poet and his readers may not be able to formulate explicitly the nature of the constraints that are operative in a given poem; there is little doubt, however, that neither the poet nor the experienced reader would find great difficulty in telling apart wildly unmetrical lines from lines that are straightforwardly metrical. Thus few people familiar with the canon of metrical English verse from Chaucer to Yeats would disagree with the proposition that (1b) and (1c) are lawful embodiments of the iambic pentameter, whereas (1a) is not, even though (1a) has the same number of syllables as (1b), but (1c) does not.

(1) a. Ode to the West Wind by Percy Bysshe Shelley
    b. O Wild West Wind, thou breath of Autumn's being
    c. The curfew tolls the knell of parting day

In addition, readers of verse possess the ability to categorize metrical lines as more or less complex. Thus, most readers would no doubt judge (1b) as a more complex iambic pentameter line than (1c).

We shall look upon these readily observable abilities of experienced poetry readers as crucial facts that must be accounted for by an adequate theory of prosody. A good theory, however, would be expected to do more than that; it would also help us to understand the nature of metrical verse and illuminate the relationship between a speaker's everyday linguistic competence and his ability to judge verses as metrical or unmetrical, as complex or simple. We restrict this study to the favorite meter of English poets, the iambic pentameter. The approach used here can readily be extended to other meters; see, for example, Halle, 'On Meter and Prosody,' and Halle and Keyser, *English Stress*.

We propose that the ability of readers and poets to judge verse lines as metrical or unmetrical, and as more or less complex, is due to their knowledge of certain principles of verse construction. This knowledge – much like the average speaker's knowledge of his language – is tacit rather than explicit. People when questioned may be unable to give a coherent account of the principles that they employ in making the above judgments of verse lines. It is, therefore, the task of the metrist to provide a coherent and explicit account of this knowledge, just as it is the task of the grammarian to make explicit what it is that the fluent speaker of a language knows about it.

We shall assume that this knowledge consists of two distinct parts: one concerns the abstract pattern underlying the meter; the other, the rules that relate the abstract pattern to concrete lines of verse. We regard this assumption as a working hypothesis to be justified by showing that insightful and important results can be obtained with its help.

The sequences of abstract entities that underlie the meter are symbol strings such as those in (2):

(2) a. xxxxxxxxxxxx
b. wswswswsws(w(w)) where parenthesized entities are optional.

These abstract patterns are related to concrete lines of verse by correspondence rules such as those illustrated in (3):

(3) a. Each abstract entity (x, w, s) corresponds to a single syllable.[2]
b. Stressed syllables occur in s positions only and in all s positions.[3]

We scan particular lines by establishing a correspondence between the syllables of the line and the abstract entities in the abstract pattern such as those in (2). Lines are judged metrical if such a correspondence can be established exhaustively without violating the applicable correspondence rules. In (4) we illustrate the scanning of a line from Robert Bridges's

'Testament of Beauty', a poem written in the pure syllable-counting meter defined by the abstract pattern (2a) and the correpondence rule (3a):

(4) Long had the homing bees plundered the thymy flanks
    x   x   x x x   x   x x   x x x x

In (5) we illustrate the scanning of an iambic pentameter line which is defined by the pattern (2b) and the correspondence rules (3a) and (3b). It should be noted that (3a) and (3b) together imply that an unstressed syllable must occur in each w position. We shall see below that the somewhat indirect formulation adopted here is actually required in order to characterize the full variety of stress patterns that may lawfully actualize the iambic pentameter pattern.

(5) The cúrfew tólls the knéll of párting dáy
     w s w   s   w   s w   s w   s

The characterization of the iambic pentameter that has been given here with the help of the pattern (2b) and the correspondence rules (3a) and (3b) is essentially a more formal statement of the description to be found in many of the standard treatises. Thus in Robert Bridges's important *Milton's Prosody* we are told that the normal iambic pentameter line can be defined as

(6) a decasyllabic line on a disyllabic basis and in rising rhythm (i.e. with accents or stresses on the alternate even syllables); and the disyllabic units may be called *feet*. (p. 1)

We discuss the question of feet below (p. 210). At this point we wish only to note that the normal iambic line defined by (6) – or equivalently by (2b), (3a), and (3b) – does not characterize (1b) or any of a huge number of lines that appear commonly in iambic pentameter verses, e.g.,

(7) As ook, firre, birch, aspe, alder, holm, popler,
Wylugh, elm, plane, assh, box, chasteyn, lynde, laurer,
Mapul, thorn, bech, hasel, ew, whippeltree—
(Chaucer, Knight's Tale, ll. 2921–3)

(8) Batter my heart, three-person'd God, for you
As yet but knock, breathe, shine, and seek to mend;
That I may rise, and stand, o'erthrow me, and bend
Your force to break, blow, burn, and make me new
(Donne, 'Holy Sonnet 14')

(9) O Wild West Wind, thou breath of Autumn's being
Thou from whose unseen presence the leaves dead
Are driven like ghosts from an enchanter fleeing, ...
(Shelley, 'Ode to the West Wind')

(10) Speech after long silence; it is right,
　　　All other lovers being estranged or dead,...
　　　　　　(Yeats, 'After Long Silence')

The existence of such lines has not escaped the attention of Bridges or of any other serious student of prosody. In fact, immediately below the definition (6) Bridges notes that in Milton one may find three types of exception to the norm:

1. Exceptions to the number of syllables being ten,
2. Exceptions to the number of stresses being five,
3. Exceptions in the position of the stresses.

In other words, each of the three properties of the line that are specifically regulated in the definition (6) is violated on some occasion in the iambic pentameter of Milton's *Paradise Lost*.

To account for these exceptions Bridges and many other metrists supplement the definition of the norm with a list of allowable deviations, which commonly includes the items below:

(11) 1. unstressed foot (pyrrhic)
　　 2. heavy foot (spondee)
　　 3. initial foot inverted (trochee)
　　 4. verse-medial foot inverted (trochee)
　　 5. extra slack syllable inserted verse-medially
　　 6. dropping of verse-initial slack syllable (headless)

We shall refer to the account based on the norm (6) and the allowable deviations (11) as the standard theory of the iambic pentameter. We examine next the lines in (7)–(10) in order to illustrate the functioning of the standard theory.

The lines from Chaucer (7) are metrical by a liberal invocation of allowable deviation (11.2), for heavy feet abound in (7). Moreover, there is an initial trochee (11.3) in the last two lines, and an extra slack syllable (11.5) in the second line.

The first line of Donne's Sonnet (8) has an initial trochee (11.3) as well as a verse-medial heavy foot (11.2) in the phrase *three-person'd God*. The second line contains a spondee (11.2), as does the fourth line; whereas the third line has an initial pyrrhic foot (11.1) and an extra slack syllable (11.5) *me and*.

The first line of Shelley's poem (9) exhibits two spondees (11.2). The second line contains an initial trochee (11.3) and the pyrrhic foot (11.1) *-ence the*, and a verse final spondee (11.2). The third line has an extra slack syllable *en* in *driven* (11.5) and a pyrrhic (11.1).

In the Yeats verses (10) the first line is headless (11.6) and contains one verse-medial spondee (11.2) and a pyrrhic foot (11.1). The second line begins with a spondee (11.2) and includes an extra slack syllable in *being* (11.5).⁴

Although the standard theory consisting of the abstract pattern (2b), the correspondence rules (3), and the list of allowable deviations (11) correctly establishes the lines in (7)–(10) as metrical, it has a number of inadequacies that suggest rather fundamental revisions. Consider first the line (1a) which we have been using as our prime example of an unmetrical line:

Óde to the West Wínd by Pércy Býsshe Shélley.

The line contains an inverted first foot (11.3), a heavy foot (11.2), and two verse-medial trochaic substitutions (11.4). Since all these are admissible deviations, the line must be judged metrical by the standard theory. But this surely is an unacceptable consequence.

The difficulty arises from the fact that the standard theory expresses allowable deviations in terms of feet. (In fact, it is only in this domain that the entity *foot* plays a significant role.) Implicit in this view is the notion that deviations in one foot are independent of deviations in adjoining feet. Deviations in one foot, however, are not independent of deviations in adjoining feet. Thus the line just scanned was unmetrical because it had two consecutive trochaic feet, and such lines are ruled out in iambic meters. It is, of course, possible to modify (11.4) so as to take account of this possibility. But if adjoining feet are not independent, there is a serious question as to the sense of setting up feet as entities intermediate between the line and the weak and strong positions that constitute the line. We shall propose below an account that does not make use of the concept *foot*, and we shall attempt to show that such an account is superior to the standard theory even where the latter is patched up to handle cases like the one just discussed.

We have already noted that an important shortcoming of the standard theory is that it deals with allowable deviations by means of a list, thus implying that there is nothing in common among the allowable deviations, for in the standard theory there are no qualifications for membership in this list. By characterizing the allowable deviations with the help of a list, the standard theory renders itself incapable of explaining certain facts about English verse which an adequate theory would be expected to explain. It was noted many years ago by Jespersen (p. 262) that whereas an iambic line could tolerate a trochee in the first two syllables,⁵ a trochaic line could not tolerate an analogous iambic substitution in the first two syllables. He cites the following lines from Longfellow:

(12) Tell me not in mournful numbers
Life is but an empty dream

and observes that the second line may not be replaced by:

(13) A life's but an empty dream

There is no explanation for this phenomenon in the standard theory.

There is a further systematic correlation which is suggested by Jespersen's observation. If iambic verse permits the dropping of an initial slack syllable (see the first line of (10)), trochaic verse admits of an extrametrical slack syllable at the beginning of a line. The following trochaic couplet is illustrative:

(14) All the buds and bells of May
From dewy sward or thorny spray

(Keats, 'Fancy')

Indeed, if one did not know that 'Fancy' was written in trochaic meter the above couplet would be metrically ambiguous since it can easily have occurred in an iambic tetrameter poem. This second correlation between iambic and trochaic verse also remains unexplained in the standard theory.

Thirdly, Jespersen (p. 255) notes that major syntactic breaks – what he refers to as pauses – appear to play an important role in the metrical behavior of a line. This break is commonly indicated orthographically by a comma, semi-colon, colon, or period. It is noteworthy that two of the categories on the allowable deviation list are commonly associated with major syntactic breaks. These two are internal trochaic substitution, which often occurs after a major syntactic break (see 28c–d), and the heavy foot, which is composed of two positions separated by a major syntactic break (see (7)). Once again a deeper generalization is hinted at here which the standard theory does not capture.

To meet the objections just sketched we propose to replace the standard theory by the account below:

(15) a. *Abstract metrical pattern* (cf. (2b))
*(w)swswswsws(x)(x)
where each x position may only be occupied by an unstressed syllable and where elements enclosed in parentheses may be omitted.
b. *Correspondence rules* (cf. (3))
(i) A position (s or w) corresponds to either a single syllable, or a sonorant sequence incorporating at most two vowels (immediately adjoining to one another, or separated by a sonorant consonant).
Definition: When a stressed syllable is located between two unstressed syllables in the same syntactic constituent within a line of verse, this syllable is called a *stress maximum*.

(ii) stressed syllables occur in s positions and in all s positions;
or
stressed syllables occur only in s positions, but not necessarily in all s positions;
or
stress maxima occur only in s positions, but not necessarily in all s positions.[6]

The order of alternatives of the correspondence rules is significant. Each earlier alternative is subsumed by each later alternative and the later alternatives can be viewed as enlarging the class of lines which are deemed metrical. For example, in (15bi) the first alternative allows only ten- to twelve-syllable lines to realize the abstract metric pattern whereas the second alternative increases to twenty the number of syllables in lines which realize the abstract metrical pattern. At first sight the correspondence rules given here with their several alternatives may appear to differ but little from the list of allowable deviations incorporated in the standard theory. This, however, disregards the very important fact that while in the standard theory there is no limitation as to what is to be included in the lists, the alternative statements of the revised theory are subject to the limitation that later statements must subsume – and hence be generalizations of – earlier statements. In addition, we propose that the order of statements in the correspondence rules reflects the complexity of a line. The order is, therefore, our formal device for capturing the important concept of tension. The intuitive basis for this is reasonably straightforward. If the means whereby a given abstract pattern is actualized are narrowly restricted, the pattern is readily perceived as being present in the data. On the other hand, when the means whereby a pattern is actualized are allowed to be of a great variety, it becomes correspondingly difficult to discern that the pattern is encoded in a given sequence of words. Thus no one can miss the iambic pentameter pattern in

The cúrfew tólls the knéll of párting dáy

whereas it takes considerable sophistication to see that the same pattern is present in Donne's line

Yet deárly I lóve you and would be lovéd fáin

This increased difficulty in perception of the pattern which results from utilizing more complex correspondence rules explains also why there are no lines in which all and only the most complex correspondence rules are utilized. Such lines exceed the threshold of the reader's ability to perceive the pattern. We return to questions of this type in the last part of the paper.

To begin our discussion of the revised theory let us simply see how the theory permits a line to be scanned. The procedure is as follows: in each line we first establish position occupancy by numbering the different syllables in the line from left to right.[7] If the number is ten, a one-to-one occupancy of positions by syllables is assumed, in accordance with the first alternative of (15bi). If the number is one less than ten, a check is made to determine if a one-to-one syllable-to-position assignment can be made by assuming a headless line. If the number of syllables is more than ten, a check is made to determine whether the line contains any extra-metrical syllables, or whether two adjacent syllables may be assigned to a single position in accordance with the second alternative of (15bi). (See also below p. 215.)

Having established the syllable-to-position assignments, we next locate stressed and unstressed syllables in the line. We then check to see if the location of stressed and unstressed syllables satisfies one of the three alternatives of (15bii). We begin by checking the first alternative and underlining all positions in which this alternative is not satisfied; i.e. we underline each position where an s is occupied by an unstressed syllable or a w by a stressed syllable. Next we examine the line by means of the second alternative of (15bii) and underline all positions where it is violated; i.e. a w occupied by a stressed syllable now receives a double underline. Finally, we check out the third alternative; if any position violates, this alternative – i.e. if any w is occupied by a stress maximum – the line is judged unmetrical. Below we illustrate the procedure just outlined:

(16) The cúrfew tólls the knéll of párting dáy
     w s w   s   w   s w s w   s

This line satisfies in its entirety the first alternative of both (15bi) and (15bii).

(17) And léaves the wórld to dárkness and to mé
     w s   w s   w s   w <u>s</u>   w s

In line (17) the fourth s violates the first but not the second alternative of (15bii).

(18) <u>Bátter</u> my héart, <u>thrée</u>-pérson'd Gód, for yóu
     w s   w s   w s w   s   w   s

In (18) the first s violates the first alternative of (15bii) but not the second, and the first and third w violate the second alternative, but are allowed by the third alternative. An example of cases where all three alternatives are violated is provided by the triply underlined and barred position in the unmetrical line (19a).

(19a) Óde to the Wést Wínd by Pércy Býsshe Shelley[8]
      W S W S   W   S W S W   S W

The revised theory provides a great deal of freedom within the iambic pattern while at the same time providing sufficient constraints to make the art form an interesting one for the poet to work in. It is for this reason that when one finds a poet moving outside of the constraints of the meter, one is tempted to search for some aesthetic reason for his doing so. Consider, in this regard, the following opening line from a sonnet by Keats:

(19b) Hów many bárds gíld the lápses of tíme
       W   S W S   W   S W   S W S

This line is unmetrical since it contains a stress maximum in the fourth w position in violation of the last alternative of (15bii). However, it seems quite clear that the poet is purposely moving outside of the meter in order to caricature metrically the sense of the line. The line is literally what it speaks of figuratively, a 'lapse of time'. This metrical joke requires that the line be treated as unmetrical.

Returning to metrical lines, we note Donne's line (20) as an instance where later alternatives of both (15bi) and (15bii) apply;

(20) Yet dearlý I lóve you and wóuld be lovèd fáin
     W   S   W S   W   S   W S W S

The second and third w in (20) violate the first alternative of (15bi) but not the second, while the third s violates the first but not the second alternative of (15bii). Note that the assignment of two syllables to a single position has to be done in the way shown. If different syllables were to be assigned to a single position the line would be unmetrical because stress maxima would occupy w positions.

The assignment of syllables to positions is, of course, a strictly metrical assignment. It does not imply that the syllables assigned to a single position should be slurred or elided when the verse is recited. The correspondence rules are not instructions for poetry recitations. They are rather abstract principles of verse construction whose effect on the sound of the recital verse is much more indirect.

It is obvious that the second alternative of (15bi) subsumes the first alternative as a special case. Poets appear to differ a great deal as to the precise extension of the second alternative. For example, Chaucer not only

The iambic pentameter 215

makes use of elision, but allows for monosyllabic words to be assigned to a single position along with an adjacent syllable under certain special conditions.[9] Other poets seem to modify elision as defined in (15bi) by allowing it to operate on two vowels separated by an optional fricative consonant (s, f, v, etc.) as well as across an optional sonorant.[10] Still other poets allow for an extra-metrical syllable internally before a major syntactic break. Examples of the latter are:

(21) And as I past I worsh<u>ipt</u>: if those you seek

(Milton, *Comus*, l. 302)

From mine own know<u>ledge</u>. As nearly as I may

(Shakespeare, *Ant.* 11.ii.91)

and Shelley as well (see (25) below).

Whatever the usages may be from one poet to another, they can readily be accounted for by suitable extensions of the correspondence rules, and, as they appear to have only limited general theoretical interest, we shall not attempt to deal further with these rules here.

We recall that in rejecting the standard theory we stressed the fact that the list of allowable deviations (11) was not otherwise restricted, and that there was no mechanism for excluding from this list such obviously absurd items as (21):

(21) 1 Insertion of a parenthetic phrase in a line
     2 Trochaic foot followed by a dactyl
     3 Elision of exactly three syllables verse finally.

We must now show that the allowed deviations of the standard theory (11) are in fact subsumed by the various alternatives of the revised theory advanced here, and that it excludes the absurdities collected in (21).

That the revised theory exludes (21) is really unnecessary to demonstrate in detail since there is no way in which even the last (i.e. most general) alternatives of (15bi) and (15bii) can be stretched so as to include (21). It is equally self-evident that (11.5) which allows an extra slack syllable in the line and (11.6) which admits headless lines are included by the revised theory. The latter is specifically allowed by (15a), where the first w is marked as optional and parenthesized. It ought to be noted here that the omission of the line-initial w contributes to the complexity of the line, whereas the omission of the line-final, extra-metrical syllable leaves the complexity of the line unaffected. We have reflected this difference between the two parenthesized sub-sequences by supplying an asterisk to he first parentheses in (15a). We have, however, at this point no explanation for this difference. Examples of headless lines in iambic pentameter are given in (23):

(23) a. – Twénty boókes clád in blák or reéd –
*(w)   s   w   s   w   s   w   s   w   s

(Chaucer, *CT* Prol., 1.294)

b. – Spéech after lóng sílence; it is ríght
*(w)   s   w s   w   s w   s w s

(Yeats)

Extra slack syllables in the line (11.5) are allowed by the later alternatives of (15bi), as we have already seen in our discussion of (20) above. The third line of (8), repeated here as (24), is an additional example:

(24) That Í may ríse and stánd, o'erthrów me and bénd
     w s   w   s   w   s   w   s   w   s

Turning now to the remaining allowable deviations, we recall that the unstressed foot (11.1), has already been illustrated in (17) above. The third line of (9), repeated here as (25), offers an additional example:

(25) Are dríven, like ghósts from an enchánter fleéing
     w   s   w   s   w s   w   s   w s   w

Here the third s contains an unstressed syllable, a realization allowed by the second alternative of (15bii). (For the assignment of *driven* to a single position, see above p. 215.)

The next allowable deviation (11.2), the heavy foot (spondee), requires invocation of the last alternative of (15bii). We have already invoked it in our discussion of (18) above. Notice, however, that it is required to accommodate all of the lines of (7), the second of which is repeated here by way of illustration:

(26) Wýlugh, élm, pláne, ássh, bóx, chásteyn, lýnde, laurér
     w   s   w   s   w   s w   s   w   s

In (26) the first w violates the first alternative of (15bi) and both the first and second alternatives of (15bii). The second and third w's violate the first two alternatives of (15bii) but are allowed by the last alternative.

The two final allowable deviations of the standard theory concern inverted feet; by (11.3) these are allowed verse-initially, by (11.4) they are allowed verse-medially. We have shown in (18) above how examples of the former type would be scanned by the revised theory. An additional example of a line beginning with an inverted foot is scanned in (27).

(27) Sı́lent upon a peak in Dárien   (Keats)
    ‾w‾s   w s   w s   w   s ‾w‾s

Verse-medially inverted feet may appear in two distinct positions, after stressed syllables (cf. (28 a–b)) and after a major syntactic boundary (cf. (28 c–d)).

(28) a. The Mı́llere was a stóut cárl for the nónes (A. Prol. 1. 545)

   b. The coúrse of trúe lóve never díd rún smóoth (*MND* 1.i.134)

   c. Appeáre in pérson hére in Coúrt. Sı́lence. (*WT* 111.i.10)
      w   s   w   s   w   s   w   s ‾w‾s

   d. Frı́ends, Rómans, coúntrymen, lénd me your eárs.
      w   s   w   s   w s   w   s w   s

(*JC* 111.ii.78)

The occurrence of two stressed syllables back to back as in *stout carl* and *true love* may correspond to any verse internal w s or s w sequence by virtue of the last alternative of (15b). To illustrate this we scan (28a) and 28b) below:

(28) a. The Mı́llere was a stóut cárl for the nónes
        w   s‾w‾   s‾w‾s   ‾w‾ s   w s w

   b. The coúrse of trúe lóve never díd rún smóoth
      w s   w s   w ‾s‾w‾ s   w ‾s‾w‾   s

Instances of two stressed syllables corresponding to a w s sequence were scanned in (18), (23b) and (26) above.

It is an interesting fact that inverted feet appear only under the following three conditions in an iambic pentameter line; verse initially, after a stressed syllable (see (18)), and after a major syntactic boundary (see p. 211 above), across which the stress subordination rules of English do not operate. In the standard theory this is just another fact, to be noted down, of course, but not to be endowed with any special significance. In the revised theory, on the other hand, these three environments are the environments where a stressed syllable will not constitute a stress maximum and hence where a stressed syllable may occupy a w position. Note, in particular, that line (28d) would be unmetrical, were there no major syntactic boundary before *lend*. Thus, is the light of the revised theory, the restriction of inverted feet to the above three environments is anything but a curious coincidence; it rather reflects a significant property of the meter. It is one of the reasons for our assertion that the revised theory is more powerful than, and hence to be preferred over the standard theory.

There is yet another odd fact noted by metrists that finds a ready explanation in the light of the revised theory, but is just a curiosity from the point of view of the standard theory. This is an asymmetry cited above between trochaic and iambic lines with regard to the admissibility of inverted feet in verse-initial position (see pp. 210–11 above.) The abstract metrical pattern for a trochaic line must be of the form.

(29) swswsws(w)

and its correspondence rules, those of (15b). If one allows an inverted foot (i.e. an iamb) at the beginning of a trochaic line, one places a stress maximum in a w position, thereby violating the last alternative of (15bii). We illustrate this with the help of the line concocted by Jespersen on the model of Longfellow's 'Psalm of Life':

(30) A life's but an empty dream
     s   w   s w s   w   s

Here the second syllable violates all three of the alternatives of (15bii), and hence renders the line unmetrical. As we have seen above the same does not happen when a trochee is substituted for the first iamb in an iambic line. Such lines (see (28a)) are allowed by the third alternative of (15bii) and are therefore perfectly metrical lines.

Notice also that the introduction of an initial extrametrical syllable will have no effect on a trochaic line, but its inclusion in an iambic line will be limited to lines without inverted first feet since, otherwise, a stress maximum will be realized in a w position in violation of the last alternatives of (15bii).[11]

Once again the revised theory shows certain facts to be lawful consequences which are deducible from certain other facts, and thus provides a more adequate explanation for the phenomena than the standard theory.

The final argument in favor of the revised theory is that, as noted above, it is relatively easy to reconstruct the notion of metrical complexity or tension within the revised theory. In the standard theory it is possible to attribute increasing complexity to each succeeding item in the list of allowable deviations. This procedure, however, is quite *ad hoc*. There is no independent justification for ordering the allowable deviations as in (11); hence nothing can be deduced from that order. This does not hold for the order of the alternatives in the correspondence rules (15b): here the alternatives are ordered in increasing generality, beginning with the least general and ending with the most general. As already remarked above, the degree of difficulty that a reader will experience in discerning the abstract metrical pattern in a line can be plausibly assumed to be directly related to the richness and variety of the means that can be employed in actualizing the pattern. It should follow, therefore, that when a greater variety of correspondences is employed, the pattern is more difficult to perceive. The number of underlines in the different lines scanned in accordance with our procedure can then be taken as a measure of the complexity of the line. As demonstrated above this measure works properly in extreme cases. Whether it works properly in all cases cannot be determined at this stage in the progress of our science. Questions can naturally be raised about our decision to assign equal complexity to later alternatives regardless of source. It is perfectly conceivable that the increase in complexity due to the need to invoke the third rather than the second alternative of the correspondence rule (15bii) should be a fraction of that resulting from the invocation of the second alternative of (15bi). Such questions, however, can be answered only when a massive body of verse has been subjected to the type of analysis proposed. The best that can be done at this point is to list in order of increasing complexity all the lines that have been analyzed above so as to show that the judgments made by our scheme are not totally implausible.[12]

(31)
	Complexity of
1. The curfew tolls the knell of parting day (16)	0
2. Twenty bookes clad in blak or reed (23a)	1
3. And leaves the world to darkness and to me (17)	2
4. Are driven like ghosts from an enchanter fleeing (25)	2
5. Yet dearly I love you and would be loved fain (20)	3
6. Appears in person here in Court. Silence (28b)	3
7. The Millere was a stout carl for the nones (27a)	4
8. Speech after long silence; it is right (23b)	5
9. Silent upon a peak in Darien (28a)	5
10. Batter my heart, three-person'd God, for you (18)	5
11. Friends, Romans, countrymen, lend me your ears (28c)	6
12. Wylugh, elm, plane, assh, box, chasteyn, lynde, laurer (26)	7

It will be observed that the lines in (31) vary in complexity from zero to seven. Lines with considerably greater complexity can be readily invented (cf. (32) with the complexity of (17)), but such lines do not appear to be attested in the poets. The theory, thus, allows for a greater variety of line than anyone ever found use for. When faced with such a fact, one may attempt to revise the theory so as to restrict the number of unattested cases that are allowed by the theory. Alternatively one may attempt to explain the unattested cases in some plausible fashion leaving the theory intact. Since we are unable at this point to come up with a significant improvement over the revised theory, we must look for an explanation for the observed facts within the theory. If it is granted that the complexity of a line is directly related to the difficulty that the line in question poses for the reader, and if one further supposes that poets normally do not wish to turn their poems into difficult crossword puzzles the artistry of which cannot be appreciated without laborious pencil and paper calculations, then it is not unreasonable to assume further that there is an upper bound on the complexity that a given poet would ever wish to impose on his lines. A supposition of this sort is perfectly natural in the case of syntax: while clearly there is no upper bound on the number of nouns that can be conjoined in a noun phrase, it would surprise no one to learn that a perusal of the collected works of all American novelists from Hawthorne to Henry James did not reveal a single conjoined noun phrase composed of more than twenty-seven (or, for that matter, none of more than sixty-nine) nouns.[13]

The case of the iambic pentameter does not appear to us so dissimilar as to rule out an analogous explanation for the absence of lines such as (32) in verses written in iambic pentameter.[14]

(32) bíllows, bíllows, seréne mírror of the maríne bóroughs, remóte

    W   S   W   S   W   S   W   S

wíllows

W S

Notes

1 This essay is a shortened version of a part of a larger study dealing with English metrics. The full study constitutes the third chapter of Halle and Keyser, *English Stress: Its Form, Its Growth, and Its Role in Verse* (Harper & Row, 1971). (Permission to reproduce material from this book granted by publisher.) This work was supported in part by National Institute of Mental Health Grant No. MH-13390-02 and in part by National Science Foundation Grant No. GS-2005 at Brandeis University. We wish to acknowledge the extremely helpful comments of Edward Weismiller and W. K. Wimsatt. We are indebted to them for many improvements in the exposition which follows; responsibility for its

imperfections is, of course, our own. For full reference for all works cited in these notes, see the selected bibliography at the end.

2 We use the term 'syllable' here as the equivalent of 'sequence of speech sounds consisting of one syllabic sound ('vowel') preceded and followed by any number of consecutive nonsyllabic sounds ('consonants').' In particular, we do not take a position on the vexing question of whether or not utterances can be unambiguously segmented into syllables.

3 By stressed syllable we mean here the syllable that has the main stress in the word; all other syllables in the word are subsumed under the term 'unstressed'. Thus in the word *instrumentality*, the antepenult syllable will be viewed as 'stressed' and all other syllables lumped together as 'unstressed'. We regret this imprecise language, but we see no ready way out of this terminological embarrassment.

4 An example of a verse medial inverted foot (11.4) can be found in (28).

5 See W. K. Wimsatt (in Thomas A. Sebeok, *Style in Language*): '... it is not at all clear to me why the trochaic substitution in the first foot is so acceptable in the iambic line. I'm never able to make up my mind whether it is because it just happened, as Mr Ransom, I think, suggests, sort of got established, or whether there is some peculiar reason' (p. 206).

6 In previous studies (see, e.g., Halle and Keyser, 'Chaucer and the study of prosody', we proposed that a stress maximum is constituted by a stressed syllable located between two syllables with lesser stress. The definition of stress maximum given here limits more severely the syllables that can be stress maxima. Since in metrical lines, stress maxima may *not* correspond to w positions, an immediate consequence of the more restrictive definition of the stress maximum is to admit as metrical certain lines that previously had been judged as unmetrical; e.g.,

from Chaucer:
1. 'With this quyksilver, shortly for to sayn' (C.Y., l. 1111); cf. 'for quyksilver, that we it hadde anon' (C.Y., l. 1103);
2. 'He was short-sholdered, brood, a thikke knarre' (A. Prol., l. 549);
3. 'Ther nas quyk-silver, lytarge, ne brymstoon' (A. Prol., l. 629);

from Spenser:
4. 'Ne let house-fyres, nor lightnings helplesse harmes' (Epithalamion xix. 7);

from John Donne:
5. 'Askt not of rootes, nor of cock-sparrows, leave' ('Progress of the Soule', l. 217);
6. 'Th'hydroptique drunkard, and night-scouting thiefe' ('Holy Sonnet III', l. 9).

Though lines of this kind are clearly unusual, they do occur and thereby provide justification for 'weakening' the theory in the manner outlined here. The need for a revision of the definition of the stress maximum given in Halle and Keyser, 'Chaucer and the study of prosody', was noted independently by J. Meadors, 'On defining the Stress Maximum'. Note, finally, that 'unstressed' in (15a) means literally 'without stress'. This may not be invariant from one poet to another but seems correct for Chaucer and the major poets of the Renaissance.

7 It is important to keep in mind that extra-metrical syllables, both in verse initial and verse final position, are not included in the numbering.

8 Edward R. Weismiller (in a personal letter) has pointed out that lines which exhibit a violation of our rules do, in fact, occur in the work of many

Renaissance poets; for example, in the metrically experimental poet Sidney's *Astrophel and Stella*:

With swórd of wít, gíving wounds of dispráise   (10.10)
 w   s   w   s   w s   w   s   w   s

It is Weismiller's belief that such lines are in imitation of an Italian model, the so-called 'double trochee'. Since we have no relevant statistical studies for the major poets of the Renaissance, we are not in a position to judge how common lines like the above are. A reading of the first thousand lines of the metrically conservative poet Spenser's *Faerie Queene* yielded three clear examples: 1.i.12.9, 1.ii.36.4, 1.iii.7.9, which suggests that the so-called 'double trochee' was far from common. They are, in any case, unmetrical in terms of (15) and, if Weismiller's contention is correct, we should expect few lines of this type to occur in poets and in periods known not to be influenced by the Italian model. For a fuller discussion of the term metricality see Halle and Keyser, 'Illustration and Defense of a Theory of the Iambic Pentameter'.

9 For a discussion of Chaucer's rule in some detail see Halle and Keyser, 'Chaucer and the study of prosody', and for a criticism of the rule as given there see Hascall, 'Some contributions to the Halle-Keyser theory of prosody'. Hascall's modification is based upon the observation that in the overwhelming number of instances in which a monosyllabic word is assigned with another syllable to a single position, the monosyllabic word is not a member of a major lexical category (i.e. not an adjective, noun, adverb, verb). This seems to us a correct observation and requires modification of the rule along the lines specified by Hascall.

10 Extensions of the class of consonants which participate in elision are suggested in Hascall and in Freeman, 'On the primes of metrical style'. It is one of the contributions of Bridges, *Milton's Prosody*, that the content of this rule actually changes in Milton between *Paradise Lost* and *Samson Agonistes*.

11 Notice that the occurrence of an extra-metrical syllable in verse-initial position in a trochaic line will have the same effect as a verse final extra-metrical syllable in an iambic line; namely, both may turn a main stress into a stress maximum. This suggests that stress maxima in these positions are not crucial to the meter, which would then be a purely internal matter. If this is so, the last position of an iambic line and the first position of a trochaic line would have to be given a rather different theoretical status. Bridges was aware of this: 'Tyrwhitt is quoted as saying that one of the indispensable conditions of English blank verse was that the last syllable should be strongly accented. The truth seems to be that its metrical position in a manner exonerates it from requiring any accent. – Whether the "last foot" may be inverted is another question. – A weak syllable can very well hold its own in this tenth place, and the last essential accent of the verse may be that of the "fourth foot"' (p. 39).

12 Recent studies (see Beaver, 'A grammar of prosody' and Freeman, 'On the primes of metrical styles') have dealt with the question of metrical style in terms other than line complexity. They have taken into account such things as the number and position of stress maxima, the number and position of unactualized s positions, and so forth. For example, in a discussion of the following lines from Pope's 'An Essay on Criticism':

1. When Ajax strives some rock's vast weight to throw
2. The line too labours, and the words move slow.

Freeman notes that the heavy stresses back to back contribute to the overall impression of slowness: 'Stress neutralization is at work even more clearly in another of Pope's deliberately and exaggeratedly "slow" lines:

 And tén lów words oft crèep in one dull line
 w s w s w s ws w s

The line is perfectly metrical, but the monosyllabic Adjective-Noun and Adverb-Verb combinations create so much stress neutralization that no stress maxima, or at most one, are actualized in the line' (p. 78).

It is perhaps worth noting that while the large number of heavy stresses back to back in this line is in part responsible for the impression of slowness, it is not in itself a sufficient condition. Thus, we can paraphrase this line by a simple permutation and while the complexity level remains the same, the line seems impressionistically quite different:

 And ten low words in one dull line oft creep.

Conversely, note that (18) above can be made to seem much slower by performing a similar inversion which leaves the complexity level unchanged:

 Batter my heart, for you, three-person'd God.

The precise relationship to a theory of metrical style of such factors as line complexity and the arrangement of syntactic structures within the line remains to be explored. The most that can be said at this juncture is that the revised theory, we hope, provides an adequate tool for such explorations.

13 We have tried to demonstrate the existence of an inverse relation between metrical complexity of a verse type and the frequency of this type by studying the statistics of different verse types in *Beowulf*; see Halle and Keyser, *English Stress*, pp. 153–5.

14 In May 1970 (see References), two articles appeared: Wimsatt: 'The Rule and the Norm', and Magnuson and Ryder, 'The Study of English Prosody', which take issue with the theory of prosody in Halle and Keyser, 'Chaucer and the study of prosody' and Keyser, 'The linguistic basis of English prosody'. The theory presented above anticipates in certain instances the objections raised. A more detailed reaction to these critics, which touches also upon a number of points not treated above, appears in Halle and Keyser, 'Illustration and defense'.

References

Beaver, Joseph C. 'A grammar of prosody'. *College English*, 29 (1968), 310–21.
Bridges, Robert. *Milton's Prosody*. Oxford: Clarendon, 1921.
—— 'A letter to a musician on English prosody'. Rpt. Gross (see below), pp. 86–101.
Freeman, Donald C. 'On the primes of metrical style'. *Language and Style*, 1 (1968), 63–101.
Gross, Harvey S., ed. *The Structure of Verse: Modern Essays on Prosody*. Greenwich, Conn.: Fawcett, 1966.
Halle, Morris, 'On meter and prosody'. In *Progress in Linguistics*. Eds. Manfred Bierwisch and Karl Erich Heidolph. The Hague: Mouton, 1970. Pp. 64–80.

—— and S. Jay Keyser. 'Chaucer and the study of prosody'. *College English*, 28 (1966), 187–219.

—— and S. Jay Keyser. *English Stress: Its Form, Its Growth, and Its Role in Verse.* New York: Harper & Row, 1971.

Hascall, Dudley. 'Some contributions to the Halle-Keyser theory of prosody'. *College English*, 30 (1969), 357–65.

Jespersen, Otto. 'Notes on meter'. *Linguistica.* Copenhagen: Levin & Munksgaard, 1933.

Keyser, S. Jay. 'The linguistic basis of English prosody'. In *Modern Studies in English: Readings in Transformational Grammar.* Ed. David Reibel and Sanford A. Schane. Englewood Cliffs, N.J.: Prentice-Hall, 1969.

—— and Morris Halle. 'Illustration and defense of a theory of the iambic pentameter'. *College English*, 33 (1971), 154–76.

Magnuson, Karl, and Frank G. Ryder. 'The study of English prosody: an alternative proposal'. *College English*, 31 (1970), 789–820.

Meadors, James. 'On defining the Stress Maximum'. MIT, 1969. Unpub. ms.

Sebeok, Thomas A., ed. *Style in Language.* Cambridge: MIT Press, 1960.

Weismiller, Edward. 'The "dry" and "rugged" verse'. In *The Lyric and Dramatic Milton.* Ed. Joseph H. Summers. New York: Columbia Univ. Press, 1965. Pp. 115–52.

Wimsatt, W. K. 'The rule and the norm: Halle and Keyser on Chaucer's meter'. *College English*, 31 (1970), 774–88.

11

Stress, syntax and meter*

Paul Kiparsky

Most theories of English metrics consider verse simply from the phonological side, as arrangements of syllables with varying degrees of stress, possibly with certain intervening pauses. They differ among themselves mainly in how they tackle the problem of reducing the huge variety of stress patterns in English to the relatively few and simple meters that they manifest.

Traditionally, English verse is analysed by dividing it into feet and classifying the feet into types called 'trochees', 'iambs', 'spondees' etc., where each of these types represents some arrangement of the two basic elements 'stressed syllable' and 'unstressed syllable'. This is not so illuminating as the corresponding approach in Greek or Latin. In those languages, the basis of versification is the distinction between long and short syllables, which really is binary – so that there are, e.g., only four possible types of two-syllable feet, and terms like 'trochee' have a well-defined meaning. But more than two degrees of stress are demonstrably significant in English verse. As a result, the traditional approach is incapable of making the necessary basic distinctions. For example, is *mídnìght* a spondee or a trochee? Both interpretations can be encountered in the scansions of the metrical literature. But neither is adequate, for the fact is that a word with this stress pattern

---

*A more satisfactory treatment of English metrics than presented here has since been worked out on the basis of a somewhat different theory of stress. See the author's 'Rhythmic Structure of English Verse', *Linguistic Inquiry* 8.189–247 (1977).

behaves quite differently from either clear spondees like $\overset{2}{dark}$ $\overset{1}{night}$ or clear trochees like $\overset{1}{rabbit}$. For such reasons, a theory modeled directly on the metrics of classical languages cannot even get off the ground in English.

I do not mean to deny that the venerable classification of feet into trochees, iambs etc. can be useful for certain purposes. My objections are rather that it is not well defined for English speech rhythms; and that it would not, even if made precise, be a fine enough classification of them for metrical purposes. In this essay, I shall mainly use the traditional terms to classify the underlying metrical patterns in the usual way (as in the terms 'iambic pentameter', 'trochaic verse'), for which they are entirely adequate. When no confusion can result, I shall also sometimes speak loosely of 'trochaic feet' and the like, in reference to particular pieces of verse.

It is in part the recognition of these shortcomings which has given rise to the tradition of 'musical' scansion (Lanier 1880) and the application of Trager–Smith or other multiple-stress systems to English metrics (Whitehall 1956, Chatman 1965). Both approaches provide notations for representing metrical structure in a way which begins to do justice to the actual rhythm of language. They have led to discerning analyses of particular poems (e.g. Frye 1957, Chatman 1956). For the most part, however, they have remained nothing more than methods of transcription. Only rarely have they been used as the basis of theories of meter that give some general account of the principles of versification. Even if we assume just two levels of stress, there are several hundred arrangements of stressed and unstressed syllables that are ordinarily encountered as instances of the iambic pentameter verse type, and also several hundred arrangements of the same length which are not. If we recognize, as we must, at least four metrically relevant degrees of stress, the figures on each side run in the hundreds of thousands. Nobody could possibly learn the distinction between metrical and unmetrical lines by memorizing the actual patterns; rather, one acquires a 'feel' for the verse in terms of some general principles. The initial task of metrical theory is just to discover these principles in particular metrical systems; at a deeper level, we can then proceed to try to explain them, and ultimately to develop a general theory of meter. But even the beginnings of this program have seldom been attempted until recently.

Among the rare exceptions in the earlier literature on metrics is Jespersen 1933, which proposed a metrical theory that takes into account the phonetic realities of English stress, but without giving up the traditional goal of discovering the principles that differentiate metrical from unmetrical verse. This project requires some new handle on the problem of stating metrical constraints. The old approach of classifying the feet and specifying their permissible combinations is not likely to work – since, with a more elaborate stress system, the number of foot types grows unmanageable (in a four-level stress system, there are sixteen possible types of disyllabic feet alone). Jespersen ingeniously tried to solve the problem by taking stress values not in absolute terms, but relative to their context: 'The pattern expected by the hearer is a sequence of ten syllables (which may be followed by an eleventh, weak syllable), arranged in such a way that the syllables occupying the even places are raised by their force above the surrounding syllables' ([1900] 1962, 653); 'the only thing required by the ear is an upward and a downward movement, a rise and a fall, an ascent and a descent, at fixed places, whereas it is of no importance whatever how great is the ascent or the descent' (1962, 654). The basic requirement, then, is to minimize 'disappointing' transitions in a line. The attractive feature of this approach is that it explains why inversion is most common after a pause: 'Here the ear is not disappointed in the first syllable: after the pause preceding the line, one does not know what general level to expect' (1962, 655).

It is doubtful whether the distinction between metrical and unmertrical lines can be drawn simply in terms of the number of 'disappointments' (and Jespersen in fact did not try to do so). Thus his example

(1) Never came poyson from so sweet a place

has two 'disappointments': a fall in the second syllable in place of the expected rise, and a rise in the third syllable instead of the expected fall – still, it is perfectly metrical. But the construct

(2) *For when came poison from so sweet flowers?

has two 'disappointments', and is unmetrical (for the basis of this unmetricality, see §2.3 below). Thus Jespersen's concept does not by itself constitute or directly lead to a metrical theory. At best, it could form an element of some metrical theory; but I shall argue below that even this is not the case.

Halle and Keyser (1966, 1971a,b) have raised the discussion to a new level by formulating a theory precise enough to make clear immediately what sort of evidence is required for its support or refutation. Their theory is also based on relative stress values; but, unlike Jespersen, they take the value of a stress to be determined by both its right and left context. They set up the abstract metrical pattern as an alternating sequence of weak and strong positions, and define a STRESS MAXIMUM as 'a fully stressed syllable [that] occurs between two unstressed syllables in the same syntactic constituent within a line of verse' (1971a, p. 169). They then propose, as the basic principle of English meters, the 'realization rule' that *stress maxima can occur only in strong positions*. I shall refer to this as the *Stress Maximum Principle*.

Among the lines that are allowed as metrical by the Stress Maximum Principle, Halle and Keyser further establish a hierarchy of metrical complexity that provides a formal reconstruction of what is sometimes referred to as the 'tension' created by the 'allowable deviations' of linguistic rhythm from the the underlying meter. Although their specific solution cannot be made to work, their idea of a hierarchy of complexity is an important advance, which I shall adopt in my own proposal below.

In some respects, however, the Halle–Keyser theory is a step backward. Their first formulation (1966) was based on the generally recognized phonetic representation of English stress as a system with multiple levels. But this resulted in so many exceptions to the Stress Maximum Principle that they were forced to revise their theory (1971a, b) – so that, in effect, it treats stress as a binary feature. In their new version, the greatest non-zero stress in each word (including members of compounds) counts as stressed for purposes of the Stress Maximum Principle, and everything else counts as unstressed. But by their definition, a stress maximum has an unstressed syllable on its right and left; it therefore follows that their theory cannot even distinguish, e.g. between the phrasal and compound stress patterns, though these are not treated at all alike in English versification. By this revision, Halle and Keyser have really returned to the binary system of stress that underlies Latin-style English metrics – and with it, to many of the inherent difficulties of that approach. We shall see (in §2.3) that certain types of metrical lines cannot be accommodated by any possible version of the Stress Maximum Principle. Its chief failing, however, as several critics have already pointed out, is that it is far too weak, and fails to rule out much that never occurs in actual poetry.

The traditional approach, as well as the new departures of Jespersen and of Halle–Keyser, are based on the assumption that meter regulates just the phonological shape of verse. This mistake is, in my judgment, the main reason for the unsatisfactory state of the field. The most important, virtually unbreakable constraints on meter in English involve the grammatical structure of the verse, notably the phrase and word units of which it is made up.

The great merit of the metrical theory proposed by Magnuson and Ryder (1970, and 1971) is to have recognized some of the role that word structure plays in meter. Their rules reflect several correct observations about the different treatment of monosyllabic and polysyllabic words. However, their observations are not general enough; consequently their metrical rules remain ad-hoc, and do not lead to any explanations.

What is more, the Magnuson–Ryder rules must be rejected simply because they rest on incorrect assumptions about the facts. Great quantities of counter-examples to them have been adduced by Halle and Keyser

1971b, to which Magnuson and Ryder have responded with a curious willingness to brand a significant part of English poetry as unmetrical. This is as if a grammarian should decide to reject an equivalent portion of English prose as ungrammatical. The analogy can be developed further: The two sources of ungrammaticality in written texts are slips of the pen, which are obviously rare in literary writing, and deliberate breaches of grammar, which always have some special expressive purpose. The situation is similar in metrics. A sound working assumption would be that a line can be taken as unmetrical only if it can plausibly be defined as either a slip or an intentional, expressive violation of meter.[1] On this view, large numbers of random metrical exceptions do not occur, except possibly in hurried compositions of inexperienced poets. In particular, they do not occur in 'experimental' poetry. Deviations in such work are always either functionally motivated breaches of the system, or else are regular within a new, less restricted system set up by the poet (though even then, part of their effect might of course be caused by the contrast with the old system). If this is correct, then students of metrics, when faced with exceptions, must either explain them or change their rules. They should neither rest their case and blame the poet, nor rest their case and challenge others to come up with a 'better theory'. In particular, since the wholesale unmetricality that Magnuson and Ryder impute to Shakespeare is too random to be expressive and too frequent to be accidental, we can only conclude that their metrical rules are incorrect.

The inordinate complexity of the Magnuson–Ryder rules is in part the result of their failure to draw the right distinction between phonology and metrics: their rules include a good bit of information that simply duplicates what is already given by the stress rules of the language. For example, they carefully specify the distinction between lexical and non-lexical categories in their metrical rules; but the metrical difference between them simply follows from the different stress assigned to them by English grammar: you do not have to be a poet to know that *boy*, but not *the*, has stress. That fact need not be included in a theory of English metrics, but can be presupposed by it. The consequences of failing to separate metrics and grammar go beyond mere redundancy. More seriously, they obscure the deep similarities between the metrical systems of languages with different phonological systems (see §3.5 below), and thus makes the general principles of metrical systems difficult, if not impossible, to discover.

The recent controversy – involving the Halle–Keyser theory, Beaver's modification of it (1971a), and the Magnuson–Ryder counter-proposal – has so far been inconclusive. At any rate, apparently none of the participants has succeeded in convincing any of the others. In the last round of debate (Halle and Keyser 1971b, Magnuson and Ryder 1971, Beaver

1971b), each of the contending views met with some strong criticism from the opposition; but the rejoinders, insofar as any were made, seemed generally unconvincing. As things now stand, both the Halle–Keyser theory (with or without Beaver's emendation) and the Magnuson–Ryder theory plainly have serious flaws. But there certainly is nothing to recommend a return to the combination of vague generalizations and aimless cataloguing of facts that was characteristic of traditional metrics. Rather, I shall try to build on the progress already achieved by formal methods in metrics. In order to do justice to the facts, however, a new theoretical approach will be required.

1. A theory of English metrics.

On one traditional view, which I follow here, *meter* is a system of correspondences between musical and linguistic rhythm. Specifically, in line with the approach to poetic form sketched in Kiparsky 1973, I take a metrical system to be characterized by four components:

(A) An inventory of *basic patterns*, each of which is some regular arrangement of a small number of phonological units. In English verse, these units are stressed and unstressed syllables. The basic pattern of the iambic pentameter, for example, is a sequence of ten alternatingly unstressed and stressed syllables. Thus the basic pattern characterizes the musical rhythm that underlies verse.

(B) A set of *metrical rules*, which take as input the basic patterns in the inventory, and generate a set of derived metrical patterns. Like the basic patterns, the derived patterns are sequences of phonological units, e.g. sequences of stressed and unstressed syllables. The derived patterns correspond to the natural rhythm of speech: thus, in English, a line is metrical if the stress pattern assigned to it by the normal stress rules of the language corresponds to a derived metrical pattern.

(C) An index of *metrical tension*, which defines *relative* metrical constraints that correspond to what is sometimes referred to as the *tension* between the abstract metrical pattern and the actual rhythm of verse, and to what Halle and Keyser and term metrical *complexity*. The index of metrical tension sets up a stylistic hierarchy among metrical lines which can also, in statistical terms, differentiate between periods or types of verse (see §§3.1–2 below).

(D) A set of *prosodic rules*, which specify HOW the derived patterns generated by the metrical rules are to be matched up with linguistic representations. This matching is not necessarily uniquely determined;

hence it is necessary to state specifically what, for metrical purposes, counts as a 'stress', what counts as a 'syllable', and so on. In so delimiting prosody from metrics, I follow usage which is well established in classical philology (Maas 1962).

1.1. In order to state our metrical rules, we need certain linguistic prerequisites. The sentences of a language are made up for WORDS, and of larger units called *phrases*. Both terms have somewhat vague meanings in ordinary usage; for our purposes we require precise definitions which pick out exactly the right linguistic units. The definitions supplied by the theory of transformational grammar turn out to meet our needs well.

The formalization of the concept 'word' has been worked out in Chomsky and Halle 1968 (§6.2), and in more detail in Selkirk 1972 (Chapter 1). It involves two rules:

> *Word boundary rule* 1 (WBR 1): The boundary ♯ is automatically inserted at the beginning and end of every string dominated by a major category, i.e., by one of the lexical categories 'noun', 'verb', 'adjective', or by a category such as 'sentence', 'noun phrase', 'verb phrase', which dominates a lexical category (Chomsky and Halle, 366).
>
> *Word boundary rule* 2 (WBR 2): In a sequence W♯]$_X$ ♯]$_Y$ Z or W $_Y$[♯ $_X$[♯Z, where Y ≠ S' [S' = the initial symbol of the grammar; I shall simply use S here – P.K.], delete the 'inner' word boundary (Selkirk, 12).

In the sentence *His friend raises sheep*, WBR 1 will give

(3) $_S$[♯ $_{NP}$[♯His $_N$[♯friend♯]$_N$ ♯]$_{NP}$ $_{VP}$[♯ $_V$[♯raises♯]$_V$ $_{NP}$[♯ $_N$[♯sheep♯]$_N$ ♯]$_{NP}$ ♯]$_{VP}$ ♯]$_S$

Applying **WBR 2** to eliminate superfluous ♯ boundaries, we get the following representation (given without brackets):

(4) ♯♯His♯friend♯♯raises♯♯sheep♯

In general, members of lexical categories – nouns (including members of compounds), adjectives, verbs, and adverbs – will be surrounded by double word boundaries (♯♯___♯♯) in the resulting surface structure; members of non-lexical categories (such as *his*, *the*, *and*, *with*) will be separated from the word or phrase with which they are in construction (usually on their right) by a single ♯ boundary. This has interesting consequences for metrics, as we shall see below (§2.5).

The division of sentences into phrases is also given by the surface syntactic structure. A phrase is everything that is dominated by one of the categories Noun Phrase, Verb Phrase, Adjective Phrase, or Prepositional

Phrase.Thus the location of phrase boundaries can be identified in surface structure by the occurrence of brackets labeled P ($_P$[ ), where P is one of the above categories.

This syntactic phrasing appears to determine, by principles which are only partially understood, the phonological phrasing of sentences, i.e. the locations of optional or obligatory intonation breaks, corresponding to caesuras in verse. It appears, as a first approximation, that intonation breaks are possible at all phrase boundaries which coincide with ♯♯, viz. at ♯] $_P$[♯ and at $_S$[♯ $_P$[♯. In what follows, I shall use ♯ $_P$[♯ to denote both cases. For example, in the sentence *John sat with the old man*,

(5) $_S$[♯ $_{NP}$[$_N$[John]$_N$ ♯]$_{NP}$ $_{VP}$[♯ $_V$[sat♯]$_V$ $_{PP}$[♯ [with] $_{NP}$[♯ [the] $_A$ [♯old♯]$_A$ $_N$[♯man]$_N$]$_{NP}$ ♯]$_{PP}$ ♯]$_{VP}$ ♯]$_S$

a break can be made between *John* and *sat*, and between *sat* and *with*. But there can be no break between *with* and *the*, or between *old* and *man*, neither of which is separated by ♯ $_P$[♯. I shall refer to an unstressed word which cannot be followed by a break as a *proclitic*, and to an unstressed word which cannot be preceded by a break as an *enclitic*. The part of a sentence between two (potential or actual) breaks is termed a (potential or actual) *phonological phrase*. Intonation breaks are of course obligatory between sentences. They are also obligatory (except in fast speech) at certain kinds of clause boundaries, which correspond to orthographical commas. I shall proceed on the assumption that versification is based on the actualization of optional intonation breaks – i.e. that sentences are divided into phonological phrases wherever possible. However, this does not mean that the same breaks must necessarily be pronounced in recitation (see below for further discussion).

The occurrence of ♯ $_P$[♯ is a sufficient condition for the occurrence of a potential break, with the proviso that the potential breaks are unlikely to be pronounced if the resulting phonological phrases are very short. Especially under conditions of hesitation or emphasis, breaks are also possible elsewhere in a sentence, e.g. *John is – a LIAR!* or *John is a – LIAR!* To what extent this happens, apart from such special conditions, is unclear.

I shall operate with four degrees of stress, as in many phonetic and 'phonemic' transcriptions (e.g. the Trager–Smith system, Jespersen). These can be obtained from the output of the Chomsky–Halle stress rules by identifying everything of degree four or less as a single weakest level. There is nothing magic about that number; the reason for ignoring stresses of degree four or weaker here is simply that I have not found them to have any metrical relevance. If it turns out that the facts after all warrant it, a lower cut-off point can easily be introduced. The system given below can operate equally well with finer gradations of weak stresses; nothing in its structure depends on there being only four.

I represent degrees of stress by numbers in the currently usual way, with 1 standing for the highest degree of stress ('primary' stress). For convenience, I represent the lowest degree as 4 rather than 0, e.g. $\overset{4\ 2\ \ \ 1\ \ 3}{\textit{alert lifeguard}}$. Furthermore, I assume that only the greatest stress in each word (i.e. in each domain ♯♯ ──── ♯♯) is metrically relevant; i.e., the fact that the first and last syllable of *pentameter* are slightly more stressed than the third appears to be of no metrical relevance – it only matters that the second has primary stress, and the others are unstressed for purposes of metrics. Otherwise, the representation of stress can be taken to be the normal output of the stress rules, including the Nuclear Stress Rule, which subordinates the stresses of the non-final members of a constituent to its final member (e.g. $\overset{2\ \ \ 1}{\textit{long night}}$). The Nuclear Stress Rule operates within phonological phrases. By the above-mentioned working assumption that versification is based on the maximal division into phonological phrases, the Nuclear Stress Rule will not operate at the sentence level, since a sentence in poetry will consist of at least two phonological phrases (unless the subject is a pronoun, in which case the Nuclear Stress Rule applies vacuously at the sentence level): thus the subject Noun Phrase will not be subordinated to the predicate Verb Phrase in stress. The metrical facts show (§2.1, end) that at least this much stress subordination is metrically relevant; they are consistent with, but do not positively support, the possibility that there is stress subordination in larger domains, such as the sentence (as assumed by Beaver 1971a) or the line. If this should prove to be the case after all, our assumption about phrasing would have to be revised.

1.2. *The metrical rules* constitute a bridge between the rhythm of music and speech, operating on the units which make up the basic metrical patterns. In English, these units are syllables with either stress ([1 stress]) or no stress ([4 stress]). Metrical rules have the form

(6) A → B in env. C────D

which may be read 'A is replaced by B in the environment after C and before D'. In such a rule, A and B may be any single unit, or zero; C and D are sequences of units and/or boundary markets. Metrical rules may be optional or obligatory; all those that we shall encounter here are optional, and we shall not specifically reiterate this for each rule below.

Examples of metrical rules that insert or delete units (i.e. rules where A or B are zero) are the rules that account for headless lines and extrametrical syllables. These rules will be discussed in §2.7.

Stress in English verse is governed by the following metrical rules:

Metrical rule 1 (MR1): [1 stress] → [α stress]
Metrical rule 2 (MR2):

[4 stress] → [β stress] in env. $\begin{cases} \# \underline{\qquad} \# & \text{(a)} \\ \# \text{ P}[\# \underline{\qquad} & \text{(b)} \end{cases}$

Here α, β are variables ranging over the relevant values of stress (1 through 4, in the present system). MR1 says that a primary stress can be freely replaced by any other stress. That is, strong positions are not constrained categorically, though they are constrained relatively, by the metrical tension index. MR2 says that, in place of no stress, we can have a stress under two conditions: in a monosyllabic word (condition a), and after an intonation break (condition b). Thus weak positions are constrained in two ways: categorically, by conditions (a) and (b), and relatively, by the metrical tension index. The former distinguishes metrical from unmetrical lines; the latter establishes the hierarchy of complexity among metrical lines.

1.3. *Metrical tension* can be construed as the degree of difference between underlying and derived metrical patterns. Since both are expressed as sequences of stresses, we can quantify the tension by totaling the difference between the underlying and derived values for each metrical position:

Index of metrical tension: The metrical tension between a derived metrical pattern $\phi_1, \ldots \phi_n$ and an underlying metrical pattern $\psi_1, \ldots \psi_n$ is the sum of differences between each ϕ_1 and ψ_1.

Since we are assuming that stress ranges over the values 1, 2, 3, 4(=0), where only 1 and 4 appear in the underlying pattern, the tension in each metrical position may have a value from 0 to 3, and the tension of a ten-syllable line varies from 0 to a theoretical maximum of 30. In practice this maximum is hardly ever reached; one example is Lear's dying

(7) Never, never, never, never, never.

Normally, a tension of about 15 already makes the underlying pattern hard to grasp, and approaches the upper limit of tolerable metrical complexity in English poetry.[2]

Other than this, there is no *absolute* meaning to the values of our tension index: they have only a *relative* meaning in comparing different lines or poems for metrical complexity, or in comparing different metrical utilizations of word or phrase.

This tension index is of course no a-priori construct, but must be justified empirically as corresponding to some real hierarchy of metrical complexity.[3] I shall attempt to do so by showing that relative tension, as here defined, corresponds to relative frequency in poetic usage and to evident stylistic differences, both over-all between periods and within single works.

1.4. The *prosodic rules* which interest us here are primarily those governing the metrical utilization of stress in English. Thus, as we have noted, subsidiary stresses within words are not metrically relevant. Formally, this fact corresponds to the following rule:

Prosodic rule (PR): Disregard all but the strongest stress in each domain ♯♯ X ♯♯, where X does not contain ♯♯.

Other prosodic rules deal with the matching of metrical positions to syllables. They must provide, e.g., that words like *being, prism, heaven* may each fill either one or two positions in most kinds of English verse; *Antonio, circumference* may fill either three or four; and so on.[4] In general, prosodic rules can be viewed as a kind of parasystem of phonology, a modification for poetic use of the regular phonological system of the language. The principal ways of modification are the disregarding of certain phonological rules and the addition of others: thus, *prism* is morphophonemically monosyllabic between a consonant and a word boundary (compare *prismatic*, where this rule cannot apply). To scan it as a monosyllable involves disregarding the operation of this rule. On the other hand, a word like *pitiful* is trisyllabic, both morphophonemically and in actual pronunciation; if we find Shakespeare scanning it as disyllabic, we should ascribe that fact to a prosodic convention that allows two syllables to be counted as one under certain conditions. In neither case does this necessarily mean that the actual pronunciation ever followed the scansion; it is unlikely that *prism* would ever have been pronounced as a monosyllable, or that *pitiful* would ever have been pronounced as a disyllable. Similarly, the stresses which PR tells us to disregard are not omitted in the actual recitation of verse.

I shall, throughout this paper, maintain the sharp distinction between the metrical organization of a poem and the way it is recited (see Jakobson 1960, Halle and Keyser 1966, 1974 for discussion of this distinction). The confusion between them is, however, endemic to the metrical study of stress-based verse. Unlike syllabic quantity, stress – and especially sentence stress – is highly variable in speech. Stress-based verse can therefore be recited in many ways. At one extreme, it can be recited 'as if it were prose', according to the natural rhythm of speech. In terms of our theory, this kind of recitation actualizes solely the derived metrical pattern; an example is Robert Frost's reading of his own poetry in his well-known recording. The other extreme is the 'schoolboy' manner of imposing a mechanical alternating rhythm on the verse, i.e. reciting according to the underlying metrical pattern: this is said to have been the prevalent manner of reciting poetry in the eighteenth century. Between these extremes (which, perhaps, are never found in absolutely pure form) are various compromises between the two levels of rhythm. In these compromises, the rhythm of recitation is 'tilted' (to use the term of Wimsatt 1970) from the derived pattern toward the underlying pattern. Chatman's analysis of recorded recitations (1965) shows that such 'tilting' is common where it involves relatively small changes in stress, as in 'spondaic' and 'pyrrhic' feet.

In no way does this mean that meter and recitation are to be identified. On the contrary, the very notion of 'tilting' implies that something (the natural speech rhythm, corresponding to the derived mechanical pattern) is being changed toward something else (the musical rhythm, corresponding to the underlying metrical pattern). The question "What is the relationship between these two levels of rhythm?" is not the same as, and indeed is presupposed by, the question 'Where, between these levels, is the rhythm of recitation determined?' Suppose, for the sake of argument, the poetry were always recited in the 'schoolboy' manner. The recitation of verse would always coincide with the underlying metrical pattern, and the derived metrical pattern would never be heard. Would this do away with the need for metrics? Of course not. The question of what is a metrical line would remain: it would now be the question of what can and what cannot be 'tilted' into an iambic pattern. To answer it, we should still need metrical rules to map out a relation between two levels of rhythm. (If we like, we could think of the arrow in the metrical rules as going in the other direction, with the speech rhythms now 'changing into' the musical iambic rhythm – so long as we realize that the rules are still the same, and that the direction of the arrow is nothing more than a metaphorical way of visualizing the conventions of recitation.)

But to say that meter and recitation are distinct is NOT to say that they are unrelated. It is quite possible that prevailing conventions of recitation may be connected in interesting ways with metrical rules and their utilization. For example, the strictness of neo-classical versification could have something to do with the custom at that period of reciting verse largely in accordance with the underlying pattern. The reader can easily convince himself that such recitation sounds much worse for Shakespeare and Donne, because of their higher level of metrical tension, than it does for Dryden and Pope. Thus we may speculate that the neo-classical style of recitation requires neo-classical metrical practice, and that neo-classical metrical practice in turn invites the neo-classical style of recitation.

2. Metrical tension

2.1. *Compounds vs. phrases.* Disyllabic compounds like *midnight* have a 1–3 stress pattern. Since the members of compounds are themselves words,

MR2a is applicable to them, and allows both the first and the second member of a compound to occur in weak position. There is, however, a great difference in the metrical tension that results from these two possible metrical uses of disyllabic compounds, as is evident from the schema in Figure 1.

$$
\begin{array}{cccc}
4 & 1 & 4 & 1 & \textit{tension} \\
& & [\#\#\overset{1}{\text{mid}}\# & \#\overset{3}{\text{night}}\#\#]_N & 5 \\
[\#\#\overset{1}{\text{mid}}\#\# & & \overset{3}{\text{night}}\#\#]_N & & 1
\end{array}
$$

Figure 1

A compound in strong–weak (even–odd) position produces the near-minimum tension of 1, whereas a compound in weak–strong (odd–even) position produces the near-maximum of 5. Accordingly, the system predicts that compounds should occur in both positions, but that strong–weak positioning should be much more frequent than weak–strong positioning in iambic verse.

This matches the facts of metrical usage exactly. The favored position of disyllabic compounds is, of course, beginning at an even syllable. It is not necessary to give many examples of this normal case:

(8) With Ap/ril's *first-/born* flowers, / and all / things rare   (Son. 21)
    And art / made *tongue-/tied* by / author/ity   (Son. 66)
    When *proud-/pied* Ap/ril, dressed / in all / his trim   (Son. 98)

And disyllabic compounds do occur also in odd–even position. This usage is much less frequent, as predicted by our theory, but is sufficiently well attested that there can be no doubt about its metrical status:

(9) As the *death-bed* whereon it must expire   (Son. 73)
    Anon he rears *upright*, curvets, and leaps   (Ven. 279)
    Grew I not faint? And fell I not *down-right*?   (Ven. 645)
    Like a *milch doe*, whose swelling dugs do ache   (Ven. 875)
    The dove sleeps fast that this *night-owl* will catch   (Luc. 360)
    With the *love juice*, as I did bid thee do?   (MND 3.2.37)
    Between our after-supper and *bedtime*   (MND 5.1.34)
    In the *line-grove* which weather-fends your cell   (Tmp. 5.1.10)
    In my *school-days* when I had lost one shaft   (MV 1.1.140)
    Yond light is not *daylight*, I know it, I   (Rom. 3.5.12)
    Or I'll be buried in the King's *highway*   (R2 3.3.155)
    Do wound the bark, the skin of our *fruit-trees*   (R2 3.4.58)

The odd–even positioning of disyllabic compounds remains a possibility throughout English iambic verse:

(10) Of fruits, and flowers, and bunches of *knot-grass*
                                                                            (Keats, 'Eve of St Agnes', st. 24)
      Half-hidden, like a mermaid in *sea-weed*   (*Ibid.*, st. 26)
      Some boy too far from town to learn *baseball*   (Frost, 'Birches')
      I'd like to go by climbing a *birch-tree*   (*Ibid.*)

Even as strict a versifier as Pope allows it (see §3.1 below).

Our theory, then accounts for both facts: the occurrence of both strong – weak and weak–strong positioning, and the great predominance of the former. How does the Halle–Keyser theory fare in this respect? The prediction which the Stress Maximum Principle makes about disyllabic compounds depends on how their stress pattern is analysed prosodically. There are two possible alternatives to consider. The first is that the tertiary stress of the second member is not counted as a stress in prosody: in that case, *blackbird* is trochaic, and should pattern like non-compounded disyllables with initial stress. But then the Halle-Keyser theory could not account for the metrical type of (9), as opposed to the non-occurring type

(11) *As the *pallet* whereon it must expire

Indeed, on this assumption, the type of (9), with a compound in odd – even position, would become a counter-example to the Stress Maximum Principle – since *death* etc. are stressed syllables in weak position between two unstressed syllables.

The second alternative, which Halle and Keyser (1971, p. 171) opt for, is that

(12) [in the *blackbird* type] 'both stresses would count metrically since both stresses are the full stresses within their respective words, namely *black* and *bird*.'

But first of all, assumption (12) leads to an insoluble contradiction within the Halle–Keyser system. They allow (1971a) for a line to contain one or two extrametrical syllables,[5] which must be unstressed. And it is quite true that there are no extrametrical syllables with primary stress. However, second members of compounds can occur as extrametrical syllables:

(13) Like to a chaos, or an unlicked bear*whelp*   (3H6 3.2.161)
      Quite overcanopied with luscious wood*bine*   (MND 2.2.251)
      Which daily grew to quarrel and to blood*shed*   (1H4 4.5.195)
      The lamps of night in revel, is not more man*like*   (Ant. 1.4.5)
      Take heed of perjury, thou art on thy death*bed*   (Oth. 5.2.51)

Since Halle and Keyser take second members of compounds to be stressed, their theory is unable to distinguish the metrical examples of (13) from the unmetrical

(14) *Quite overcanopied with luscious green *vines*.

The rule is that an extrametrical syllable must have a weaker than primary stress. No system that equates the tertiary stress of compounds with primary stress can state this rule.

Prosodic convention (12) also leaves us with no way of accounting for the asymmetry in the positioning of compounds. It admits the lines in (9) as metrical, but at the price of destroying the whole basis for explaining why that type is vastly outnumbered by the type of (8). On the hypothesis that compounds simply have the prosodic value of two stressed syllables, we should expect them to occur with similar frequency in both strong–weak and weak–strong position, instead of being overwhelmingly preferred in strong–weak position.

Another patently false consequence of (12) is that strings of disyllabic compounds should be equally well analysable as trochaic or iambic. But clearly the natural scansion of (15) is trochaic:[6]

(15) Blackbird, peacock, bullfinch, titmouse, nighthawk

To summarize, the Halle–Keyser theory cannot explain the metrical behavior of disyllabic compounds, no matter which of the two possible prosodic valuations of the compound stress pattern they choose. The root of their problem is the impoverished prosodic basis of their system, which in essence operates with only two degrees of stress.

Concerning the Magnuson–Ryder (1971) rules, it is sufficient to note that they are inconsistent with the facts about disyllabic compounds. Most of the lines in (9) would be unmetrical by their 'Base Rule 1'. This is not due to an accidental misformulation, but to an error of fact, since they explicitly state that a (constructed) line

(16) *Making driftwood more blest than living lips

is unmetrical (because of the second foot). In reality, lines of that type do occur:

(17) Hear a foot-fall: we are now near his cell   (Tmp. 4.1.195)

We may now compare the patterning of compounds with that of phrases. How should a phrase such as *long night* behave according to our system? The prediction we make is that both positionings ought to be metrical (though putting the more strongly stressed head in strong position should give a lesser degree of metrical tension), while the difference between the two positionings is not nearly as great as in the case of compounds – as shown in Figure 2.

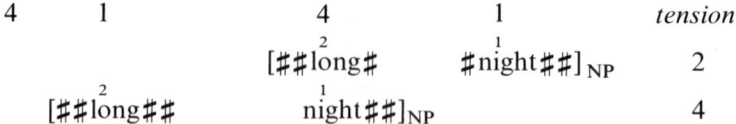

Figure 2

Again, the system makes the correct predictions. Of course, both positionings are used; and Beaver (1971b) reports that he and his co-workers have compiled statistics for different periods of English poetry which show that 'occurrences of adj.–noun with back-to-back stress are well over twice as frequent in the weak–strong configuration'.

2.2. *The monosyllable constraint: Trisyllabic compounds.* Our theory makes an equally specific prediction about the treatment in iambic verse of compounds of the type *grandfather, swift-footed, housekeeping*, with disyllabic second members: see Figure 3.

```
              4            1            4            1        tension
              1            3            4
a. [##house   ##keep       ing##]_N                            5
              1            3            4
b.           [##house      keep         ing##]_N     unmetrical
```

Figure 3

In case (a), the compound occurs in weak–strong–weak position. The first syllable is accepted in weak position by MR2a, since it is a monosyllabic word. The second syllable is accepted in strong position by MR1, and the third syllable fits in its weak position directly. This positioning is therefore metrical, with a tension index of 5.

Next consider the same type of compound shifted into strong–weak–strong position (b). The first syllable fits into its strong position directly, and the third by MR1. But the second syllable cannot undergo either branch of MR2, and the metrical pattern is therefore not derivable by our rules. Consequently, this positioning is unmetrical.

We predict, then, that in iambic pentameter, such trisyllabic compounds should begin only in *odd* positions. Remarkably, this is indeed the case, as has been noted by Magnuson and Ryder 1971.[7] They can begin in first, third, fifth, seventh, or ninth position (the last possibility involving an extrametrical syllable at the end of the line):

(18) *Love-lacking* vestals and *self-loving* nuns   (Ven. 752)
     The hot *scent-snuffing* hounds are driven to doubt   (Ven. 692)

> And sometime where *earth-delving* conies keep (Ven. 687)
> To say within thine own *deep-sunken* eyes (Son. 2)
> Melodious discord, heavenly tune *harsh-sounding* (Ven. 431)

I find that this restriction holds with no exceptions in Shakespeare's *Sonnets*, in *Venus and Adonis*, and in *The rape of Lucrece*. It also seems to hold almost completely in the middle and late plays (the three exceptions I found are MV 2.5.40, 5.1.284, and Mac. 3.2.97). This is astonishing in view of the frequency with which Shakespeare uses these compounds. In the early plays, the restriction also holds in the majority of cases, but a fair number of exceptions are found:

> (19) A knot you are of dammnèd *bloodsuckers* (R3 3.3.6)
> Rude ragged nurse, old sullen *playfellow* (R3 4.1.102)
> Which now, two tender *playfellows* for dust (R3 4.4.385)
> Under our tents I'll play the *eavesdropper* (R3 5.3.221)
> Full of *rose water* and bestrewed with flowers (TS Ind. 1.56)
> Dread prince of plackets, king of *codpieces* (LLL 3.1.186)

This is interesting in view of the fact that Shakespeare was in the generation of poets who established this restriction in English verse (cf. §3 below).

In trochaic verse, of course, such trisyllabic compounds can begin in even positions – and indeed must begin there, for exactly the same reasons, though Shakespeare does not have enough trochaic verse to test this side of the claim:

> (20) Nose of Turk and Tartar's lips
> Finger of *birth-strangled* babe (Mac. 4.1.29–30)

Halle and Keyser are in the same dilemma here as with the disyllabic compounds. They can make one of two predictions, depending on what they decide about secondary stress, and both predictions are wrong. If secondary stress counts as metrical stress, then there is no way to exclude the trisyllabic compounds in question from occurring in strong–weak–strong position. The second syllable can never constitute a stress maximum, as it is always preceded by a stressed syllable:

> (21) hóuse kéep ing
>   s   w   s

And if secondary stress is said not to count as a metrical stress, the situation is even worse. The fact that strong–weak–strong positioning does not occur still lacks an explanation, since the second syllable must again fail to constitute a stress maximum, this time because it is taken to be unstressed:

> (22) house keep ing
>   s   w   s

And on the contrary, most of the lines that DO occur would on this assumption violate the Stress Maximum Principle; e.g.,

(23) Were an *all-eating* shame and thriftless praise (Son. 2)
And his *love-kindling* fire did quickly steep (Son. 153)
Or as *sweet-seasoned* showers are to the ground (Son. 75)
If the true concord of *well-tunèd* sounds (Son. 8)
Some fresher stamp of the *time-bettering* days (Son. 82)
In true plain words by thy *true-telling* friend (Son. 82)
E'en so, being full of your *ne'er-cloying* sweetness (Son. 118)
Which works on leases of *short-numbered* hours (Son. 124)
Simply I credit her *false-speaking* tongue (Son. 138)
Some in their garments, though *newfangled* ill (Son. 91)
This sour informer, this *bate-breeding* spy (Ven. 655)
O Night, thou furnace of *foul-reeking* smoke (Luc. 799)

Magnuson and Ryder 1971 deal with such compounds in an inconsistent manner. On p. 212 they treat them as unmetrical in any position; but on p. 216 they say they are 'clearly within the English iambic tradition' in weak–strong–weak position, and a rule is given to admit them there. This rule, however, is nothing more than a summary of the facts about the metrical behavior of this type of compound. The rule is an ad-hoc addition to the system; a simpler system would result if the facts about trisyllabic compounds were different. In the system advocated here, just the reverse is true: the facts considered in this section are a special case of a more general metrical regularity. They are, in fact, predicted by MR2a, whose main motivation is the completely different set of observations to be treated in the next section. Nothing need be added to our rules specially for the compounds. On the contrary, if these behaved in any other way, such additions would be necessary. It is in this sense that our theory explains, rather than merely accounts for, their metrical treatment.

2.3. *The Monosyllable Constraint: Phrases.* MR2a requires that a stressed syllable in weak position must constitute a monosyllabic word. We have already seen what consequences this restriction has for the positioning of compounds; let us consider now how it limits the metrical use of polysyllabic simple words.

First, MR2a implies that, in iambic verse, the first syllable of a 'spondaic' foot must be a word. For example, a line like

(24) With cold *pale weak*ness numbs *each feel*ing part (Ven. 892)

represents the typical case of the spondaic foot (italicized). If we rewrite the line, putting polysyllabic words in its spondees, the result is contrary to Shakespeare's metrical practice:

(25) *With ma*lign weak*ness ben*umbs feel*ing parts

This fact shows that meter does not depend on stress alone. For example, we have

(26) Pluck the keen teeth from the fierce tiger's jaws (Son. 10)

But because of the monosyllable condition on MR2a we could not have

(27) *Pluck immense teeth from enraged tigers' jaws

even though the disposition of stresses is identical. If we are to account for the different metrical status of (26) and (27), we must abandon traditional stress-bound metrics in favor of a new approach which takes account of word and phrase structure.

Second, MR2a implies that, in iambic verse, the first syllable of a trochaic foot must be a word, except (thanks to MR2b) after an intonation break. The latter proviso holds in principle also for spondees; but it cannot in practice arise there, since there are no single words with spondaic stress patterns. The following lines illustrate the types that do occur.

(28) a. Suff'ring my friend for my *sake to* approve her (Son. 42)
    Better becomes the gray *cheeks of* the east (Son. 132)
    Oh me, what eyes hath love *put in* my head (Son. 148)
    That dogs *bark at* me as I halt *by them* (R3 1.1.23)
    If yet your gentle souls *fly* in the air (R3 4.4.11)
    Our strong *arms be* our conscience, swords our law (R3 5.3.311)
    A black *day will* it be to somebody (R3 5.3.280)
  b. Thou dost *love her*, because thou knowst I love her (Son. 42)
    For how do I *hold thee* but by thy granting? (Son. 87)
    From hence your memory *death can*not take (Son. 81)
    Since I *left you* mine eye is in my mind (Son. 113)
    Let me *not to* the marriage of true minds (Son. 116)
    Whoe'er *keeps me*, let my *heart be* his guard (Son. 133)
    She may *help you* to many fair preferments (R3 1.3.95)
    Shall we *hear from* you, Catesby, ere we sleep? (R3 3.1.188)
    I do suspect I have *done some* offense (R3 3.7.111)
    I am *not in* the giving vein today (R3 4.2.119)
    Bear thee *well in* it, and *leave us* alone (Ado 3.1.13)
    When I *come where* he calls, then he is gone (MND 3.2.416)
    Speak no *more of* her. Give me a bowl of wine (JC 4.3.158)
    If I *quench thee*, thou flaming minister (Oth. 5.2.8)
    How thou *lov'st us*, show in our brother's welcome (WT 4.1.23)

What is excluded by MR2a is a trochaic foot whose first syllable is not a word, viz. any of the following types:

(29)   4   1   4   1
  a.   ♯   ´ ♯
  b.   ♯   ´   ♯
  c.   ♯   ´ ♯

Examples are:

(30) a. *To re/stóre to / old age / what youth / hath lost
     b. *And to / bánish / old age / where youth / hath lost
     c. *And re/stóring / old age / where youth / hath lost

Lines of this type do not in fact occur.

A number of restrictions on inverted feet have been suggested in previous metrical studies, none of which receive clear support from the facts:

(i) Jespersen claimed that inverted feet must contain a syntactic boundary corresponding to a phonological pause. Such a boundary is present in many examples, such as Jespersen's

(31) Like to a step-dame or a dowager

But in most of the lines of (28), no such boundary is justified, and a phonological pause between the first and second syllable of their trochees would be quite unnatural. Moreover, violations of type (29a) are not repaired by a syntactic pause after the stressed syllable.

(ii) Halle and Keyser (1971a, b) propose the Stress Maximum Principle, whose effect is to disallow inverted feet which are preceded by an unstressed syllable (unless they are line- or clause-initial). Constructed lines like (25) and (27), which are unmetrical although allowed by the Stress Maximum Principle, show that it is too weak. Examples as in (28b) show that it is too strong in that it fails to allow for attested kinds of verse. The fact seems to be that MR2a operates independently of the stress in the preceding metrical position, and the Stress Maximum Principle is irrelevant in Shakespeare's verse.

(iii) Magnuson and Ryder's position on inverted feet is confusing: at 1971, p. 207–8 they label them unmetrical, but at 1971, p. 216 they recant partially, and allow some of them back in. Their suggestion is that the metrical constraints are 'weakened' across the fourth and fifth syllables in a line (the caesural point in the Romance decasyllabic line). This simply isolates an arbitrary subclass of lines, and does not apply to most of the examples in (28). I know of nothing to show that metrical constraints are weakened at this position in the line, and it is plainly false that inverted feet occur only there.

Note that none of these three additional conditions proposed by Jespersen, by Halle and Keyser, or by Magnuson and Ryder is in itself incompatible with the rules I have proposed. If any of them were factually correct, they could be incorporated into this system by a modification of the metrical rules, although this would in each case constitute a complication of their present form. However, the conditions are in the first place not borne out by Shakespeare's actual versification; and second, they would not by themselves, even if correct, constitute a sufficient restriction on the use of trochaic feet. MR2a would still be needed to account for the absence of lines like (25), (27), and (30).

One generalization about inverted feet does appear to have some validity, however, and is not accounted for in our rules. A glance at (28) shows that trochaic feet (aside from the first foot, where they are allowed for by MR2b) occur mainly in *even* feet (second and fourth) and less often in odd feet (third and fifth). Also, they appear to be more frequent (other things being equal) toward the *beginning* of the line – e.g. more frequent in the second foot than in the fourth, more frequent in the third than in the fifth. This can only in part be explained historically by reference to the model of the 'double trochee' of Italian Renaissance poetry. It also seems that the distribution of *spondees* is rather similar to that of trochees just described. The preference for even feet, and for the beginning of the line, would thus hold for the application of MR2a, rather than for any specific foot type. If so, then we may conjecture that these facts basically reflect two general principles of poetic form which in one way or another impinge on the poetry of nearly all languages:

(a) A tendency toward dipodic structure. The second and fourth feet are strong – as opposed to the first, third and fifth, which are weak. This higher-level pattern is super-imposed on the pattern of alternating syllable strength. Thus the very common line type

(32) *For the four winds* blow in from every coast   (MV 1.2.168)
     I will feed fat the ancient grudge I bear him   (MV 1.3.48)

begins with a kind of 'super-iamb' made up of the first (weak) and second (strong) foot.

(b) A tendency to reduce metrical tension toward the end of a line. This itself is of course only a special case of the principle of closure, insightfully examined by Smith (1968).

2.4. *Some apparent counter-evidence.* The above conclusions depend on an assessment of the metrical evidence which recognizes the commonplace that some disyllabic and polysyllabic words were accented differently in Shakespeare's time than they are today. Obviously, Shakespeare's meter must be determined on the basis of what, to the best of our knowledge, was Shakespeare's pronunciation. This must be established by a careful analysis of the philological evidence for each word. For example, the fourth foot of the line

(33) He in the worst sense con*strues their* denial (Luc. 324)

has a stressed syllable in odd position, and it is not a monosyllabic word. Instead of concluding that MR2a is wrong, we must take into account the earlier pronunciation of *construe*, about which the OED says: 'At an early date the stress was put on the first syllable, and the final reduced to *-stre*, *-ster*: conster continued to be the pronunciation down to the nineteenth century, even after it had disappeared as a written form. Walker (1791) called this 'a scandal to seminaries of learning'. A similar apparent difficulty in the line

(34) Do I *envy* those jacks that nimble leap (Son. 128)

is removed by the information that 'The older accentuation (envəí) survived into the seventeenth century and is still common dialectally, esp. In Sc[ots]' (OED). Because of the known historical fact that there has been much fluctuation in what words were subject to the Noun/Verb accent alternation of the type *subjéct/súbject* (Halle and Keyser 1971a, p. 117), very little significance can be attributed to such apparently unmetrical lines as

(35) In pur*suit of* the thing she would have stay (Son. 143)
     The vacant leaves thy mind's *imprint* will bear (Son. 77)

Here an earlier accentuation *púrsuit, imprínt* is the most plausible interpretation, especially where other contemporary instances requiring the same stress can be adduced:

(36) Was this the *pursuit* of thy policy (Marlowe, Jew of Malta 3.3.43)

Many words, such as *aspéct*, occur so frequently in metrical positions that contradict their present stress, and so consistently, that there can be no doubt that they have undergone a shift in stress. Under these circumstances it is more reasonable to assume a parallel stress fluctuation in deverbal nouns like *imprint* than to take (35) as isolated exceptions to MR2a. Evidence against MR2a would have to come from cases where such stress changes are, for phonological or morphological reasons, unlikely or impossible.

Shakespeare's accentuation is also likely to have differed from ours in the extent of application of the so-called Rhythm Rule, which reverses a 3–2 stress pattern before a primary stress in the next word within a phrase, e.g.

$\overset{3}{\text{Tennessee}}\ \overset{2}{\text{Williams}} \rightarrow \overset{2}{\text{Tennessee}}\ \overset{3}{\text{Williams}}$; $\overset{3}{\text{sixteen}}\ \overset{2}{\text{tons}} \rightarrow \overset{2}{\text{sixteen}}\ \overset{3}{\text{tons}}$; $\overset{3}{\text{unknown}}\ \overset{2}{\text{author}} \rightarrow \overset{2}{\text{unknown}}\ \overset{3}{\text{author}}$:[8]

(37) [+stress]→[2 stress] / ___ X [2 stress] Y [1 stress]
where X, Y contain no 1 or 2 stress, and no ₚ[
(P = any phrase-level constituent)

The rule does not now apply to all phrases that fit its structural analysis, e.g. *ex*$\overset{3}{t}$*reme* $\overset{2}{f}$*ear*, *an*$\overset{1}{t}$*ique* $\overset{3}{f}$*ur*$\overset{2}{n}$*i*$\overset{1}{t}$*ure*. Its scope seems to have been steadily shrinking; Bridges mentions the phrase *éxtreme únction* as a survival in Irish speech. Given its more widespread application in Shakespeare's time, we can conclude that lines of the following type were probably not exceptions to MR2a:

(38) And *extreme fear* can neither fight nor fly   (Luc. 230)
     And from the for*lorn world* his visage hide   (Son. 33)
     The pangs of des*pised love*, the law's delay   (Ham. 3.1.73)
     The life of purity, the s*upreme fair*   (Luc. 780)
     These an*tique fables*, nor these fairy toys   (MND 5.1.3)

Of course, this assumption about stress needs some justification other than the fact that it is required in order to save the monosyllable constraint on MR2a. Otherwise our reasoning would be circular and our conclusions worthless.

We can arrive at such justification through the following considerations. If the monosyllable constraint on MR2a is wrong, then counter-examples to it should occur randomly in all sorts of cases, including those to which Rhythm Rule (37) would be inapplicable. But if our metrical rule is correct, and our phonological treatment of the apparent counter-examples is also correct, then the apparent counter-examples should all be of a specific type, namely those subject to rule (37). In fact, the latter seems to be true. In the first place, the remaining counter-examples to MR2a involve mostly non-final elements of phrases, adjectives and participles before a noun, as in (37). On the theory that the monosyllabic word condition does not hold, it is a mystery why lines of the following type do not occur:

(39) *To re*fuse* Virtue in thy nakedness
     *As ga*zelles* leap a never-resting brook

Their absence follows from my proposal, since rule (37) is not applicable across a phrase boundary.

A second argument is based on the observation that certain frequent adjectives like *antique*, *extreme* are ALWAYS found in strong–weak position when preceding a noun with initial stress. That is, we have the configuration (40a), and never (40b):

(40) a. ... extreme fear
       s   w   s
   b. *extreme fear
       w   s   w

This could be explained only on the assumption that the actual pronunciation was *éxtreme féar*. If it was *extréme féar*, then the non-occurring case (40b) would be permissible under any metrical theory (and indeed, the only possible one under mine, which would then exclude (40b) by MR2a). These facts indeed permit an even stronger conclusion to be drawn. They show not only that (37) was an operative rule, but that it was obligatory, at least in poetic language and for a certain group of words, such as *extreme*, *supreme*. That conclusion is further strengthened by the spelling in

(41) The famous warriors of the anticke world   (Spenser, Son. 79)

since *-ic(k)*, *-icke* is a spelling otherwise found only in initially stressed words, such as *music(k)*, *comic(k)*.

A final piece of evidence in favor of rule (37) would be the line

(42) My cóncealed lady to our cancelled love   (Rom. 3.3.98)

which loses its pun (as well as its meter) if we suppose the stress to have been *concéaled*.

Beaver (1971a, b) goes far beyond the rather conservative position which I have tried to secure here. He not only assumes a lexically unrestricted Rhythm Rule, but favors beefing it up so that it will reduce virtually any sequence of stresses to an alternating pattern. Moreover, he takes this generalized form of the rule to apply not just in earlier English, but in all English poetry. In ordinary language, this certainly does not happen, and almost certainly never did. Beaver's rule would thus have the status of a prosodic rule, taking the form of a generalized version of a phonological rule of the language, viz. the Rhythm Rule proper. This is not in itself unreasonable: in much the same way, the prosodic rule of synaloepha looks like a generalization of vowel deletion in ordinary language. The problem with Beaver's rule is that it would predict the occurrence not only of (38), but also of the type (39), which is not found. Also, since Beaver's rule is optional, the absence of (40b) could not be acounted for under his proposal. On these grounds the phonological treatment seems better founded.

2.5. *The role of the prosodic rule*: In §1 we set up PR, stating that only the strongest of the stresses in each domain ♯ ♯ X ♯ ♯ (where X contains no ♯♯) is metrically relevant. The immediate motivation for this is that, in polysyllabic uncompounded words, syllables with subsidiary stress are not distinguished metrically from completely unstressed syllables. For example,

Stress, syntax and meter 249

$\overset{1}{main}\overset{1}{tain}$ is metrically equivalent to $\overset{1}{attain}$, and $\overset{1}{in}\overset{3}{cest}$ is metrically equivalent to $\overset{3}{mod}\overset{}{est}$. Were it not for our prosodic convention, positionings of the type shown in Figure 4 would be inadmissible by the monosyllable constraint on MR2a – and would thereby constitute outright metrical violations, which they clearly are not.

$$\begin{array}{ccc} s & w & s \\ & \overset{3}{main} & \overset{1}{tain} \\ \overset{1}{in} & \overset{3}{cest} & \end{array}$$

Figure 11.4

PR has another remarkable consequence. As Halle and Keyser (1971b, p. 163) and Beaver (1971b, p. 189, fn. 12) point out, disyllabic prepositions (e.g. *among*, *against*, *upon*, *over*, *under*, *after*) function as if they were unstressed. Otherwise, lines like

(43) And I will comment up*on* that offense   (Son. 89)

would violate MR2. The usage appears even in such a strict versifier as Pope:

(44) Pride, Malice, Folly *against* Dryden rose (*Essay on Criticism* 2.458)

Magnuson and Ryder (1971, p. 205) further note that we cannot simply say that they have no inherent stress, for then constructs like

(45) *Inbetween, before, beneath and beyond

are wrongly admitted as iambic pentameter lines. Thus the stress on prepositions is disregarded metrically when they are in construction with a noun phrase, but taken into account when they occur in isolation. And exactly this behavior is predicted by PR in conjunction with the usual conventions on word boundaries which were also outlined in §1. In (44), WBR1 gives

(46) ... ♯]$_{NP}$ $_{VP}$[♯ $_{PP}$[♯against $_{NP}$[♯ $_N$[♯Dryden♯]$_N$ ♯]$_{NP}$]$_{PP}$ $_{VP}$[♯ ...

Simplification by WBR2 gives (omitting brackets)

(47) ... ♯♯against♯Dryden♯♯ ...

Even though *against* will be assigned a stress on the second syllable, this stress will not count when the preposition is proclitic, as in (47), since PR provides that all but the strongest stress in each domain ♯♯ X ♯♯ (where X does not contain ♯♯) should be disregarded. Hence ♯♯ $\overset{3}{against}$♯$\overset{1}{Dryden}$♯♯

will be metrically valued as ♯♯ *against* ♯ *Dryden* ♯♯, and lines like (43)–(44) will not violate the monosyllable constraint on MR2a. But when *against* is not proclitic, it is alone dominated by a phrasal category, and will therefore be enclosed by ♯♯ on each side – so PR cannot have an effect on it. Also, when a preposition stands before an unstressed head, it will have the strongest stress in its phrase, and therefore not be subject to PR. Thus we predict that the type *against him* should occur in weak–strong–weak position only, as in

(48) To see you here *before me*. O my soul's joy!   (Oth. 2.1.186)

2.6. *Further evidence for the monosyllable constraint.* In arguing for their Stress Maximum Principle, Halle and Keyser (1971b) have concocted the unmetrical line

(49) *Ode to the West Wind by *Percy* Bysshe Shelley.

This line is correctly designated as unmetrical by our rules, since MR2 is violated by the italicized syllable – a stressed syllable in a weak position which does not constitute a word. Magnuson and Ryder (1971) have, in their turn, made up a series of equally unmetrical lines which the Stress Maximum Principle wrongly fails to rule out:

(50) a. A little con*ceit*? What a dangerous thing!
     b. Intro*duc*ed grànd*fa*ther to a*muse* friends
     c. If it be be*tray*ed, slander doth approve.
     d. Fly a*way*! fly away! you dangerous thing!

These examples likewise violate MR2, and are therefore correctly rejected in our theory. Finally, the metrical lines which Halle and Keyser cite (1971a, p. 169–70) as counter-examples to the Magnuson–Ryder rules are fully accounted for by ours. In general, then, the rules given here fit all the crucial data, both negative and positive, given by Halle and Keyser in favor of their theory or by Magnuson and Ryder in favor of theirs. However, the explanation which we give for both sets of data is different. The deviance of (49) has nothing to do with the Stress Maximum Principle, and the deviance of (50a) has nothing to do with the availability of an alternative (anapestic) scansion for it, contrary to what Magnuson and Ryder maintain (1971, p. 203). There are lines with the same rhythm as (50a) in impeccably iambic poetry:

(51) Or keep / him from / heart-eas/ing words / so long   (Luc. 1782)

In general, it is perfectly possible for a line to have two or more metrical interpretations out of its metrical context (occasionally, the ambiguity may persist even in context: as in language, ambiguity of sentences is not always resolved by context). In iambic verse we also encounter lines whose most obvious scansion is dactylic, but which are still understood as iambic because the context leads us to expect iambic scansion and they satisfy the metrical rules under that interpretation as well:

(52) Love-lack/ing ves/tals and / self-lov/ing nuns   (Ven. 752)
    Simply / I cred/it her / false-speak/ing tongue   (Son. 138)

Conversely, dactylic verse can contain lines which happen to scan as perfect iambic verse, e.g. the second line in Dryden's dactylic tetrameter song from 'An Evening's Love':

(53) After the pangs of a desperate Lover,
    When day and / night I have / sighed all in / vain ...

2.7. *The role of phrase boundaries.* Phrase structure is relevant to at least three aspects of versification: the application of MR2b, the division of verse into lines, and the insertion of extrametrical syllables.

MR2b says that a stressed syllable can occur in weak position after a phrase boundary which coincides with a double word boundary, viz. #] ₚ[# or [# ₚ[#. In monosyllabic words, this option is always permissible by MR2a, but MR2b extends it to polysyllabic non-compounded words in the indicated environment. The force of MR2b is to allow inverted feet after a break in the verse.

Specifically, MR2b is applicable after any sentence boundary–

(54) Listen great things. *Brutus* and Cassius   (JC 4.2.41)

and after any clause boundary (internal sentence boundary), whether this corresponds to an obligatory break, represented by an orthographic comma, or merely an optional break:

(55) a. When that the poor have cried, *Caesar* hath wept   (JC 3.2.96)
    b. I shall find time, *Cassius*, I shall find time   (JC 5.5.105)
(56) a. I heard him say *Brutus* and Cassius
    Are rid like madmen through the gates of Rome.   (JC 3.2.273)
    b. Yet who knows not *conscience* is born of love?   (Son. 151)

It is also applicable at the beginning of a phrase (Noun Phrase, Verb Phrase, or Adjective Phrase):

(57) Within whose face *beauty* and virtue strived   (Luc. 52)
    But now is black *beauty's* successive heir   (Son. 127)
    His eye, which scornfully *glisters* like fire   (Ven. 275)
    When lofty trees I see *barren* of leaves   (Son. 12)

Her breasts, like ivory globes *circled* with blue	(Luc. 407)
And peace proclaims *olives* of endless age	(Son. 107)
On horror's head *horrors* accumulate	(Oth. 3.3.370)
And I *nothing* to back my suit at all	(R3 1.2.236)
Whom God preserve *better* than you would wish	(R3 1.3.59)
To make *William* Lord Hastings of our mind	(R3 3.1.162)

In reading each of these lines aloud in their context, a break could be made rather naturally before the inverted foot. Our conclusion is, then, that MR2b can apply at points where an intonation break is either obligatory or possible. These are at least those points where a phrase boundary ₚ[coincides with a double word boundary ♯♯. Excluded thereby are, on the one hand, phrase-internal syllables – even if preceded by ♯♯ – and, on the other, those preceded by proclitics, even if phrase-initial (subject to the reservations of §1):

$$
\begin{array}{cccc}
& S & W\ S & W\ S \\
(58)\ *_{NP}[\sharp\ _A[\overset{2}{\text{green}}\ \sharp]_A\ _N[\ \overset{1}{\text{ol}}\ \overset{4}{\text{ives}}]_N\ \sharp]_{NP} & & & \\
*_{PP}[\ \sharp\ \text{in}\ _{NP}[\sharp\ _A[\overset{4}{\text{bar}}\ \overset{2}{\text{ren}}\ \sharp]_A\ _N[\sharp\ \overset{4}{\text{a}}\ \text{bodes}]_N\ ]_{NP}\ \sharp]_{PP} & & &
\end{array}
$$

The favored location for inverted feet is, of course, the beginning of the line:

(59)	a. *Nothing*, sweet boy. But yet like prayers divine	(Son. 108)
	b. *Making* dead wood more blest than living lips	(Son. 128)

The question arises whether such line-initial inversions require a third branch of MR2. If we introduce a special symbol (say, ||) to denote the beginning of a line, then we would add to MR2 the environment

    MR2c: ... in env. || ─────

But it is not clear that this new case is actually necessary. In Shakespeare's verse, the beginning of a line generally coincides with a potential or obligatory break, in fact exactly with what we designate as ♯] ₚ[♯ or [♯ ₚ[♯. Of course, the strongest boundaries can be left inside the line, and often are – with great effect, as in this marvelous passage:

(60) Age cannot wither her, nor custom stale
     Her infinite variety. Other women cloy
     The appetites they feed, but she makes hungry
     Where most she satisfies. For vilest things
     Become themselves in her, that the holy priests
     Bless her when she is riggish.   (Ant. 2.2.240–45)

In all such lines, MR2b suffices to provide for initial inverted feet:

(61) a. ... Epicurean cooks
Sharpen with cloyless sauce his appetite (Ant. 2.1.24–5)
b. ... her impatience, which not wanted
Shrewdness of policy too, ... (Ant. 2.2.68–9)
c. ... I have a ship
Laden with gold. (Ant. 3.11.4–5)

In fact, in Shakespeare's poems, and in the early and middle plays, all lines begin at a point where a break is possible or obligatory. This must be incorporated into the specification of the basic patterns, e.g. for the iambic pentameter:

Basic pattern 1: A line is a sequence of ten syllables, alternatingly with [4 stress] and [1 stress], beginning at a syntactic configuration ♯] ₚ[♯ or [♯ ₚ[♯.

Because of this fact, MR2b is automatically applicable at the beginning of every line, and the new MR2c is simply not needed.

But in the later plays – especially *Coriolanus, Antony and Cleopatra, Cymbeline, A Winter's Tale,* and *The Tempest* – a characteristic new type of line division begins to appear. Proclitic elements, such as conjunctions (*and, but, or*), prepositions, and complementizers (*that, which, as*) which are phonologically grouped with the following phrase, are now allowed to be stranded at the end of a line:

(62) a. Thy mother was a piece of virtue, and
She said thou wast my daughter (Tmp. 1.2.56–7)
b. A freckled whelp hag-born – not honored with
A human shape ... (Tmp. 1.2.283–4)
c. Some food we had, and some fresh water, that
A noble Neapolitan, Gonzalo ... (Tmp. 1.2.160–61)

From a syntactic point of view, this freer enjambment amounts to dropping the requirement that lines must begin with ♯♯. Accordingly, we assume this basic pattern for late Shakespeare:

Basic pattern 2: A line is a sequence of ten syllables, alternatingly with [4 stress] and [1 stress], beginning at a syntactic configuration ₚ[.

It seems clear that, in such cases, no break is possible between the lines, even optionally. Let us refer to a line which does not begin with ♯♯ as a *run-on line.* The question about MR2c now reduces to the question whether run-on lines ever begin with stressed syllables in polysyllabic words. If they do, then MR2c is necessary; if they do not, then MR2c is not necessary –

and indeed, not possible, since it would permit a non-occurring type of line.

The somewhat surprising fact seems to be that run-on lines do NOT begin with stressed syllables in polysyllabic words. If they begin with stressed syllables, these are monosyllabic words, as permitted by MR2a:

(63) a. ... the common liar, who
    Thus speaks of him at Rome; (Ant. 1.1.60–61)
 b. ... his glory which
    Brought them to be lamented. (Ant. 5.2.364–5)
 c. That valor is the chiefest virtue, and
    Most dignifies the haver. (Cor. 2.2.88–9)
 d. Pray you, go fit you to the custom and
    Take to you, as your predecessors have (Cor. 2.2.147–8)
 e. Hath an aspect of intercession which
    Great nature cries, 'Deny not!' (Cor. 5.3.32–3)
 f. ... A woman that
    Bears all down with her brain, (Cymb. 2.1.58–9)
 g. ... Why, that was when
    Three crabbèd months had soured themselves to death
    (WT 1.2.101–2)
 h. ... that nuptial which
    We two have sworn shall come. (WT 4.4.50–51)
 i. Hides not his visage from our cottage but
    Looks on alike. (WT 4.4.455–6)
 j. Might thus have stood begetting wonder as
    you, gracious couple, do. (WT 5.1.133–4)
 k. ... did give us, with
    Rich garments, linens, stuffs; and necessaries (Tmp. 1.2.163–4)

If they begin with polysyllabic words, their first syllable is unstressed:

(64) a. My hazards still have been your solace, and
    Believe't not lightly – though I go alone (Cor. 4.1.28–9)
 b. Your stinking greasy caps in hooting at
    Coriolanus' exile. Now he's coming; (Cor. 4.6.132–3)
 c. The city ports by this hath entered and
    Intends t'appear before the people, hoping (Cor. 5.6.6–7)

With stranded auxiliaries, and with *not*, however, we find a fair number of examples:

(65) a. ... the full Caesar will
    Answer his emptiness! (Ant. 3.13.35–6)
 b ... that mine own servant should
    Parcel the sum of my disgraces by (Ant. 5.2.162–3)

c. ... not frenzy, not
   Absolute madness could so far have raved   (Cym. 4.2.134–5)

We might speculate that auxiliaries and *not*, unlike prepositions and complementizers, are not proclitics in Shakespeare's language. Note that they can be followed freely by parenthetical elements.

If the above observations are correct, then we can conclude that we need not add MR2c to the metrical system of Shakespeare's earlier verse, and that we *cannot* add it to that of Shakespeare's later verse. The second part of this conclusion must remain tentative until a closer examination of all the texts confirms the facts, and the special status of auxiliaries and *not* can be supported on syntactic grounds.

Finally, there are some metrical rules that change the number of positions in the basic pattern. One rule deletes the initial, weak position in iambic verse, creating so-called 'headless lines.' These are of rather marginal importance in Shakespeare and later English poetry. More frequently applied is a rule that inserts a weak 'extrametrical' syllable before a syntactic boundary and at the end of a line:

(66) Laugh at / me, make / their pas/time at / my sorrow   (WT 2.3.2–4)
     As check/ing at / his voyage, / and that / he means   (Ham. 4.7.63)
     That is / the mad*man*. / The lov/er, all / as fran*tic*   (MND 5.1.10)

If such extrametrical syllables occurred only at the end of a line, they could easily be made optional elements of the basic pattern. The fact that they also occur within a line before a break could not be accounted for in that way. The two cases are easily derived, however, by the metrical rule which inserts the extra position:

Metrical rule 3 (MR3): ø → [α stress] in env. ____ # ₚ[# where α ≠ 1, 2

This formulation combines the line-internal and line-final cases. Moreover, it makes the interesting (and apparently correct) prediction that a line-final stranded proclitic in cases like (62)–(64) should never be extrametrical – i.e., that such a proclitic should always be in the tenth position, rather than in an eleventh position inserted by MR3, for that rule cannot operate before a single #.

We do not want the output of MR3 to be subject to MR2, which could introduce a stronger stress than is allowed in extrametrical position. I shall assume that this is done by ordering MR3 after MR2, though simultaneous application of the three rules is also consistent with the facts.

In the Halle–Keyser approach, which has no metrical rules in my sense, I cannot find a natural way of relating line-final and line-internal extrametrical syllables to each other. They give no formal account of the line-internal case, although they mention its existence (1971a, p. 172); and indeed I cannot see how they would account for it without some modification of their framework. In addition to these difficulties, their treatment of extrametrical syllables also faces those mentioned in §2.1 above.

Finally, a rule with the opposite effect from MR3 will be required in trochaic (and dactylic) verse, in order to delete a weak position under conditions similar to those in which MR3 inserts one.

3. Extending the system

Freeman (1968a) has discussed the frequency with which strong positions are realized as stress maxima, and has shown that this is a useful index of metrical style. His results can be reformulated, and indeed made somewhat more precise, in terms of the index of metrical tension defined in §1 above. Most of English poetry – e.g. that of Spenser, Shakespeare, Pope, Wordsworth, Keats, Tennyson, Dryden, Frost, and Thomas – is governed by Metrical Rules 1 and 2; and the diversity within this tradition is reducible in large part to statistical variation in use of the options allowed by them.

Even where this metrical system remains fixed, there is much change in the prosodic conventions. It is well known that the conditions for synaloepha, syllabic value of syllabic nasals and liquids, and desyllabification of prevocalic *i* vary rather widely in different periods, and do not always coincide even in contemporary poets. This prosodic variation is independent of the metrical rules, and I shall not attempt to deal with it here.

The metrical system characterized by MR1–2 seems to emerge for the first time in Sidney, Marlowe, Shakespeare, Spenser, and many of their contemporaries. Earlier poets, such as Wyatt, have a different metrical system, showing a conspicuous absence of the monosyllable constraint on MR2a. This less restricted system persists in the poetry of Donne and, to a lesser extent, in Milton. After a gap of two centuries, it reappears in some nineteenth and twentieth century poetry.

3.1. *Pope.* Probably the strictest type of iambic pentameter in English poetry is the neo-classical heroic couplet, especially that of Alexander Pope. An analysis in terms of the system proposed in §1 makes clear the nature of this strictness.[9] First, Pope never violates the monosyllable constraint (MR2a), either in simple words or in compounds. The only exception which I have found is deviant by design, and is in fact a joke on certain metrists. It occurs in a passage lambasting hack critics and philologists whose only pleasure in poetry is to find metrical faults:

(67) Each wight, who reads not, and but scans and spells,
    Each *Word-catcher*, that lives on syllables
                                   ('Epistle to Dr Arbuthnot', 165–6)

It is pretty clear that the meter (and perhaps also the rhyme) are intended to provide an example of what a pedantic 'Word-catcher' would be looking for. The example is interesting because it suggests that Pope was aware of the principle embodied in MR2a, rather than simply following it unconsciously.

Second, the environment of MR2b must for Pope be construed more strictly as an obligatory break corresponding to at least a comma, i.e. generally at clause or sentence boundary. Phrase boundaries do not ordinarily suffice for inversion in Pope. Similarly, Pope divides lines only at obligatory breaks. Thus it is true for both Pope and early Shakespeare that the points of possible line division are the same as the points of possible inversion in polysyllables. But Pope's versification is based on tight phrasing, where weaker syntactic boundaries cannot be implemented as breaks, as opposed to Shakespeare's loose, 'cantabile' phrasing.

Third, the over-all level of metrical tension in Pope is appreciably lower than in Shakespeare. The following lines approach the upper limit for Pope:

(68) To the first good, first perfect, and first fair (Tension: 12)
   ('Essay on Man' 2.24)
   Grafts on this passion our best principle (Tension: 14) (ibid. 2.176)
   Fans clap, silks rustle, and tough whalebones crack (Tension: 10)
   ('Rape of the Lock' 5.50)

Lines of this complexity are ordinary in Shakespeare, but infrequent in Pope. The lower level of tension is also reflected in the rarity of the more complex positionings discussed in §2 above. The trochaic foot par excellence, of the form |1 4|, with the maximal tension of 6, is rare inside a line:

(69) On the rich quilt *sinks with* becoming woe ('Rape of the Lock' 4.35)
   And the pale ghosts *start at* the break of day   (ibid. 5.52)
   Thus wit, like faith, by each *man* is applied
   (Essay on Criticism 1.394)
   They love themselves, a third *time, in* their race,
   ('Essay on Man' 3.124)
   See the sole bliss *Heaven could* on all bestow   (ibid. 4.327)
   An angel tongue, which no *man can* persuade   (Moral Essay 1.199)

Somewhat more frequent are trochaic feet with compounds beginning in odd position (metrical tension: 5).

(70) Nor is Paul's church more safe than Paul's *churchyard*
   ('Essay on Criticism' 3.623)
   Charmed the *smallpox*, or chased old age away
   ('Rape of the Lock' 5.20)
   Friendly at Hackney, faithless at *Whitehall*   ('Moral Essay' 1.76)

But Wisdom's triumph is *well-timed* Retreat	(ibid. 2.225)
Spleen, Vapours, or *Smallpox*, above them all	(ibid. 2.267)
'Twas no *Court badge*, great Scrivener! *fired thy brain*	(ibid. 3.145)
And heads the bold *Trainbands*, and burns a Pope	(ibid. 3.214)
May some choice patron bless each grey *goose quill*	('Epistle to Dr Arbuthnot', 249)
And suckle Armies, and *dry-nurse* the land	('Dunciad' 1.316)

It is only by virtue of this possibility that trisyllabic compounds are usable at all in Pope's verse:

(71) As to soft gales *top-heavy* pines bow low	('Dunciad' 2.391)
Some, deep *Freemasons*, join the silent race	(ibid. 4.571)

Inverted feet can also appear when the second member of a disyllabic compound is followed by an unstressed word (tension: 4):

(72) Of showers and sun*shine, as* of Man's desires	('Essay on Man' 1.152)
From dirt and sea*weed as* proud Venice rose	(ibid. 4.327)
In a dun night*gown of* his own loose skin	('Dunciad' 2.38)
Others a sword-*knot and* laced suit inflame	(ibid. 2.52)
He dies, sad out*cast of* each church and state	('Moral Essay' 1.204)
Shine, buzz, and fly*blow in* the sun	(ibid. 2.28)

By Pope's time, the stress system of English had reached nearly its present form, so in general we can consider Pope's meter from the viewpoint of modern pronunciation. This fact, together with the stringency of Pope's versification, puts our metrical rules and tension hierarchy to a demanding test, which they pass with distinction. Lines which violate the categorical restrictions of MR2 do not occur (except for the deliberate exception (67), which literally proves the rule). And, as we have seen, the tension index suggested in §1 closely matches the relative frequencies of usage in Pope.

3.2. *Poets not observing the monosyllable constraint.* It is well known that Donne was declared by Ben Jonson to have deserved hanging for writing unmetrical verse. As far as I know, the charge was never made more specific than that. I would like to rectify the situation here. What so bothered the contemporary champions of 'correctness' was that Donne's poetry contains, in numbers too great to blame on carelessness or textual inaccuracy, lines that violate the monosyllable condition on MR2. Donne seems to apply MR2 rather freely in *polysyllabic words:*

(37) Weav'd in my low devout *mel*ancholie	('La corona', 1)
Weake en*ough*, now into our world to come	(ibid. 3)
That would have need to be *pi*tied by thee	(ibid. 3)
Which him*selfe* on the Doctors did bestow	(ibid. 4)

Nor had time mellowed him to this *ripe*nesse	(ibid. 4)
But first hee, and hee first *en*ters the way	(ibid. 7)
By sicknesse, deaths *her*ald, and champion	('Holy sonnets', 4)
Shall be*hold* God, and never taste deaths woe	(ibid. 7)
If faithfull soules be a*like* glorified	(ibid. 8)
Make sinnes, else equal, in mee more *hei*nous	(ibid. 9)
But is *cap*tiv'd, and proves weake or untrue	(ibid. 14)
First tra*vail* we to seeke and then make Love	(ibid. 18)

For Donne, then, the monosyllable condition on MR2 does not hold. It is quite possible, of course, that some less restrictive condition on MR2 takes its place in Donne, though I cannot at present see what this condition would be. I also leave it for further investigation to decide whether the monosyllable condition is completely inoperative, or whether it has gone from a categorical to a relative condition, functioning in some way to determine metrical tension. What is clear so far is merely that the monosyllable condition cannot be categorical in Donne, and that his metrical rules are thus different from those of the main tradition of English poetry.

In a sense, Donne's violations of MR2a are proof of its validity elsewhere. The fact that lines as in (73) are encountered at every step in Donne is further proof that their absence in Shakespeare, Pope, Wordsworth, and other 'mainstream' poets cannot possibly be accidental, but must be due to the requirement of their metrical system. This conclusion is strengthened by a further correct prediction that is made by dropping the monosyllable constraint. We have seen that this constraint explains why trisyllabic compounds of the *earth-shaking* type must begin in weak position. It follows that Donne, who lacks the monosyllable constraint, should allow these compounds even beginning in strong position. And this is indeed the case:

(74) To *peace-teaching* Lawyer, Proctor, or brave ('Elegy', 14)
None doth; but *all-healing* grace and spirit[10] ('Holy sonnets', 16)

Violations of the monosyllable constraint are also found in Milton's blank verse:

(75) Before thy fellows, amb*itious* to win (PL 6.160)
Beyond all past example and *future* (PL 10.840)
Uni*versal* reproach, far worse to bear (PL 6.34)

They are frequent enough that the monosyllable condition cannot have been categorical in Milton's verse, but still not so frequent that MR2 could have been simply unrestricted. In this respect, Milton's metrics is transitional between the disappearing Renaissance system and the new system with the categorical monosyllable condition.

Milton also extends enjambment, but in a different way than Shakespeare does in his late plays. Milton allows lines to end in the middle of a phrase:

(76) a. But all that fair and good in thy divine
      Semblance, and in thy beauty's heavenly ray   (PL 9.606–7)
   b. ... These, these and many more
      Causes import your need of this fair fruit   (PL 9.730–31)
   c. Great joy he promis'd to this thought, and new
      Solace in her return, so long delay'd   (PL 9.846–7)
   d. To judgment he proceeded on the accursed
      Serpent, though brute ...   (PL 10.164–5)

However, there is apparently always a ♯♯ boundary between lines in Milton; i.e., the kind of stranding of proclitics that occurs in late Shakespeare is not attested in Milton. We can summarize the variation in enjambment as follows:

in the poetry of	*line division requires at least*
(77) early Shakespeare	ₚ[coinciding with ♯♯
late Shakespeare	ₚ[
Milton (*Paradise lost*)	♯♯

Note that the examples of (76) are not sufficient to prove the need for MR2c (see §2.7) in Milton's verse: as (75) shows, such inversion is possible even line-internally with no preceding boundary of any kind.

Among some of the Renaissance poets, the monosyllable constraint is frequently broken; at best it figures as a tendency. This is well illustrated by the following lines of Wyatt:

(78) Wherewith Love to the harts *forest* he fleeth
    Leaving the enterprise with pain and cry,
    And there him hideth and not *appeareth*.
    What may I do? When my *master feareth*,
    But in the field with him to live and die,
    For good is the life ending faithfully.

Auden (1962, p. 46–7) has discussed these lines appreciatively, declaring that they had influenced the rhythm of some of his own lines.[11] Though Auden does not explicitly say it, what is 'irregular' about them is that they violate the monosyllable constraint in the italicized syllables of lines 1, 3, and 4. As far as I can see, lines 2 and 5 might have come straight from Shakespeare; line 6 violates a constraint on the caesura which most later poets observe strictly.[12]

3.3. *Trochaic meter.* The metrical rules given in §1 have been justified here, up to now, only on the basis of iambic verse. But nothing in the rules limits their scope to this type of meter: they should also operate, where applicable, to characterize the permissible varieties of trochaic, dactylic, and anapestic verse in English. In this and in the next section, I shall try to show that this expectation is generally borne out, though a few minor additions to the system appear to be needed.

The applicability of MR1 in trochaic verse needs no documentation. As to MR2, the situation is a good bit more complicated than either traditional or more recent metrical studies would indicate. When it applies alone, it turns trochees into spondees; when it applies jointly with MR1, the result is an iambic foot. To what extent are such feet actually found in trochaic verse?

In order to arrive at a precise answer, we shall first have to make certain essential distinctions. In the case of iambic meter, blank verse and Hudibrastics are governed by the same metrical rules; but for stylistic reasons, they show greatly differing degrees of complexity in their utilization of these rules. The over-all metrical tension constitutes an index of this complexity. A similar observation can be made about trochaic verse. We may make a rough division of trochaic poems into two classes (without implying that the two are always sharply distinguishable). The first is a relatively complex type, familiar from numerous songs and from such poems as Shelley's 'To a Skylark' or Longfellow's 'Psalm of Life'. It can be termed *lyric trochaic*. The second is a relatively simple type, *narrative trochaic*, which is exemplified by 'Hiawatha,' 'The Raven,' and 'Locksley Hall.'

The principal difference between the two is in how often MR2 applies. In lyric trochaic verse, it applies with about the same frequency as in most iambic verse. Even a short lyric poem will have 'spondaic' feet generated by the application of MR2 to weak positions:

(79) Hail to / thee, *blithe* / spirit ('To a Skylark')
Whose in/tense *lamp* / narrows (ibid.)
In the / white *dawn* / clear (ibid.)
In its / own *green* / leaves (ibid.)
In the / world's *broad* / field of / battle ('A Psalm of Life')
Lives of / great *men* / all re/mind us (ibid.)
Let the / dead *past* / bury its / dead (ibid.)

But other trochaic poems – typically, longer narrative poems – have a very low percentage of spondaic feet. There are only a couple of them in 'The Raven' and in 'Locksley Hall':

(80) But the / Raven / still be/guiling / all my / sad *soul* / into / smiling ('The Raven')
Leave no / black *plume* / as a / token / of that / lie thy / soul hath / spoken (ibid.)

Catch the / wild *goat* / by the / hair, and / hurl their / lances / in
  the / sun   (Locksley Hall)
Let the / great *world* / spin for / ever / down the / ringing / grooves
  of / change   (ibid.)

Then what about iambic feet in trochaic verse? It is commonly said that they do not occur at all. This is repeated both in the traditional metrical literature (Bridges, p. 54; Jespersen) and in more recent works (Halle & Keyser 1971a, Hascall 1971). A look at the poetry shows that this is an oversimplification. A more accurate statement of the facts is that inverted feet occur in all kinds of trochaic verse; and that they are moderately frequent in lyric trochaic verse, but quite rare in narrative trochaic verse. Examples from lyric trochaics:

(81) *The blue* / deep thou / wingest   ('To a Skylark')
     Soothing / *her Love-*/laden   (ibid.)
     By warm / winds de / flowered   (ibid.)
     And sinks / down, down / like that / sleep (Shelley, 'Euganean Hills')
     To find / refuge / from di/stress   (ibid.)
     In the / waters / *of wide* / Agony   (ibid.)
     Wilt thou / be when / *the sea-*/mew   (ibid.)
     Like thought-/winged / Liber/ty   (ibid.)
     Sailing / *o'er life's* / solemn / main   ('A Psalm of Life)
     Be not / *like dumb* / driven / cattle   (ibid.)

But there are no examples in 'The Raven', and only one in 'Locksley Hall':

(82) Summer / isles of / Eden / lying / *in dark* / purple / spheres of / sea
                                                                (1.164)

This is, of course, exactly the situation which we would predict. One of the basic claims that our system makes is that inverted feet, in both iambic and trochaic poetry, arise through the joint application of MR1 and MR2 in the same foot: thus the conditions under which inverted feet appear should (unless special restrictions intervene) be a summation of the conditions under which 'pyrrhic' and 'spondaic' feet appear. Pyrrhic feet are unrestricted: and so we end up with the prediction that iambic feet should be possible in trochaic verse in proportion as spondaic feet are – though they should be more complex, and consequently less frequent, inasmuch as they involve the application of the additional rule MR1. Since this appears to be correct, we can conclude that trochaic verse confirms the metrical theory of §1.

Our rules for iambic verse have still another consequence for trochees. Because of the condition placed on MR2a, a stressed syllable in weak position must be a monosyllabic word. This means that the *second* syllable of a 'spondaic' or 'iambic' foot in trochaic verse must be a word. This holds true of all the examples given above, and I have found no exceptions so far.

The upshot of the preceding is that, in order to account for trochaic verse, we do not need to change anything in the metrical rules that govern iambic verse. These rules, when applied to basic patterns of a trochaic form (i.e. $[1,4]^n$) will generate the actually occurring prosodic variants – and, as far as we can now tell, no unmetrical ones. We need only take note of the fact that the over-all metrical tension in trochaic verse varies, like that of any other kind of verse, depending on the stylistic level.

3.4. *Ternary meters.* How do our metrical rules fare in dactylic and anapestic verse? I shall concentrate here on the later – which, in tetrameter lines, has at times been a popular form in songs and light lyrics. The basis of my discussion will be Byron's poetry, where this meter is rather frequently used. It is my impression that the conclusions that can be drawn from this corpus have general validity for ternary meters in English, though this would of course have to be checked by a systematic investigation.

In ternary meters, the application of MR1 produces long sequences of unstressed syllables, and is for that reason disfavored. This is not an absolute prohibition which could be built into the metrical rules, but a stylistic factor which is analysable separately from the abstract system. Lines which do show MR1 at work are:

(83) And redeemed, if they *have* not retarded, thy fall
('The Irish Avatar')
But *thou* wert not fated affection to share
('To an Oak at Newstead')
'Tis *but* as a dead-flower with May-dew besprinkled
('Stanzas Written on the Road between Florence and Pisa')

MR2 applies frequently in anapestic meter. The word-boundary condition on MR2a holds for the second weak position:

(84) *Such*, such was my hope, when in infancy's years
('To an Oak at Newstead')
Remembrance *still* hallows the dust of the dead (ibid.)
That dog thy *young* growth, and assist thy decay (ibid.)
The *deep* thoughts that dwell in that silence of heart
('Stanzas for Music')
Flashed back on the last glance I gave to thy wall
('On the Day of the Destruction of Jerusalem by Titus')
And the eyes of the sleepers *wax'd* deadly and chill
('The Destruction of Sennacherib')
And their hearts but *once* heaved, and for ever grew still! (ibid.)
And the tents were *all* silent, the banners alone (ibid.)

Tears fall on his chain, though it drops from his hands
('The Irish Avatar')
Even Tyranny listening *sate* melted or mute (ibid.)
Spread – spread, for Vitellius, the royal repast (ibid.)

In the first weak position, the monosyllabic word constraint is waived. MR2a, as it now stands, allows the unstressed syllable to be replaced by a monosyllabic word with either primary or secondary stress:

(85) From the last *hill* that looks on thy once holy dome
('On the Day of the Destruction of Jerusalem by Titus')
Flashed back on the last *glance* I gave to thy wall (ibid.)
Had reflected the last *beam* of day as it blazed (ibid.)
For the Angel of Death *spread* his wings on the blast
('The Destruction of Sennacherib')
Of ages, the first, *last* the saviour, the one! ('The Irish Avatar')
But back to our theme! *Back* to despots and slaves! (ibid.)
On his right *hand* behold a Sejanus appears! (ibid.)
(86) On thy leaves yet the day-*beam* of ages may shine
('To an Oak at Newstead')
I beheld but the death-*fire* that fed on thy fare
('On the Day of the Destruction of Jerusalem by Titus')
The hosts with their banners at sun*set* were seen
('The Destruction of Sennacherib')
'Tis but as a dead-*flower* with May-*dew* besprinkled
('Stanzas Written on the Road between Florence and Pisa')

But there are also numerous examples with polysyllabic words in the equivalent metrical position, either with primary or secondary stress:

(87) Uninjured by time, or the rude *winter's* breath
('To an Oak at Newstead')
For still in thy bosom are life's *ear*ly seeds (ibid.)
For centuries still may thy boughs *light*ly wave (ibid.)
And here, will they say, when in life's *glow*ing prime (ibid.)
Perhaps he has poured forth his young *sim*ple lay (ibid.)
From the last hill that looks on thy once *ho*ly dome
('On the Day of the Destruction of Jerusalem by Titus')
Let the poor *squa*lid splendour thy wreck can afford
('The Irish Avatar')
Till, like Babel, the new *roy*al dome hath arisen! (ibid.)
Without one *sin*gle ray of her genius, without (ibid.)
I have known *no*ble hearts and great souls in thy sons (ibid.)
Yes, happy are they in their cold *Eng*lish graves! (ibid.)

(88) That thy dark-*wa*ving branches would flourish around
                    ('To an Oak at Newstead')
And the fast-*fet*tered hands that made vengeance in vain
                    ('On the Day of the Destruction of Jerusalem by Titus')
As cold as the spray of the rock-*beat*ing surf
                    ('The Destruction of Sennacherib')
Could that long-*with*ered spot but be verdant again
                    ('The Irish Avatar')

I have been unable to find any examples breaking the monosyllabic word condition in the *second* weak position of a foot; and it is also my intuition that this would constitute a metrical violation. Thus the line

(89) Oh, say, can you see by the dawn's early light

sounds really wretched if we replace *early* with an end-stressed disyllabic word:

(90) *Oh, say, can you see by the dawn's *intense* light

This shows the need for revising MR2. We add to it another branch which generates the attested anapestic patterns:

Metrical rule 2d: [4 stress] → [β stress] in env. ____ [4 stress]

This formulation requires either that MR1 and MR2 should apply simultaneously, or that MR2 should precede MR1 in the ordering. We do not want a [4 stress] from MR1 to provide an environment for the application of MR2d, which would mean that trochaic feet would be freely generated in iambic verse, even in polysyllabic words. Thus, while it is evident that some rule with the effect of MR2d is required, we must leave open here, for lack of relevant evidence, the question of how that rule is to be formally incorporated into the system. The general parallelism of metrical and phonological rules which has become apparent at every step would naturally suggest that linear ordering is the right mechanism, although nothing in our data is incompatible with the other alternative of simultaneous application.

I likewise leave open the question of whether MR2d applies in dactylic meter. If a study of that meter shows that it is inapplicable there, or applies in a different way than suggested by the above formulation, then it will be necessary to modify the rules accordingly.

Of course, MR2 can apply twice in a foot:

(91) When the blue *wave rolls* nightly on deep Galilee
                    ('The Destruction of Sennacherib')
But I marked not the twi*light beam* melting away
                    ('On the Day of the Destruction of Jerusalem by Titus')

But the contiguous application of MR1 and MR2 is as rare in ternary meters as it is in trochaic meter:

(92) a. And if *not* / *shot* or hanged, / you'll get knight/ed
                                              ('When a Man hath no Freedom')
   b. Lo, George, / the triumph/ant *speeds ov*/er the wave
                                                    ('The Irish Avatar')
   c. I left / thee, my Oak, / and, since *that* / *fa*tal hour
                                                  ('To an Oak at Newstead')

Note that, in all these cases, a stressed syllable in weak position stands between two unstressed syllables. Thus even ternary meters contradict the Stress Maximum Principle.

3.5. *Intimations of universal metrics.* Systematic relationships of the sort we have been finding justify treating the whole metrical repertoire of English as a unified system, allowing us to describe changes in it in terms of that system. But we must go even further: a theory of meter cannot restrict itself to one poetic tradition, any more than a theory of grammar can restrict itself to one language. We must make our theory account for metrical systems of other languages, and begin to construct a 'universal metrics'. The increased scope of the theory will limit the range of possible hypotheses, and decide many questions which would remain moot if we stuck to English alone. Only when the foundations have been laid for a general theory of meter will we be able to begin raising seriously such questions as the relationship of poetic meter to rhythm in music and other arts, and to rhythm in biological organisms in general.

It is clear that English shares at least some of the elements of its metrical system with other languages; e.g. the monosyllable constraint appears in one form or another in the stress-based verse of many languages. Chisholm (1973), citing work by Magnuson and Ryder, finds that German trisyllabic compounds of the type *Stammtische* always occur in weak–strong–weak position, as in English (cf. §2.2 above); this suggests that the monosyllable constraint may also be valid in German. Chisholm finds further that derivational suffixes fall into two types. One type includes -*heit*/-*keit*, -*fach*, -*los*, -*voll*, -*tum*, -*falt*, -*kunft*, -*wart*/-*wärts*, -*haft*, -*lein*, -*arm*, -*reich*, -*wert*: trisyllabic words with this type of suffix are placed in weak–strong–weak position. The other type includes suffixes like -*ig*, -*ling*, -*ich*, -*nis*, -*at*, -*icht*, -*sal*, -*rich*, -*ing*, -*lich*, -*e*, -*isch*, -*ung*, -*sam*, -*in*:[13] words with these suffixes are placed in a strong–weak–strong position. Chisholm assumes that this difference in positioning reflects a stress difference between the suffix types, and argues that the stress rules of Kiparsky (1966) must be revised to assign a stress to the suffixes of the first type, but not the second. Ultimately, he claims, the difference between the suffix classes has historical causes: the first class contains the suffixes which were retained as independent lexical items at least into Middle High German, while the second class contains the suffixes which disappeared as independent lexical items before Middle High German.

This historical correlation is suggestive; but of course etymology cannot in this case directly influence meter, since it is neither relevant nor even known to the poet. Historical facts can directly account for a regularity in a living poetic tradition only when they correspond to synchronically valid derivations in the grammar of a language (for some such cases, see Zeps 1963, 1973; Kiparsky 1968, 1972). The MHG or post-MHG origin of some suffixes could not directly determine modern German verse structure, though it could do so indirectly via some reflex in the synchronic grammatical system of modern German. What could this reflex be?

The suggestion that stress is the mediating factor is unsatisfactory; it is simply not true that there is a consistent stress difference between the two suffix types. The words *einfache* (Type 1) and *langsame* (Type 2) are stressed alike. In general, suffixes with reduced vowels ([ə], and [ɪ] before palatals) have no stress, and suffixes with full vowels have some degree of secondary stress. While all suffixes of Type 1 have full vowels, suffixes of Type 2 have both full and reduced vowels.

There is an alternative synchronic explanation which does not rely on dubious stress distinctions. Given the fact that the monosyllable constraint holds in German – at least in its relevant portion, as evinced by the behavior of compounds like *Stammtische* – we can suppose that the suffixes of Type 1 are morphologically like second members of compounds, whereas those of Type 2 are not. Now MR2a and PR directly predict the observed positioning, on the basis of the usual assumption that suffixes with full vowels have a subsidiary stress, while suffixes with reduced vowels have none:

(93) Type 1   ## Gott ## heit en ##   metrical

   ## Gott ## heit ## en   unmetrical
                                 (*heit* violates MR2a)

Type 2   ## lang sam e ##   unmetrical
                                 (*lang* violates MR2a)

          ## lang sam e ##   metrical

Gottheiten will violate the monosyllable condition when its (accented) suffix is placed in weak position. Note that this requires that all Type 1 suffixes have unreduced vowels, which is in fact true. The type *langsame* will, on the other hand, violate the monosyllable condition when its stem is in weak position, since the stem is not a monosyllabic word in the required sense of standing between ## boundaries. The suffix in *langsame*, even though stressed, will not violate the monosyllable condition by virtue of PR, which directs us to disregard all but the highest stresses in each domain ## X ## (where X contains no ##). For Type 2 suffixes, then, it does not matter whether the suffix is stressed or not – and in fact, this type is represented by suffixes with both full and reduced vowels.

Of course this explanation, however neat, remains conjectural until the required ## boundaries are justified on linguistic grounds. What evidence is there to suppose that Type 1 suffixes are morphologically structured like compounds? One fact which points in that direction is that Type 1 suffixes, like second members of compounds, can generally be factored out in conjunction: like *Ess- und Schreibtische* 'dining- and writing tables', we have *zwei- und dreifach* 'two- and threefold', *öl- und erzreich* 'rich in oil and ore', *vor- und rückwärts* 'forward and backward', *König- und Kaisertum* 'kingship and emperorship', *flegel- und stümperhaft* 'boorish and bungling'. Admittedly, this does not seem equally possible for all Type 1 suffixes, e.g. *-heit* and *-lein*; and of course it is possible only when the suffixes are used in a parallel way: **König- und Altertum* 'kingship and antiquity'. But not even under complete parallelism is such factoring out permissible for Type 2 suffixes: **lang- und sorgsam* 'slowly and carefully', *Güt- und Stärke 'goodness and strength', **klapper- und wackelig* 'rattling and shaky'.

A close examination of the suffixes would allow my proposal to be tested in other ways. For example, Chisholm finds some inconsistency in *-bar*, which behaves like a Type 2 suffix in 80 per cent of the cases and a Type 1 suffix in the remaining cases. I would conjecture that the reason is the double function of *-bar* as (a) a lexicalized unproductive suffix, as in *dankbar* 'grateful', *sonderbar* 'strange'; and (b) a productive suffix corresponding to Eng. *-able*, e.g. *trinkbar* 'drinkable', *undenkbar* 'unthinkable', which is factorable (*trink- und essbar* 'drinkable and eatable'). I would thus predict that the bulk of Type 1 cases should be of the latter, productive type, while the bulk of Type 2 cases should be of the lexicalized type.

Russian meter is, like that of English and German, based on stress rather than quantity. A detailed comparison of Russian and English would undoubtedly be highly instructive, judging from the analysis presented in Zhirmunsky 1966. Russian shares MR1 with English. Iambic verse allows spondaic feet if the first position in the foot is a monosyllabic word. Inverted feet require, in addition, that a verse or sentence boundary precede. It is evident that this is a system made up of the same basic elements as English metrics, but assembled in a different way. Variations parallel to those in the English tradition are found; e.g. some twentieth-century poets drop the monosyllable condition.

In languages like classical Greek and Latin, we find no analogs to the MR1 and MR2a of English. However, a process comparable to MR2b or 2c does exist. Consider the iambic trimeter of classical Greek poetry, with the basic structure

(94) $\underline{\smile} \_ \smile \_ \underline{\smile} \mid \_ \smile \mid \_ \underline{\smile} \_ \smile \underline{\smile}$

Here a word boundary must occur in one of the two places marked by |, viz. either between the fifth and sixth positions or between the seventh and eighth positions. The free choice between strong and weak in the final position is a constant option of Greek (as well as of Latin and Sanskrit) verse of every metrical form. To be distinguished from this neutralization – which seems to be found only in languages with quantitative verse (but in all these?) – is the neutralization in the first, fifth, and ninth positions. This is a characteristic of iambic verse only, and has no counterpart in trochaic verse, where /_/ in the corresponding positions cannot be replaced by /∪/.

It is well-known that Greek verses containing even numbers of feet have a dipodic internal structure (hence the term trimeter for a six-foot line). We can represent this dipodic internal structure by assuming verse boundaries before each odd-numbered foot, i.e. before positions 1, 5, and 9. (We will want to postulate that the initial boundary is stronger than the internal ones, but this will not be relevant here.) To express the quantitative neutralization of these positions we need the rule

(95) $\smile \rightarrow \_$ after verse boundary

The same rule can be motivated for the Vedic poetry of ancient India – which, like Greek and Latin poetry, is based on the distinction between long and short syllables, and also has verse-initial neutralization of quantity everywhere. This correlates with the fact that Vedic meter is fundamentally iambic throughout (Arnold, 1905).

The general impression thus seems to emerge that MR1 and MR2a are characteristic of stress-based metrical systems, whereas MR2b (or 2c) recurs in quantitative meter as well. This fact supports the conjecture that the monosyllable constraint (MR2a) is functionally motivated by its effect of preventing word-internal stress relations from conflicting with meter.*

---

*This work was supported in part by a grant from the National Institute of Mental Health (5 PO1 MH13390). Thanks to Ann Banfield for spotting an inadequacy in my earlier version of MR2.

Notes

1 As in Pope's line discussed in §3.1 below (ex. 67), or that of Keats cited by Halle and Keyser 1971a.
2 Thus there are lines which are metrical, but unacceptable because of their complexity. This is no different from the fact that there are sentences which are grammatical, but unacceptable for a variety of stylistic reasons, including syntactic complexity. The limits of complexity vary with style and period.

Note that even lines with zero tension need not be doggerel; considerable variety of rhythm can still be introduced by syntactic means, e.g.:

> ... By the fire
> That quickens Nilus' slime, I go from hence
> Thy soldier, servant, making peace or war
> As thou affect'st. (Ant. 1.3.68–71)

All examples here, unless otherwise indicated, are from Shakespeare (with titles abbreviated in the style of the *Shakespeare Quarterly*).

3 The tension index is here defined only for lines that preserve the underlying number of syllables in the derived pattern. Presumably, the application of the metrical rules that create extrametrical syllables or headless lines gives an additional boost to the metrical tension of a line. But in the absence of clear facts about the stylistic function of these processes, assigning a definitive quantitative value to their operation would be mere numerology. There is also the question whether the prosodic component makes a contribution to the tension index. For example, when two syllables fill a single metrical position, does this increase the complexity of a line? Some observations of Sipe 1968 suggest a way in which this question might be answered. She finds that Shakespeare systematically uses lexical doublets of different syllabic value (such as *gainst* and *against*, *get* and *beget*) to impose a decasyllabic iambic pattern on his verse. However, there is no apparent effort to minimize synaloepha by these means. It could easily have been avoided in lines such as

> To *emblaze* the Honor that thy Master got (2H6 4.10.76)
> To *enforce* the pained impotent to smile (LLL 5.2.864)

by replacing *emblaze, enforce* by *blaze, force* (elsewhere used by Shakespeare in the same meanings). The fact that the disyllabic form of the verb could be used in such cases shows that synaloepha, whether or not it corresponded to a real phonetic elision, was at any rate not viewed as a desperate last resort. Perhaps a thorough comparison of the possibilities with Shakespeare's actual practice will tell us to what extent synaloepha was stylistically marked.
4 A recent detailed study of the evolution of these prosodic conventions in English poetry is Tarlinskaya 1973.
5 Actually, two extrametrical syllables are generally adjacent vowels or other sequences which the prosodic rules must in any case permit to occupy a single metrical position (Bridges 1921:5–6). If this is always true, then only one extrametrical position need be allowed – indeed, more than one cannot be allowed.
6 Strictly speaking, an iambic analysis is possible, as in Lear's line quoted as ex. 7 above. But with a tension index of 25, its complexity under that scansion goes well past what is normally found in iambic verse.

7 A first formulation (Magnuson and Ryder 1970) was slightly incorrect, prompting Halle and Keyser 1971b wrongly to reject the whole claim. The correct formulation was given in Magnuson and Ryder 1971.
8 In stating this rule I use the convention that assigning a stress of degree n is accompanied by automatic reduction of stresses equal to or weaker than n in the same constituent (Kiparsky 1966). A somewhat more complex rule is required in the framework of Chomsky and Halle. A better treatment of this phenomenon is possible with the revision suggested by Halle 1973, where both syllables in *sixteen* (cf. also Lee 1969) first receive a primary stress, and then either the first or the second is reduced depending on the context. Some problems remain, such as *állied ármies*, where the first syllable of *allied* lacks a stress in isolation and thus should not be subject to the Rhythm Rule.
9 The following discussion is based on the works contained in W. K. Wimsatt's *Alexander Pope: Selected Poetry and Prose* (Rinehart edition).
10 Here *spirit* rhymes with *yet*, and so must be disyllabic. Note that both lines have three successive trochaic feet. On the basis of stress alone, the second has a tension of 18, not counting what the multiple violations of the monosyllable condition might contribute.
11 I owe this reference to Andrew Carstairs.
12 I discuss this constraint in my forthcoming *Syntax of Verse*.
13 Chisholm also found six examples with *-schaft*, which were divided equally between the two types.

References

Arnold, E. Vernon. 1905. *Vedic Metre*. Cambridge: University Press.
Auden, W. H. 1962. *The Dyer's Hand*. New York: Random House.
Beaver, Joseph C. 1971a. 'The rules of stress in English verse'. *Language* 47.486–614.
——. 1971b. 'Current metrical issues'. *College English* 33.177–97.
Bridges, Robert. 1921. *Milton's Prosody*. Oxford: Clarendon Press.
Chatman, Seymour. 1956. 'Robert Frost's *Mowing*: an inquiry into prosodic structure.' *Kenyon Review* 18.421–51.
——. 1965. A *Theory of Meter*. The Hague: Mouton.
Chisholm, David H. 1973. 'Lexicality and German derivational suffixes: a contribution to the Magnuson–Ryder theory of prosody.' *Language and Style* 6.27–38.
Chomsky, Noam, and Morris Halle. 1968. *The Sound Pattern of English*. New York: Harper & Row.
Freeman, Donald. 1968a. 'On the primes of metrical style.' *Language and Style* 1.63–101.
—— (ed.) 1970. *Linguistics and Literary Style*. New York: Holt, Rinehart & Winston.
Frye, Northrop. 1957. 'The Rhythm of Recurrence: Epos.' In his *Anatomy of Criticism*, 251–62. Princeton: Princeton University Press.
Halle, Morris. 1973. 'Stress rules in English: a new version.' *Linguistic Inquiry* 4.451–64.
——, and J. Keyser. 1966. 'Chaucer and the study of prosody.' *College English* 28.187–219.

———, ———. 1971a. *English Stress: Its Form, Its Growth, and Its Role in Verse.* New York: Harper & Row.
———, ———. 1971b. 'Illustration and defense of a theory of the iambic pentameter.' *College English* 33.154–76.
———, ———. 1974. 'On the theoretical bases of metrical verse.' To appear.
Hascall, Dudley. 1971. 'Trochaic meter.' *College English* 33.217–26.
Jakobson, Roman. 1960. 'Linguistics and Poetics.' *Style in Language,* ed. by T. A. Sebeok, 350–85. Cambridge, Mass.: MIT Press.
Jespersen, Otto. 1933. 'Notes on metre.' In his *Linguistica,* 249–74. Copenhagen: Levin & Munksgaard.
Kiparsky, Paul. 1966. 'Über den deutschen Akzent.' *Studia Grammatica* 7.69–98.
———. 1968. 'Metrics and morphophonemics in the Kalevala.' *Studies Presented to Professor Roman Jakobson by his Students,* ed. by C. Gribble, 137–48. Cambridge, Mass.: Slavica.
———. 1972. 'Metrics and morphophonemics in the Rigveda.' *Contributions to Generative Phonology,* ed. by M. Brame, 171–200. Austin: University of Texas Press.
———. 1973. 'The role of linguistics in a theory of poetry.' *Daedalus,* Summer, 231–44. [Reprinted in this volume, pp. 9–23]
Lanier, Sidney. 1880. *The Science of English Verse.* New York.
Lee, Gregory. 1969. 'English word-stress.' *Papers from the 5th Regional Meeting,* Chicago Linguistic Society, 389–96.
Maas, Paul. 1962. *Greek Metre.* Oxford: Clarendon Press.
Magnuson, Karl, and Frank Ryder. 1970. 'The study of English prosody: an alternative proposal. *College English* 31.789–820.
———, ———. 1971. 'Second thoughts on English prosody.' *College English* 33.198–216.
Selkirk, Lisa. 1972. *The Phrase Phonology of English and French.* MIT dissertation.
Sipe, Dorothy L. 1968. *Shakespeare's Metrics.* New Haven: Yale University Press.
Smith, Barbara Herrnstein. 1968. *Poetic Closure: a Study of how Poems End.* Chicago: University of Chicago Press.
Tarlinskaya, Marina. 1973. 'The syllabic Structure and meter of English Verse from the thirteenth through the nineteenth century'. *Language and Style* 6.249–72.
Whitehall, Harold. 1956. 'From Linguistics to Criticism.' *Kenyon Review* 18.411–21.
Wimsatt, W. K. 1970. 'The rule and the norm: Halle and Keyser on Chaucer's meter.' *College English* 31.774–88.
Zeps, Valdis. 1963. 'The meter of the so-called trochaic Latvian folksongs.' *International Journal of Slavic Linguistics and Poetics* 7.123–8.
———. 1973. 'Latvian folk meters and styles.' *A Festschrift for Morris Halle,* ed. by S. Anderson & P. Kiparsky, 207–11. New York: Holt, Rinehart & Winston.
Zhirmunsky, Viktor. 1966. *Introduction to Metrics.* The Hague: Mouton.

12
Towards a formal poetics: metrical patterning in 'The Windhover'

Charles T. Scott

For Archibald A. Hill

In general, literary critics have not taken kindly to Harold Whitehall's assertion that 'no criticism can go beyond its linguistics.'[1] Whitehall's claim, first made in 1951, to this day smacks of an intellectual arrogance that some have regarded as insufferable, since it clearly seems to insist that the discipline of linguistics must serve as a *controlling* theory for criticism. Such a position, moreover, implies that non-linguistic considerations, e.g. the relationship of the literary text to cultural factors outside the text, have no place in the activities and conclusions of literary criticism. Students of literature, therefore, have frequently dismissed the efforts of those who would assert a necessary connection between linguistics and literary study as little more than a terminologically different version of the principles of the New Criticism.

Since Whitehall's provocative statement, a number of linguists have attempted to argue the case for linguistics as a discipline which is crucially necessary to sound literary criticism.[2] Though this work, as might be expected, varies considerably in quality and persuasiveness, a central assumption in all of these efforts has been that rigorous analysis of the primary data is the best means of obviating vapid and 'impressionistic conclusions. This assumption follows naturally from the principal charge that linguistics has leveled against much of what purports to be literary criticism: that too often criticism fails to recognize, or perhaps disregards, systematic (i.e. apparently non-accidental) regularities in the data and relies instead on unverifiable intuitions for its interpretations. The linguist prefers the point of view that the critic's conclusion is best regarded as analogous to the scientist's theory; that in both endeavors a theory is constructed which consistently, completely, and simply accounts for the observed data; and that in both cases the theory is true and vulnerable in the sense that it must be viewed as the best theory unless a new theory is proposed which more consistently, more completely, and more simply accounts for the same observed data. It is in this context that we might understand Freeman's recent claim that 'a good critic is perforce a good linguist.'[3]

One purpose of this paper is to lend support to Freeman's contention that 'linguistics gives literary criticism a theoretical underpinning as necessary to that undertaking as mathematics is to physics.'[4] Put another way, the paper purports to show that an intuitively unsatisfying and demonstrably wrong *literary* conclusion could have been avoided if proper attention had been given to linguistic-stylistic detail. The question of metrical patterning in Hopkins's 'The Windhover' is selected for examination and for re-analysis. On re-analysis, a further insight to the structure of the poem is proposed. Thus, a second purpose of the paper is to contribute to the literary scholarship on Hopkins and on 'The Windhover'.

In the introduction to his casebook edition of 'The Windhover',[5] John Pick briefly surveys a number of details of the poem which have elicited widely diverse interpretations on the part of scholars and critics. To judge simply from the number of commentaries on the poem in scholarly journals and books, Pick is clearly right in concluding that 'few poems in the English language will bear such careful analysis as "The Windhover" – and few will yield such riches.'[6] The richness of 'The Windhover' has been amply demonstrated by the many critics who have chosen to 'revisit' the poem – always presumably with the conviction that some new clue to its structure or meaning will be discovered and elucidated. Hopefully, then, still another visitor may be forgiven for believing that not all has been said of 'The Windhover' that might be said.

This paper concentrates on an aspect of the poem's structure that has been hinted at in many ways, but has never, to my knowledge, been convincingly explained. This structural aspect is the metrical patterning of the poem, though in the course of the following discussion it will also be necessary to refer to related matters of poetic ornamentation such as rhyme and alliteration. The poem, as it is usually printed, appears below for convenient reference:

The Windhover:
To Christ our Lord
I caught this morning morning's minion, king-
    dom of daylight's dauphin, dapple-dawn-drawn Falcon, in his riding
    Of the rolling level underneath him steady air, and striding

High there, how he rung upon the rein of a wimpling wing
In this ecstasy! then off, off forth on swing,
    As a skate's heel sweeps smooth on a bow-bend: the hurl and gliding
    Rebuffed the big wind. My heart in hiding
Stirred for a bird, – the achieve of, the mastery of the thing!

Brute beauty and valour and act, oh, air, pride, plume, here
    Buckle! AND the fire that breaks from thee then, a billion
Times told lovelier, more dangerous, O my chevalier!

    No wonder of it: shéer plód makes plough down sillion
Shine, and blue-bleak embers, ah my dear,
    Fall, gall themselves, and gash gold-vermilion.

First, it will be helpful to restate some of the formal features of the poem that have been accepted without question by most critics. There is general agreement, for example, that the poem is a sonnet with a Petrarchan rhyme scheme, and George Pace has pointed out the interesting unconventional realization of the conventional rhyme pattern in Hopkins's use of stressed and unstressed *-ing* syllables for the *abbaabba* format of the octave.[7] Though the term 'sonnet' is regularly applied to the poem (obviously because of the fourteen lines and the apparent traditional rhyme scheme), there remains the anomalous fact that the metrical pattern does not appear to conform to the iambic meter that is characteristically expected of the sonnet form. John Pick accommodates this difficulty by reference to Hopkins's personal view of the uniqueness of each poem. In elucidating Hopkins's view, Pick says: 'Indeed, each sonnet must have a metrical pattern different from any other sonnet in the history of mankind. Hopkins rediscovered a metrical system in which this is possible.'[8] Pick then goes on to point out that the metrical system that Hopkins rediscovered was a variation of the Old English alliterative system, which required four accented syllables in each line, though the number of unaccented syllables could vary. 'Hopkins reintroduced this system but with some important differences. Each one of Hopkins's poems has a set number of accented syllables in each line, though that number is not necessarily four, and Hopkins wrote various poems in three, five, six or even eight accented syllables. The number of unaccented syllables is different in each line and may fall in any position. Thus in "The Windhover" each line has five accented syllables, but the total number of accented and unaccented syllables in each line varies all the way from nine to sixteen.'[9] A further traditionally accepted feature of Hopkins's metrical practice is his use of what he himself termed a 'sprung rhythm'. Pick describes this as follows: 'To his system Hopkins gave the name "sprung rhythm", because it was possible for two accented syllables to follow immediately upon one another

276   *Essays in Modern Stylistics*

giving a sprung or "abrupt" effect similar to the emphasis in impassioned speech. Thus in "The Windhover" one comes across such instances as "big wind", "sheer plod", and "gash gold-".[10]

These commonly accepted 'facts' concerning Hopkins's poetic practice in general, and formal features of 'The Windhover' in particular, require some scrutiny because there are difficulties associated with all of them. Consider first the validity of the notion 'sprung rhythm'. Is there any basis for it, other than simply Hopkins's idiosyncratic instructions concerning how his poems should be read, i.e. *performed*? A metrical pattern, precisely because it is an abstract structure, cannot be a set of instructions for performing a poem, and it would appear that a failure to distinguish between 'metrical pattern' and 'performance directions' lies at the heart of much of the confusion surrounding Hopkins's metrical practice.[11] If the distinguishing characteristic of 'sprung rhythm' is the possibility for two accented syllables to follow immediately upon one another, then there is no way of designating 'sprung rhythm' as a metrical pattern distinctly different from either the Old English alliterative system or the iambic system, since the possibility for two accented syllables to follow immediately upon one another can also be found in both of those systems.[12] More generally, the question is whether 'sprung rhythm' refers to a metrical system which is linguistically possible for English and which has a linguistic basis that is different from either the supposed isochronous nature of the Old English alliterative system (or of various types of folk literature and of popular songs) or the syllable-counting, stress-alternating nature of the iambic system. This seems not to be the case. That is, the term 'sprung rhythm' would appear to designate nothing more than Hopkins's way of indicating how he felt his poems should be read.

This brings us to the question of the number of accented syllables in each line of 'The Windhover' – five per line, according to Pick. Is this really the case, or is this, too, simply a contrived presumption on the part of Hopkins? This question, of course, involves assumptions about which categories of lexical items may be supposed to carry strong stress. Adjectives, nouns, and verbs characteristically present no problems, but what of various adverbials like *here, there, down, then,* and interjection like *oh, O,* and *ah*? A line such as

Rebúffed the bíg wínd. My héart in híding

seems straightforward, since it is doubtful whether the indicated accent assignments would be disputed. But is the assignment of accent so clear in the line

Shíne, and blúe-bleak émbers, ah my déar,

in which the fifth accent might be assigned to either *-bleak* or to *ah*? And how do we compute the necessary five accented syllables of

> Brute beauty and valour and act, oh, air, pride, plume, here

or

> As a skate's heel sweeps smooth on a bow-bend: the hurl and gliding?

On the other hand, in the much-discussed line

> Buckle! AND the fire that breaks from thee then, a billion

it is reasonable to assume that Hopkins used the typographical device of capitalized letters to inform the reader that *AND* should be the fifth accented syllable of the line (*Buck-*, *fire*, *breaks*, *bill-* must be the other four) rather than the more plausible adverbial *then*. If this interpretation is correct, then we have here a clear instance of the use of a purely superficial device, a typographical convention, to provide a kind of stage direction for properly *performing* the poem – a device, in other words, which is as contrived as the notion 'sprung rhythm'. It should be apparent, then, that at least on the surface, we cannot accept at face value John Pick's assertion that Hopkins employed a system of five accented syllables in each line of 'The Windhover'.

In fairness to both Hopkins and Pick, however, the matter of alliteration must also be considered in this context, since (1) alliteration is a principal characteristic of the Old English system and (2) Hopkins supposedly employed a variation on the Old English system in 'The Windhover'. In other words, alliterating consonants could provide an additional constraint on which of the possible accented syllables of each line should be computed as part of the necessary five. These data can be summarized in tabular form, and are presented in the Appendix.

Even with an analysis that recognizes alliteration as a formal constraint, it should be clear that there are still doubts concerning which five of the possible accented syllables of each line are to be considered the ones that presumably sustain Pick's assertion that Hopkins uses five accented syllables in each line of 'The Windhover'. To put the matter more generally: there is good reason to be skeptical of the traditional claim that Hopkins 'reintroduced' the Old English alliterative system as the basic metrical pattern of 'The Windhover', even though we may properly recognize certain similarities between formal features of 'The Windhover' and the general rules of the Old English system.

It should also be observed that all of the traditionally accepted 'facts' pertaining to the formal structure of 'The Windhover' depend, in one way or another, on unquestioned assumptions concerning the boundaries – indeed, the nature – of the poetic 'line'. Thus, the assertion that 'The Windhover' is a sonnet is clearly based on the recognition of fourteen 'lines' for the poem. The Petrarchan rhyme scheme, associated formally with the generic term 'sonnet', is described as an *abbaabba cdc dcd* pattern on the basis of a recognition of 'line ends'. Further, the entire argument which maintains that Hopkins employed a variation of the OE alliterative system for his metrical pattern presupposes the identification of 'lines', since it is only with this presupposition that one can speak of Hopkins's use of five accented syllables per line.

The nature of the poetic 'line' is a fundamental issue of poetic theory, but the issue is one which cannot be explored in detail here. For our present purposes, it is sufficient to note that the application of linguistic-stylistic criteria to this issue could demonstrate rather convincingly that the typographical practices associated with poetic discourses must be viewed with some skepticism. In the course of the following discussion, some of the reasons for this skepticism will become clear.

Thus far, it has been shown that some of the traditionally accepted conclusions concerning the formal characteristics of 'The Windhover' are dubious at best. In particular, we can now view with skepticism any claim that the metrical pattern of the poem is a contemporary representation of the Old English alliterative system. Two other alternative views of the poem's metrical pattern are possible: (1) that the metrical pattern is iambic, since this is the other major pattern in the history of English versification and the one that has been particularly associated with the sonnet form; and (2) that the metrical pattern is one which can be conveniently identified as 'sprung rhythm' and which is, by definition, distinct from either the Old English pattern or the iambic pattern.

This paper argues that the second alternative can be rejected by showing that the first alternative, under a revised theory of the iambic meter, correctly accounts for the metrical patterning of the poem. In addition, after demonstrating that the underlying metrical pattern of 'The Windhover' is iambic, it is shown that that conclusion leads to a further insight concerning the formal structure of the poem.

The revised theory of the iambic meter that is adopted here is one that has been proposed by Morris Halle and Samuel Jay Keyser.[13] Halle and Keyser have claimed that the abstract metrical pattern for the iambic pentameter line can be expressed as follows:

$$(w) * s \ ws \ ws \ ws \ ws \ (x) \ (x)$$

where elements enclosed in parentheses may be omitted and where each x position may be occupied only by an unstressed syllable.[14]

The asterisk following the initial (w) means that, if the initial weak syllable is omitted, i.e., if the line is headless, then the line is a more, rather than a less, complex actualization of the abstract metrical pattern. Since the difference between iambic pentameter and other iambic lines is presumably a matter of length only, and not of basic regularity of pattern, then for our purposes we may assume that the formal expression of the pattern can be revised to expand or to reduce the number of medial ws units without modifying the special conditions that apply to line beginnings and line ends. The *correspondence rules* established by Halle and Keyser to relate the abstract metrical pattern to actualizations of this pattern in lines of verse can be restated in full:

(i) A position (s, w, or x) corresponds to a single syllable
OR
to a sonorant sequence incorporating at most two vowels (immediately adjoining or separated by a sonorant consonant).

DEFINITION: When a fully stressed syllable occurs between two unstressed syllables in the same syntactic constituent within a line of verse, this syllable is called a 'stress maximum'.

(ii) Fully stressed syllables occur in s positions only and in all s positions
OR
Fully stressed syllables occur in s positions only but not in all s positions
OR
Stress maxima occur in s positions only but not in all s positions.[15]

Space will not allow a full explication of the analysis for each of the fourteen lines of 'The Windhover'. Instead, the analysis is given in summary presentation in which underlinings refer to permitted elisions of syllables in accordance with the second alternative of correspondence rule (i), numbers refer to syllable-to-position assignments, and the symbols s, w, and x refer to the abstract metrical pattern (i.e., the resulting sequence of symbols, plus the syllable-to-position assignment, is an assertion as to whether the given line is metrical or not). Fully stressed syllables are marked in the usual way, and major syntactic breaks are marked by vertical slashes.

1. I caught this morning morning's minion, king-
   1 2   3   4   5   6   7   8 9   10
   w s   w   s   w   s   w   s w   s

2. dom of daylight's dauphin, dapple-dawn-drawn Falcon, in his riding
   (1) 2   3   4   5   6   7   8   9   10   11   12 13 14 15 16 17
   (W) S   W   S   W   S   W   S   W   S   W   S W   S   W S X

280 *Essays in Modern Stylistics*

3. of the rólling lével underneáth him steády aír, and stríding
    (1) 2 3 4 5 6 7 8 9 10 11 12 13 14 15 16 17
    (W) S W S W S W S W S   W   S W W   S   X

4. Hígh there, how he rúng upon the reín of a wímpling wíng
    (1) 2 3 4 5 6 7 8 9 10 11 12 13 14
    (W) S W S W S W S W S   W S   W   S

5. In his écstasy! then off, off fórth on swíng,
    (1) 2 3 4 5 6 7 8 9 10 11 12
    (W) S W S W S| W S W S   W S

6. As a skáte's heel sweéps smooth on a bów-bend: the húrl and glíding
    (1) 2 3 4   5 6   7 8 9   10 11 12 13 14 15
    (W) S W S   W S   W S W   X | S   W   S   X

7. Rebúffed the big wínd. My heart in hídíng
    1 2   3 4   5 6 7 8 9
    W Z   W S | W S W S X

8. Stírred for a bírd, – the achíeve of, the mástery of the thíng!
    (1) 2 3 4 5 6 7   8 9 10 11 12
    (W) S W S| W S W   S W S   W S

9. Brúte beaúty and válour and áct, oh, aír, príde, plúme, here
    1 2 3 4 5 6 7 8 9 10 11
    W S W S W S W S W S   X

10. Búckle! AND the fíre that breáks from thee then, a bíllion
    (1) 2 3 4 5 6 7 8 9 10 11 12 13
    (W) S X| S W S W S W S   W   S X

11. Tímes told lóvelier, more dángerous, O my chevalíer!
    (1) 2 3 4 5 6 7   8 9 10 11 12 13 14
    (W) S W S W S W   S W S W   S W S

12. No wónder of it: sheer plód makes plough dówn síllion
    1 2   3 4 5   6 7 8   9   10 11
    W S   W S W   S W S   W   S X

13. Shíne, and blue-bleak émbers, ah my deár,
    (1) 2 3 4 5 6 7 8 9 10
    (W) S W S W S W S W S

14. Fáll, gáll themselves, and gásh góld-vermílion.
    1 2 3 4 5 6 7 8 9 10
    W S W S W S W S W S

(This line is not metrical, because the 7th and 9th positions are filled by fully stressed syllables and the 8th and 10th positions by unstressed syllables).

In the above analysis, all lines except the 14th are interpreted as metrical within the rules that govern iambic meters. These rules allow for certain variant actualizations of the abstract pattern: e.g. headless lines, extra-metrical syllables at line ends or at major syntactic breaks, and elisions of syllables under limited phonetic conditions.[16] Since the correspondence rules permit various options, it is clear that there can be more or less complex actualizations of the abstract metrical pattern. Compare, for example, lines 1 and 9:

(1) I caught this morning morning's minion, king-

(9) Brute beauty and valour and act, oh, air, pride, plume, here

Both lines are iambic pentameter, though line 9 is a much more complex actualization of the pattern than line 1, since it contains one extra-metrical syllable, two instances of elided syllables, and two instances of fully stressed syllables occurring in metrically weak (w) positions. Line 1 reveals the simplest actualization of the iambic pattern in the entire poem. All other lines show additional complexities in the actualization of the iambic pattern, including variation in the lengths of the pattern. Lines 1, 5, 9, 12, and 13 are pentameter lines. Lines 2 and 3 are octameter; lines 4, 6, and 11 heptameter; lines 8 and 10, hexameter; and line 7, tetrameter. With the exception of line 14, the metrical pattern of the poem, however, is iambic throughout. We may conclude, therefore, that there is no basis for claiming that Hopkins either (1) reintroduced a variation of the Old English alliterative metrical system or (2) invented a distinctly different metrical system called 'sprung rhythm'.

Nevertheless, we intuitively recognize that 'The Windhover' represents a singular achievement in the exploitation of formal poetic structures, and that this achievement seems to rest on more than a particularly ingenious manner of actualizing the basic iambic meter of each line. Consider now the possibility that there is a second *form* of the poem, a second *shape of presentation*, so to speak. We revise the format of 'The Windhover' in the following way:

Lines	Syllables	Rhyme
1. The Windhover: To Christ our Lord	8	a
2. I caught this morning morning's minion,	9	b
3. kingdom of daylight's dauphin,	7	b
4. dapple-dawn-drawn Falcon,	6	b
5. in his riding of the rolling level	10	c
6. underneath him steady air,	7	d
7. and striding high there,	5	d
8. how he rung upon the rein	7	b/d

9.	of a wimpling wing in his ecstasy!	10	e
10.	then off, off forth on swing,	6	f
11.	As a skate's heel sweeps smooth on a bow-bend:	10	g
12.	the hurl and gliding rebuffed the big wind.	10	g
13.	my heart in hiding stirred for a bird, –	9	a
14.	the achieve of, the mastery of the thing!	11	f
15.	Brute beauty and valour and act, oh, air, pride, plume	12	a
16.	here buckle! AND the fire that breaks from thee then,	11	a
17.	a billion times told lovelier, more dangerous	12	b
18.	O my chevalier! No wonder of it:	10	c
19.	sheer plod makes plough down sillion shine,	8	a
20.	and blue-bleak embers, ah my dear, fall,	9	d
21.	gall themselves, and gash gold-vermillion.	9	a

The first fourteen lines of the revised format correspond to the 'octave' of the poem (plus the title and dedication) as normally printed. Lines 15–21 correspond to the 'sestet' of the poem. Let us first consider the 'octave' part of the revised format.

Notice first that, by interpreting the 'dedication' – 'To Christ our Lord' – as an integral part of the title of the poem, we are presented with a perfectly admissible iambic tetrameter line, a fact which might be construed as the first clue to the underlying metrical pattern of the lines that follow. Second, if we think of the 'title line' of the poem as an integral part of the entire 'octave', then we find that we have *fourteen* iambic tetrameter lines – a sub-unit of the total poem, in other words, which suggests, in spite of the tetrameter nature of the lines and the unusual rhyme pattern that emerges, a kind of 'sonnet' – a sonnet within a sonnet, so to speak. Third, it should be noticed that the fourteen 'lines' of the revised format are established on a principled basis rather than simply in terms of typographical conventions. That is, the 'lines' are identified as sequences of words comparable in terms of number of syllables, supported in most instances by end rhymes and also by correspondence with major syntactic constituents. In short, the convergence of these criteria – comparability of length in terms of number of syllables, end rhymes, and correlation with major syntactic constituents – can hardly be regarded as accidental. Finally, notice the curious patterning of the rhyme scheme which emerges, particularly the *b/d* status of *rein* in line 8. *Rein* is so marked because it shares the consonantal /n/ of the *b* items and also the stressed vowel quality /ey/ of the *d* items. If priority is given to the vowel quality, then the 'octave' of this 'sub-sonnet' has the rhyme scheme *abbb cddd*, a pattern which also appears to be too designed to be accidental.

Towards a formal poetics 283

Let us turn now to the claim that the underlying metrical pattern of the 'octave' of 'The Windhover' is basically iambic tetrameter. Once again, we adopt the Halle-Keyser theory for iambic meters and present the analysis in summary fashion as above:

1. The Wíndhover: To Chríst our Lórd
   1 2 3 4 5 6 7 8
   W S W S | W S W S

2. I cáught this mórning mórning's mínion
   1 2   3 4 5 6 7   8 9
   W S   W S W S W   S X

3. kingdom of dáylight's daúphin
   (1) 2 3   4 5   6 7
   (W) S W   S W   S X

4. dápple-dáwn-dráwn Fálcon
   (1) 2 3 4   5   5 7
   (W) S W S   S   S X

5. in his ríding of the rólling lével
       1 2 3 4 5 6 7 8 9
       W S W S W S W S X

6. underneáth him stéady áir
   (1) 2 3 4   5   6 7 8
   (W) S W S   W   S WS

7. and stríding hígh there
   1 2 3 4 5
   W S W S X

8. how he rúng upon the réin
   (1) 2 3 4 5 6 7 8
   (W) S W S W S W S

9. of a wímpling wíng in his écstasy
   1 2 3 4 5 6 7 8
   W S W S W S W S

10. then óff, off fórth on swíng
    1 2 3 4 5 6
    W S W S W S

11. As a skáte's héel swéeps smóoth on a bów-bend
    (1) 2 3 4 5 6 7 8 9 10 11
    (W) S W S W S W S W S X

12. the húrl and glíding rebúffed the bíg wínd
    1 2 3 4 5 6 7 8
    W S W S W S W S

284 *Essays in Modern Stylistics*

13. My héart in híding stírred for a bírd
    1 2 3 4 5 6 7 8
W S W S W S W S

14. the achíeve of, the mástery of the thíng
    1 2 3 4 5 6 7 8
W S W S W S W S

Of the fourteen lines examined, one (line 11) may be regarded as an iambic pentameter line; nine (lines 1, 2, 5, 6, 8, 9, 12, 13, and 14) as iambic tetrameter lines; three (lines 3, 4, and 10) as iambic trimeter lines; and one (line 7) as iambic dimeter. The prevailing metrical pattern is clearly iambic, and the further claim that the underlying pattern is basically iambic tetrameter is well supported. As in the previous analysis, there are variant actualizations of the abstract iambic pattern as a result of headless lines, extra-metrical syllables, and certain elisions of syllables. Line 12 involves one elision that has not been previously identified; this occurs in the sequence '... glid*ing* r*e*buffed ...' i.e. [-Iŋ rə-], in which the sonorant sequence of two vowels is separated by *two* sonorant consonants rather than the *one* required by the second alternative of correspondence rule (i).[17]

In several instances where an unmarked syllable fills an s position, there is some reason for regarding the syllable as stressed, even if not 'fully stressed' in the terms of Halle and Keyser. For example, in line 5 the preposition *of* fills the second s position. Metrically, there is some justification for this because the phrasal stress pattern on syntactic constructions of Preposition-Article-(Adjective)-Noun characteristically involves a 'tertiary' stress on the preposition, 'weak' stress (or absence of stress) on the article, 'secondary' stress on the adjective, and 'primary' stress on the head noun; e.g. òf the rólling lével. Similarly, in line 8 we would have upòn the réin, where the second syllable of *upon* fills the third s position. Conversely, in line 11 the compound *bow-bend* has the stress pattern bów-bènd, where the 'tertiary' stress on *-bend* functions as lack of stress for metrical purposes. In the much-disputed line 4, notice that *drawn* fills a w position. In Halle-Keyser terms, a verbal should be regarded as having a fully stressed vowel. In this case, however, the metrical position of *drawn* demands that it be considered the second element of a compound *dáwn-dràwn*. Thus, the whole construction has the stress pattern *dápple-dáwn-dràwn Fálcon*. Here, the metrical analysis resolves the dispute over the meaning of this line because it provides a syntactic interpretation of the construction: Adjectival-Adjectival Compound-Noun. The falcon is dapple in appearance and is drawn toward the dawn, the emerging light of day.

The 'sestet' of the poem (lines 15–21 of the revised format) shows a rhyme scheme – posited on the basis of final nasal consonants – that is not

Towards a formal poetics 285

very convincing. But neither, for that matter, is the rhyme scheme of this part of the poem in its usual presentation, because of obvious stress differences and varying phonological juncture phenomena. More convincing is the evidence of syntactic constituents, since line beginnings and line ends now correspond more closely to meaningful syntactic boundaries. For the purposes of metrical analysis, the data may be summarized in the same manner as above:

15. Brute beauty and valour and act, oh, air, pride, plume
```
     1   2   3   4   5   6   7   8   9   10
     W   S   W   S   W   S   W   S   W   S
```

16. here buckle! AND the fire that breaks from thee then,
```
     1   2   3   4   5   6   7   8   9   10  11
     W   S   X | S   W   S   W   S   W   S   X
```

17. a billion times told lovelier, more dangerous,
```
     1  2 3   4   5   6  7 8  9   10  11
     W  S W   S   W   S  W S  W   S   X
```

18. O my chevalier! No wonder of it:
```
     (1)  2   3   4 5 6   7   8   9 10
     (W)  S   W   S W S | W   S   W S
```

19. sheer plod makes plough down sillion shine,
```
     1   2   3   4   5   6 7   8
     W   S   W   S   W   S W   S
```

20. and blue-bleak embers, ah my dear, fall,
```
     1   2   3   4   5   6 7 8   9
     W   S   W   S   W   S W S   X
```
(This line is not metrical because of the fully stressed syllable in the extra-metrical position x).

21. gall themselves, and gash gold-vermilion.
```
     (1)  2   3   4   5   6   7   8   9 10
     (W)  S   W   S   W   S   W   S   W S
```
(This line is not metrical because of the unstressed syllables in the fourth and fifth s positions).

Lines 15, 16, 17, 18, and 21 are pentameter lines, though line 21 is unmetrical. Lines 19 and 20 are tetrameter lines, though line 20 is unmetrical because of the stressed extra-metrical syllable. The iambic pattern is clearly evident in all lines, even if only partially so in lines 20 and 21. In line 16, Hopkins's use of capital letters for AND can be verified as a simple 'stage direction' for demanding full stress on a normally unstressed lexical item which occurs in a metrically strong position.

In lines 20 and 21 there appears to be a purposeful convergence of the metrical pattern and the semantic reference. Notice that line 20 is unmetrical only because of the last syllable 'fall', which is the extra-metrical position. Just as the blue-bleak embers fall (as from a grate), so also the iambic pattern, for the first time in the entire poem, begins to break down. And in line 21, just as the embers crash down into chaotic disintegration, so also the iambic metrical pattern collapses completely and decisively. The jarring but exhilarating breakdown of the metrical pattern thus becomes an echo of Hopkins's message.

There are several conclusions that one might draw from this analysis of metrical patterning in 'The Windhover'. Perhaps the most obvious one is that the poem is indeed worth 'revisiting', as so many critics have suggested. It appears, in fact, that the formal poetic structure of 'The Windhover' is immensely more complex and sophisticated than has been previously recognized. In particular, the realization that the underlying metrical pattern of the poem is iambic suggests that Hopkins achieved a masterful interweaving of the two basic metrical traditions in the history of English poetry: the Old Engligh alliterative (and essentially isochronous) system and the iambic (syllable-counting and stress-alternating) system. On the *surface*, 'The Windhover' appears to conform to the essential characteristics of the Old English system. Of course, it does not really do so – not any more than Swinburne's poetry does – but superficial similarities with the Old English system have clearly led some scholars to this mistaken conclusion. The present analysis, however, demonstrates that the *underlying* metrical pattern is actually the iambic system, the system that has been practiced by virtually every major poet from Chaucer to Yeats. In 'The Windhover', however, Hopkins appears to have consciously capitalized on characteristics of the two historical systems and to have constructed a poem with the appearances of one of the systems but with the structure of the other. It is perhaps in this sense that we can agree with W. H. Gardner's appraisal that Hopkins 'led poetry forward by taking it back'.[18]

This analysis has also shown that appearances are deceiving with respect to line structure as well as metrical structure, raising questions about the nature of the poetic line vis-à-vis the typographical conventions associated with the line. We have seen that there are two different versions of the format of 'The Windhover' – the fourteen-line 'sonnet', which is the one in print, and a twenty-one line format in which the title and dedication combine with the 'octave' of the 'sonnet' to form a second 'sonnet'. Which of the two versions is 'The Windhover'? Or is it both of them? More generally, what, then, is the poem?

It may be possible to conclude that this analysis demonstrates to some extent Whitehall's statement that 'no criticism can go beyond its linguistics.' The analysis of metrical patterning in 'The Windhover' was possible only

Towards a formal poetics 287

because of the relative richness of the Halle-Keyser theory compared to previous theories of the iambic system. Literary critics had reached certain conclusions about the formal structure of 'The Windhover'. These conclusions were shown to be incorrect in the light of a new linguistic theory of meter. Re-analysis of the poem within the framework of this theory has yielded new *critical* conclusions about the poem. It should not be unreasonable to suppose, then, that as linguistics contributes to the development of a formal poetics, the resultant findings of such a poetics can only enhance the accuracy and persuasiveness of literary criticism.

Appendix

(Each (?) in the third column indicates an additional required accented syllable, though it is not clear which of the remaining accented syllables of the line are to be included.)

Line	Possible Number Accented Syllables	Possible Accented Syllables Defined by Alliteration	Alliterating Consonants	Note
1	5	caught, morn-, morn-, min-, king-	/k, m/	
2	7	day-, dauph-, dap-,? ?	/d/	a
3	5 (6?)	stead-, strid-, ? ? ?	/st-/	b
4	5 (7?)	rung, rein, wimp-, wing,?	/r, w/	c
5	5	ec-, off, off, ? ?	/Vwl/	d
6	8	skate's, sweeps, smooth, heel, hurl	/s, h/	e
7	5	-buffed, big, wind, heart, hid-	/b, h/	f
8	5	stirred, bird, -chieve, mas-, thing		g
9	7 (9?)	brute, beau-, val-, pride, plume	/b, v, p/	h
10	5 (6?)	Buck-, breaks, bill-, fire, AND	/b/	i
11	5 (6?)	Times, told, lov-, dan-, (cheva)lier	/t, l/	j
12	6 (7?)	won-, sheer, plod, plough, sill-	/p, s, s/	k
13	5 (6?)	blue, -bleak, ? ? ?	/b/	l
14	5	fall, gall, gash, gold-, -mil-	/g/	m

(a) It is impossible to compute which five of the possible accented syllables are to be included. The possible syllables must include at least *day-, dauph-, dap-, dawn, drawn, Falc-, rid-*. Even though there are several interpretations of the 'dapple-dawn-drawn Falcon' construction, with differing stress reductions depending on the compound interpretation chosen, all of these syllables must be considered as possible accented syllables because they bear the main stress of the word in which they occur. Thus, the necessary five accented syllables might be *day-, dauph-, dap-, dawn,* and *drawn* because of /d/ alliteration. On the other hand, a secondary feature of assonance links *dauph-, dawn, drawn,* and *Falc-*, which suggests that *Falcon* is foregrounded for this reason as well as for the more obvious reason of its being the head of a syntactic construction. In short, in this line there is no obvious clue as to why one set of five accented syllables should be identified in favor of another set of five syllables.

(b) In this line, two of the five accented syllables are clear because of /st-/ alliteration. The remaining three are dubious, but must be selected from *roll-, lev-,* and *air,* and possibly *un-*. Distinctive features shared by vowels and sonorant consonants (/r l/) suggest a linking of *roll-, lev,* and *air,* but one might make a similar case for linking *air, un-,* and either *roll-* or *lev-*.

(c) *there* and *how* might be included as possible accented syllables. If not, then *high* is one of the five by elimination, since the alliterating /r/ and /w/ identify *rung, rein, wimp-,* and *wing* as the others. But the /h/ alliteration in *high, how* virtually demands the inclusion of *how* as a sixth accented syllable.

(d) Here, as in the OE system, stressed vowels regardless of quality could alliterate. Thus, *ec-, off,* and *off* constitute an alliterative set for three of the accented syllables, leaving *forth* and *swing* as the other two, only possible, syllables.

(e) These are probably the intended five accented syllables, because of the alliterative sets, but *bow-bend* suggests still another set. Do we in fact have seven accented syllables in this line?

(f) Note here that *wind* shares the initial labial feature of *-buffed* and *big*.

(g) Alliteration here must be viewed wholly in terms of shared phonetic features: (1) the labial features of /b, m/ in *bird* and *mas-,* and (2) the voiceless fricative features of /s, č, θ/ in *stirred, -chieve,* and *thing*.

(h) In this line, the five possible accented syllables are identified by an alliterative labial set. On the other hand, a second alliterative set consisting of *act, oh, air,* and *here* could be identified on the basis of initial vowels (including the vowel-like qualities associated with /h/). In short, there is no strong reason here for assuming that there are just five accented syllables in this line.

(i) The /f/ of *fire* shares the labial feature of the alliterating /b/s, and the fifth accented syllable must be assumed to be *AND* because of the capitalization, unless the adverbial *then* is to be admitted.

(j) A sixth possible accented syllable is the interjection *O*.

(k) The /w/ of *won-* is linked to the /p/ of *plod* and *plough* by a shared labial feature. The (š) of *sheer* and the /s/ of *sill-* are linked as voiceless sibilants.

(l) The possible accented syllables can only be those of *shine, blue, -bleak, em-, ah,* and *dear*. Two are easily identified by the alliterating /b/s. If the interjection *ah* is included, it would alliterate with *em-*; if not, then the remaining three syllables are identified by a process of elimination.

(m) The alliterating /g/s identify *gall, gash, gold,* easily. *Fall* and *-mil-* are the only other possible candidates. It should be noted that the apparent alliteration seen in *fall* and in *vermilion* (i.e. /f v/) is inadmissible, since it is not the first syllable of *vermilion* that is stressed but the second one.

Notes

1 'From linguistics to criticism,' *Kenyon Review,* 13 (1951), p. 713. I wish to acknowledge helpful comments on an earlier draft of this paper by my colleagues Todd K. Bender, Charles Read, and Peter Schreiber and also by Samuel Jay Keyser. My greatest debt of gratitude, however, is to Archibald A. Hill, teacher, mentor, friend. I am, of course, wholly responsible for errors of analysis or judgment in this paper.

2 Most of this discussion is in the form of scholarly papers, many of which have been collected in such volumes as: Donald C. Freeman, ed., *Linguistics and Literary Style* (New York: Holt, Rinehart & Winston, 1970); Seymour Chatman and Samuel R. Levin, eds., *Essays on the Language of Literature* (New York: Houghton Mifflin, 1967); and Thomas A. Sebeok, ed., *Style in Language* (Cambridge, Mass.: The MIT Press, 1960).

3 Freeman, p. 3.

4 Freeman, p. 3.
5 John Pick, *The Windhover* (Columbus, Ohio: Charles E. Merrill Publishing Co., 1969).
6 Pick, p. 9.
7 George Pace, 'On the octave rhymes of *The Windhover*', *English Language Notes*, 2 (1956) pp. 285–6.
8 Pick, p. 2.
9 Pick, p. 2
10 Pick, p. 3.
11 To say, as some might, that a metrical pattern can be derived from lexical clues in the text, and that, therefore, cues for performance are in the text, only confuses the issue. The metrical pattern is an abstract structure precisely because it may have different actualizations. Textual data include many kinds of data, of which lexical items are only one. As we will see below, *typographical* data may be used as performance cues, e.g. to indicate emphatic stress.
12 E.g.: (1) Fýrst fórð gewāt; flóta waes on ýðum
(B. 210)
(2) And ten low words oft creep in one dull line
(Pope)
These examples are taken from Morris Halle and Samuel Jay Keyser, *English Stress: Its Form, Its Growth, and Its Role in Verse* (New York: Harper and Row, 1971). (1) is an instance of the OE alliterative system and (2) is an instance of the iambic system.
13 Halle and Keyser.
14 Halle and Keyser, p. 169.
15 Halle and Keyser, p. 169.
16 In the Halle-Keyser proposal, two successive syllables may be elided if they are separated by a sonorant consonant, normally nasals, liquids, and resonants. This analysis of 'The Windhover' suggests that the class of permissible consonants may be expanded to include voiced fricatives (e.g. *of a* in line 4) and occasionally voiced stops (e.g. *the big* in line 7).
17 If this elision is disallowed, then the line is unmetrical. Of course, the metricality of the line is already somewhat problematic because of the other elision which has been accepted, i.e. '... the big ...', in which the sonorant sequence of two vowels is separated by a voiced stop consonant [b].
18 Quoted in Pick, p. 1.

13
A generative metrical analysis of 'Sir Gawain and the Green Knight'

Justine T. Stillings

Introduction

'Sir Gawain and the Green Knight' (SG) is a Middle English narrative poem of approximately 2500 lines.[1] The author of the poem is unknown, as is the date of its composition, but dialect and other internal evidence suggests that the poem was written in the north Midland area of England, possibly Lancashire, in the last quarter of the fourteenth century.[2] The poem is an Arthurian romance describing the adventures of Sir Gawain in his quest for the Green Knight and his ultimate encounter with the enchanted knight after a series of challenges devised by the sorceress Morgan Le Fay. Metrically the poem has presented a fascinating puzzle to scholars, not only because of the two distinct stanza forms employed by the poet, but because of the difficulty in determining the precise characteristics of the meter used by the poet within each stanza form.

SG is composed in unrhymed stanzas of 12 to 38 lines alternating with 5-line rhymed stanzas. The unrhymed stanzas are formed of alliterative lines roughly 12 syllables long, while the rhymed stanzas are composed of a short 2-syllable first line (the 'bob') followed by 4 lines of roughly 6 syllables each (the 'wheel'). Stanzas of long alliterative lines alternate regularly throughout the poem with stanzas of short rhymed lines. It has been generally assumed that the long alliterative lines are a lineal descendant of Old English verse, and all metrical treatments of these lines utilize some variation of OE tonic meter in their analyses. The short rhymed lines, on the other hand, appear to be written in iambic trimeter, i.e. in the modern syllabotonic tradition, and are generally analyzed in that fashion.[3] Thus from even the most superficial observation SG occupies an important place as a transitional poem between two metrical traditions, and a careful analysis of the meters employed by the poet may shed more light on the way in which linguistic (including metrical) processes change over time.

The present paper investigates the way in which modern theories of metrics might be applied to SG, and comes to the conclusion that such theories are unable to elucidate the meters employed by the SG poet. A new generative theory of meter is therefore proposed which not only provides a satisfactory means of analyzing the complex metrical style of the poem but appears to have interesting theoretical consequences for the analysis of modern syllabotonic poetry as well. From the analysis of SG certain tentative conclusions are reached about the nature of the diachronic shift from OE meter to syllabotonic meter in English poetry; the paper concludes with a brief summary of the differences between other metrical theories and the generative theory proposed here.

The Appendix contains data on the pronunciation, stress, and orthographic rules employed in this analysis of SG. Section 1.4 and the Appendix contain detailed information on the scansion principles employed. Only two stress levels, strong and weak, are used for scansion in the present paper; multiple stress distinctions are felt to belong to the realm of poetic correspondence rules and thus fall beyond the scope of the paper. Section 4 presents additional comments on this point.

1 The iambic lines of Sir Gawain

With chynne and cheke ful swete
Both white and red in blande
Ful lufly can ho lete
With lippes smal lachande (1204–1207)

1.1 Inadequacies of current metrical theories

While the iambic lines of SG are generally quite regular, as in the example above, the SG poet nevertheless employs a number of metrical deviations which current metrical theories cannot account for. Both major constraints of the Halle-Keyser theory of metrics are frequently broken by the SG poet, while the central thesis of Paul Kiparsky's recent analysis of meter is equally inapplicable to SG.[4]

The first difficulty which SG presents to the Halle-Keyser theory of meter concerns the extreme variation in foot-length permitted in the iambic verse of the SG poet. The iambic foot is a fixed two-syllable foot consisting of a weak position followed by a strong position (ws). All of the iambic feet in the above lines are of this form. However, in other iambic lines the SG poet freely lengthens the iambic foot to wws, wwws, and occasionally even to wwwws. The only way such expansion is permitted in the Halle-Keyser theory is via the Sonorant Sequence Condition: 'A sonorant sequence incorporating at most two vowels (immediately adjoining or separated by a sonorant consonant) may be treated as a single syllable' (*English Stress*, p. 169). Yet the SG poet apparently did not use the SSC as a rule for foot expansion, as can be seen from a typical wwws foot in SG such as

A sem/loker that ev/er he sye (83)
    w w   w s

where *k*, *th*, and *t* cannot in any fashion be subsumed under the sonorant elision theory. (D. C. Freeman, on p. 453 of *Linguistics and Literary Style* [New York: Holt, Rinehart & Winston, 1970], discusses sonorant elision from the point of view of a diachronic continuum, with the most extreme elision occurring over ð and z: $VV \rightarrow V_l^r V \rightarrow V_n^m V \rightarrow V_z^{\circ} V$. In no case does this continuum extend over voiceless stops, however.)

The second constraint of the Halle-Keyser theory, the Stress Maximum Condition (SMC) is apparently equally inapplicable to the SG poet. The SMC states: 'When a stressed syllable is located between unstressed syllables in the same syntactic constituent within a given line of verse, this syllable is called a stress maximum. w positions cannot be filled by stress maxima' (*English Stress*, p. 169). Yet in the iambic lines of SG what appear to be two contiguous trochees are fairly common, as in

/Couples / huntes / of kest (1147)
  s   w   s   w

where the second s in this line is a stress maximum occupying a weak position.

Thus, with respect to the iambic lines of SG, the Halle-Keyser theory is not able to provide a satisfactory analysis of the iambic meter employed by the poet and in fact results in the undesirable conclusion that many of the iambic lines of the poem are unmetrical.

Paul Kiparsky's recent theory of meter is equally unable to account for the iambic lines of SG. According to Kiparsky's Metrical Rule 2 (the Monosyllable Rule), two-syllable nouns with strong stress on the first syllable do not begin in odd positions within an iambic line in normal, e.g., Shakespearean, English iambic verse ('Stress, syntax, and meter', p. 583).

With reference once again to line 1147, the noun 'huntes' has strong stress in position 3 of the line. Thus MR2 is obviously inapplicable to the SG poet (just as it is inapplicable to the verse of Donne, as is pointed out by Kiparsky). Since Kiparsky's rules are poet-oriented, rather than universal, the fact that the SG poet does not use MR2 cannot be taken as a counterexample to Kiparsky's theory. But a problem does remain: Kiparsky's rules are unable to elucidate the meter which the SG poet *does* use; a poetic style cannot be defined solely in terms of what it is not.

This difficulty arises in Kiparsky's treatment of extrametrical syllables. His Metrical Rule 3, an epenthesis rule, adds one extra syllable line-medially or line-finally before a constituent break: 'MR3: ø→[α stress] in the environment ___ [$^{\#}_{P}$ where P is a constituent label and α ≠ strong stress (1 or 2)' ('Stress, syntax, and meter', p. 602). This rule is as inapplicable to the SG poet as MR2, since the SG poet freely adds one or two or even three extra syllables to any given foot, requires no constituent break in the environment of the rule, and can add either strong or weak syllables:

A sem/loker that ev/er he sye   (83)
   w w w s

  i. Two extra syllables are added
  ii. -lo- is added word-medially (no constituent break)

/Quoth that luf/sum under lyne   (1814)
 s   w s

  iii. A strong syllable is added line-initially

As these lines illustrate, the iambic verse of the SG poet is a counterexample to Kiparsky's MR3 in three separate ways. But the difficulty here is not simply that Kiparsky's rule MR3 is inapplicable to the SG poet. Rather, if one attempts to write a rule which does account for syllable epenthesis in SG, one finds that the formal tools provided by Kiparsky's theory are not flexible enough to write the desired revised rule at all. Kiparsky has provided an epenthesis rule which does not work for SG but has not provided a theory which will permit writing a new rule of epenthesis which does work.

The reason for this is that the only contexts permitted for stress deviation in Kiparsky's theory are constituent structure contexts (i.e. labeled brackets and word-boundary symbols). As (83) above illustrates, the SG poet does not use constituent structure to determine where syllable epenthesis can occur. Weak syllables can be added freely in any foot-initial position. Strong syllables, however, can only be added when at most one weak syllable intervenes between the epenthesized strong syllable and foot-final strong position of the normal iambic foot. (See Section 1.2 for a discussion of this characteristic of the SG poet's verse.) Thus for the SG poet line 1814 is metrical, but a line of the following form would be unmetrical:

Unmetrical in SG: *s wws ws ws

Since there is a difference between weak syllable epenthesis and strong syllable epenthesis for the SG poet, the rules governing syllable epenthesis must be able to distinguish between the metrical contexts for one rule and the metrical contexts for the other rule. It turns out that the difference in context for strong and weak syllable epenthesis is solely a matter of the number of weak syllables occurring after the epenthesized syllable. But Kiparsky's theory of meter does not permit the formulation of rules which rely solely on syllable count in a metrical context. Instead, as has been pointed out, his rules can make reference only to constituent structure contexts. Yet line 83 illustrates that constituent structure is not used as an epenthesis environment by the SG poet. Thus we are left with the paradox of having to write an epenthesis rule for SG which uses syllable count rather than constituent structure as an environment, but we have no means other than constituent structure to specify rule environments within the formal framework established by Kiparsky.

Since Halle and Keyser's theory of meter rests on two presumably universal constraints on iambic verse, the Stress Maximum Condition and the Sonorant Sequence Condition, neither of which is followed by the SG poet, their theory is not flexible enough to describe early iambic verse. Kiparsky's formalism, which relies crucially on the importance of constituent structure, is basically a more flexible theory than the Halle-Keyser theory, since it is poet-oriented rather than universal, but it is still unable to account for the metrical practices of the SG poet because the SG poet does not make use of constituent structure as a rule context.

From these observations it is argued that a new formal theory of meter is required to account for the iambic lines of SG, and the outline of such a theory is sketched in the following section.

1.2 Metrical base rules

The generative theory to be developed here is similar to Kiparsky's theory in that it is poet-oriented (different poets use different metrical rules) and relies on the notion that there is an underlying abstract metrical foot in the iambic line from which deviations are created by the application of metrical rules. The difference is that the present theory makes no reference to constituent or phonological structure in its rules. The only contexts specified for rules in the present theory are the placement of line boundaries, foot boundaries, and abstract markers for weak and strong positions within the iambic foot. In effect the present theory is completely abstract: it deals with possible permutations of metrical patterns before any correspondence between these patterns and the stress contours of poetic lexical material is considered. In this respect the rules proposed are similar to the phrase structure rewriting rules of Noam Chomsky's syntactic theory, and thus the rules proposed in the present paper will be called Metrical Base Rules. The present theory assumes that each poet has, as part of his poetic 'competence', a unique set of metrical base rules which permit him to generate deviations from an underlying abstract metrical pattern, and that the lexical material of a poem falls only into such metrical patterns as are permitted by the underlying metrical base rules.

The conception of a poem's meter as having both an underlying pattern and a surface or derived pattern has been a characteristic of all recent theories of metrics. Hypothesizing the existence of an underlying abstract metrical pattern (e.g. iambic trimeter) permits a means of accounting for our intuitions that a poem has a regular meter even though the surface realization of that meter may itself be very irregular. Thus the present postulation of underlying abstract metrical patterns in SG is well within the bounds of current discussions of metrical rules. What differs in the present treatment is the means by which metrical deviations are to be accounted for. Previous theories ascribe such deviations solely to rules of correspondence between stressed lexical material and underlying metrical patterns. This approach, as has been argued above, is unable to account for the verse of the SG poet. The present paper thus takes the other alternative, that of ascribing metrical deviations to the abstract level of Metrical Base Rules.

With respect to SG, it is proposed that there is an underlying abstract metrical foot in the iambic line, namely the iambic foot ws, and that the poet creates deviations from this foot by applying to it various metrical rewriting rules. These metrical rewriting rules, or metrical base rules, apply at the abstract metrical level prior to the insertion of lexical material into the line. Thus the 'w' and 's' symbols here are to be taken not as features of syllables in words, but simply as abstract metrical place markers which will later be filled by words. 'w' stands for a weak position in the foot and 's' for a strong position. Neither symbol has any reference to word stress at this point.

It is assumed that lines are generated as sequences of identical feet. Thus the iambic trimeter lines of SG are generated by the following rules:

L→F F F (w)   L = line   F = foot
F→ws   (w) = an optional extrametrical weak syllable

Note that foot boundary symbols and line boundary symbols are considered elements of the underlying base metrical system just as are weak and strong position markers. In other words, it is asserted here that both the foot and the line are of theoretical importance in the metrical system, as against, for example, Halle and Keyser, who dispense with the notion of the foot. The necessity for a line boundary follows from the fact that the poet deletes weak syllables only line-initially (see the Decrease rule below). The use of a foot boundary is intended to capture our intuitive notions that a line of iambic verse is composed of a series of repeating elements, and that the number of repetitions determines whether the line is to be considered trimeter, tetrameter, pentameter, etc. It is not clear how Halle and Keyser can account for our intuitions of 'repetitions' in metrical verse, since for them a line is simply composed of a fixed number of positions which happen to alternate between weak and strong syllables.

To account for metrical deviations in the iambic verse of SG, four metrical base rules are attributed to the SG poet. These are:

(i) The Spondee rule $\quad$ w→s/____(w)s}
Elements in parentheses are optional
} is a right foot boundary
The Spondee rule states that a weak position can be rewritten as a strong position when
a. it immediately precedes a foot-final strong position,
b. or, when it precedes a foot-final strong position with at most one weak position intervening. (This option will be discussed after the other metrical base rules have been introduced.)
If the poet applies the Spondee rule directly to an underlying ws foot, the rule rewrites the ws foot as ss. Thus in the iambic trimeter line, ws ws ws→ws ss ws:

$$\text{A grene / hors gret / and thikke} \quad (1175)$$
$$\quad\quad\quad\quad\text{s}\quad\text{s}$$

(ii) The Pyrrhus rule $\quad$ s→w/w____
A foot-final strong position can be rewritten as a weak position following another weak position. If the Pyrrhus rule applies to an underlying ws foot, a ww foot is derived:

$$\text{For woth / that thou / ne wonde} \quad (488)$$
$$\quad\quad\quad\text{w}\quad\quad\text{w}$$

(iii) The Decrease rule $\quad$ w→Ø/[{____
$\quad\quad\quad\quad\quad\quad\quad\quad\quad\quad$ ⌊

[is a left line boundary
⌊ is a left foot boundary
A weak position may be dropped line-initially before s or w.

A generative metrical analysis 297

If the Decrease rule is applied to a line-initial ws foot, an s foot is derived:

/ Hey / with hunt and hornes   (1417)
   s

(iv)   The Increase rule   w→ww / {——
A weak position may be expanded to two weak positions foot-initially. If the Increase rule applies to an underlying ws foot, a wws foot is derived:

That breme / was and brayn/wod both   (1580)
              w   w   s

N.B. Kiparsky's Increase Rule MR3 is written as an epenthesis rule, while the present rule is written as a reduplication rule. It is difficult to determine which of these rule formalizations is more appropriate, and thus the issue is not argued here. Note that the most important distinction between the Increase rule and Kiparsky's MR3 is that the latter requires reference to the constituent structure of the words in a poem, while the Increase rule refers only to the abstract metrical entity of the foot boundary.

The metrical base rule are context-sensitive (i.e. they can apply only in certain foot and position environments), but as long as their environmental conditions are met there is no reason why several rules cannot apply to the same foot. The rules are unordered and a rule may apply to its own output. The only restriction is that no rule can operate to 'undo' the effects of a previous rule (e.g. the Decrease rule cannot be followed by the Increase rule). The examples given above are all cases where a single rule has applied to an underlying ws foot to generate a derived foot type. However, feet derived from the application of two and three metrical rules also occur in the iambic lines of SG.

Examples of feet derived in two steps in the iambic lines

	ws→ww	via the Pyrrhus rule
	ww→w	via the Decrease rule
	Example: / Thus / to the derk night (1177)	
	w	
www	ws→ww	via the Pyrrhus rule
	ww→www	via the Increase rule
	Example: More lyk/erwys on/to lyk (968)	
	w w w	

298 *Essays in Modern Stylistics*

wwws	ws→wws	via the Increase rule
	wws→wwws	via the Increase rule

Example: He hur/tes of the hound/es and they   (1452)
w   w   w   s

wss	ws→wws	via the Increase rule
	wws→wss	via the Spondee rule

Example: To the king/es burg busk/es bold   (2476)
w   s   s

sws   This foot utilizes the (b) option of the Spondee rule and in the iambic lines is filled most often by 'Quoth that x'.

ws→wws	via the Increase rule
wws→sws	via the Spondee rule

Example: / Quoth that luf/som under lyne   (1814)
s   w   s

Examples of feet derived in three steps in the iambic lines

www	ws→ww	via the Pyrrhus rule
	ww→www	via the Increase rule
	www→wwww	via the Increase rule

Example: Dar / any hereinne / aught say   (300)
ww   w   w

wwwws	ws→wws	via the Increase rule
	wws→wwws	via the Increase rule
	wwws→wwwws	via the Increase rule

Example: Let / es me overtake / your wylle   (2387)
w   w   w w   s

Note that given the conditions on the rules, the Spondee rule and the Pyrrhus rule can never both apply to the same foot in SG. Thus trochees (sw) will never be a derived foot form in the short lines. Whenever this sequence occurs, it must be analyzed as some other scansion not involving a trochee. To write the rules in this fashion was a device to reduce ambiguous foot derivations. There may be no principled reason why some other option could not be chosen by which trochees could be generated and ambiguities reduced in some other manner. However, the following evidence suggests that the SG poet may truly not have used trochees himself:

> The lorde sayde, 'By saynt Gile
> Ye ar the best that I knowe!
>
> Ye ben ryche in a whyle,
> Such chaffer and ye drowe!'   (1644–1647)

If line 1646 were to be scanned as obligatorily beginning with two trochees, one would predict the possibility of pausing slightly after *ben* and *in*. Yet

A generative metrical analysis 299

this in no way corresponds to the normal stress assigned to emphatic phrases such as 'You'll be rich in a while!' in which the pauses occur after *you'll* and *rich*. Thus an analysis correctly corresponding to the colloquial speech of the passage requires that line 1646 be scanned without trochees. Hence in this case case of apparent ambiguity between a trochaic and a non-trochaic reading, only the non-trochaic reading is permissible, and this is exactly what is predicted by the present analysis.

From the example lines used to illustrate the two-step and three-step foot derivations, it can be seen that the four basic metrical rules ascribed to the SG poet are capable, singly and in combination, of generating a large number of complex derived foot types, including all of those which find expression in various of the iambic lines of the poem. It is exactly this wide variation in foot-types which causes difficulties for the Halle-Keyser theory of meter, and which the generative theory proposed in this section accounts for as a direct formal consequence of the metrical base rules. Note that the Spondee rule permits a weak syllable to rewrite as a strong syllable only if at most one weak syllable intervenes before the next strong syllable. This accounts for the fact that an extrametrical strong syllable can occur line-initially before ws or s but not before wws, a fact which Kiparsky's theory of meter cannot handle.

Given the metrical base rules, two typical iambic stanzas of SG can be scanned as follows:

/They lan/ced word/es gode/
  w s   w   s   w   s
/Much wele / then was / thereinne;/
  w   s   w   w   w   w
/Gret per/ile bitween / hem stod,/
  s s   w w   w   w   s
/Nif Mar/e of hir / knyght mynne./   (1766–1769)
  s s   ww   w   s   s

/A hun/dreth hound/es kym hent,/
 ws   w   s   w w   s
/That breme/ly con / hym bite,/
  w   s   w   s   w   s
/Burn/es him brought / to bent/
  s   w w   s   w s
/And dog/ges to dethe / endite./   (1597–1600)
  w   s   ww   s   w s

1.3 The Complexity Measure

It is not enough simply to generate all of the foot-types employed by the SG poet; one must simultaneously provide some method of evaluating the SG poet's tendency to choose certain of these foot-types over certain others. Thus, in conjunction with the metrical base rules, a complexity measure is proposed for the generative metrical theory:

Complexity Measure

The metrical complexity of a given foot is a function of the number of metrical base rules required to generate the foot. The greater the number of steps in the derivation, the more complex the foot. Less complex feet will tend to occur more frequently than more complex feet.

The Complexity Measure in effect predicts that the most frequent foot type will be the basic iambic foot ws to which no metrical base rules have applied. Feet derived by one metrical base rule will tend to occur less frequently than ws. Feet derived by two metrical base rules will tend to occur less frequently than feet derived by one rule, and so on. The Complexity Measure, in other words, is an empirical measure, and as such its predictions should be capable of empirical verification.

That the Complexity Measure does in fact correctly predict the frequency of foot types in the iambic lines of SG is clear from the following chart. There are 404 lines of iambic trimeter in the poem, and the frequencies of foot types occurring in these lines are as follows:

Foot-type frequencies in the iambic lines

Foot	# of Rules	Rules	# of Occurences
ws	0		707
ss	1	S	122
ww	1	P	125
wws	1	I	146
s	1	D	35
w	2	P,D	14
www	2	P,I	24
wss	2	I,S	19
sws	2	I,S	8
wwws	2	I,I	9
wwww	3	P,I,I	1
wwss	3	I,I,S	1
wwwws	3	I,I,I	1

S = Spondee   P = Pyrrhus   I = Increase   D = Decrease

Note that the s foot appears much less frequently than the other foot types derived by one rule. This is because s can occur only line-initially and thus has only one-third as many possible places for ocurring as do the other foot-types derived by one rule.

1.4 Consequences of the Complexity Measure: the line scansion principle

One of the most difficult problems for any metrical analysis is the problem of ambiguous line scansions. Under the generative metrical theory proposed here, certain of the iambic lines of SG are capable of multiple scansions because of the flexible length of the iambic foot for the SG poet. With respect to ambiguous line scansions, the Complexity Measure predicts that if one scansion is more complex and another scansion less complex, the poet had a tendency to choose the less complex realization and to maximize ws feet when possible. Thus a Scansion Principle follows directly from the Complexity Measure:

Scansion Principle

If a line is capable of various scansions, choose the least complex scansion – i.e. the scansion which derives from the fewest number of metrical rules. If two ambiguous scansions are equally complex, choose the scansion which maximizes the number of iambic feet.[5]

A general algorithm for determining the scansion of the rhymed iambic lines of the SG poet can be based on the Scansion Principle as stated.

1. Determine the strong and weak stresses in the line: primary stress in nouns, verbs, adjectives, and adverbs is rewritten as s. All other stresses are rewritten as w. (See Appendix.)
2. Insert foot boundaries between each syllable in a sequence sw. (The rhymed lines often end with an extrametrical weak syllable; this syllable is to be ignored when inserting foot boundaries.)

$$sw \rightarrow s)(w$$

3. Insert foot and line boundaries line-initially and line-finally.

$$xxxxxx \rightarrow [(xxxxxx)]$$

4. If three feet are demarcated by steps (2) and (3), the scansion is complete. If four feet are demarcated by steps (2) and (3) and the first two

feet are s and ws, the initial foot will be an expanded Spondee foot and the scansion is complete. If fewer than three feet are demarcated, use the Scansion Principle to determine the least complex scansion, and insert foot boundaries accordingly.

In practice this algorithm works out as follows for an ambiguous line such as line 58:

Hit were now gret nye to neven

1. Determine strong and weak stress positions.

   Hit were now gret nye to neven
    w   w   s   s   s   w s(w)

2. Insert foot boundaries.

   Hit were now gret nye) (to neven
    w   w   s   s   s   w s(w)

3. Insert line boundaries.

   [(Hit were now gret nye) (to neven)]
     w   w   s   s   s   w s(w)
   L

4. Since the first five syllables are capable of various scansions, determine the complexity of each scansion (i.e., the total number of metrical rules required to derive the scansion).

   a. (Hit)(were now gret nye) = 6 rules P,D and I,I,S,S
       w   w   s   s   s

   b. (Hit were)(now gret nye) = 4 rules P and I,S,S
       w   w   s   s   s

   c. (Hit were now)(gret nye) = 2 rules I and S
       w   w   w   s   s

The preferred scansion is (c.) and thus the entire line is scanned as:

[(Hit were now)(gret nye)(to neven)]
  w   w s   s   s   w s(w)
L

There are a few examples of lines in SG where two alternate scansions result in the same metrical complexity. For example:

a. /Yet brev/ed was it / ful bare/ (465) Complexity = 2
   w   s w   w w   w s

b. /Yet brev/ed was / it ful bare/   Complexity = 2
   w   s w   w   w w s

A generative metrical analysis 303

The Complexity Measure in this case indicates the choice of scansion (a.) because scansion (a.) maximizes the number of ws feet in the line. (It should be emphasized that the Scansion Principle cannot determine the exact meter used by the poet in any given ambiguous case, but only the meter that he had the greatest probability of using – in this respect the Scansion Principle is a 'best guess' principle based on probabilities.)

1.5 Perspectives on the generative metrical theory

The purpose of any metrical theory must be, ultimately, to account not only for the various metrical patterns which occur in verse but also for our intuitions about those patterns. How, for example, do we understand what the meter of a poem is? How do we distinguish between the underlying meter of a poem and deviations from that meter? What, in fact, is meter? These are large questions, far beyond the scope of this paper; yet this paper takes stands on these issues by virtue of its theoretical framework.

With respect to meter itself, the generative metrical theory presented here contains an implicit commitment to the notion of meter as the regular repetition of particular sound patterns. In this theory lines are composed of some number of identical feet which are demarcated by abstract foot boundaries. The repetition of these feet in a line corresponds to the notion of meter as rhythmic repetition. This approach can be distinguished from the Halle-Keyser theory of meter in which the perceived metrical unit is not the foot but the line and which therefore appears to take an implicit stand against the notion that metrical regularity should be defined primarily in terms of repetition.

A related question is the puzzling one of 'unmetrical verse'. Kiparsky takes the ontological position that there is no such thing as an unmetrical line. The Halle-Keyser theory takes the opposite stand, that not only can unmetrical lines occur but there are well-defined reasons for their unmetricality: i.e. iambic lines are unmetrical if they break the Stress Maximum Condition. The present theory has a notion of unmetrical line, but it is far weaker than the Halle-Keyser approach. Under the generative metrical analysis, a line whose deviations must be accounted for by metrical rules which are not part of the set of metrical base rules of the poet in question will be an unmetrical line *for that poet*. Thus what a poet writes is metrical for his verse; what he would not write is unmetrical for his verse.

With respect to intuitions of the underlying meter of a poem, the Halle-Keyser theory of meter implicitly argues that the underlying metrical pattern of a poem is inviolable. The fact that a given line contains a single fixed underlying metrical pattern accounts for our ability to perceive that pattern in spite of surface deviations, since surface deviations are a result only of lexical correspondence rules such as the Sonorant Sequence Condition. This paper argues that our intuitions of the underlying meter of a poem come not only from our perception of basic metrical patterns but also from our intuitive ability to recognize abstract rules which can change metrical patterns in certain well-defined ways. Thus the present theory holds not that underlying metrical patterns are inviolable, but that they are changeable in well-defined but still abstract ways. Our intuitive knowledge of poetic meter thus encompasses not only an abstract notion of meter but an abstract notion of possible metrical deviations.

The present theory thus can account with a single explanation for our ability to scan metrically complex poems and our ability to write metrically complex poems: we have intuitions of complexity as a function of the application of abstract rules of metrical deviation. Whether or not this is an appropriate psychological model is outside the realm of prosodic studies; in terms of evaluation measures on formal systems, however, it meets the criterion that the most highly valued of a set of systems will be that which accounts for seemingly widely diverse phenomena with a unified conception of formal strategies, while lesser-valued systems will be those which require recourse to multiple strategies. Whether or not the Halle-Keyser theory of metrics can account for scansion and complexity remains an open question, since as of the present time that theory has not yet been extended to these areas for syllabotonic verse.

In the absence of further extensions of the Halle-Keyser approach to meter, the theory proposed here can in any event account for a variety of facts left unexplained by earlier work. For example:

1. The proposed generative metrical theory accounts for all of the diverse foot-types occurring in the iambic lines of SG, which the Halle-Keyser and Kiparsky theories cannot do. Yet in terms of number of rules it is no more complex than the earlier theories.
2. The generative metrical theory correctly predicts the relative frequencies of foot-types employed by the SG poet. Other theories of syllabotonic verse contain complexity measures, but these are too imprecise to make factual numerical frequency predictions for iambic verse.
3. The generative metrical theory provides a principled method for scansion, which has not been possible for other metrical theories.

With respect to the value of a generative metrical analysis of SG, perhaps the greatest argument lies in a comparison of the iambic lines of the poem with the long alliterative lines. This argument will be developed in detail in Section 2.

2 The long alliterative lines of Sir Gawain

They tan him between hem, with talking him leden
To chambre, to chemné, and chefly they asken ... (977–978)

2.1 The standard Old English analysis

All prior analyses of the long lines of SG have attributed their meter solely to the OE tonic tradition. The alliteration in the long lines is much freer than in OE poetry, and the number of strong syllables per half-line varies much more than in OE verse, but these facts have been accounted for by hypothesizing that SG was a very late example of OE meter and that by the end of the fourteenth century the OE tradition itself had changed.

The strengths of an OE analysis of SG similar to that of the Halle-Keyser theory of OE poetry are obvious. With very little revision the Halle-Keyser theory of OE verse (as in *English Stress*, pp. 153–54) accounts for the long lines of SG as follows:

OE metrical theory of Sir Gawain (after Halle and Keyser)

a. Abstract Metrical Pattern Rules
   i. A couplet consists of two half-lines
   ii. One half-line consists of (x) x x (w) (w)
   iii. The other half-line consists of (x) (x) x (w) (w)
   Elements in parentheses are optional. w is a weak syllable.
b. Correspondence Rules
   An x corresponds to a syllable-sequence which ends with a primary-stressed vowel.
c. At least two x's in each couplet must alliterate, although not necessarily one in each half-line. (Other analyses of this aspect of SG are possible. Missing alliterations may be due to faulty transcription, for example, or to the 'promotion' of function words to full alliterative status.)

However, the deficiencies of this analysis are also clear with respect to the overall metrical pattern of the long lines. As can be seen from the two lines introducing this section, the long lines of SG have a strong feeling of metrical regularity about them which is simply not captured by the OE analysis. In addition, the OE theory has no predictive power about common and uncommon patterns of weak and strong syllables occurring in the long lines because it makes no reference to weak syllables at all (except those occurring optionally in half-line final position). Intuitions about the metrical regularity of the long lines have plagued scholars approaching these lines from the standpoint of OE meter, yet the OE tonic tradition has continued to be the standard of analysis for the long lines. In this paper a different tack will be taken: it will be argued that our intuitions about the metrical regularity of the long lines arise from the fact that these lines *are* metrically regular. It will be argued that the alliteration and number of feet per line in the long lines of SG are determined by the requirements of OE meter, but that the feet themselves are modern syllabotonic anapests. (Such an analysis is not without precedent. D. C. Freeman has argued that certain of the poems of Emily Dickinson exemplify a similar interplay of OE and modern English verse elements.[6])

The OE component of the long lines, particularly the alliteration and strong stress requirements, can be observed with reference to the long lines given as examples of other points in this section. The modern syllabotonic component of the long lines will be discussed in the following section with respect to the metrical base rules established for the iambic lines of the poem.

2.2 The Metrical Base Rules applied to the alliterative lines

By far the most frequent foot-type occurring in the long lines of SG is the anapest, wws. However, any attempt to treat the long lines as anapestic verse has not been possible with other current theories of metrics for the same reasons as those which render other theories unable to account for the iambic lines of the poem:

1. The SG poet freely adds extrametrical positions to the basic anapestic foot without observing the Sonorant Sequence Condition or any constituent structure context:

    The lord la/*ch*es hym *by the* lappe / and ledes him to sitte   (936)
            w   w w w s

2. The SG poet freely violates the Stress Maximum Condition:

    And fer over the French Flod, / Felix Brutus /   (13)
                            s   w   s w

The weak position occupied by the strong syllable *Bru* is surrounded by weak syllables within the same syntactic constituent, which violates the SMC.

However, making allowances for the extra weak syllable in the anapestic foot, the set of metrical base rules attributed to the SG poet for the iambic

A generative metrical analysis 307

lines also generates all deviations from the anapestic foot occurring in the long lines.

The line expansion rules for the long alliterative lines will be:

L→HL HL
HL→(F) F (F) (w) (w)
F→wws

L = Line HL = Half-line F = Foot w = weak position s = strong position. Elements in parentheses are optional elements. Condition: Each line must contain at least three s positions.

From these underlying structures the metrical base rules operate to generate metrical deviations as follows:

        Feet Derived in One Step in the Anapestic Lines of SG

ws   wws→ws in line-initial position via the Decrease rule.
        /The tulk / that the trammes of tresoun ther wrought (3)
         w   s

N.B. In the long lines, the Decrease rule can apply either line-initially or half-line-initially. Thus the Decrease rule can be modified as follows:

       (iii) Decrease rule w→ø / [{——
                       L, HL

s   wws→s in half-line initial position.
      /Tic/ius to Tuskan and teldes biginnes (11)
       s

N.B. This requires a new rule which deletes both initial positions of the anapestic foot. This is the only additional rule required in the long lines and not used in the iambic lines.

       (v) Radical Decrease rule ww→ø / [{——
                         HL

wwws wws→wwws via the Increase rule.
       /With all the mete / and the mirthe that men couthe avyse (45)
        w   w   w s

wss   wws→wss via the Spondee rule.
       /The borg brit/tened and brent to brondes and askes (2)
        w   s   s

sws   wws→sws via the Spondee rule.
       /Nowel nay/ted onewe, nevened ful oft (65)
        s   w   s

308   *Essays in Modern Stylistics*

www   wws→www via the Pyrrhus rule.
   That he beknew cortaysly of the court / that he were /   (903)
                                                   w   w   w

N.B.. In the long lines the SG poet uses this rule only at the end of a half-line. Thus the Pyrrhus rule can be modified as follows for the anapestic feet:

(ii) Pyrrhus rule s→w/   a. {w____   for iambs
                         b.   ww____}] for anapests
                              {HL

No other changes in the metrical base rules are required for the anapestic feet of the long lines. However, two comments should be made on the way in which the rules have been formulated here. First, the restriction of the Decrease rule to half-line initial position in the long lines may appear to be unmotivated. For example, half-lines of the form ws ws ws fairly frequently appear in the long lines. It may be asked why this half-line cannot simply be derived from three anapests by three applications of the Decrease rule, one initial, one medial, and one final. The reason this option was not chosen was to reduce ambiguities. Given an iterative non-restricted Decrease rule plus the (b.) alternative of the Spondee rule, a ws ws ws line would be more than ten ways ambiguous (e.g., w/sws/ws, w/s/wsws, ws/w/sws, ws/ws/ws, ws/w/s/ws, etc.).

Second, it has been suggested (Lisa Selkirk and Don Freeman, personal communication) that the Radical Decrease rule be eliminated and simple iteration of the regular Decrease rule be permitted line-initially. This is a possible alternative. See Section 3 for another possible alternative: that some anapestic half-lines may begin underlyingly with an iambic foot. If this is the case, the Radical Decrease rule would be unnecessary, since one application of the simple Decrease rule would account for the s feet in the long lines.

Using the metrical base rules as they have at present been formulated, the following complex anapestic foot types can be derived in two and three steps:

Examples of Feet Derived in Two Steps in the Long Lines of SG

ww   wws→ws half-line initially via the Decrease rule.
     ws→ww via option (a.) of the Pyrrhus rule.
       /For to / bring this burn with blys into halle   (825)
              w   w

ss   wws→ss via the Decrease rule.
     ws→ss via the Spondee rule.
       /Fayre fyl/yoles that fyged, and ferlyly long   (796)
              s   s

A generative metrical analysis 309

wsws   wws→wwws via the Increase rule.
           wwws→wsws via the Spondee rule.
              With rych revel oryght / and rechles merth/es   (40)
                       w   s   w   s   (w)

wwss   wws→wwws via the Increase rule.
           wwws→wwss via the Spondee rule.
              If they hade herde any karp / of a knyght grene/   (704)
                            w   w   s   s

sss   wws→wss via the Spondee rule.
           wss→sss via the Spondee rule.
              And al was rayled on red, / ryche gold nayl/es   (603)
                        s   s   s   (w)

         Examples of Feet Derived in Three Steps in the Long Lines of SG

wwsws   wws→wwws via the Increase rule.
           wwws→wwwws via the Increase rule.
           wwwws→wwsws via the Spondee rule.
              And sy/then a crafty cap/ados closed aloft   (572)
                  w   w   s   w   s   (w) (w)

wwwss   wws→wwws via the Increase rule.
           wwws→wwwws via the Increase rule.
           wwwws→wwwss via the Spondee rule.
              Fal/les upon fayre flat, / flowres ther schewen   (507)
                w   w   w   s   s

wsss   wws→wwws via the Increase rule.
           wwws→wwss via the Spondee rule.
           wwss→wsss via the Spondee rule.
              And sythen the brawden bryné / of bryght stele ring/es   (580)
                        w   s   s   s   (w)

    The Scansion Principle proposed in Sectiion 1.4 can be used to analyze the long lines of SG with only one change – 'Scan so as to maximize the number of anapestic feet.' Note that the scansion algorithm for the long lines of SG will be almost identical to that for the iambic lines, with only the following changes:

a. Determine the half-line boundary as well as the line boundary.
b. Insert a foot boundary in every sequence sww (a change from iambs to anapests):

    sww→s)(ww

310 *Essays in Modern Stylistics*

c. Since the number of feet per half-line is not fixed, determine if the scansion demarcates only single feet. If so, the scansion is complete. If not, proceed as in Section 1.4 to demarcate foot boundaries based on the Scansion Principle.

Using this scansion algorithm in conjunction with the metrical base rules, the first stanza of long alliterative lines in SG can now be scanned as follows:

/Sith/en the sege / and the assaut / was ses/ed at Troye,/
  S   W W S   W   W W   S   W   S W W   S
/The borg brit/tened and brent / to bron/des and ask/es,
  W   S   S   W   W   S   W S   W   W   S (W)
/The tulk / that the tram/mes of tre/soun ther wrought/
  W   S   W   W   S   (W) W S   W   W   S
/Was tried / for his trich/erie, the trew/est on erthe:/
  W   S   W   W   S   (W) (W) W   S   W W   S
/Hit was Enn/ias the ath/el and his highe kynde,/
  W   W   S   W W   S (W) W   W   S   S
/That sith/en depreced prov/inches, and pat/rounes bicome/
  W   S   W   W   S W   S (W) (W) W S   W   WS
/Welnegh / of al the wele / in the West Il/es.
  W   S   W W W   S   W   W   S S (W)
/Fro riche Rom/ulus to Rome / ric/chis hym swythe,/
  W   S   S   W W W   S   S   W   W   S
/With gret bob/baunce that Burg / he big/es upon fyrst,/
  W   S   S   W   W   S   W S   W W W   S
/And nev/enes hit his aune nome, / as hit now hat./
  W   S   W W W   S   S   W W S   S
/Tic/ius to Tus/kan and tel/des bigyn/nes,
  S   W W   S (W) W   S   W W   S (W)
/Lang/aberde in Lum/bardie lyft/es up hom   /es,
  S   W W W   S (W)(W) S W W   S   (W)
/And fer / over the French Flod, / Felix Bru/tus
  W   S   W W W   S   S   S W S (W)
/On mony bonk/kes ful brode / Bret/ayn he set/tes.   (1-14)
  W W   W   S   W   W W   S   W   W S (W)

From these lines it is clear that the meter of the long alliterative lines, while obviously extremely complex, is nonetheless derivable in a very predictable fashion from five quite simple metrical base rules, four of which are needed on independent grounds to account for the meter of the iambic lines of SG and the fifth of which is simply an anapestic variation of the Decrease rule. It is possible that one of the reasons the long alliterative lines have for so long eluded metrical analysis is that while the modern reader is accustomed to iambic verse and its allowable deviations (as exemplified in Section 1), modern anapestic verse is quite uncommon. Thus our perceptions of allowable deviations from the anapest are not nearly so well-defined, and when faced with anapestic feet derived from a series of rules we are unable to recover at all precisely the underlying metrical pattern, even though we intuit its presence in reading the long lines of SG. The intuited underlying pattern is, however, made clear when its metrical 'deviations' are expressed by means of the generative metrical base rules.

2.3 The Complexity Measure applied to the long lines of SG

As in the case of the foot-types appearing in the iambic lines, the Complexity Measure provides a testable prediction about the relative frequency of foot-types occurring in the long alliterative lines. The anapestic foot ought to occur most frequently; feet derived from wws by a single metrical rule ought to have a tendency to appear less frequently than wws; feet derived by two rules ought to have a tendency to appear less frequently than feet derived by one rule, and so on.

Again the predictions of the Complexity Measure are borne out, and in fact in a far more interesting fashion than with respect to the frequencies of the iambic feet. The following chart contains a listing of all of the foot-types occurring in the long lines of Book II of *Sir Gawain* (approximately 600 lines). Note that the wwws foot occurs much more frequently than the wss foot within the second complexity group. It is interesting to speculate that while relative frequencies between complexity groups are a function of the metrical rules employed by the poet, variation within a group is attributable solely to stylistic preference – i.e., the poet's deliberate preference for one metrical pattern over another.

Foot-Type Frequencies in the Long Lines of SG

Foot	*♯ of Rules*	*Rules*	*♯ of Occurrences*
wws	0		596
ws	1	D	328
s	1	D(v)	162
wwws	1	I	192
sws	1	S	101
wss	1	S	102
www	1	P	72
wsws	2	I,S	99
ww	2	D,P	90
wwss	2	I,S	82
ss	2	D,S	34

Foot	# of Rules	Rules	# of Occurrences
wwwws	2	I,I	24
sss	2	S,S	10
wwww	2	I,P	10
wsss	3	I,S,S	14
wwwss	3	I,I,S	8
wwsws	3	I,I,S	9
wwwww	3	I,I,P	4
wwwwss	4	I,I,I,S	1

I = Increase   D = Decrease   S = Spondee   P = Pyrrhus

It is apparent that the overall proportion of derived anapestic feet to basic anapestic feet is much higher than the proportion of derived iambic feet to basic iambic feet. This difference captures the reader's intuitions that the iambic lines are much more regularly 'iambic' than the anapestic lines are 'anapestic'. The perceived metrical complexity of the long lines is a function of the number of deviant feet, and the number of deviant feet is quite high in the long lines.

The ws and s feet can be generated only in half-line initial position. With the ww feet, over 500 of these occur in Book II, indicating that almost half of the half-lines begin with iambs. Given such a high proportion, it is possible to speculate that the precise metrical half-line format favored by the SG poet was actually something corresponding to

HL→ws wws (w) (w)

Note that all four of the half-lines given at the beginning of this section, for example, are of this form. In Section 2.1 it was proposed that the half-line format of the long lines was due strictly to OE requirements on the number of strong syllables per half-line and had nothing to do with the number of feet per half-line. The high proportion of ws and s feet in the long lines argues the contrary – that even in the long lines, the SG poet had a tendency to prefer a fixed number of feet over a variable number of feet.

The relatively low frequencies of www and wwww feet can be explained by the fact that these feet could be derived by the SG poet only in half-line final position and were seldom necessary there, since the half-line format employed by the poet already allowed him two optional extra-metrical weak syllables in those positions, which he was much more likely to make use of than of the more complex derived feet. A more interesting problem is that the sss foot derived by two metrical rules occurs less frequently than the wsss foot derived by three metrical rules. In both of these cases the derived foot occupies an entire half-line with its maximum of three strong

A generative metrical analysis 313

positions. The three strong positions in these feet have to be filled by three stressed monosyllables, since only primary stress in each word counts as a strong syllable. The most likely syntactic candidate for this half-line type is probably the sequence ADJ – ADJ – NOUN (as in the examples given in Section 2.2). However, in most cases such a sequence, unless set off as an appositive Noun Phrase to some prior Noun Phrase, requires a determiner which occupies a weak position before the strong positions. Thus syntactic considerations dictate that while it may be metrically simpler to derive an sss foot than a wsss foot, linguistically it is preferable to make use of the wsss foot. Hence, although both of these foot types occur seldom, wsss occurs slightly more frequently. Similar reasoning probably accounts for the fact that the half-line initial ss foot is one of the less frequent of the two-rule foot types.

2.4 The interaction of syllabotonic and OE meter in the long lines

While the basic meter of the long alliterative lines is anapestic, the number of feet per line is quite free. The line expansion rules given in Section 2.2 are essentially OE in character. One half-line in each couplet of SG must have two or three strong stresses, and the other must have one, two or three strong stresses. Thus the number of feet per line of SG can vary from two to, presumably, six or more, depending on the number of times the Spondee rule and the Pyrrhus rule have applied to the underlying anapestic feet in the line. The anapestic tetrameter line is most highly favored by the SG poet, but examples of dimeter, trimeter, and pentameter lines also occur:

Two-foot lines:

/The lede lay lurk/ed a ful long while/   (1195)
 w s   s s (w) w w s   s
/Auther to long lye / or to long sitte/   (88)
 w w w s   s   w w s   s

Three-foot lines:

/Welnegh / of al the wele / in the West Il/es   (7)
 w s   w w w s   w w   s s (w)

Four-foot lines:

/The tulk / that the tram/mes of tre/soun ther wrought/   (3)
 w s   w   w s   (w) w s   w   w   s

Five-foot lines:

/When Zef/erus syf/les himself / on sed/es and herb/es   (517)
 w s   w w s w   w w w s   w w s   (w)

314 *Essays in Modern Stylistics*

The Old English character of the long lines is further heightened by the SG poet's use of alliteration, although the alliteration appears not to be so integral to the meter of SG as to the meter of strict OE verse. Nonetheless the essential syllabotonicity of the underlying anapestic feet imposes a character of regularity in the long lines of SG which is perceptibly different from the regularity of strict OE verse.

3 Summary of the Proposed Analysis of Sir Gawain

The conclusions reached about the meter of SG in the preceding sections may be summarized as follows:

1. The entire poem is written in syllabotonic meter. The short rhymed lines are written in iambic feet and the long alliterative lines in anapestic feet. This conclusion differs from prior analyses of SG, which attribute the meter of the long alliterative lines solely to the OE tradition in which there is no regular fixed-syllable foot apparent in the linguistic material of a verse line.
2. The SG poet had, as part of his poetic style, a set of five metrical base rules which permitted him to generate deviations from the basic syllabotonic meters which he employed. The same set of metrical base rules could be applied either to the basic ws foot or to the basic wws foot, the first in the short rhymed lines of the poem and the second in its long alliterative lines.
3. The short rhymed lines of the poem contain not only a fixed basic number of syllables per foot, but a fixed number of feet per line in the trimeter pattern.
4. The long alliterative lines contain a fixed basic number of syllables per foot, but a free number of feet per line, ranging from two to five or six. The number of feet per line in the long lines of SG is determined by OE requirements on the number of strong stresses per line rather than by modern syllabotonic requirements of a fixed number of feet,
5. Thus the present analysis of SG agrees with prior analyses in attributing part of SG to OE meter and part to modern syllabotonic meter, but disagrees as to where the division is made. In the present analysis the use of OE meter in SG is restricted to determining the number of syllabotonic feet per line in the long lines of the poem, and even so the SG poet had a tendency to prefer a fixed number of feet per line (four) in a fixed half-line format of ws wws (w) (w), rather than a tendency to make full use of the freedom granted him by the loose OE stress requirements of three to six strong stresses per line.

A generative metrical analysis 315

If one were to make a chart based on these conclusions showing the diachronic progresssion from OE meter to a modern meter such as iambic pentameter, with SG in the middle, it would come out something like the following:

	♯ *of Syllables/Foot*	♯ *of Feet/Line*
OE meter	free within limits; no fixed-syllable foot	free within limits;[7] depending only on number of strong stresses per line
SG long lines	fixed at three but allowing extensive deviation; the basic foot is wws	free within limits of the number of strong stresses, but with a tendency toward four
Modern iambic pentameter	fixed at two and allowing little deviation; the basic foot is ws	fixed at five

SG is obviously a transitional poem since the metrical base rules employed by the SG poet permit far more deviation in the fixed-syllable foot than is characteristic of modern verse, while within the loose OE requirements of a free number of feet per line the SG poet still had a tendency to choose the four-foot line over any other. Yet it is interesting in this context that in English poetry as exemplified by SG the fixed meter apparently could be said to have 'begun' at the level of the fixed syllable foot.

4 Summary of the proposed generative metrical theory

The generative metrical theory proposed here is viewed not so much as a counter-proposal to Halle and Keyser's theory of metrics but as the formal development of various theoretical notions suggested by that work. For the analysis of SG the advantage of the more formal approach is obvious: Halle and Keyser's metrical constraints do not apply to the verse of the SG poet. On the other hand, the verse of the SG poet can be accurately described by abstract metrical base rules which are formal counterparts of Halle and Keyser's suggested correspondence rules for the formation of spondaic and pyrrhic feet.

A crucial difference between Halle and Keyser's theory and the generative metrical theory proposed here is the range of metrical rules. As in Kiparsky's theory of meter, the metrical base rules developed here are assumed to be a part of the metrical competence of the individual poet,

316   *Essays in Modern Stylistics*

rather than a characteristic of all syllabotonic verse (as opposed to Halle and Keyser, whose theory of meter is assumed to be valid for an entire verse form – e.g. all of iambic verse – regardless of its author or date of composition). Thus each poet presumably has a distinct set of metrical base rules which distinguish his work from that of other poets.

The advantages of this approach over the Halle-Keyser cross-verse approach are threefold:

1. By comparing the metrical base rules of two different poets, it is possible to characterize formally the way in which the two poets' approach to meter differs. For example, the Pyrrhus rule in the long anapestic lines of SG applies only half-line finally:

$$s \rightarrow w/ww\_\_\_\}]$$
$$HL$$

   while for Byron's anapestic verse the Pyrrhus rule applies freely to any foot:

$$s \rightarrow w/ww\_\_\_\}$$

   And redeemed, / if they have / not retarded, thy fall
   ('The Irish Avatar')

   The metrical base rules permit formal characterization of this stylistic difference very precisely, and in addition give rise to the empirical prediction that Byron's poems will contain a higher proportion of pyrrhic feet than does SG due to Byron's use of a less contextually constrained Pyrrhus rule. (It is unclear how Kiparsky's Metrical Rule 1: 1 stress $\rightarrow$ [α stress] could be modified to account for Pyrrhic feet in SG – Kiparsky's formalism contains no provision for line boundaries. Thus within Kiparsky's theory the formal comparison between Byron and SG could not be carried out by simply comparing two 'versions' of MR1. This is similar to the objection raised in Section 1.1 against Kiparsky's epenthesis rule.) Since one of the goals of stylistics is to make precise the reader's aesthetic intuitions about differences in style, the addition of poet-oriented metrical base rules to the formal apparatus of stylistics can be of great assistance to the student of prosody.

2. The metrical base rules are formally precise and thus are capable of serving as a criterion or diagnostic for disputed authorship. One of the questions about SG, for instance, concerns whether the SG poet was also the author of the *Pearl*. Given the metrical base rules established for SG along with the predictions of the Complexity Measure which hold for SG, it ought to be possible to determine whether the same rules also generate the meter of *Pearl*. If both poems derive from the same

(idiosyncratic) set of metrical base rules, a strong piece of evidence will be added to the argument for identical authorship.[8]
3. Finally, the study of diachronic change in metrical style is made possible with poet-oriented metrical base rules in a manner which has not previously been possible. The reason that the Halle-Keyser theory of metrics is unable to elucidate the meter of SG is that the Halle-Keyser metrical constraints apply to modern iambic verse but did not apply to the iambic verse of the SG poet. Thus the Halle-Keyser theory is not flexible enough to compare widely differing (but presumably equally valid) examples of the same verse type. Kiparsky's formalism, which makes reference only to constituent structure, is similarly unable to serve as a comparative tool for poems whose metrical deviations rely on non-linguistic contexts. The metrical base rules, on the other hand, are a flexible enough tool to describe a wide variety of syllabotonic verse equally precisely, and thus comparison of differing approaches to the same verse form is possible without recourse to the unsatisfactory conclusion that one or the other of the approaches is unmetrical (or undescribable).

This paper has attempted to argue that neither the Halle-Keyser nor the Kiparsky theory of meter is capable of adequately representing the metrical practices of the SG poet and that an entirely different formalism is required to do justice to the metrical deviations in SG. However, no attempt has been made to argue that the generative metrical theory proposed in this paper can account fully for all syllabotonic verse. In fact, even with respect to the verse of the SG poet, an entire area of metrical theory has been glossed over – the problem of 'fitting' the lexical material of a poem into an underlying derived metrical pattern. For example, the SG poet could put any sequence of weak syllables into a derived wws foot in his iambic lines. By the time of Wyatt, a constraint has been added to this process of fitting lexical material into the derived wws pattern, such that two weak syllables could occur foor-initially only if they were not separated by consonantal stops such as *t*, *d*, *p* (cf. Section 1.1). This particular constraint on 'poetic lexical insertion' continued to strengthen to the point that the only allowable consonants between two foot-initial weak positions became the glides *r* and *l*. The thesis of the present paper is that even though sonorant elision thus became the standard approach to the use of the wws foot in iambic verse, the derived foot still contains three metrical positions, two weak and one strong. It is only the way in which these metrical positions are filled by lexical material which has changed over time.

This approach differs from other metrical theories, which say that an iambic foot containing, e.g., the words 'to a hill', consists of only two metrical positions, ws, and that the w position is filled by two elidible syllables. This paper takes the stand that if an iambic foot contains three syllables, its underlying metrical representation contain three metrical positions. At various times different 'lexical insertion' rules then put different constraints on the syllables which can occur in these positions. From this point of view, all rules concerning the lexical/phonological realization of an underlying abstract metrical pattern fall into the realm of correspondence rules: rules affecting the correspondence between an abstract derived metrical pattern and the linguistic material which is arranged in this pattern in a poem. Since Kiparsky's Monosyllable Rule MR2 makes reference to syntactic constituent structure for its operation, it is here considered to be a correspondence rule (or rule of poetic lexical insertion) rather than a generative metrical rule. Similarly the Sonorant Sequence Condition of Halle and Keyser is viewed as a diachronically changing phonological constraint on correspondence rules rather than as an essential element of the underlying generative metrical component of poetic competence. Correspondence rules are an essential part of any theory of poetic meter and thus, although it has been pointed out in this paper that the Halle-Keyser and Kiparsky theories of meter are unable to account for SG, no attempt has been made to argue that the generative metrical theory can replace the Halle-Keyser and Kiparsky rules. On the contrary, it is assumed that the metrical base rules operate prior to but along with lexical correspondence rules and that neither rule type can be a complete replacement for the other.

Appendix: Pronunciation, stress, and orthography

I   In analyzing the meter of SG, the following rules of pronunciation were used, as proposed in Chapter 5 of Marie Borroff's *Sir Gawain and the Green Knight* (1962; rpt. Hamden, Conn: Archon, 1973). Note that pronunciation rules cannot be more precisely defined for the SG poet's dialect, due to the problematic circle between poetic meter and word stress. Without detailed knowledge of the SG poet's metrical practices, it has been impossible for scholars to determine exact pronunciation rules for his dialect. Similarly, the lack of detailed pronunciation rules has made analysis of the meter of SG quite difficult in the past. (The present analysis of the poem is by and large neutral with respect to disputed pronunciation, since the meter employed by the poet is so flexible.)

   1. Gawain usually receives stress on the first syllable (Gáwain, Wáwan) unless the second syllable is artificially emphasized, e.g. for purposes of rhyme in the short rhymed lines.

2. Final unaccented -e is not usually pronounced.
3. Final past tense -ed and present tense or plural -es
   a. are usually pronounced when they follow a primary stressed syllable as in stónes, wérres, tákes, blámes, lérned (all two-syllable words); bihéstes, bicómes, avísed (all three-syllable words);
   b. are usually not pronounced when the preceding syllable has secondary or tertiary stress, as in ládies, lóveres, ánswered (two-syllable words);
   c. are usually not pronounced in unstressed words such as elles, whennes, youres (all one-syllable words.)
4. Words derived from OE are stressed according to the rules developed in Chapter 2 of Halle and Keyser's *English Stress* (New York: Harper & Row, 1971):
   a. nouns, adjectives, and compound nouns receive primary stress on the first syllable;
   b. other words receive primary stress on the first syllable of the stem.
5. Words derived from ME are stressed according to the rules developed by Borroff in Chapter 5:
   a. stem-suffix derivatives: accent tended to be shifted to the first syllable, as in prísun, mírour, cástel, bátaille:
   b. prefix-stem derivatives: stress was retained on the stem if the prefix ended with a vowel: aréi, debát, destrésse, repáire; words whose prefixes ended with a consonant were sometimes stressed on the initial syllable and at other times on the stem, as in párdon/pardón, pértain/pertáin, cómfort/comfórt;
   c. stem-initial words of three or more syllables received primary stress on the first syllable, as in córtesie, prísonnier;
   d. words of the form prefix-stem-suffix tended to have two accentual forms, one with stress on the prefix and the other with stress on the stem: désirous/desírous, déspitous/despítous, áventure/avénture.

II Sentence stress (e.g., the Nuclear Stress rule) is not taken into account in the present analysis of SG since this analysis does not depend on the constituent structure of the verse lines.

III With respect to line scansion in the present analysis, only the primary stressed syllable in each word is specifically marked. All other stresses count as weak stresses. Specifically, the following rules are used for scansion:

$$\begin{bmatrix} V \\ 1\ \text{stress} \end{bmatrix} \quad N, A, V, Adv \quad \rightarrow s\ \text{(strong syllable)}$$

$$[V]\ \text{elsewhere} \quad \rightarrow w\ \text{(weak syllable)}$$

IV Alliteration: While alliteration usually coincides with strong stresses in the long lines of SG, it need not necessarily coincide.

And hit lyfte up the eye-liddes and loked ful brode   (446)
 w   w s w w s w   w s w w   s

The word *liddes* alliterates in this line but does not count as a strong stress. There are many examples in SG where a similar situation prevails; thus alliteration is not generally used in the present paper for determining stress placement.

V Orthography: The orthography of SG contains two symbols not used in Modern English, ȝ and ƿ (yogh and wen). For ease in reading examples, these have been changed throughout the paper to their closest modern equivalent (*g*, *y*, or *w*), and ð (eth) has been changed to *th*.

Notes

1 I am indebted to Don Freeman, Lisa Selkirk, and Jay Keyser for their helpful criticism of this paper; to Sally Hollens for her encouragement; and to Professor Philip Damon, in whose class I first studied *Sir Gawain and the Green Knight* in 1966. Work on the paper was supported by a National Science Foundation Graduate Fellowship.
2 J. R. R. Tolkien and E. V. Gordon, 'Introduction', *Sir Gawain and the Green Knight*, ed. J. R. R. Tolkien and E. V. Gordon (1925; rpt. Oxford: Clarendon, 1966), pp. xx–xxiii. Subsequent references will be to this edition.
3 See, e.g., Tolkien and Gordon, pp. 118–21.
4 The theories under discussion are presented in Morris Halle and S. J. Keyser, *English Stress: Its Form, Its Growth, and Its Role in Verse* (New York: Harper & Row, 1971) and in Paul Kiparsky, 'Stress, syntax, and meter', *Language*, 51 (1975), [Reprinted in this volume, pp. 225–72]. Subsequent references will be to this edition.
5 The chart of foot-type frequencies given in Section 1.3 was scanned according to the Line Scansion Principle. If in each case the most complex rather than the least complex scansion had been chosen, the foot-type frequencies in the chart would have been shifted downward, but the ordering of the metrical complexity groups would have remained unchanged.
6 'Current trends in metrics', *Current Trends in Stylistics*, ed. B. Kachru and H. Stahlke (Champaign: Linguistic Research, 1972), pp. 67–81.
7 This proposal is in accordance with the Halle-Keyser theory of OE verse. For an alternate analysis which proposes that OE verse contains four isochronous feet per line, see R. P. Creed, 'A new approach to the rhythm of Beowulf', *PMLA*, 81 (1966), 23–33.
8 I am indebted to Tim Austin for this suggestion.

V
Approaches to prose style

Introduction

Most recent studies in prose style have concerned themselves more than earlier work with the social, interpersonal implications of prose narrative. Such studies have primarily been programmatic rather than practical, an emphasis reflected in the essays which follow.

In 'Linguistic function and literary style', M. A. K. Halliday stresses the place of semantics in the study of style. He adopts a functional theory of language which seeks to explain linguistic phenomena 'by reference to the notion that language plays a certain part in our lives'. Language, for Halliday, has three main functions: the 'ideational' (expression of content), the 'interpersonal' (the relationship which the speaker establishes between himself and his interlocutor), and the 'textual', in which language 'makes links with itself and with the situation'. The text, in Halliday's view, is the appropriate locus for stylistic studies. In an analysis of passages from William Golding's *The Inheritors*, he shows how a 'foregrounding of everyday syntactic options' makes clear the 'vision of things' of the novel's two tribal groups. For 'the people', the less advanced Neanderthal tribe, the language depicts a world in which people act intransitively, reflecting the theme of the Neanderthal limitation of understanding. Halliday constructs a grammar of 'the people's' language, showing sentences unlikely to occur in that grammar, and in the people's world, in which there 'is no cause and effect'. In the language of the new, more powerful tribe, the 'inheritors' of the novel's title, however, most clauses have a human subject, and the syntax shows much greater action and transitivity. Such a comparative analysis of the novel's syntactic patterning is, Halliday argues, central to our understanding of the major themes of *The Inheritors*.

Richard Ohmann's 'Speech, literature, and the space between' builds on the theoretical precepts of J. L. Austin's *How to Do Things With Words* and John Searle's *Speech Acts* in a discussion of 'illocutionary acts', acts performed in speaking, in literature. Rules of illocutionary acts, unlike rules of grammar, involve interpersonal relationships. Most linguistic studies of literature, Ohmann argues, have focused on locutionary acts – *acts* of speaking – or perlocutionary acts – the *effects* of speaking. Ohmann proposes that analysis of illocutionary acts be added to the critical endeavor. In literature, he suggests, the rules for illocutionary acts – appropriateness of circumstance, speaker, intentions, and behavior – are suspended. The act of literary interpretation therefore relies in part on the reader's attributing appropriate illocutionary conditions to literary statements. In so doing, the reader constructs or infers the world of the literary work.

'Literary cooperation and implicature', a chapter of Mary Louise Pratt's *Toward a Speech Act Theory of Literary Discourse* (1977), seeks to apply to literature Searle's speech act theory and the Cooperative Principle for discourse of the philosopher H. Paul Grice. The calculations which a listener must go through in order to make sense of an utterance, given the observation of the Cooperative Principle, Grice calls *conversational implicatures*. Narrativity, for Pratt, necessitates the implicatures of causality and time sequence. Along with the Cooperative Principle are maxims of conversation – Quantity, Quality, Relation, and Manner – which literary works often flout for particular effects, and which implicature – calculations in order to make sense – must resolve. Pratt illustrates this principle in extended analyses from, among others, Sterne, Faulkner, Camus, Borges, and Defoe.

14
Linguistic function and literary style: an inquiry into the language of William Golding's 'The Inheritors'

M. A. K. Halliday

My main concern, in this paper, is with criteria of relevance. This, it seems to me, is one of the central problems in the study of 'style in language': I mean the problem of distinguishing between mere linguistic regularity, which in itself is of no interest to literary studies, and regularity which is significant for the poem or prose work in which we find it. I remember an entertaining paper read to the Philological Society in Cambridge some years ago by Professor John Sinclair, in which he drew our attention to some very striking linguistic patterns displayed in the poetry of William McGonagall, and invited us to say why, if this highly structured language was found in what we all agreed was such very trivial poetry, we should be interested in linguistic regularities at all.[1] It is no new discovery to say that pattern in language does not by itself make literature, still less 'good literature': nothing is more regular than the rhythm of *Three Blind Mice*, and if this is true of phonological regularities it is likely to be true also of syntactic ones. But we lack general criteria for determining whether any particular instance of linguistic prominence is likely to be stylistically relevant or not.

This is not a simple matter, and any discussion of it is bound to touch on more than one topic, or at the least to adopt more than one angle of vision. Moreover the line of approach will often, inevitably, be indirect, and the central concern may at times be lost sight of round some of the corners. It seems to me necessary, first of all, to discuss and to emphasize the place of semantics in the study of style; and this in turn will lead to a consideration of 'functional' theories of language and their relevance for the student of literature. At the same time these general points need to be exemplified; and here I have allowed the illustration to take over the stage: when I reexamined for this purpose a novel I had first studied some four years ago, *The Inheritors* by William Golding, there seemed to be much that was of interest in its own right.[2] I do not think there is any antithesis between the 'textual' and the 'theoretical' in the study of language, so I hope the effect of this may be to strengthen rather than to weaken the general argument. The discussion of *The Inheritors* may be seen either in relation to just that one work or in relation to a general theory; I am not sure that it is possible to separate these two perspectives, either from each other or from various intermediate fields of attention such as an author, a genre, or a literary tradition.

The paper will fall into four parts: first, a discussion of a 'functional theory of language'; second, a reference to various questions raised at the Style in Language conference of 1958 and in other current writings; third, an examination of certain features of the language of *The Inheritors*; and fourth, a brief résumé of the question of stylistic relevance. Of these, the third part will be the longest.

The term *function* is used, in two distinct though related senses, at two very different points in the description of language. First it is used in the sense of 'grammatical' (or 'syntactic') function, to refer to elements of linguistic structures such as actor and goal or subject and object or theme and rheme. These 'functions' are the roles occupied by classes of words, phrases, and the like in the structure of higher units. Secondly, it is used to refer to the 'functions' of language as a whole: for example in the well-known work of Karl Bühler, in which he proposes a three-way division of language function into the representational, the conative and the expressive.[3]

Here I am using 'function' in the second sense, referring, however, not specifically to Bühler's theory, but to the generalized notion of 'functions of language'. By a functional theory of language I mean one which attempts to explain linguistic structure, and linguistic phenomena, by reference to the notion that language plays a certain part in our lives, that it is required to serve certain universal types of demand. I find this approach valuable in general for the insight it gives into the nature and use of language, but particularly so in the context of stylistic studies.

The demands that we make on language, as speakers and writers, listeners and readers, are indefinitely many and varied. They can be derived, ultimately, from a small number of very general headings; but what these headings are will depend on what questions we are asking. For example, if we were to take a broadly psychological viewpoint and consider the functions that language serves in the life of the individual, we might arrive at some such scheme as Bühler's, referred to above. If on the other hand we asked a more sociological type of question, concerning the functions that language serves in the life of the community, we should probably elaborate some framework such as Malinowski's distinction into a pragmatic and a magical function.[4] Many others could be suggested besides.

These questions are extrinsic to language; and the categorizations of language function that depend on them are of interest because, and to the extent that, the questions themselves are of interest. Such categorizations therefore imply a strictly instrumental view of linguistic theory. Some would perhaps reject this on the grounds that it does not admit the autonomy of linguistics and linguistic investigations. I am not myself impressed by that argument, although I would stress that any one particular instrumental view is by itself inadequate as a general characterization of language. But a purely extrinsic theory of language functions does fail to take into account one thing, namely the fact that the multiplicity of function, if the idea is valid at all, is likely to be reflected somewhere in the internal organization of language itself. If language is, as it were, programmed to serve a variety of needs, then this should show up in some way in an investigation of linguistic structure.

In fact this functional plurality is very clearly built into the structure of language, and forms the basis of its semantic and 'syntactic' (i.e. grammatical and lexical) organization. If we set up a functional framework that is neutral as to external emphasis, but designed to take into account the nature of the internal, semantic, and syntactic patterns of language, we arrive at something that is very suggestive for literary studies, because it represents a general characterization of semantic functions – of the meaning potential of the language system. Let me suggest here the framework that seems to me most helpful. It is a rather simple catalogue of three basic functions, one of which has two sub-headings.

In the first place, language serves for the expression of content: it has a representational, or, as I would prefer to call it, an *ideational* function. (This is sometimes referred to as the expression of 'cognitive meaning,' though I find the term *cognitive* misleading; there is, after all, a cognitive element in all linguistic functions.) Two points need to be emphasized concerning this ideational function of language. The first is that it is through this function that the speaker or writer embodies in language his experience of the phenomena of the real world; and this includes his experience of the internal world of his own consciousness: his reactions, cognitions, and perceptions, and also his linguistic acts of speaking and understanding. We shall in no sense be adopting an extreme pseudo-Whorfian position (I say 'pseudo-Whorfian' because Whorf himself never was extreme) if we add that, in serving this function, language lends structure to his experience and helps to determine his way of looking at things. The speaker can see through and around the settings of his semantic system; but he is aware that, in doing so, he is seeing reality in a new light, like Alice in Looking-glass House. There is, however, and this is the second point, one component of ideational meaning which, while not unrelatable to experience, is nevertheless organized in language in a way which marks it off as distinct: this is the expression of certain fundamental logical relations such as are encoded in language in the form of co-ordination, apposition, modification, and the like. The notion of co-ordination, for example, as in *sun, moon, and stars*, can be derived from an aspect of the speaker's experience; but this and other such relations are realized through the medium of a particular type of structural mechanism (that of linear recursion) which takes them, linguistically, out of the domain of experience to form a functionally neutral, 'logical' component in the total spectrum of meanings. Within the ideational function of language, therefore, we can recognize two sub-functions, the *experiential* and the *logical*; and the distinction is a significant one for our present purpose.

In the second place, language serves what we may call an *interpersonal* function. This is quite different from the expression of content. Here, the speaker is using language as the means of his own intrusion into the speech event: the expression of his comments, his attitudes, and evaluations, and also of the relationship that he sets up between himself and the listener – in particular, the communication role that he adopts, of informing, questioning, greeting, persuading, and the like. The interpersonal function thus subsumes both the expressive and the conative, which are not in fact distinct in the linguistic system: to give one example, the meanings 'I do not know' (expressive) and 'you tell me' (conative) are combined in a single semantic feature, that of question, typically expressed in the grammar by an interrogative; the interrogative is both expressive and conative at the same time. The set of communication roles is unique among social relations in that it is brought into being and maintained solely through language. But the interpersonal element in language extends beyond what we might think of as its rhetorical functions. In the wider context, language is required to serve in the establishment and maintenance of all human relationships; it is the means whereby social groups are integrated and the individual is identified and reinforced. It is, I think, significant for certain forms of literature that, since personality is dependent on interaction which is in turn mediated through language, the 'interpersonal' function in language is both interactional and personal: there is, in other words, a component in language which serves at one and the same time to express both the inner and the outer surfaces of the individual, as a single undifferentiated area of meaning potential that is personal in the broadest sense.[5]

These two functions, the ideational and the interpersonal, may seem sufficiently all-embracing; and in the context of an instrumental approach to language they are. But there is a third function which is in turn instrumental to these two, whereby language is, as it were, enabled to meet the demands that are made on it; I shall call this the *textual* function, since it is concerned with the creation of text. It is a function internal to language, and for this reason is not usually taken into account where the objects of investigation are extrinsic; but it came to be specifically associated with the term 'functional' in the work of the Prague scholars who developed Bühler's ideas within the framework of a linguistic theory (cf. their terms 'functional syntax', 'functional sentence perspective'). It is through this function that language makes links with itself and with the situation; and discourse becomes possible, because the speaker or writer can produce a text and the listener or reader can recognize one. A *text* is an operational unit of language, as a sentence is a syntactic unit; it may be spoken or written, long or short; and it includes as a special instance a literary text, whether haiku or Homeric epic. It is the text and not some super-sentence that is the relevant unit for stylistic studies; this is a functional-semantic concept and is not definable by size. And therefore the 'textual' function is not limited to the establishment of relations between sentences; it is concerned just as much with the internal organization of the sentence, with its meaning as a message both in itself and in relation to the context.

A tentative categorization of the principal elements of English syntax in terms of the above functions is given in Table 1. This table is intended to serve a twofold purpose. In the first place, it will help to make more concrete the present concept of a functional theory, by showing how the various functions are realized through the grammatical systems of the language, all of which are accounted for in this way. Not all the labels may be self-explanatory, nor is the framework so compartmental as in this bare outline it is made to seem: there is a high degree of indeterminacy in the fuller picture, representing the indeterminacy that is present throughout language, in its categories and its relations, its types and its tokens. Secondly it will bring out the fact that the syntax of a language is organized in such a way that it expresses as a whole the range of linguistic functions, but that the symptoms of functional diversity are not to be sought in single sentences or sentence types. In general, that is to say, we shall not find whole sentences or even smaller structures having just one function. Typically, each sentence embodies all functions, though one or another may be more prominent; and most constituents of sentences also embody more than one function, through their ability to combine two or more syntactic roles.

Table 14.1

rank	function	IDEATIONAL — Experiential	IDEATIONAL — Logical	INTERPERSONAL	TEXTUAL
				COHESION ('above the sentence': non-structural relations) reference; substitution & ellipsis; conjunction; lexical cohesion	
CLAUSE		TRANSITIVITY types of process participants and circumstances (identity clauses) (things, facts, and reports)	condition addition report	MOOD types of speech function modality (the WH-function)	THEME types of message (identity as text relation) (identification, predication, reference, substitution)
		PARATACTIC COMPLEXES (all ranks) co-ordination apposition			
Verbal GROUP		TENSE (verb classes)	POLARITY catenation secondary tense	PERSON ('marked' options)	VOICE ('contrastive' options)
Nominal GROUP		MODIFICATION epithet function enumeration (noun classes) (adjective classes)	classification sub-modification	ATTITUDE attitudinal modifiers intensifiers	DEIXIS determiners 'phoric' elements (qualifiers) (definite article)
		HYPOTACTIC COMPLEXES OF CAUSE, GROUP, AND WORD			
Adverbial (incl. prepositional) GROUP		'MINOR PROCESSES' prepositional relations (classes of circumstantial adjunct)	narrowing sub-modification	COMMENT (classes of comment adjunct)	CONJUNCTION (classes of discourse adjunct)
WORD (incl. lexical item)		LEXICAL 'CONTENT' (taxonomic organization of vocabulary)	compounding derivation	LEXICAL 'REGISTER' (expressive words) (stylistic organization of vocabulary)	COLLOCATION (collocational organization of vocabulary)
INFORMATION UNIT				TONE intonation systems	INFORMATION distribution & focus

Let us introduce an example at this point. Here is a well-known passage from *Through the Looking-Glass, and What Alice Found There*:

'I don't understand you,' said Alice. 'It's dreadfully confusing!'

'That's the effect of living backwards,' the Queen said kindly: 'it always makes one a little giddy at first –'

'Living backwards!' Alice repeated in great astonishment. 'I never heard of such a thing!'

'– but there's one great advantage in it, that one's memory works both ways.'

'I'm sure *mine* only works one way,' Alice remarked. 'I can't remember things before they happen.'

'It's poor sort of memory that only works backwards,' the Queen remarked.

'What sort of things do *you* remember best?' Alice ventured to ask.

'Oh, things that happened the week after next,' the Queen replied in a careless tone.

To illustrate the last point first, namely that most constituents of sentences embody more than one function, by combining different syntactic roles: the constituent *what sort of things* occupies simultaneously the syntactic roles of 'theme', of 'phenomenon' (that is, object of cognition, perception, etc.) and of 'interrogation point'. The theme represents a particular status in the message, and is thus an expression of 'textual' function: it is the speaker's point of departure. If the speaker is asking a question he usually, in English, takes the request for information as his theme, expressing this by putting the question phrase first; here, therefore, the same element is both theme and interrogation point – the latter being an expression of 'interpersonal' function since it defines the specific communication roles the speaker has chosen for himself and for the listener: the speaker is behaving as questioner. *What sort of thing* is the phenomenon dependent on the mental process *remember*; and this concept of a mental phenomenon, as something that can be talked about, is an expression of the 'ideational' function of language – of language as content, relatable to the speaker's and the listener's experience. It should be emphasized that it is not, in fact, the syntactic role in isolation, but the structure of which it forms a part that is semantically significant: it is not the theme, for example, but the total theme-rheme structure which contributes to the texture of the discourse.

Thus the constituents themselves tend to be multivalent; which is another way of saying that the very notion of a constituent is itself rather too concrete to be of much help in a functional context. A constituent is a particular word or phrase in a particular place; but functionally the choice of an item may have one meaning, its repetition another, and its location in structure yet another – or many others, as we have seen. So, in the Queen's remark *it's a poor sort of memory that only works backwards*, the word *poor* is a 'modifier', and thus expresses a subclass of its head-word *memory* (ideational); while at the same time it is an 'epithet' expressing the Queen's attitude (interpersonal), and the choice of this word in this environment (as opposed to, say, *useful*) indicates more specifically that the attitude is one of disapproval. The words *it's . . . that* have here no reference at all outside the sentence, but they structure the message in a particular way (textual), which represents the Queen's opinion as if it was an 'attribute' (ideational), and defines one class of *memory* as exclusively possessing this undesirable quality (ideational). The lexical repetition in *memory that only works backwards* relates the Queen's remark (textual) to *mine only works one way*, in which *mine* refers anaphorically, by ellipsis, to *memory* in the preceding sentence (textual) and also to *I* in Alice's expression of her own judgment *I'm sure* (interpersonal). Thus ideational content and personal interaction are woven together with, and by means of, the textual structure to form a coherent whole.

Taking a somewhat broader perspective, we again find the same interplay of functions. The ideational meaning of the passage is enshrined in the phrase *living backwards*; we have a general characterization of the nature of experience, in which *things that happened the week after next* turns out to be an acceptable sentence. (I am not suggesting it is serious, or offering a deep literary interpretation; I am merely using it to illustrate the nature of language.) On the interpersonal level the language expresses, through a pattern of question (or exclamation) and response, a basic relationship of seeker and guide, in interplay with various other paired functions such as yours and mine, for and against, child and adult, wonderment and judgment. The texture is that of dialogue in narrative, within which the Queen's complex thematic structures (e.g. *there's one great advantage to it, that . . .*) contrast with the much simpler (i.e. linguistically unmarked) message patterns used by Alice.

A functional theory of language is a theory about meanings, not about words or constructions; we shall not attempt to assign a word or a construction directly to one function or another. Where then do we find the functions differentiated in language? They are differentiated semantically, as different areas of what I called the 'meaning potential'. Language is itself a potential: it is the totality of what the speaker can do. (By 'speaker' I mean always the language user, whether as speaker, listener, writer, or reader: *homo grammaticus*, in fact.) We are considering, as it were, the dynamics of the semantic strategies that are available to him. If we represent the language system in this way, as networks of interrelated options which define, as a whole, the resources for what the speaker wants to say, we find empirically that these options fall into a small number of fairly distinct sets. In the last resort, every option in language is related to every other; there are no completely independent choices. But the total network of meaning potential is actually composed of a number of smaller networks, each one highly complex in itself but related to the others in a way that is relatively simple: rather like an elaborate piece of circuitry made up of two or three complex blocks of wiring with fairly simple interconnections. Each of these blocks corresponds to one of the functions of language.

In Table 14.1, where the columns represent our linguistic functions, each column is one 'block' of options. These blocks are to be thought of as wired 'in parallel'. That is to say, the speaker does not first think of the content of what he wants to say and then go on to decide what kind of a message it is and where he himself comes into it – whether it will be statement or question, what modalities are involved and the like.[6] All these functions, the ideational, the interpersonal and the textual, are simultaneously embodied in his planning procedures. (If we pursue the metaphor, it is the rows of the table that are wired 'in series': they represent the hierarchy of constituents in the grammar, where the different functions come together. Each row is one constituent type, and is a point of intersection of options from the different columns.)

The linguistic differentiation among the ideational, interpersonal and textual functions is thus to be found in the way in which choices in meaning are interrelated to one another. Each function defines a set of options that is relatively – though only relatively – independent of the other sets. Dependence here refers to the degree of mutual determination: one part of the content of what one says tends to exert a considerable effect on other parts of the content, whereas one's attitudes and speech roles are relatively undetermined by it: the speaker is, by and large, free to associate any interpersonal meanings with any content. What I wish to stress here is that all types of option, from whatever function they are derived, are meaningful. At every point the speaker is selecting among a range of possibilities that differ in meaning; and if we attempt to separate meaning from choice we are turning a valuable distinction (between linguistic functions) into an arbitrary dichotomy (between 'meaningful' and 'meaningless' choices). All options are embedded in the language system: the system *is* a network of options, deriving from all the various functions of language. If we take the useful functional distinction of 'ideational' and 'interpersonal' and rewrite it, under the labels 'cognitive' and 'expressive', in such a way as sharply to separate the two, equating cognitive with meaning and expressive with style, we not only fail to recognize the experiential basis of many of our own intuitions about works of literature and their impact – style as the expression of what the thing is about, at some level[7] (my own illustration in this paper is one example of this) – but we also attach the contrasting status of 'non-cognitive' (whatever this may mean) to precisely these options that seem best to embody our conception of a work of literature, those whereby the writer gives form to the discourse and expresses his own individuality.[8] Even if we are on our guard against the implication that the regions of language in which style resides are the ones which are linguistically non-significant, we are still drawing the wrong line. There are no regions of language in which style does not reside.

We should not in fact be drawing lines at all; the boundaries on our map consist only in shading and overlapping. Nevertheless they are there; and provided we are not forced into seeking an unreal distinction between the 'what' and the 'how', we can show, by reference to the generalized notion of linguistic functions, how such real contrasts as that of denotation and connotation relate to the functional map of language as a whole, and thus how they may be incorporated into the linguistic study of style. It is through this chain of reasoning that we may hope to establish criteria of relevance and to demonstrate the connection between the syntactic observation which we make about a text and the nature of the impact which that text has upon us. If we can relate the linguistic patterns (grammatical, lexical, and even phonological) to the underlying functions of language, we have a criterion for eliminating what is trivial and for distinguishing true foregrounding from mere prominence of a statistical or an absolute kind.

Foregrounding, as I understand it, is prominence that is motivated. It is not difficult to find patterns of prominence in a poem or prose text, regularities in the sounds or words or structures that stand out in some way, or may be brought out by careful reading; and one may often be led in this way towards a new insight, through finding that such prominence contributes to the writer's total meaning. But unless it does, it will seem to lack motivation; a feature that is brought into prominence will be 'fore-grounded' only if it relates to the meaning of the text as a whole. This relationship is a functional one: if a particular feature of the language contributes, by its prominence, to the total meaning of the work, it does so by virtue of and through the medium of its own value in the language – through the linguistic function from which its meaning is derived. Where that function is relevant to our interpretation of the work, the prominence will appear as motivated. I shall try to illustrate this by reference to *The Inheritors*. First, however, a few remarks about some points raised at the 1958 Style in Language Conference and in subsequent discussions, which I hope will make slightly more explicit the context within which Golding's work is being examined.

There are three questions I should like to touch on: Is prominence to be regarded as a departure from or as the attainment of a norm? To what extent is prominence a quantitative effect, to be uncovered or at least stated by means of statistics? How real is the distinction between prominence that is due to subject matter and prominence that is due to something else? All three questions are very familiar, and my justification for bringing them up once more is not that what I have to say about them is new but rather that some partial answers are needed if we are attempting an integrated approach to language and style, and that these answers will be pertinent to a consideration of our main question, which is that of criteria of relevance.

I have used the term *prominence* as a general name for the phenomenon of linguistic highlighting, whereby some feature of the language of a text stands out in some way. In choosing this term I hoped to avoid the assumption that a linguistic feature which is brought under attention will always be seen as a departure. It is quite natural to characterize such prominence as departure from a norm, since this explains why it is remarkable, especially if one is stressing the subjective nature of the highlighting effect; thus Leech, discussing what he refers to as 'schemes' ('foregrounded patterns ... in grammar or phonology'), writes 'It is ultimately a matter of subjective judgment whether ... the regularity seems remarkable enough to constitute a definite departure from the normal functions of language.'[9] But at the same time it is often objected, not unreasonably, that the 'departure' view puts too high a value on oddness, and suggests that normal forms are of no interest in the study of style. Thus Wellek: 'The danger of linguistic stylistics is its focus on deviations from, and distortions of, the linguistic norm. We get a kind of counter-grammar, a science of discards. Normal stylistics is abandoned to the grammarian, and deviational stylistics is reserved for the student of literature. But often the most commonplace, the most normal, linguistic elements are the constituents of literary structure.'[10]

Two kinds of answer have been given to this objection. One is that there are two types of prominence, only one of which is negative, a departure from a norm; the other is positive, and is the attainment or the establishment of a norm. The second is that departure may in any case be merely statistical: we are concerned not only with deviations, ungrammatical forms, but also with what we may call 'deflections', departures from some expected pattern of frequency.

The distinction between negative and positive prominence, or departures and regularities, is drawn by Leech, who contrasts foregrounding in the form of 'motivated deviation from linguistic, or other socially accepted norms' with foregrounding applied to 'the opposite circumstance, in which a writer temporarily renounces his permitted freedom of choice, introducing uniformity where there would normally be diversity.'[11] Strictly speaking this is not an 'opposite circumstance', since if diversity is normal, then uniformity is a deviation. But where there is uniformity there is regularity; and this can be treated as a positive feature, as the establishment of a norm. Thus, to quote Hymes, '... in some sources, especially poets, style may not be deviation from but achievement of a norm.'[12]

However, this is not a distinction between two types of prominence; it is a distinction between two ways of looking at prominence, depending on the standpoint of the observer. There is no single universally relevant norm, no one set of expectancies to which all instances may be referred. On the one hand, there are differences of perspective. The text may be seen as 'part' of a larger 'whole', such as the author's complete works, or the tradition to which it belongs, so that what is globally a departure may be locally a norm. The expectancies may lie in 'the language as a whole', in a diatypic variety or register[13] characteristic of some situation type (Osgood's 'situational norms'[14]), in a genre or literary form, or in some special institution such as the Queen's Christmas message; we always have the choice of saying either 'this departs from a pattern' or 'this forms pattern'. On the other hand, there are differences of attention. The text may be seen as 'this' in contrast with 'that', with another poem or another novel; stylistic studies are essentially comparative in nature, and either may be taken as the point of departure. As Hymes says, there are egalitarian universes, comprising sets of norms, and 'it would be arbitrary to choose one norm as a standard from which the others depart'.[15] It may be more helpful to look at a given instance of prominence in one way rather than in another, sometimes as departure from a norm and sometimes as the attainment of a norm; but there is only one type of phenomenon here, not two.

There is perhaps a limiting case, the presence of one ungrammatical sentence in an entire poem or novel; presumably this could be viewed only as a departure. But in itself it would be unlikely to be of any interest. Deviation, the use of ungrammatical forms, has received a great deal of attention, and seems to be regarded, at times, as prominence *par excellence*. This is probably because it is a deterministic concept. Deviant forms are actually prohibited by the rules of whatever is taken to be the norm; or, to express it positively, the norm that is established by a set of deviant forms excludes all texts but the one in which they occur. But for this very reason deviation is of very limited interest in stylistics. It is rarely found; and when it is found, it is often not relevant. On the contrary, if we follow McIntosh (who finds it 'a chastening thought'), '... quite often ... the impact of an entire work may be enormous, yet word by word, phrase by phrase, clause by clause, sentence by sentence, there may seem to be nothing very unusual or arresting, in grammar or in vocabulary....'[16]

Hence the very reasonable supposition that prominence may be of a probabilistic kind, defined by Bloch as 'frequency distributions and transi-

Linguistic function and literary style 337

tional probabilities [which] differ from those ... in the language as a whole'.[17] This is what we have referred to above as 'deflection'. It too may be viewed either as departure from a norm or as its attainment. If, for example, we meet seven occurrences of a rather specific grammatical pattern, such as that cited by Leech '*my* + noun + *you* + verb',[18] a norm has been set up and there is, or may be, a strong local expectancy that an eighth will follow; the probability of finding this pattern repeated in eight successive clauses is infinitesimally small, so that the same phenomenon constitutes a departure. It is fairly easy to see that the one always implies

Table 14.2 Frequencies of transitivity clause types

A Process;	ACTION intransitive movement	ACTION intransitive other	ACTION transitive movement	ACTION transitive other	location/ possession	mental process	attribution	other (equation, event)	
A									
human {people	9		1	1	1	12			24
human {tribe	2		1			1			4
part of body	2				1	3	2		8
inanimate	4		1		12		3		20
	17		3	1	14	16	5		56
B (i)									
human {people	4		1	3*	2	1			11
human {tribe	5		1	1	2				9
part of body									
inanimate	13	1	2		5			2	23
	22	1	4	4	9	1		2	43
B (ii)									
human {people	13	2	1		2	4			22
human {tribe									
part of body	3				1		2		6
inanimate	3	1	1	2	4		6	2	19
	19	3	2	2	7	4	8	2	47
C									
human {people	1		1	2		4			8
human {tribe	3	2	5	11	3	11	3	2	40
part of body	2	1					5		8
inanimate	2	1			3		4	1	11
	8	4	6	13	6	15	12	3	67

*including two passives, which are also negative and in which the actor is not explicit: *The tree would not be cajoled or persuaded.*

the other; the contravention of one expectation is, at the same time, the fulfillment of a different one. Either way, whether the prominence is said to consist in law-breaking or in law-making, we are dealing with a type of phenomenon that is expressible in quantitative terms, to which statistical concepts may be applied.

In the context of stylistic investigations, the term 'statistical' may refer to anything from a highly detailed measurement of the reactions of subjects to sets of linguistic variables, to the parenthetical insertion of figures of occurrences designed to explain why a particular feature is being singled out for discussion. What is common to all these is the assumption that numerical data on language may be stylistically significant; whatever subsequent operations are performed, there has nearly always been some counting of linguistic elements in the text, whether of phonological units or words or grammatical patterns, and the figures obtained are potentially an indication of prominence. The notion that prominence may be defined statistically is still not always accepted; there seem to be two main counterarguments, but whatever substance these may have as stated they are not, I think, valid objections to the point at issue. The first is essentially that, since style is a manifestation of the individual, it cannot be reduced to counting. This is true, but, as has often been said before, it misses the point. If there is such a thing as a recognizable style, whether of a work, an author, or an entire period or literary tradition, its distinctive quality can in the last analysis be stated in terms of relative frequencies, although the linguistic features that show significant variation may be simple and obvious or extremely subtle and complex. An example of how period styles may be revealed in this way will be found in Josephine Miles's 'Eras in English poetry', in which she shows that different periods are characterized by a distinction in the dominant type of sentence structure, that between 'the sort which emphasizes substantival elements – the phrasal and co-ordinative modifications of subject and object – and the sort which emphasizes clausal co-ordination and complication of the predicate'.[19]

The second objection is that numbers of occurrences must be irrelevant to style because we are not aware of frequency in language and therefore cannot respond to it. This is almost certainly not true. We are probably rather sensitive to the relative frequency of different grammatical and lexical patterns, which is an aspect of 'meaning potential'; and our expectancies, as readers, are in part based on our awareness of the probabilities inherent in the language. This is what enables us to grasp the new probabilities of the text as local norm; our ability to perceive a statistical departure and restructure it as a norm is itself evidence of the essentially probabilistic nature of the language system. Our concern here, in any case, is not with psychological problems of the response to literature but with the linguistic options selected by the writer and their relation to the total meaning of the work. If in the selections he has made there is an unexpected pattern of frequency distributions, and this turns out to be motivated, it seems pointless to argue that such a phenomenon could not possibly be significant.

What cannot be expressed statistically is foregrounding: figures do not tell us whether a particular pattern has or has not 'value in the game'.[20] For this we need to know the rules. A distinctive frequency distribution is in itself no guarantee of stylistic relevance, as can be seen from authorship studies, where the diagnostic features are often, from a literary standpoint, very trivial ones.[21] Conversely, a linguistic feature that is stylistically very relevant may display a much less striking frequency pattern. But there is likely to be some quantitative turbulence, if a particular feature is felt to be prominent; and a few figures may be very suggestive. Counting, as Miller remarked, has many positive virtues. Ullmann offers a balanced view of these when he writes 'Yet even those who feel that detailed statistics are both unnecessary and unreliable [in a sphere where quality and context, aesthetic effects and suggestive overtones are of supreme importance] would probably agree that a rough indication of frequencies would often be helpful'.[22] A rough indication of frequencies is often just what is needed: enough to suggest why we should accept the analyst's assertion that some feature is prominent in the text, and to allow us to check his statements. The figures, obviously, do not alone constitute an analysis, interpretation, or evaluation of the style.

But this is not, be it noted, a limitation on quantitative patterns as such; it is a limitation on the significance of prominence of any kind. Deviation is no more fundamental a phenomenon than statistical deflection: in fact there is no very clear line between the two, and in any given instance the most qualitatively deviant items may be among the least relevant. Thus if style cannot be reduced to counting, this is because it cannot be reduced to a simple question of prominence. An adequate characterization of an author's style is much more than an inventory of linguistic highlights. This is why linguists were so often reluctant to take up questions of criticism and evaluation, and tended to disclaim any contribution to the appraisal of what they were describing: they were very aware that statements about linguistic prominence by themselves offer no criterion of literary value. Nevertheless some values, or some aspects of value, must be expressed in linguistic terms. This is true, for example, of metrical patterns, which linguists have always considered their proper concern. The question is how far it is also true of patterns that are more directly related to meaning: what factors govern the relevance of 'effects' in grammar and vocabulary? The significance of rhythmic regularity has to be formulated linguistically, since it is a phonological phenomenon, although the ultimate value to which it relates is not 'given' by the language – that the sonnet is a highly valued pattern is not a linguistic fact, but the sonnet itself is.[23] The sonnet form defines the relevance of certain types of phonological pattern. There may likewise be some linguistic factor involved in determining whether a syntactic or a lexical pattern is stylistically relevant or not.

Certainly there is no magic in unexpectedness; and one line of approach has been to attempt to state conditions under which the unexpected is *not* relevant – namely when it is not really unexpected. Prominence, in this view, is not significant if the linguistically unpredicted configuration is predictable on other grounds; specifically, by reference to subject matter, the implication being that it would have been predicted if we had known beforehand what the passage was about. So, for example, Ullmann warns of the danger in the search for statistically defined key-words: 'One must carefully avoid what have been called contextual words whose frequency is due to the subject-matter rather than to any deep-seated stylistic or psychological tendency.'[24] Ullmann's concern here is with words that serve as indices of a particular author, and he goes on to discuss the significance of recurrent imagery for style and personality, citing as an example the prominence of insect vocabulary in the writings of Sartre;[25] in this context we can see that, by contrast, the prevalence of such words in a treatise on entomology would be irrelevant. But it is less easy to see how this can be generalized, even in the realm of vocabulary; is lexical foregrounding entirely dependent on imagery?

Can we in fact dismiss, as irrelevant, prominence that is due to subject-matter? Can we even claim to identify it? This was the third and final question I asked earlier, and it is one which relates very closely to an interpretation of the style of *The Inheritors*. In *The Inheritors*, the features that come to our attention are largely syntactic, and we are in the realm of syntactic imagery, where the syntax, in Ohmann's words, 'serves [a] vision of things.... since there are innumerable kinds of deviance, we should expect that the ones elected by a poem or poet spring from particular semantic impulses, particular ways of looking at experience.'[26] Ohmann is concerned primarily with 'syntactic irregularities', but syntax need not be deviant in order to serve a vision of things; a foregrounded selection of everyday syntactic options may be just as visionary, and perhaps more effective. The vision provides the motivation for their prominence; it makes them relevant, however ordinary they may be. The style of *The Inheritors* rests very much on foregrounding of this kind.

The prominence, in other words, is often due to the vision. But 'vision' and 'subject matter' are merely the different levels of meaning which we expect to find in a literary work; and each of these, the inner as well as the outer, and any as it were intermediate layers, finds expression in the syntax. In Ruqaiya Hasan's words, 'Each utterance has a thesis: what it is talking about uniquely and instantially; and in addition to this, each utterance has a function in the internal organization of the text: in combination with other utterances of the text it realizes the theme, structure and other aspects....'[27] Patterns of syntactic prominence may reflect thesis or theme or 'other aspects' of the meaning of the work; every level is a potential source of motivation, a kind of semantic 'situational norm'. And since the role of syntax in language is to weave into a single fabric the different threads of meaning that derive from the variety of linguistic functions, one and the same syntactic feature is very likely to have at once both a deeper and a more immediate significance, like the participial structures in Milton as Chatman has interpreted them.[28]

Thus we cannot really discount 'prominence due to subject-matter', at least as far as syntactic prominence is concerned; especially where vision and subject-matter are themselves as closely interwoven as they are in *The Inheritors*. Rather, perhaps, we might think of the choice of subject-matter as being itself a stylistic choice, in the sense that the subject-matter may be more or less relevant to the underlying themes of the work. To the extent that the subject-matter is an integral element in the total meaning – in the artistic unity, if you will – to that extent, prominence that is felt to be partly or wholly 'due to' the subject-matter, far from being irrelevant to the style, will turn out to be very clearly foregrounded.

To cite a small example that I have used elsewhere, the prominence of finite verbs in simple past tense in the well-known 'Return of Excalibur' lines in Tennyson's *Morte d'Arthur* relates immediately to the subject-matter: the passage is a direct narrative. But the choice of a story as subject-matter is itself related to the deeper preoccupations of the work – with heroism and, beyond that, with the *res gestae*, with deeds as the realization of the true spirit of a people, and with history and historicalism; the narrative register is an appropriate form of expression, one that is congruent with the total meaning, and so the verb forms that are characteristically associated with it are motivated at every level. Similarly, it is not irrelevant to the *style* of an entomological monograph (although we may not be very interested in its style) that it contains a lot of words for insects, if in fact it does. In stylistics we are concerned with language in relation to all the various levels of meaning that a work may have.

But while a given instance of syntactic or lexical prominence may be said to be 'motivated' either by the subject-matter or by some other level of the meaning, in the sense of deriving its relevance therefrom, it cannot really be said to be 'due to' it. Neither thesis nor theme imposes linguistic patterns. they may set up local expectancies, but these are by no means always fulfilled; there might actually be very few insect words in the work on entomology – and there are very few in Kafka.[29] There is always choice. In *The Inheritors*, Golding is offering a 'particular way of looking at experience', a vision of things which he ascribes to Neanderthal man; and he conveys this by syntactic prominence, by the frequency with which he selects certain key syntactic options. It is their frequency which establishes the clause types in question as prominent; but, as Ullmann has remarked, in stylistics we have *both* to count things *and* to look at them, one by one, and when we do this we find that the foregrounding effect is the product of two apparently opposed conditions of use. The foregrounded elements are certain clause types which display particular patterns of transitivity, as described in the next section; and in some instances the syntactic pattern is 'expected' in that it is the typical form of expression for the subject-matter – for the process, participants, and circumstances that make up the thesis of the clause. Elsewhere, however, the same syntactic elements are found precisely where they would not be expected, there being other, more likely ways of 'saying the same thing'.

Here we might be inclined to talk of semantic choice and syntactic choice: what the author chooses to say, and how he chooses to say it. But this is a misleading distinction; not only because it is unrealistic in application (most distinctions in language leave indeterminate instances, although here there would be suspiciously many) but more because the combined effect is cumulative: the one does not weaken or cut across the other but reinforces it. We have to do here with an interaction, not of meaning and form, but of two levels of meaning, both of which find expression in form, and through the same syntactic features. The immediate thesis and the underlying theme come together in the syntax; the choice of subject-matter is motivated by the deeper meaning, and the transitivity patterns realize both. This is the explanation of their powerful impact.

The foregrounding of certain patterns in syntax as the expression of an underlying theme is what we understand by 'syntactic imagery', and we assume that its effect will be striking. But in *The Inheritors* these same syntactic patterns also figure prominently in their 'literal' sense, as the expression of subject-matter; and their prominence here is doubly relevant, since the literal use not only is motivated in itself but also provides a context for the metaphorical – we accept the syntactic vision of things more readily because we can see that it coincides with, and is an extension of, the reality. *The Inheritors* provides a remarkable illustration of how grammar can convey levels of meaning in literature; and this relates closely to the notion of linguistic functions which I discussed at the beginning. The foregrounded patterns, in this instance, are ideational ones, whose meaning resides in the representation of experience; as such they express not only the content of the narrative but also the abstract structure of the reality through which that content is interpreted. Sometimes the interpretation matches our own, and at other times, as in the drawing of the bow in passage A below, it conflicts with it; these are the 'opposed conditions of use' referred to earlier. Yet each tells a part of the story. Language, because of the multiplicity of its functions, has a fugue-like quality in which a number of themes unfold simultaneously; each of these themes is apprehended in various settings, or perspectives, and each melodic line in the syntactic sequence has more than one value in the whole.

The Inheritors[30] is prefaced by a quotation from H. G. Wells's *Outline of History*:

> We know very little of the appearance of the Neanderthal man, but this ... seems to suggest an extreme hairiness, an ugliness, or a repulsive strangeness in his appearance over and above his low forehead, his beetle brows, his ape neck, and his inferior stature.... Says Sir Harry Johnston, in a survey of the rise of modern man in his *Views and Reviews*: 'The dim racial remembrance of such gorilla-like monsters, with cunning brains, shambling gait, hairy bodies, strong teeth, and possibly cannibalistic tendencies, may be the germ of the ogre in folklore.'

The book is, in may opinion, a highly successful piece of imaginative prose writing; in the words of Kinkead-Weekes and Gregor, in their penetrating critical study, it is a 'reaching out through the imagination into the unknown'.[31] The persons of the story are a small band of Neanderthal people, initially eight strong, who refer to themselves as 'the people'; their world is then invaded by a group of more advanced stock, a fragment of a tribe, whom they call at first 'others' and later 'the new people'. This casual impact – casual, that is, from the tribe's point of view – proves to be the end of the people's world, and of the people themselves. At first, and for more than nine-tenths of the book (pp. 1–216), we share the life of the people and their view of the world, and also their view of the tribe: for a long passage (pp. 137–80) the principal character, Lok, is hidden in a tree watching the tribe in their work, their ritual and their play, and the account of their doings is confined within the limits of Lok's understanding, requiring at times a considerable effort of 'interpretation'. At the very end (pp. 216–38) the standpoint shifts to that of the tribe, the inheritors, and the world becomes recognizable as our own, or something very like it. I propose to examine an aspect of the linguistic resources as they are used first to characterize the people's world and then to effect the shift of world-view.

For this purpose I shall look closely at three passages taken from different parts of the book; these are reproduced below (pp. 355–8). Passage A is representative of the first, and longest, section, the narrative of the people; it is taken from the long account of Lok's vigil in the tree. Passage C is taken from the short final section, concerned with the tribe; while passage B spans the transition, the shift of standpoint occurring at the paragraph division within this passage. Linguistically, A and C differ in rather significant ways, while B is in certain respects transitional between them.

The clauses of passage A [56][32] are mainly clauses of action [21], location (including possession) [14], or mental process [16]; the remainder [5] are attributive.[33] Usually the process is expressed by a finite verb in simple past tense [46]. Almost all of the action clauses [19] describe simple movements (*turn, rise, hold, reach, throw forward*, etc.); and of these the majority [15] are intransitive; the exceptions are *the man was holding the stick, as though someone had clapped a hand over her mouth, he threw himself forward*, and *the echo of Liku's voice in his head sent him trembling at this perilous way of bushes towards the island*. The typical pattern is exemplified by the first two clauses, *the bushes twitched again* and *Lok steadied by the tree*, and there is no clear line, here, between action and location: both types have some reference in space, and both have one participant only. The clauses of movement usually [16] also specify location, e.g. *the man turned sideways in the bushes, he rushed to the edge of the water*; and on the other hand, in addition to what is clearly movement, as in *a stick rose upright*, and what is clearly location, as in *there were hooks in the bone*, there is an intermediate type exemplified by [*the bushes*] *waded out*, where the verb is of the movement type but the subject is immobile.

The picture is one in which people act, but they do not act on things; they move, but they move only themselves, not other objects. Even such normally transitive verbs as *grab* occur intransitively: *he grabbed at the branches* is just another clause of movement (cf. *he smelled along the shaft of the twig*). Moreover a high proportion [exactly half] of the subjects are not people; they are either parts of the body [8] or inanimate objects [20], and of the human subjects half again [14] are found in clauses which are not clauses of action. Even among the four transitive action clauses, cited above, one has an inanimate subject and one is reflexive. There is a stress set up, a kind of syntactic counterpoint, between verbs of movement in their most active and dynamic form, that of finite verb in independent clause,[34] in the simple past tense characteristic of the direct narrative of events in a time sequence, on the one hand, and on the other hand the preference for non-human subjects and the almost total absence of transitive clauses. It is particularly the lack of transitive clauses of action with human subjects (there are only two clauses in which a person acts on an external object) that creates an atmosphere of ineffectual activity: the scene is one of constant movement, but movemet which is as much inanimate as human and in which only the mover is affected – nothing else changes. The syntactic tension expresses this combination of activity and helplessness.

No doubt this is a fair summary of the life of Neanderthal man. But Passage A is not a description of the people. The section from which it is taken is one in which Lok is observing and, to a certain extent, interacting with the tribe; they have captured one of the people, and it is for the most part their doings that are being described. And the tribe are not helpless. The transitivity patterns are not imposed by the subject-matter; they are the reflection of the underlying theme, or rather of one of the underlying themes – the inherent limitations of understanding, whether cultural or biological, of Lok and his people, and their consequent inability to survive when confronted with beings at a higher stage of development. In terms of the processes and events as we would interpret them, and encode them in our grammar, there is no immediate justification for the predominance of intransitives; this is the result of their being expressed through the medium of the semantic structure of Lok's universe. In our interpretation, a goal-directed process (or, as I shall suggest below, an externally caused process) took place: someone held up a bow and drew it. In Lok's interpretation, the process was undirected (or, again, self-caused): *a stick rose upright* and *began to grow shorter at both ends.* (I would differ slightly here from Kinkead-Weekes and Gregor, who suggest, I think, that the form of Lok's vision is perception and no more. There may be very little processing, but there surely is some; Lok has a theory – as he must have, because he has language.)

Thus it is the syntax as such, rather than the syntactic reflection of the subject-matter, to which we are responding. This would not emerge if we had no account of the activities of the tribe, since elsewhere – in the description of the people's own doings, or of natural phenomena – the intransitiveness of the syntax would have been no more than a feature of the events themselves, and of the people's ineffectual manipulation of their environment. For this reason the vigil of Lok is a central element in the novel. We find, in its syntax, both levels of meaning side by side: Lok is now actor, now interpreter, and it is his potential in both these roles that is realized by the overall patterns of prominence that we have observed, the intransitives, the non-human subjects, and the like. This is the dominant mode of expression. At the same time, in passage A, among the clauses that have human subjects, there are just two in which the subject is acting on something external to himself, and in both these the subject is a member of the tribe; it is not Lok. There is no instance in which Lok's own actions extend beyond himself; but there is a brief hint that such extension is conceivable. The syntactic foregrounding, of which this passage provides a typical example, thus has a complex significance: the predominance of intransitives reflects, first, the limitations of the people's own actions; second, the people's world view, which in general cannot transcend these limitations – but within which there may arise, thirdly, a dim apprehension of the superior powers of the 'others', represented by the rare intrusion of a transitive clause such as *the man was holding the stick out to him.* Here the syntax leads us into a third level of meaning, Golding's concern with the nature of humanity; the intellectual and spiritual developments that contribute to the present human condition, and the conflicts that arise within it, are realized in the form of conflicts between the stages of that development – and, syntactically, between the types of transitivity.

Passage A is both text and sample. It is not only these particular sentences and their meanings that determine our response, but the fact that they are part of a general syntactic and semantic scheme. That this passage is representative in its transitivity patterns can be seen from comparison with other extracts.[35] It also exemplifies certain other relevant features of the language of this part of the book. We have seen that there is a strong preference for processes having only one participant: in general there is only one nominal element in the structure of the clause, which is therefore the subject. But while there are very few complements,[36] there is an abundance of adjuncts [44]; and most of these [40] have some spatial reference. Specifically, they are (a) static [25], of which most [21] are place adjuncts consisting of preposition plus noun, the noun being either an inanimate object of the immediate natural environment (e.g. *bush*) or a part of the body, the remainder [4] being localizers (*at their farthest, at the end,* etc.); and (b) dynamic [15], of which the majority [10] are of direction or non-terminal motion (*sideways, [rose] upright, at the branches, towards the island,* etc.) and the remainder [5] perception, or at least circumstantial to some process that is not a physical one (e.g. *[looked at Lok] along his shoulder, [shouted] at the green drifts*). Thus with the dynamic type, either the movement is purely perceptual or, if physical, it never reaches a goal: the nearest thing to terminal motion is *he rushed to the edge of the water* (which is followed by *and came back!*).

The restriction to a single participant also applies to mental process clauses [16]. This category includes perception, cognition, and reaction, as well as the rather distinct sub-category of verbalization; and such clauses in English typically contain a 'phenomenon', that which is seen, understood, liked, etc. Here however the phenomenon is often [8] either not expressed at all (e.g. *[Lok] gazed*) or expressed indirectly through a preposition, as in *he smelled along the shaft of the twig;* and sometimes [3] the subject is not a human being but a sense organ (*his nose examined this stuff and did not like it*). There is the same reluctance to envisage the 'whole man' (as distinct

Linguistic function and literary style 347

from a part of his body) participating in a process in which other entities are involved.

There is very little modification of nouns [10, out of about 100]; and all modifiers are non-defining (e.g. *green drifts, glittering water*) except where [2] the modifier is the only semantically significant element in the nominal, the head noun being a mere carrier demanded by the rules of English grammar (*white bone things, sticky brown stuff*). In terms of the immediate situation, things have defining attributes only if these attributes are their sole properties; at the more abstract level, in Lok's understanding the complex taxonomic ordering of natural phenomena that is implied by the use of defining modifiers is lacking, or is only rudimentary.

We can now formulate a description of a typical clause of what we may call 'Language A', the language in which the major part of the book is written and of which passage A is a sample, in terms of its process, participants and circumstances:

(1) There is one participant only, which is therefore subject; this is
  (a) actor in non-directed action (action clauses are intransitive), or participant in a mental process (the one who perceives, etc.), or simply the bearer of some attribute or some spatial property;
  (b) a person (*Lok, the man, he*, etc.), or a part of the body, or an inanimate object of the immediate and tangible natural environment (*bush, water, twig*, etc.);
  (c) unmodified, other than by a determiner which is either an anaphoric demonstrative (*this, that*) or, with parts of the body, a personal possessive (*his*, etc.).
(2) The process is
  (a) action (which is always movement in space), or location-possession (including e.g. *the man had white bone things above his eyes* = 'above the man's eyes there were ...'), or mental process (thinking and talking as well as seeing and feeling – a 'cunning brain'! – but often with a part of the body as subject);
  (b) active, non-modalized, finite, in simple past tense (one of a linear sequence of mutually independent processes).
(3) There are often other elements which are adjuncts, i.e. treated as circumstances attendant on the process, not as participants in it; these are
  (a) static expressions of place (in the form of prepositional phrases), or, if dynamic, expressions of direction (adverbs only) or of non-terminal motion, or of directionality of perception (e.g. *peered at the stick*);
  (b) often obligatory, occurring in clauses which are purely locational (e.g. *there were hooks in the bone*).

A grammar of Language A would tell us not merely what clauses occurred in the text but also what clauses could occur in that language.[37] For example, as far as I know the clause *a branch curved downwards over the water* does not occur in the book; neither does *his hands felt along the base of the rock*. But both of them could have. On the other hand, *he had very quickly broken off the lowest branches* breaks four rules: it has a human actor with a transitive verb, a tense other than simple past, a defining modifier, and a non-spatial adjunct. This is not to say that it could not occur. Each of these features is improbable, and their combination is very improbable; but they are not impossible. They are improbable in that they occur with significantly lower frequency than in other varieties of English (such as, for example, the final section of *The Inheritors*).

Before leaving this passage, let us briefly reconsider the transitivity features in the light of a somewhat different analysis of transitivity in English. I have suggested elsewhere that the most generalized pattern of transitivity in modern English, extending beyond action clauses to clauses of all types, those of mental process and those expressing attributive and other relations, is one that is based not on the notions of actor and goal but on those of cause and effect.[38] In any clause, there is one central and obligatory participant – let us call it the 'affected' participant – which is inherently involved in the process. This corresponds to the actor in an intransitive clause of action, to the goal in a transitive clause of action, and to the one who perceives, etc., in a clause of mental process; *Lok* has this function in all the following examples: *Lok turned away*, *Fa drew Lok away*, *Lok looked up at Fa*, *Lok was frightened*, *curiosity overcame Lok*. There may then be a second, optional participant, which is present only if the process is being regarded as brought about by some agency other than the participant affected by it: let us call this the 'agent'. This is the actor in a transitive clause of action and the initiator in the various types of causative; the function of *Tuami* in *Tuami waggled the paddle in the water* and *Tuami let the ivory drop from his hands*. As far as action clauses are concerned, an intransitive clause is one in which the roles of 'affected' and 'agent' are combined in the one participant; transitive clause is one in which they are separated, the process being treated as one having an external cause.

In these terms, the entire transitivity structure of Language A can be summed up by saying that there is no cause and effect. More specifically: in this language, processes are seldom represented as resulting from an external cause; in those instances where they are, the 'agent' is seldom a human being; and where it is a human being, it is seldom one of the people. Whatever the type of process, there tends to be only one participant; any other entities are involved only indirectly, as circumstantial elements (syntactically, through the mediation of a preposition). It is as if doing was as

Linguistic function and literary style 349

passive as seeing, and things no more affected by actions than by perceptions: their role is as in clauses of mental process, where the object of perception is not in any sense 'acted on' – it is in fact the perceiver that is the 'affected' participant, not the thing perceived – and likewise tends to be expressed circumstantially (e.g. *Lok peered at the stick*). There is no effective relation between persons and objects: people do not bring about events in which anything other than they themselves, or parts of their bodies, are implicated.

There are, moreover, a great many, an excessive number, of these circumstantial elements; they are the objects in the natural environment, which as it were take the place of participants, and act as curbs and limitations on the process. People do not act on the things around them; they act within the limitations imposed by the things. The frustration of the struggle with the environment, of a life 'poised ... between the future and the past',[39] is embodied in the syntax: many of the intransitive clauses have potentially transitive verbs in them, but instead of a direct object there is a prepositional phrase. The feeling of frustration is perhaps further reinforced by the constant reference to complex mental activities of cognition and verbalization. Although there are very few abstract nouns, there are very many clauses of speaking, knowing and understanding (e.g. *Lok understood that the man was holding the stick out to him*); and a recurrent theme, an obsession almost, is the difficulty of communicating memories and images (*I cannot see this picture*) – of transmitting experience through language, the vital step towards that social learning which would be a precondition of their further advance.

Such are some of the characteristics of Language A, the language which tells the story of the people. There is no such thing as a 'Language B'. Passage B is simply the point of transition between the two parts of the book. There is a 'Language C': this is the language of the last sixteen pages of the novel, and it is exemplified by the extract shown as passage C below. But passage B is of interest because linguistically it is also to some extent transitional. There is no doubt that the first paragraph is basically in Language A and the second in Language C; moreover the switch is extremely sudden, being established in the first three words of B (ii), when Lok, with whom we have become closely identified, suddenly becomes *the red creature*. Nevertheless B (i) does provide some hints of the change to come.

There are a few instances [4] of a human 'agent' (actor in a transitive clause); not many, but one of them is Lok, in *Lok ... picked up Tanakil*. Here is Lok acting on his environment, and the object 'affected' is a human being, and one of the tribe! There are some non-spatial adjuncts, such as *with an agonized squealing, like the legs of a giant*. There are abstract nominal: *demoniac activity, its weight of branches*. And there are perhaps more modifiers and complex verb forms than usual. None of these features is occurring for the first time; we have had forward-looking flashes throughout, e.g. (p. 191) *He had a picture of Liku looking up with soft and adoring eyes at Tanakil, guessed how Ha had gone with a kind of eager fearfulness to meet his sudden death* and (pp. 212–3) '*Why did you not snatch the new one?*' and '*We will take Tanakil. Then they will give back the new one*', both spoken by the more intelligent Fa (when transitive action clauses do occur in Language A, they are often in the dialogue). But there is a greater concentration of them in B (i), a linguistic complexity that is also in harmony with the increased complexity of the events, which has been being built up ever since the tribe first impinged on the people with the mysterious disappearance of Ha (p. 65). The syntax express the climax of the gradual overwhelming of Lok's understanding by new things and events; and this coincides with the climax in the events themselves as, with the remainder of the people all killed or captured, Lok's last companion, Fa, is carried over the edge of the waterfall. Lok is alone; there are no more people, and the last trace of his humanity, his membership of a society, has gone. In that moment he belongs to the past.

Lok does not speak again, because there is no one to speak to. But for a while we follow him, as the tribe might have followed him, although they did not – or rather we follow *it*; there can be no *him* where there is no *you* and *me*. The language is now Language C, and the story is that of *homo sapiens*; but for a few paragraphs, beginning at B (ii), as we remain with Lok, the syntax harks back to the world of the people, just as in B (i) it was beginning to look forward. The transition has taken place; *it was a strange creature, smallish, and bowed* that we had come to know so well. But it is still the final, darkening traces of this creature's world that we are seeing, fleetingly as if in an escaping dream.

A brief sketch of B (ii): There are very few transitive clauses of action [4]; in only one of these is Lok the agent – and here the 'affected' entity is a part of his own body: *it put up a hand*. The others have *the water* and *the river* as agent. Yet nearly half [22] the total number of clauses [47] have Lok as subject; here, apart from a few [4] mental process clauses, the verb is again one of simple movement or posture, and intransitive (*turn, move, crouch*, etc.; but including for the first time some with a connotation of attitude like *sidle* and *trot*; cf. *broke into a queer, loping run*). The remaining subjects are inanimate objects [19] and parts of the body [6]. But there are differences in these subjects. The horizons have widened; in addition to *water* and *river* we now have *sun* and *green sky* – a reminder that the new people walk upright; cf. (p. 143) *they did not look at the earth but straight ahead*; and there are now also human evidences and artifacts: *path, rollers, ropes*. And the parts of the body no longer see or feel; they are subjects only of intransitive verbs of movement (e.g. *its long arms swinging*), and mainly in non-finite clauses, expressing the dependent nature of the processes in which they participate. A majority [32] of the finite verbs are still in simple past tense; but there is more variation in the remainder, as well as more non-finite verbs [8], reflecting a slightly increased proportion of dependent clauses that is also a characteristic of Language C. And while in many clauses [21] we still find spatial adjuncts, these tend to be more varied and more complex (e.g. *down the rocks beyond the terrace from the melting ice in the mountains*).

This is the world of the tribe; but it is still inhabited, for a brief moment of time, by Lok. Once again the theme is enunciated by the syntax. Nature is no longer totally impenetrable; yet Lok remains powerless, master of nothing but his own body. In passages A and B taken together, there are more than fifty clauses in which the subject is Lok; but only one of these has Lok as an agent acting on something external to himself, one that has already been mentioned: *Lok picked up Tanakil*. There is a double irony here. Of all the positive actions on his environment that Lok might have taken, the one he does take is the utterly improbable one of capturing a girl of the tribe – improbable in the event, at the level of subject-matter (let us call this 'level one'), and improbable also in the deeper context ('level two'), since Lok's newly awakened power manifests itself as power over the one element in the environment that is 'superior' to himself. It is at a still deeper 'level three' that the meaning becomes clear. The action gets him nowhere; but it is a syntactic hint that his people have played their part in the long trek towards the human condition.

By the time we reach passage C, the transition is complete. Here, for the first time, the majority of the clauses [48 out of 67] have a human subject; of these, more than half [25] are clauses of action, and most of these [19] are transitive. Leaving aside two in which the thing 'affected' is a part of the body, there is still a significant increase in the number of instances [17, contrasting with 5 in the whole of A and B together] in which a human agent is acting on an external object. The world of the inheritors is organized as ours is; or at least in a way that we can recognize. Among these are two clauses in which the subject is *they*, referring to the people ('the devils': e.g. *they have given me back a changeling*); in the tribe's scheme of things, the people are by no means powerless. There is a parallel here with the earlier part. In passage A the actions of the tribe are encoded in terms of the world-view of the people, so that the predominance of intransitive clauses is interpreted at what we called 'level two', although there is a partial reflection of 'level one' in the fact that they are marginally less predominant when the subject-matter concerns the tribe. Similarly, in passage C references to the people are encoded in terms of the world-view of the tribe, and transitive structures predominate; yet the only member of the people who is present – the only one to survive – is the captured baby, whose infant behaviour is described in largely intransitive terms (pp. 230–31). And the references to the people, in the dialogue, include such formulations as *'They cannot follow us, I tell you. They cannot pass over water'*, which is a 'level one' reassurance that, in a 'level two' world of cause and effect whose causes are often unseen and unknown, there are at least limits to the devils' power.

We can now see the full complementarity between the two 'languages', but it is not easy to state. In Language A there is a level-two theme, that of powerlessness. The momentary hints of potency that we are given at level one represent an antithetic variation which, however, has a significance at level three: the power is ascribed to the tribe but signifies Lok's own incipient awareness, the people's nascent understanding of the human potential. This has become a level-two theme in Language C; and in like fashion the level-two theme of Language A becomes in Language C a level-one variation, but again with a level-three significance. The people may be powerless, but the tribe's demand for explanations of things, born of their own more advanced state, leads them, while still fearfully insisting on the people's weakness in action, to ascribe to them supernatural powers.

While there are still inanimate subjects in the clause [11], as there always are in English, there is no single instance in passage C of an inanimate agent. In A and B we had *the echo of Liku's voice in his head sent him trembling ..., the branches took her, the water had scooped a bowl out of the rock*; in C we have only *the sail glowed, the sun was sitting in it, the hills grow less*. Likewise all clauses with parts of the body as subject [8] are now intransitive, and none of them is a clause of mental process. Parts of the body no longer feel or perceive; they have attributes ascribed to them (e.g. *his teeth were wolf's teeth*) or they move (*the lips parted, the mouth was opening and shutting*). The limbs may move and posture, but only the whole man perceives and reacts to his environment. Now, he also shapes his environment: his actions have become more varied – no longer simply movements; we find here *save*, *obey*, and *kiss* – and they produce results. Something, or someone, is affected by them.

Just as man's relation to his environment has altered, so his perception of it has changed; the environment has become enlarged. The objects in it are no longer the *twig, stick, bush, branch* of Language A, nor even the larger but still tangible *river, water, scars in the earth*. In passage B (ii) we already had *air* and *sun* and *sky* and *wind*; in C we have *the mountain ... full of golden light, the sun was blazing, the sand was swirling* (the last metaphorically); and also human artifacts: *the sail, the mast*. Nature is not tamed: the features of the natural environment may no longer be agents in the transitivity patterns, but neither are they direct objects. What has happened is that the horizons have broadened. Where the people were bounded by tree and river and rock, the tribe are bounded by sky and sea and mountain. Although they are not yet conquered, the features that surround them no longer circumscribe all action and all contemplation. Whereas Lok *rushed to the edge of the water and came back*, the new people *steer in towards the shore*, and *look across the water at the green hills*.

The Inheritors has provided a perspective for a linguistic inquiry of a kind whose relevance and significance is notoriously difficult to assess: an inquiry into the language of a full-length prose work. In this situation syntactic analysis is unlikely to offer anything in the way of new interpretations of particular sentences in terms of their subject-matter; the language as a whole is not deviant, and the difficulties of understanding are at the level of interpretation – or rather perhaps, in the present instance, re-interpretation, as when we insist on translating *the stick began to grow shorter at both ends* as 'the man drew the bow'. I have not, in this study, emphasized the use of linguistic analysis as a key; I doubt whether it has this function. What it can do is to establish certain regular patterns, on a comparative basis, in the form of differences which appear significant over a broad canvas. In *The Inheritors* these appear as differences within the text itself, between what we have called 'Language A' and 'Language C'. In terms of this novel, if either of these is to be regarded as a departure, it will be Language C, which appears only briefly at the very end; but in the context of modern English as a whole it is Language A which constitutes the departure and Language C the norm. There is thus a double shift of standpoint in the move from global to local norm, but one which brings us back to more or less where we started.

The focus of attention has been on language in general, on the language system and its relation to the meanings of a literary work. In the study of the text, we have examined instances where particular syntactic options have been selected with a greater than expected frequency, a selection that is partly but not wholly explained by reference to the subject-matter; and have suggested that, by considering how the meaning of these options, taken in the context of the ideational function of language as a whole, relates to an interpretation of the meaning of the work, one can show that they are relevant both as subject-matter and as underlying theme. Each sentence in the passages that were observed in detail is thus potentially of interest both in itself and as an instance of a general trend; and we have been able to ignore other differences, such as that between dialogue and narrative, although a study of these as subvarieties would almost certainly yield further points of interest. Within the present context, the prominence that we have observed can be said to be 'motivated'; it is reasonable to talk of foregrounding, here, as an explanation of stylistic impact.

The establishment of a syntactic norm (for this is what it is) is thus a way of expressing one of the levels of meaning of the work: the fact that a particular pattern constitutes a norm *is* the meaning. The linguistic function of the pattern is therefore of some importance. The features that we have seen to be foregrounded in *The Inheritors* derive from the ideational component in the language system; hence they represent, at the level at which they constitute a norm, a world-view, a structuring of experience that is significant because there is no *a priori* reason why the experience should have been structured in this way rather than in another. More particularly, the foregrounded features were selections in transitivity. Transitivity is the set of options whereby the speaker encodes his experience of the processes of the external world, and of the internal world of his own consciousness, together with the participants in these processes and their attendant circumstances; and it embodies a very basic distinction of processes into two types, those that are regarded as due to an external cause, an agency other than the person or object involved, and those that are not. There are, in addition, many further categories and subtypes. Transitivity is really the cornerstone of the semantic organization of experience; and it is at one level what *The Inheritors* is about. The theme of the entire novel, in a sense, is transitivity: man's interpretation of his experience of the world, his understanding of its processes and of his own participation in them. This is the motivation for Golding's syntactic originality; it is because of this that the syntax is effective as a 'mode of meaning'.[40] The particular transitivity patterns that stand out in the text contribute to the artistic whole through the functional significance, in the language system, of the semantic options which they express.

This is what we understand by 'relevance' – the notion that a linguistic feature 'belongs' in some way as part of the whole. The pursuit of prominence is not without significance for the understanding and evaluation of a literary work; but neither is it sufficient to be a rewarding activity in itself.[41] It has been said of phonological foregrounding that 'there must be appropriateness to the nexus of sound and meaning';[42] and this is no less true of the syntactic and semantic levels, where, however, the relationship is not one of sound and meaning but one of meaning and meaning. Here 'relevance' implies a congruence with our interpretation of what the work is about, and hence the criteria of belonging are semantic ones. We might be tempted to express the relevance of syntactic patterns, such as we find in *The Inheritors*, as a 'unity of form and meaning', parallel to the 'sound and meaning' formulation above; but this would, I think, be a false parallel. The

Linguistic function and literary style 355

syntactic categories are *per se* the realizations of semantic options, and the relevance is the relevance of one set of meanings to another – a relationship among the levels of meaning of the work itself.

In *The Inheritors*, the syntax is part of the story. As readers, we are reacting to the whole of the writer's creative use of 'meaning potential'; and the nature of language is such that he can convey, in a line of print, a complex of simultaneous themes, reflecting the variety of functions that language is required to serve. And because the elements of the language, the words and phrases and syntactic structures, tend to have multiple values, any one theme may have more than one interpretation: in expressing some content, for example, the writer may invite us at the same time to interpret it in quite a different functional context – as a cry of despair, perhaps. It is the same property of language that enables us to react to hints, to take offence and do all the other things that display the rhetoric of everyday verbal interaction. A theme that is strongly foregrounded is especially likely to be interpreted at more than one level. In *The Inheritors* it is the linguistic representation of experience, through the syntactic resources of transitivity, that is especially brought into relief, although there may be other themes not mentioned here that stand out in the same way. Every work achieves a unique balance among the types and components of meaning, and embodies the writer's individual exploration of the functional diversity of language.

Appendix: Extracts from *The Inheritors*

A (pp. 106–7.)

The bushes twitched again. Lok steadied by the tree and gazed. A head and a chest faced him, half-hidden. There were white bone things behind the leaves and hair. The man had white bone things above his eyes and under the mouth so that his face was longer than a face should be. The man turned sideways in the bushes and looked at Lok along his shoulder. A stick rose upright and there was a lump of bone in the middle. Lok peered at the stick and the lump of bone and the small eyes in the bone things over the face. Suddenly Lok understood that the man was holding the stick out to him but neither he nor Lok could reach across the river. He would have laughed if it were not for the echo of the screaming in his head. The stick began to grow shorter at both ends. Then it shot out to full length again.

The dead tree by Lok's ear acquired a voice.

'Clop!'

His ears twitched and he turned to the tree. By his face there had grown a twig: a twig that smelt of other, and of goose, and of the bitter berries that

Lok's stomach told him he must not eat. This twig had a white bone at the end. There were hooks in the bone and sticky brown stuff hung in the crooks. His nose examined this stuff and did not like it. He smelled along the shaft of the twig. The leaves on the twig were red feathers and reminded him of goose. He was lost in a generalized astonishment and excitement. He shouted at the green drifts across the glittering water and heard Liku crying out in answer but could not catch the words. They were cut off suddenly as though someone had clapped a hand over her mouth. He rushed to the edge of the water and came back. On either side of the open bank the bushes grew thickly in the flood; they waded out until at their farthest some of the leaves were opening under water; and these bushes leaned over.

The echo of Liku's voice in his head sent him trembling at this perilous way of bushes towards the island. He dashed at them where normally they would have been rooted on dry land and his feet splashed. He threw himself forward and grabbed at the branches with hands and feet. He shouted:

'I am coming!'

B. (pp. 215–17.)
(i) Lok staggered to his feet, picked up Tanakil and ran after Fa along the terrace. There came a screaming from the figures by the hollow log and a loud bang from the jam. The tree began to move forward and the logs were lumbering about like the legs of a giant. The crumplefaced woman was struggling with Tuami on the rock by the hollow log; she burst free and came running towards Lok. There was movement everywhere, screaming, demoniac activity; the old man was coming across the tumbling logs. He threw something at Fa. Hunters were holding the hollow log against the terrace and the head of the tree with all its weight of branches and wet leaves was drawing along them. The fat woman was lying in the log, the crumpled woman was in it with Tanakil, the old man was tumbling into the back. The boughs crashed and drew along the rock with an agonized squealing. Fa was sitting by the water holding her head. The branches took her. She was moving with them out into the water and the hollow log was free of the rock and drawing away. The tree swung into the current with Fa sitting limply among the branches. Lok began to gibber again. He ran up and down on the terrace. The tree would not be cajoled or persuaded. It moved to the edge of the fall, it swung until it was lying along the lip. The water reared up over the trunk, pushing, the roots were over. The tree hung for a while with the head facing upstream. Slowly the root end sank and the head rose. Then it slid forward soundlessly and dropped over the fall.
(ii) The red creature stood on the edge of the terrace and did nothing. The hollow log was a dark spot on the water towards the place where the sun had gone down. The air in the gap was clear and blue and calm. There was

no noise at all now except for the fall, for there was no wind and the green sky was clear. The red creature turned to the right and trotted slowly towards the far end of the terrace. Water was cascading down the rocks beyond the terrace from the melting ice in the mountains. The river was high and flat and drowned the edge of the terrace. There were long scars in the earth and rock where the branches of a tree had been dragged past by the water. The red creature came trotting back to a dark hollow in the side of the cliff where there was evidence of occupation. It looked at the other figure, dark now, that grinned down at it from the back of the hollow. Then it turned away and ran through the little passage that joined the terrace to the slope. It halted, peering down at the scars, the abandoned rollers and broken ropes. It turned again, sidled round a shoulder of rock and stood on an almost imperceptible path that ran along the sheer rocks. It began to sidle along the path, crouch, its long arms swinging, touching, almost as firm a support as the legs. It was peering down into the thunderous waters but there was nothing to be seen but the columns of glimmering haze where the water had scooped a bowl out of the rock. It moved faster, broke into a queer loping run that made the head bob up and down and the forearms alternate like the legs of a horse. It stopped at the end of the path and looked down at the long streamers of weed that were moving backwards and forwards under the water. It put up a hand and scratched under its chinless mouth.

C. (pp. 228–29.)

The sail glowed red-brown. Tuami glanced back at the gap through the mountain and saw that it was full of golden light and the sun was sitting in it. As if they were obeying some signal the people began to stir, to sit up and look across the water at the green hills. Twal bent over Tanakil and kissed her and murmured to her. Tanakil's lips parted. Her voice was harsh and came from far away in the night.

'Liku!'

Tuami heard Marlan whisper to him from by the mast.

'That is the devil's name. Only she may speak it.'

Now Vivani was really waking. They heard her huge, luxurious yawn and the bear skin was thrown off. She sat up, shook back her loose hair and looked first at Marlan then at Tuami. At once he was filled again with lust and hate. If she had been what she was, if Marlan, if her man, if she had saved her baby in the storm on the salt water –

'My breasts are paining me.'

If she had not wanted the child as a plaything, if I had not saved the other as a joke –

He began to talk high and fast.

'There are plains beyond those hills, Marlan, for they grow less; and there will be herds for hunting. Let us steer in towards the shore. Have we water – but of course we have water! Did the women bring the food? Did you bring the food, Twal?'

Twal lifted her face towards him and it was twisted with grief and hate.

'What have I to do with food, master? You and he gave my child to the devils and they have given me back a changeling who does not see or speak.'

The sand was swirling in Tuami's brain. He thought in panic: they have given me back a changed Tuami; what shall I do? Only Marlan is the same – smaller, weaker but the same. He peered forward to find the changeless one as something he could hold on to. The sun was blazing on the red sail and Marlan was red. His arms and legs were contracted, his hair stood out and his beard, his teeth were wolf's teeth and his eyes like blind stones. The mouth was opening and shutting.

'They cannot follow us, I tell you. They cannot pass over water.'

Notes

1 J. McH. Sinclair, 'Linguistic meaning in a literary text'. Paper read to the Philological Society, Cambridge, March 1965.
2 The results were presented in a paper read to the Conference of University Teachers of English, London (Bedford College), April 1965.
3 Karl Bühler, *Sprachtheorie* (Jena, 1934). See also Chapter 2 of Josef Vachek, *The Linguistic School of Prague* (Bloomington, Ind., and London: Indiana University Press, 1966).
4 See Bronislaw Malinowski, *Coral Gardens and their Magic*, Volume II (London: Allen & Unwin, 1935).
5 Paul Zumthor suggests (private communication) that a particular literary tradition may be characterized by the emphasis and value placed on one particular function, a shift in emphasis being associated with a major break in the tradition.
6 Nor the other way round, at least in the typical instances. There are certain linguistic activities in which one or other function is prescribed and the speaker required to supply the remainder: 'language exercises' such as 'Now ask your neighbour a question' (in foreign language classes) and 'Write a sonnet' (in school).
7 Cf. the discussion by Tzvetan Todorov in 'The place of style in the structure of the text,' in *Literary Style: A Symposium*, ed. Seymour Chatman (New York; Oxford University Press, 1971), pp. 29–44.
8 Including those which specify types of communication role, or illocutionary force, which Richard Ohmann proposes to use in a definition of literature. See Ohmann, 'Speech, action, and style,' in Chatman, pp. 241–259.
9 Geoffrey N. Leech. 'This Bread I Break – Language and Interpretation,' *A Review of English Literature*, VI (April 1965), 70.

10 René Wellek, 'Closing statement (retrospects and prospects from the viewpoint of literary criticism)', in *Style in Language*, ed. by T. A. Sebeok (New York, 1960), pp. 417–18.
11 As n. 9 (p. 69).
12 Dell H. Hymes, 'Phonological aspects of style: some English sonnets', in *Style in Language*, 109–31.
13 On diatypic variation see Michael Gregory, 'Aspects of Varieties Differentiation', *Journal of Linguistics*, III (1967), 177–98.
14 Charles E. Osgood, 'Some effects of motivation on style of encoding,' in *Style in Language*, p. 293.
15 As n. 12.
16 Angus McIntosh, 'Saying', *A Review of English Literature*, VI (April 1965), 19. It is worth quoting further from the same paragraph: 'It is at least clear that any approach to this kind of problem which looks at anything less than the whole text as the ultimate unit has very little to contribute. Whatever it may be in linguistic analysis, the sentence is not the proper unit here. If there are any possibilities of progress, they must, I think, be on the lines of the old recognition, e.g. by the rhetoricians, of elements or strands of something or other which permeate long stretches of text and produce a gradual build-up of effect.'
17 Bernard Bloch, 'Linguistic structure and linguistic analysis' in A. A. Hill (ed.), *Report of the Fourth Annual Round Table Meeting on Linguistics and Language Study* (Monograph Series on Languages & Linguistics IV, Washington, DC, 1953), pp. 40–44.
18 As n. 9 (p. 70).
19 Josephine Miles, 'Eras in English poetry' in *Essays on the Language of Literature*, pp. 175–6.
20 Cf. George A. Miller, 'Closing statement (retrospects and prospects from the viewpoint of psychology)' in *Style in Language*, p. 394.
21 See Louis Milic, 'Rhetorical choice and stylistic option' in Chatman, pp. 77–88, in which he suggests that the diagnostic features of an author's style are generally to be found among the 'unconscious' elements.
22 See Stephen Ullmann, 'Style and personality', *A Review of English Literature*, VI (April 1965), p. 22.
23 Cf. Samuel Levin, 'The conventions of poetry', in Chatman, pp. 177–193.
24 As n. 22 (p. 27).
25 As n. 22 (p. 29). See also Stephen Ullmann, *Language and Style* (Language and Style Series, Oxford, 1964), pp. 186–8.
26 Richard Ohmann, 'Literature as sentences' in *Essays on the Language of Literature*, p. 237.
27 Ruqaiya Hasan, 'Linguistics and the Study of Literary Texts', *Études de Linguistique Appliquée*, V (1967), pp. 109–10. See also Hasan, 'Rime and reason in literature', in Chatman, pp. 299–326.
28 See Seymour Chatman, 'Milton's participial style', *PMLA*, LXXXIII (1968), 1386–99.
29 'Metamorphosis' has, I believe, only two occurrences of an insect name, although 'crawl' is frequent.
30 William Golding, *The Inheritors* (London, 1955; paperback edition, 1961). The pagination is the same in both editions.
31 Mark Kinkead-Weekes and Ian Gregor, *William Golding: A Critical Study* (London, 1967).

32 Figures in square brackets show numbers of occurrences. The most important of these are summarized in Table 2.
33 For a discussion of clause types see M. A. K. Halliday, 'Language structure and language function', in John Lyons (ed.), *New Horizons in Linguistics* (Harmondsworth: Penguin Books, 1970), pp. 140–65.
34 Cf. M. A. K. Halliday, 'Descriptive linguistics in literary studies', in A. Duthie (ed.), *English Studies Today, Third Series* (Edinburgh, 1964), p. 29.
35 The other extracts examined for comparison were three passages of similar length: p. 61 from *He remembered the old woman*; pp. 102–3 from *Then there was nothing more*; p. 166 from *At that the old man rushed forward*.
36 By 'complement' is understood all nominal elements other than the subject: direct object, indirect object, cognate object, and adjectival and nominal complement. 'Adjuncts' are non-nominal elements (adverbs and prepositional phrases).
37 Cf. James Peter Thorne, 'Stylistics and generative grammars', *Journal of Linguistics*, I (1965), 49–59.
38 For discussions of transitivity see Charles J. Fillmore, 'The case for case', in Emmon Bach and Robert T. Harms (eds.), *Universals in Linguistic Theory* (New York, 1968), 1–88; M. A. K. Halliday, *Grammar, Society and the Noun* (London, 1967); M. A. K. Halliday, 'Notes on transitivity and theme in English' (Parts I and II), *Journal of Linguistics*, III (1967), 37–81, and IV (1968), 179–215.
39 As n. 31 (p. 81).
40 See J. R. Firth, 'Modes of Meaning', *Essays and Studies* (*The English Association*, 1951). Reprinted in J. R. Firth, *Papers in Linguistics 1934–1951* (London, 1957), pp. 190–215.
41 Cf. Roger Fowler, 'Linguistic theory and the study of literature', in *Essays on Style and Language: Linguistic and Critical Approaches to Literary Style*, ed. by Roger Fowler (London, 1966), pp. 1–28.
42 As n. 12 (p. 53).

15

Speech, literature and the space between

Richard Ohmann

I

Our lives are glutted with words, and surfeit prompts revulsion from time to time. Then people cry down words and demand action instead. When Tom Hayden's sense of urgency lowered his tolerance for demonstrations and rallies some time back, it was typical of him to express impatience (in a speech, at a rally) by saying that he would probably never make another speech. When the time for guns is at hand, the time for words is past, we think. It is perfectly natural to draw this distinction between talking and more purely physical action. But doing so conceals the fact that speech is also action, distorts our understanding of both, and thus leads to confusion about how the world runs.

A semiofficial newspaper like *The New York Times* undertakes to transform mere events into history, by selecting those that are significant enough – fit to print – to bear recording in this instant archive. It is interesting to see how the *Times* exercises its sifting task, how many of the front-page stories on a random day report 'real' action and how many report speech acts. In the *Times* of 10 March 1972 (picked up at the airport on my way to lecture about these matters – so runs science), nine stories were about verbal acts, and three about other kinds of events. The proportion is customary.

First, consider the three: (1) the dollar plunged further on the international market, (2) Israeli jets renewed raids on Lebanon, and (3) in a raid on a card game, Detroit police killed a sheriff's deputy and wounded three others. Why are these news? The dollar's decline (hardly a physical happening, by the way) on a given day has little importance by itself, but indexes the evolution of the monetary crisis. Similarly, although the bombing killed people and wrecked homes, its news value is to tell the temperature of the war, not to report these sad events; death by violence is commonplace, not in itself historical. Only the shooting in Detroit even approximates the image many have of news as floods and hurricanes, 'natural disasters', physical events that senselessly just happen. It is interesting, further, that the *Times* does not get fifty words into any of these stories before linking the nonverbal event to a verbal one. Specialists 'predicted' that the dollar's plunge was the beginning of 'a new crisis of confidence'; Israeli military headquarters 'describes' the bomb raids as 'a response' to guerrilla rocket attacks; the Detroit Police Department and the Sheriff's Office 'called the shootings a "tragic mix-up"'. The nonverbal events begin to take on historical meaning as they are placed under one or another concept, labeled and so characterized by unnamed but qualified spokesmen. Similarly, as I write, the news about bombing in North Vietnam is not lives lost and dikes broken, but what Hanoi and Washington, Jane Fonda and Ramsey Clark, *say* is the meaning of these acts. And the bombing of South Vietnam and Laos, historically unprecedented in violence, is barely news at all.

I'll quote now from the opening paragraphs of the nine stories on 10 March that reported verbal action, putting in italics the verbs that specify the nature of that action.

1 Clifford Irving's notorious 'autobiography' of Howard R. Hughes was officially discredited yesterday as the expatriate author ... [was] indicted here.... a New York County grand jury *charged* [Irving and accomplices] with grand larceny, conspiracy, and possession of forged instruments.... *allegations* of a bold scheme to sell McGraw-Hill, Inc., what was *described* as a 'bogus autobiography'....

2 The Price Commission *announced* today new regulations providing relief from price controls for companies incurring losses or low profits. Under the new *rules*, the ... companies with sales of $1-million or more a year may raise prices.... However the commission *ruled* that the price of any individual product or service could be raised by no more than 8 per cent....

3 President Nixon *ordered* all airlines today to adopt new and tighter security measures immediately to prevent the sabotage of American commercial aircraft.

4 Premier Eisaku Sato of Japan *predicted* today that China would voluntarily limit her support of the Vietnamese Communists as a result of President Nixon's discussions in Peking.

5 Prince Norodom Sihanouk ... *said* today that Premier Chou En Lai of China had met North Vietnamese leaders since President Nixon's visit and *assured* them of China's full support 'until total victory'.
6 Dita D. Beard, a Washington lobbyist, was *quoted* today as having *said* that former Attorney General John N. Mitchell had *told* her that President Nixon *ordered* him to "make a reasonable settlement" of three antitrust cases against [ITT].
7 Authoritative sources here *say* that although they believe there was nothing improper about the agreement [between ITT and San Diego Republicans], the Republican National Committee ... *regards* it as prudent to *break off* the controversial arrangement.
8 TWA *announced* yesterday that there had been no contact since Tuesday night with the extortionists ... and that "no ransom has been paid." The line's president ... *said:* "TWA believes that the bomb threat that caused this situation has run its course."
9 The authenticity of a published memoir ... by a man *claiming* to be a 101-year-old Sioux chief is being seriously *questioned* by some of the country's leading authorities on American Indians, and *challenged* in a lawsuit *charging plagiarism.*

These acts performed with words share some characteristics that make them newsworthy. In each event, first, the speaker's identity – especially his or her social and institutional connections – was important. Many had charged Clifford Irving with fraud, but the grand jury's doing so had altogether greater consequence for Irving's life, and his implication in the social network. The secret 'sources' of number 7 are 'authoritative': that is, by a familiar convention we are to know that someone with the right institutional powers is behind the statement. And notice that the ultimate issue in numbers 1 and 9 is whether the extended speech acts – Irving's manuscript and Red Fox's book – were issued with proper authority. A second feature of these acts is that most of them imply further action by the participants; they bind the future in one way or another. The Price Commission's ruling will be enforced, changing the future acts of companies. Airlines and government bureaucrats will find their conduct defined by Nixon's order. Third, most of the acts constituted official or authoritative takings-of-positions, shifts in the web of our social arrangements and our ties to one another. McGraw-Hill and Red Fox are in legal jeopardy. TWA's potential customers have official reassurance. And Nixon is indirectly put under a cloud of accusation by Dita Beard. Since an order of this sort by the President of the United States would be a significant misuse of power, the *Times* allows itself to report evidence removed by three layers of speech acts from the alleged critical speech act itself – someone quoted

Dita Beard as saying that Mitchell told her that Nixon ordered him.... Except for the institutional impact, such gossip would hardly be granted the dignity of print by the *Times*.

To see why the verbal events reported on 10 March share these features, consider the verbs that name the acts, such verbs as *charged, described, predicted, ordered, assured, announced*. These are all common names for what J. L. Austin called 'illocutionary acts': acts performed *in* speaking.[1] Not the act *of* speaking one or another sentence (which Austin called the locutionary act), nor an act like frightening, pleasing, or convincing, which is performed *by means* of uttering the sentence, and which Austin called a perlocutionary act, but the act performed *in* speaking the sentence, provided that certain conditions are met. Example:

> Locutionary act: saying the English sentence, 'I order you to make a reasonable settlement.'
> Illocutionary act: ordering the hearer to make a reasonable settlement.
> Perlocutionary act: getting the hearer to make the settlement, pleasing ITT, etc.

Now why should illocutionary acts be precisely those that constitute news, those that nudge history along in its course? The answer is bound up in the kinds of conditions – *rules* might be more accurate – that must be met in order to perform an illocutionary act fully and happily by speaking a given sentence. For our purposes the critical ones are these:

1. The circumstances must be appropriate.
2. The persons must be the right ones.
3. The speaker must have the feelings, thoughts, and intentions appropriate to his act.
4. Both parties must behave appropriately afterward.

The rules for illocutionary acts determine whether performance of a given act is well-executed, in just the same way as grammatical rules determine whether the product of a locutionary act – a sentence – is well-formed. Doing an illocutionary act is acting by virtue of conventions, socially established and understood rules. But whereas the rules of a grammar concern the relationships among sound, syntax, and meaning, the rules for illocutionary acts concern relationships among people. They depend, for instance, on the relative status of people (command vs. request), on their institutional connections (ruling, firing), on their official roles (marrying), on acts previously performed (accepting), on relative experience (advising, telling), on the degree of commitment made (promise vs. prediction), on the interests of the participants (promise vs. threat), on the psychological states of the participants (stating vs. asking), on their future inclinations toward one another (betting), on ethical judgments (praising, criticizing), on people's past conduct to one another (apologize, thank), and many other such.[2] John Searle distinguishes between 'brute facts' (e.g. a stone on the ground) and 'institutional facts' (e.g. Mary and George are married), and rightly says that illocutionary acts have to do deeply with institutional facts.[3] To participate in discourse is to set in motion one's whole awareness of institutions, social ties, obligations, responsibilities, manners, rituals, ceremonies.

Furthermore, illocutionary acts all have a contractual character. This is explicit in acts like hiring and firing, but true in a less legal way for such acts as accepting, promising, and proposing, and even, loosely, for acts like stating: when I tell you that your tire is flat you have a right to infer that I believe it, and I have at least a vague obligation to tell you if I find I was mistaken, so long as my mistake makes any difference to you. As Austin said, illocutionary acts are the clearest proof that our word is our bond. Much of the ethical nature of human life is embedded in and carried by illocutionary acts.

And, to return to the starting point, illocutionary acts also have the power to *change* a friendship or a society, to alter the institutional structure out of which they rise. The front page of the *Times* is ample illustration. But recall too that the fabric of lives ignored by the *Times* is patterned with illocutionary acts like inviting, agreeing, refusing, proposing, denying, accusing, joining, forgiving, buying, asking, giving.

II

So far I have been referring to speech in what I might call the direct mode. There is also an indirect mode of speech, apparently, in all human cultures. We are *homo ludens* in our use of words; we joke, use irony, tell fictions. I'll call this mode of speech *literary*, for reasons I hope to make plausible forthwith.

Austin remarked that philosophers of language were constantly slipping off to one side or the other of illocutionary acts – fixing either on locutionary acts, as with logicians, or on perlocutionary acts, as with students of ethics. The slippage was to the detriment of the subject; in particular, in this century it encouraged an obsession with *true* and *false* as categories which, along with the category *meaningless*, should neatly embrace all utterances. Austin's work helped show the poverty of this view of language.

Linguistics itself has suffered an impoverishment of the same sort, concentrating almost exclusively on the rules for well-formedness of sentences, and ignoring the rules governing the acts performed in the speaking of sentences. Meanwhile, on the other side of the watershed, the study of rhetoric has been preoccupied with the study of perlocutionary acts, of how people are influenced by words. Chomsky notes this in a recent paper,[4] and he, Fillmore, and others in the generative group are apparently trying to extend the domain of linguistics to illocutionary acts.

The situation in literary theory is not dissimilar. Many theorists, Jakobson foremost among them, have seen literature as differing from other discourse mainly in the high degree of structuring that characterizes it. This is to focus on the locutionary acts of literature, and, accepting the spatial metaphor that seems to come with all locutionary analysis, to think of literature as consisting in verbal structures. Another way of thinking is that of Richards, who held that literature was special for the peculiar effects it had on people – a perlocutionary theory of literature. Both are helpful but limited perspectives, to which the illocutionary should be added. That it has not is the more surprising in that practical criticism has sometimes been keenly aware of illocutionary acts. Examples are the last study in Auerbach's *Mimesis* and Booth's *The Rhetoric of Fiction*.

Austin provided some hints, in distinguishing serious uses of language, with illocutionary force intact, from special uses, as in poems. An illocutionary act in a poem is '*in a peculiar way* hollow or void', but intelligibly so, because the use of language in these circumstances is 'parasitic' upon its normal use (p. 22). Waiving the unfortunate tone of the term, we can follow this suggestion with profit.

As Austin says, the imperative sentence 'Go and catch a falling star', as written by Donne or recited by anyone, does not convey a command: the normal illocutionary force is suspended. Likewise with the apparent command in 'Call me Ishmael', or the apparent statement in 'That is no country for old men', or 'In a sense, I am Jacob Horner', or 'Buffalo Bill's defunct', or 'Whose woods these are I think I know', or the question in 'Oh what is that sound which so thrills the ear', or for that matter, 'There was this traveling salesman', or 'Once upon a time....' All of these utterances fail to execute the acts that in normal circumstances they would, and for a simple reason: the rules I listed earlier cannot be applied, or, if we *were* to apply them in the usual way, we would entirely misconstrue the utterances in question.

Take 'That is no country for old men', and try to determine whether the statement comes off successfully – not whether it is *true*, bear in mind, but whether its saying is felicitous. Were the circumstances appropriate for making this statement? For instance, did Yeats have reason to think his hearer or reader ignorant of its import? And was Yeats the proper person to make the statement? If 'that country' is Ireland, had Yeats in fact left it?

Did he have the appropriate beliefs? Did he afterward conduct himself in accordance with those beliefs? To ponder these questions is to see that they are the wrong ones to ask. If Yeats's writing of the sentence *could* meet these conditions, he would not have been writing a poem, but perhaps an autobiographical narrative. On the other hand, the near certainty that the poem fails to meet the conditions for illocutionary acts in no way impedes its functioning well as a poem.

Writing (or speaking) a literary work is evidently an illocutionary performance of special type, logically different from the seeming acts that make it up. The contract between poet and reader or hearer does not put the poet behind the various statements, rejoinders, laments, promises, or whatever, that he seemingly voices. His word is not his bond, in just this way. Perhaps the *only* serious condition of good faith that holds for literary works and their authors is that the author not give out as fact what is fiction. But that's a complicated matter, as witness all the novels which elaborately pretend to be plain truth, without on that account 'really' meaning to deceive the reader.

The main point here is that if we attend to illocutionary acts, we can identify a perfectly clean cognitive break between literature – poems, plays, novels, jokes, fairy tales, fantasies, etc. – and discourses that are not literature. Literary works are discourses with the usual illocutionary rules suspended. If you like, they are acts without consequences of the usual sort, sayings liberated from the usual burden of social bond and responsibility. Even small children quickly learn this distinction – not that they can always *tell* when they are in the presence of a fiction, but they know to ask, and know how to respond once they are sure. It's as if 'once upon a time' were a ghostly presence at the beginning of all literary works, to indicate the contract that obtains between writer and reader.

But it would be a great mistake, of course, to suppose that illocutionary acts play *no* role in literature. Saying, as Austin did, that poems are parasitic on regular speech acts is a long way from saying how this works. And the *how* is of interest. If, when a poet puts forth a declarative sentence, he is not actually stating it, what then is he doing? He is doing something like putting words in another person's mouth, pretending to be someone else. But neither of these descriptions quite fits, because the other person – the persona or speaker or narrator – does not actually exist, and the pretense is not intended to deceive. More exactly, the writer puts out imitation speech acts, *as if* they were being performed by someone. This is clearest in a play, or a dramatic poem like Auden's 'Oh what is that sound which so thrills the ear.' Here there is an answer to each question, and obviously Auden has created two characters, by giving them speech acts to perform in alternation. Let me insist on the formulation: neither he nor a playwright creates characters and *then* gives them lines; rather, the assignment of speech acts is the means of creating characters. The same holds true, though less plainly, in a lyric poem like 'Sailing to Byzantium', where Yeats gives out a series of purported speech acts, all evidently performed by one character, and so creates the man who has sailed from one country to another. In novels with omniscient narrators this process is least dramatic, yet we have long since learned that even in such fictions the saying of the story is itself part of the story. The narrator may not become a vivid character, but he is nonetheless entirely distinct from the author; the logical gap between them opens up as soon as we apply the usual conditions for illocutionary acts.

I have been regarding this matter from the author's point of view. The importance of illocutionary acts is still greater for the reader/hearer, who in the standard case has literally nothing to guide him *except* the purported locutionary and illocutionary acts of one or more personae. From those acts the reader makes inferences of many kinds: who the speaker is, what roles he plays, what kind of a society he lives in, whether he is reliable, what relationship he intends to establish between himself and his hearer or reader, what nonverbal actions he is supposedly involved in, and so on. The reader makes these judgments in large part by putting to work his tacit knowledge of the conditions for performance of illocutionary acts. If a novel begins, 'In a sense, I am Jacob Horner' (Barth, *The End of the Road*), the reader is immediately forced into hypotheses about the circumstances that would make such a statement appropriate, about what person might properly so identify himself, with the odd qualifier 'in a sense', and most importantly, about what beliefs and feelings would legitimate his statement. As the reader proceeds, he will be able to determine whether Jacob Horner conducts himself appropriately afterward (i.e., whether his narrative is consistent), whether he is to be trusted, and whether the story he tells is to be taken at face value. In short, the reader works from the familiar conventions for illocutionary acts to judgments about what acts are being performed within the world of the novel, and how successfully, and from there to an imaginative construction of the world of the novel itself, verbal and nonverbal.

It may seem odd to claim that illocutionary acts play a part in our constructing the fictional world of a novel which begins 'On an evening in the latter part of May a middle-aged man was walking homeward from Shaston to the village of Marlott, in the adjoining Vale of Blakemore or Blackmoor.' The 'facts' about this place and this man seem so directly rendered. But of course the very estimate that they are to be taken *as* facts, and held in mind as part of the fictional world, is an estimate of illocutionary force. The reader begins to construct a world around Shaston,

Marlott, and the Vale of Blakemore only if he judges that the statement is to be taken as felicitous, and that the speaker does in fact have the proper beliefs to accompany it – including the belief that these places exist.

We might say that the building of a fictional world to accompany a novel, play, poem, or other fictional form is an exchange between writer and reader through the medium of illocutionary acts. In fact, the imitation of reality that takes place in literature can only happen in this way. It was unfortunate for literary theory that Aristotle fixed the term *mimesis* with reference to the performance of a tragedy, since dramatic performance is a special kind of imitation, and to focus on it is to miss the deeper similarities in mimesis that connect all genres and their written *and* spoken forms.[5]

III

Literary mimesis reverses the usual direction of inference for the reader. As we participate in ordinary speech we use what we know of the speaker and of circumstances to assess the felicity of the speech acts. As we participate in mimesis we assume the felicity of the hypothetical acts, and infer a world from the circumstances required for this felicity. Once this is clear, some generalizations about literary discourse become available. McLuhan says that 'speech is a cool medium of low definition, because so little is given and so much has to be filled in by the listener.'[6] As often, it is hard to tell what comparison McLuhan has in mind in making such a judgment, and in what sense both speech and, say, the telephone could be media. But if ordinary speech *is* a medium, then literature certainly is one in just the same sense, and the comparison is interesting. Literature, of course, is a much cooler medium than speech, because even less is directly given. Notably, the speaker himself is not present – even in a direct recitation or public reading it's only the poet or the performer who is visible, not the persona who is supposedly responsible for the speech acts. In the absence of the speaker, the reader misses gesture, intonation, facial expression, the physical setting, physical actions the speaker is performing, and many other kinds of information which in regular speech help the hearer know how to take the words he hears. All this data the reader must supply himself, in addition to data about the social situation, historical period, geography, and so on. Such, I have said, is mimesis. This is one reason that literature is harder to read well than are newspaper stories.

McLuhan would probably say that literature is 'high in participation'. And indeed the reader's work, which I have just been describing, is participation of a demanding sort. But the concept of participation is not so simple, nor its measurement so lineal, as McLuhan often implies. For literature sharply *reduces* another kind of participation, as compared to speech. To be criticized, invited, ordered, offered, promised, threatened, praised, or any of the thousand others is to be drawn into the act. The hearer participates in the illocutionary act in all the social and moral ways earlier discussed. His relations to family, friends, fellow citizens, employer, enemy, are fixed and altered by illocutionary acts. For him, words have consequences. Literature lifts these burdens and pleasures from the reader. As he reads, he enters a different dispensation, with consequences suspended. He is neither contractually nor morally implicated, nor in any way bound by the act in which he participates. His participation is entirely cognitive and imaginative, an act of the mind and heart. For this reason the enemies of literature call it escapist. And it is. Any defense of poesy has to meet this charge one way or another, for literature excuses us from participation, in the basic sense outlined here.

My own defense, upon which I won't dwell here, would acknowledge that reading literature is a form of play, and would stress the fact that the fictional worlds we construct in this game constitute a judgment on our own real world. Literature preserves the function of criticism, as Matthew Arnold said, and activates our sense of possibility, of alternatives – some of them better – to the way things are done here. Furthermore, literature is in a good way disinterested. The better works, anyhow, put forth their comment on our world as a whole, rather than advancing petty morals or special pleas.

Let me mention one more aspect of literature, whose pertinence will appear soon. Although the writer is in a way hidden, so that we meet only his surrogate and carry on no intercouse with the author himself, through our sharing of the act of mimesis we do get at something like the world he meant to create, and in this way we move close to his wishes and fears. Although hidden, he gives us access to his imaginative worlds, and to that much of himself.

IV

I have been speaking of literature and ordinary talk in an idealized way, imagining the contexts of acts as uncomplicated, and ignoring effects of the media of communication. What I have said is I hope true, but it is not a full account of literature and speech acts: the distinctions I have drawn would more nearly have exhausted the domain in a preliterate society than in our own. Now it is time to draw closer to the speech environment most of us actually inhabit, in a country like the United States.

Even with the arrival of print the relations I have outlined became blurred. The writer of a factual newspaper narrative – distinctly not a literary work – does not concretely know who his audience is, nor whether every one of them is an appropriate partner in the act of informing. Moreover, he cannot give them warrant to believe him in the usual ways, cannot stand personally behind his words. And his subsequent conduct will be hard to connect with the original act of stating. Add to this his frequent anonymity, and it is evident how thin the tie between him and his readers has become. In these circumstances, language undergoes what Austin called an 'etiolation', a fading of its usual forces and presuppositions. Not that a newspaper story is a *cross between* literature and ordinary talk: it is still nonliterary discourse, for the usual rules of illocutionary action all apply. They simply are harder to apply in detail, and the guesswork required gives the reader a slightly fictionalized experience.[7]

Much the same is true of another typical, though very different, media experience, watching a public figure on television. Take an ordinary State of the Union message. In conveying it the President addresses millions of people who are strangers to him. And although they 'know' him, and are close indeed to his screen image, the relationship is entirely one-sided: they have no way of responding, no way of completing the contract, no chance to follow up on his challenges and requests. Their participation is cognitively high, socially low. The experience is not like that of reading a literary work, but it moves in that direction from regular speech.

The speech situation is even further complicated at such moments by the fact that the President has a live audience of senators and congressmen, and technically it is at them that he aims his illocutionary acts. Yet in another sense they are not his target audience. He speaks *through* or *around* them, *to* the rest of us. Our relation to his speech is that of overhearing it, acting as a shadow audience. The social relationship that exists between him and us has become attenuated, weak, in spite of the very serious ways our lives may be affected by what the President says.

But the loss of bearings that mass media have caused by such complications are minor compared with what happens to speech acts in the mouth of commerce. Even the direct-sell commercial, featuring one speaker explicitly addressing 'you' out there is a far cry from the standard speech act. The man on TV says 'Now it's possible to relieve your tension without using drugs or pills', and, looking me in the eye, he goes on the explain that I can keep up with such bracing developments by subscribing to the *Reader's Digest*. But of course all the difficulties that beset illocutionary acts broadcast through the media affect his explanation and advice, and some others in addition. For one thing, in speaking of 'your' tension he makes a presupposition that may invalidate the act for many viewers. There is an oddity in seeming to know what kind of person you are addressing when in fact your audience is unseen and no doubt polymorphous. But the gravest issue of good faith arises when we ask whether the speaker believes what he says, and whether he wants us to know it. For he is simply voicing the sentences in a plausible-sounding way, and need not actually endorse them at all. Is this commercial, then, a work of literature like 'Sailing to Byzantium'? No, because *some* measure of accountability still remains. If the commercial misrepresents reality – e.g. if it is *not* possible to relieve tension without pills or drugs, or if the *Reader's Digest* contains no such article – the advertiser is culpable and may be brought to account in court. Plymouth's 'We'll throw in the automatic transmission free' is a binding promise. Poets cannot be held to blame for falsehoods or broken promises.[8]

The complexities deepen when the mode is not direct sell, but a staged scene with a narrator – Danny Thomas with a row of women behind him who, he says, have just tested Instant Maxwell House coffee against the leading freeze-dried; or an unseen narrator saying 'You're about to see a man open a can of dog food with his bare hands'; or the Contac commercials whose narrator describes the rigors of life in Alaska while they are enacted before our eyes by fishermen or a bush pilot and family. Commercials in this mode have larger tolerance for fiction. We do not require that the visible scene be documentary (unless, of course, the narrator says it is), and the narrator's claims about the scene need not therefore be true. But *some* of what he says must stand reality-testing: for instance, Danny Thomas's claim that 45 per cent of people who compared coffees preferred Instant Maxwell House. That must be true, even if the women we see are not really performing the test. The viewer's illocutionary role in such commercials is puzzling indeed.

Or take the pure dramatic sketch. Badgerman descends from above and says 'Hey, what happened to my Badgermobile?' His interlocutor explains that a Toyota Corolla has been substituted for it and is, as a matter of fact, superior to the Badgermobile. No viewer would think he was eavesdropping on a real conversation. The mimetic situation is that of a literary work. Yet some vestige of the regular rules for speech remains, since claims made about the Toyota Corolla will be subject to scrutiny for misrepresentation, even though spoken by a character in a patent fiction. To add one more twist, some of the dramatic sketches have as characters well-known people playing themselves. A young woman's runaway grocery cart is rescued in the parking lot by a man. She says 'Say, you're George Kirby.' He admits it, and goes on to administer a brief encomium to Ivory liquid dishwashing soap. The encounter is plainly fictional, but does George Kirby have *no* responsibility for the things he says about Ivory? What is his bond with the observer? Somewhere at about this point, the art of the television ad man meets that of Borges, Barthelme, and Beckett coming from the other direction.

There are many other genres within television alone, and the other media have their peculiar ways of transferring speech acts. But this is enough to permit some hypotheses about the environment of speech acts in which we now live.

For all of human history until the last few hundred years, speech acts were face-to-face encounters, mainly of people who knew each other and whose relative positions were clear. When brother speaks to sister, parent to child, subject to ruler, apprentice to master, judge to prisoner, the contracts and entitlements of their illocutionary acts take effect within a community already established. Such communities are likely to be stable, and their structures evident to all. Relations within them are concrete. Verbal meetings have high social and ethical content.

Life among the media is different in a number of ways. For one thing, as I hope my examples have shown, social connections undergo severe dilation as illocutionary acts stretch over media channels. Through radio, television, print, and the rest we find ourselves constantly in one-sided discourse with people whose social links to us are obscure. There is a loss in social clarity, and in relatedness itself. This observation runs directly counter to a main point of McLuhan's. As usual, I think his view acute but limited. Many times he suggests that the electric age will create a global village, a 'single consciousness' (p. 67). The electric media, he says, pour in on us 'the concerns of all other men' (p. 156), so that we 'wear all mankind as our skin' (p. 56). But seeing the pain of a Vietnamese or the desolation of an East Pakistani village is not the same as being socially connected to these other people and their concerns; on the contrary, much in the media conceals our relation to them.[9] And an opposite tendency to the one McLuhan describes is strongly at work. As long as you have the television on, you relinquish the binding ties to people you know, and enter instead a shadowy community of people whose words come *at* you but act *upon* you in enigmatic ways. That community's likenesses to a village are fewer than its differences.

The deterioration of community closely parallels a decline in authenticity. Illocutionary acts, on the my-word-is-my-bond principle, carry much of the ethical content of social life. When the performance of these acts is attenuated, when the participants who join in them are separated by unbridgeable physical and social differences, when responsibility for sincerity and follow-up is diffused or even totally concealed – then the ethical force of speech is pretty well lost. For the TV pitchman, authenticity reduces to having an honest face and an unpretentious accent. I don't know how far this process would have to go to be truly perilous, but clearly if the rules were *never* adhered to, they would cease to be the rules. Speakers can break grammatical rules many times without changing the grammar, but if no one ever followed a particular rule it would drop from the language.

Perhaps there is an appetite for authenticity in people such that if they lose it in one area of experience they will compensate in another. Let us hope so.

A third consequence of these great shifts in the basis of speech is that we spend less time acting, less time actively participating in the transactions of talk. As literature is talk without consequences (in the sense I defined earlier), the movement *toward* literature of talk channeled through television lessens our involvement in it. *They act upon* us; we can scoff, or turn off the set, but we can't act *back* upon them. The barrier falls between doing and being done to, as well as between the illocution and the perlocution. McLuhan says that the electric implosion of the culture is making us aware of our 'total interdependence with the rest of human society' (p. 59). Maybe, but to a disquieting degree this interdependence has the savor of mutual helplessness. Marcuse is closer to the mark, I think, in writing of the intimidating, hypnotic character of language in the media. If there is truth in my analysis, it supports his, and helps explain it. The repressive effect of public language is enforced by the remoteness of those who speak to us, by our consequent loss of the power to act, and by the attendant conviction that 'everything is being taken care of.' Whose *is* the 'single consciousness' in which McLuhan says we all join? The ordinary person's remarkable faith in our society's managers has something to do with accepting necessity; and this attitude finds its sophisticated parallel in the value set on detachment, disinterestedness, by liberals and intellectuals. But these are perhaps general characteristics of bourgeois culture, not causally tied to the diminishing of our power to act.

Finally, and most vaguely, speech acts in the media, as they have taken on some of the characteristics of literature, have helped us to fictionalize the reality in which people live. To much of what we hear and read, we are related almost as to a poem or story. It is not surprising that some people confuse the two orders – perceive themselves as more intimately related to a disc jockey or a politician, for instance, than to people they can see and speak to. Conversely, recall that a significant number of Americans, after the first moon landing was done as a TV spectacular, did not believe that those events were real. Moreover, while literature itself compensates the reader for loss of active participation by affording him a criticism of life and a vision of alternate reality, commercials and ads try to pin him to a diminished reality where all problems resolve themselves in a timely purchase.

V

Postscript: To bright people like McLuhan, the media offer a splendid intellectual playground. It is not at all evident that they represent such a lark for most of technological society. Given the changes wrought in illocutionary acts by the media, the growing place of mass media in our lives, and the fact that the media are paid for directly by corporations and government, and indirectly by our willingness to consume things we don't need, it is no surprise if people-in-general suffer certain *losses* in freedom through expansion of the media, along with undeniable gains. McLuhan is apposite:

> Once we have surrendered our senses and nervous systems to the private manipulation of those who would try to benefit from taking a lease on our eyes and ears and nerves, we don't really have any rights left. Leasing our eyes and ears and nerves to commercial interests is like handing over the common speech to a private corporation, or like giving the earth's atmosphere to a company as a monopoly. (p. 73)

He need only have added, to his list of what we have surrendered, our role in speech acts and our stake in literature, and he would have ended up close to where I am ending. Literature, like talk itself, has been appropriated by commercial interests for gain, and the reduction in human size that accompanies that appropriation is told well enough by a book like Vance Packard's *The Hidden Persuaders*.

For reasons that are hard to accept, McLuhan rejects the implications of the passage I have just quoted. He believes that the electric technology will, if it hasn't already, reverse the movement of older, mechanical technology toward ruthless competition, individualism, privacy, and consuming as an end in itself. But these wretched traits of our culture did not originate only in technology, and will not vanish with a newer technology. They follow in part, I believe, on the economic premises of this society: private property and the free market. Competition, individualism, privacy, and irrational consumption are rooted in our social system and in bourgeois consciousness; and since *all* the media are dominated by bourgeois interests, I think it unlikely that a shift from mechanical to electric technology, or a serendipitous greening of America, will save literature, speech, and society for mere people. To do that it will be necessary to reunite word and deed, to reclaim for ourselves the media of speech and action and level the great heights of power that block the speech of equals.

Notes

1 J. L. Austin, *How to Do Things with Words* (Cambridge, Mass., 1962).
2 For pertinent discussion, see Charles. J. Fillmore, 'Verbs de jugement; essai de description sémantique' and Zeno Vendler, 'Les performatifs en perspective,' *Langages*, 5 (March 1970), 56–72, 73–90.

3 See *Speech Acts* (Cambridge, 1969).
4 'Deep structure, surface structure, and semantic interpretation', in *Semantics: An Interdisciplinary Reader in Philosophy, Linguistics, Anthropology and Psychology*, ed. L. A. Jakobovits and P. Steinberg (Cambridge, 1971).
5 This discussion of literary mimesis in part recapitulates the argument of my 'Speech acts and the definition of literature', *Philosophy and Rhetoric*, 4 (Winter 1971), 1–19.
6 *Understanding Media* (New York: Signet Books, 1964), p. 36. Page references in the text are to this edition.
7 There are, of course, many illocutionary acts that a newspaper reporter would not or could not perform on his reader – e.g. welcoming, appointing. But inability to perform all speech acts is a limitation on all speakers and all writers, not a special difficulty with writing.
8 On the contrary, they can be blamed for reporting the insufficiently varnished truth, as in a libel suit.
9 The favorite reasons for getting American troops out of Vietnam have been to save American lives, to cut our losses in an unwinnable war, to redirect our priorities, win the war on poverty, etc. Only among radical activists and peace people have the sufferings of the Vietnamese figured as the main reason; and such opponents of the war do not seem to have taken their line from television, by and large.

16
Literary cooperation and implicature
Mary Louise Pratt

If a writer omits something because he does not know it then there is a hole in the story.

Ernest Hemingway,
Interview, *Paris Review*, 1958

So far I have discussed what are probably the three most obvious factors which an account of the literary speech situation would have to include: literary works belong to the class of utterances addressed to an audience; within this class they belong to the subclass of utterances that presuppose a process of preparation and selection prior to the delivery of the utterance; and they belong to the subclass of utterances whose relevance is tellability and whose point is to display experience. In establishing these features, I have relied on both psychological evidence – people's attitudes toward what is said in a given context – and grammatical evidence – what actually does get said. I have suggested that these features represent information which is presupposed by participants in a literary speech situation, and I have tried to stress that they are features which also form part of the context of other utterance types. From the linguist's point of view, this latter observation means that there is independent motivation for including such features as these in a grammar of discourse; from the critic's point of view, it means that, at least so far, no motivation has been found for viewing literary discourse as generically distinct from our other linguistic activities or as exploiting any kind of communicative competence other than that which we rely on in nonliterary speech situations.

I propose now to explore further the view of utterance or text interpretation that Grice derives from his concept of the Cooperative Principle and to examine its applicability to literature. In keeping with my own general concerns, I will be looking in what follows at how the Cooperative Principle (hereafter referred to as CP) works in narrative utterances, what special cooperation is required for fictional utterances, and how we handle and interpret deviance in display texts. I am assuming, as I think we must, that the CP (formulated by Grice as 'Make your contribution such as is required at the stage at which it occurs, by the accepted purpose or direction of the talk-exchange in which you are engaged') does hold for representative discourse whose purpose is not or not only informative, even though we do need to expand or alter Grice's maxims to accommodate such assertions. In the case of literature, the assumption that the writer is trying to communicate *something* is obviously a crucial one.

1 Text interpretation and implicature

Any description of text interpretation or decoding has to make use of some concept of construction, reconstruction, or 'filling in'. Ohmann's view of reading, for example, is typical in this respect: 'The reader constructs (imagines) a speaker and a set of circumstances to accompany the quasi-speech-act,' and so on. Fillmore (1974 IV, 4) offers the following description of the interpretive act:

> A text induces its interpreter to construct an image, or maybe a set of alternative images. The image the interpreter creates early in the text guides his interpretation of successive portions of the text and these in turn induce him to enrich or modify that image. While the image-construction and image-revision is going on, the interpreter is also trying to figure out what the creator of the text is doing – what the nature of the communication situation is. And that, too, may have an influence on the image-creating process.

Let me stress that Fillmore's description is intended to apply to our interpretation of any discourse, not just literary works.

On the basis of his CP model of conversation, Grice derives an approach to text interpretation which allows us to be somewhat more specific about how this image-construction process comes about linguistically. The view Grice proposes is simply this: in a given speech situation, if the hearer knows that the speaker is observing the CP and its attendant maxims, the hearer, in decoding the speaker's utterance, will make all the deductions and inferences necessary to maintain the assumption that the speaker is observing the CP. Hence, to return to Grice's example, if A says to B 'Bill is in Oxford or in London', then B, in order to maintain the assumption that A is observing the CP, will infer that A does not know exactly where Bill is. Grice adopts the general term *implicature* to refer to the various kinds of calculations by which we make sense of what we hear. The speaker who says 'Bill is in Oxford or in London' is thus said to have *implicated* (as opposed to having *said*) that he does not know exactly where Bill is. Implicatures which are required to maintain the assumption that the CP is in force are called *conversational implicatures*. Conversational implicata, then, are 'the assumptions required in order to maintain the supposition that the CP and maxims are being observed on a given occasion' (III, 1). What a speaker implicates on a given occasion is distinguishable from what he says, that is, from the literal and conventional meaning of the words he uses; what is said and what is implicated together form the meaning of the utterance in that context.

The coherence of any conversation, text, or extended utterance almost invariably depends a great deal on implicatures. Consider the simple exchange:

A: I have a headache
B: I have some aspirin in my purse.

B here implicates, among other things, that he/she is willing to make the aspirin available to *A*. *A* is entitled to assume *B*'s willingness, since otherwise *B*'s remark would be a violation of the maxim of relation. In the following more bizarre exchange:

A: I have a headache
B: What time is it?

B could be implicating that he believes the time of day has something to do with *A*'s headache, or that he does not wish to discuss *A*'s headache, or that it may be a suitable time for *A* to leave off doing whatever has given him the headache. Here, as in many cases of implicature, more than one explanation is possible, a fact which is exploited a great deal by writers of literature and also by politicians, press agents, advertisers, and other speakers interested in multiple meanings. Notice that *B*'s odd response in this exchange could also be due to the fact that *B* has not heard *A*'s remark or has not heard it correctly. In this case, *B* implicates nothing at all.

Causal and chronological sequence are frequently established by implicature. On Grice's account, in a sentence like 'I wrote some letters, attended a meeting, and had lunch with a friend', an implicature is present to the effect that I did the actions in that order. If I do not wish to implicate this, I must explicitly cancel the implicature by adding a clause like 'but not necessarily in that order'. In a sentence like 'Bill dropped the plate and it broke' both temporal and causal sequence are implicated. Where the temporal interpretation is absent, causation alone can be implicated as in 'they were busy talking and missed the boat.' Here, an implicature of temporal sequence is ruled out because the first clause is a progressive, denoting a state of affairs rather than an event. Again, the causal implicature may be canceled. I could say 'they were busy talking and missed the boat, though they may have intended to miss it anyway.'

The question of how causal and chronological links are established between clauses is one that has troubled linguists a great deal, and I will not enter into a detailed discussion of it here. Suffice it to say that any analysis of narrativity will ultimately have to give an account of our ability to implicate causality and time sequence. The rudiments of such an account may be found in the following algorithm proposed by C. Ruhl. Although Ruhl is addressing himself to sequences of clauses lexically joined by *and*, I think we can agree with Grice that 'in many cases the idea of conjunction might be regarded as present even without an explicit conjunctive device' (IV, 3). Ruhl proposes:

> If a structure A-*and*-B can be analyzed as a temporal sequence, it will be. If it can further be analyzed that A is a precondition for B, it will be. And if A can be analyzed as a decisive condition – that is, a cause – of B, it will be. Only if the first stage – the temporal sequence – is not reached, will the co-ordinate structure be analyzed as symmetric. (quoted by Schmerling, 1975, p. 214n)

(Symmetric conjunction means a logical conjunction that implicates no priority relations between the conjoined clauses, as in 'Bill is in London and Jane is in Rio.') Ruhl's rule is not accurate in detail, as Schmerling (1975) points out, and it is obviously in need of elaboration.[1] I offer it only as an example of the kind of statement we may eventually want to make about the pragmatics of narrative and of the kind of generalization the implicature analysis allows us to make.

Evaluated narrative of the type found in display texts relies on a far greater range of implicatures than those required to establish narrativity. According to Labov's analysis, a natural narrator is required to supply not only narrative sequence (Labov's complicating action and resolution) but also evaluative and orientative information, as well as abstract and coda. In Gricean terms, we would probably want to say that the CP and maxims as defined for narrative display texts require that the speaker know and reveal the whole story and that he enable us to understand the sequence of events and to adopt the desired attitude toward them. Given these obligations, for each expression he uses a storyteller must either say or implicate whether that expression is part of the narrative sequence, serves as background information required to understand the narrative sequence (orientation), or is evaluative information intended to influence our attitude to the sequence. Most of the time, narrators merely implicate what kind of relevance a given expression has. For example, in this sequence of nonnarrative orientation clauses from narrative (1) above,

1. I was gunnin' one night with that dog
2. we had to use live decoys in those days
3. a fellow named Jack Bumpus was with me

the relations among the clauses and their relationship to the narrative are not at all apparent; however, since the CP is in force, we calculate by implicature that the speaker believes this information will be useful later. If the live decoys, the dog, and Jack Bumpus played no role in what followed, to mention them would count as a violation of the maxims of Quantity and Relation and thus as a violation of the CP. Since we have no reason to think the speaker is trying to violate the CP and the maxims, we assume the information is preparatory to what follows. The narrator, furthermore, assumes we will calculate this implicature. Given the definition of a story and the assumption that the CP is in force, we calculate countless implicatures of this highly generalized and straightforward type in our dealings with narrators. On the basis of the maxim of Relation, we interpret information as narrative, orientative, or evaluative. Given the maxim of Quantity, we understand time gaps not as violations of sequence but as spaces where nothing important to the story happened; if we are not told how a character got from point A to point B, we assume he did so in some normal and untellable way.

2 Rule-breaking and implicature

I have so far dealt only with rather routine cases of implicature, in which it is clear that the speaker is not knowingly violating any of the maxims or the CP. More detailed analysis would show, I believe, that such implicatures are the mainstay of conventional narrative, both natural and literary, and indeed form the basis of all routine decoding, as the Fillmore passage quoted earlier suggests. It ought to be clear that this reconstruction by implicature is not peculiar to fictive utterances or to literature, as many reader-oriented critics seem to think (see, for example, Ong 1975). Without implicature, it would take us a long time indeed to say anything at all. It is possible and very common, however, for speakers to fail to fulfill the conversational maxims. In conversation, unintentional failures occur all the time. Speakers get carried away on a subject and violate the maxim of Quantity, they make mistakes, become confused or incoherent, under- and overestimate what the hearer already knows, and so on. Errors of this type do not threaten the assumption that the CP is in force, that the speaker is at least trying to 'make his contribution such as is required by the purposes of the exchange.' They mean only that he isn't succeeding very well at the moment, whether for lack of verbal skill or for some other reason. On the whole, unintentional failures aren't very serious in conversation because the turn-taking system allows the hearer to correct the offending speaker, interrupt him, or break off the exchange. As might be expected, such unintended failures are much more serious in speaker/audience situations where turn-taking is not in force and where the speaker is consequently indebted to the audience and in a position of being judged. In these cases, unintentional failure can finally lead to a breakdown of the CP, usually attested to be illegitimate interruptions, indignant departures from the scene of the offense, or some other outbreak of hostility.

Cases in which a speaker *knowingly* fails to fulfill a maxim are much more interesting. Grice outlines four such cases:

1. He [a speaker] may quietly and unostentatiously *violate* a maxim; if so, in some cases he will be liable to mislead.
2. He may *opt out* from the operation both of the maxim and of the CP; he may say, indicate or allow it to become plain that he is unwilling to co-operate in the way in which the maxim requires. He may say, for example, 'I cannot say more, my lips are sealed.'
3. He may be faced by a *clash*; he may be unable, e.g., to fulfill the first maxim of Quantity ('Be as informative as is required') without violating the second maxim of quality ('Have adequate evidence for what you say').
4. He may *flout* a maxim; that is, he may *blatantly* fail to fulfill it. On the assumption that the speaker is able to fulfill the maxim and do so without violating another maxim (because of a clash), is not opting out, and is not, in view of the blatancy of his performance, trying to mislead, the hearer is faced with a minor problem: how can his saying what he did say be reconciled with the supposition that he is observing the overall CP? This situation is one which characteristically gives rise to a conversational implicature; and when a conversational implicature is generated in this way, I shall say that a maxim is being *exploited*.

(Grice, II, 12)

The first three cases, violation, opting out, and clashes, put the CP in jeopardy, and if serious enough they may cause it to break down. In the first two cases, it could be said that there is a lack of agreement about purposes of the exchange. In the third case there is agreement but inability to fulfill the purpose. Only in the fourth case, flouting, is the CP not ultimately in danger. This case is the most interesting to the present discussion, first because it is one of our favorite kinds of verbal play and second because it is the only kind of intentional nonfulfillment possible in the literary speech situation. In literary works, intentionally failing to observe a maxim always counts as flouting. I will elaborate on this claim shortly, but first, for purposes of clarity, I will offer a few nonliterary examples of how speakers exploit (or flout) maxims. The following are taken from or modeled on those Grice provides:

1 Flouting the maxims of Quantity

a. *A* is writing a testimonial about a pupil who is a candidate for a philosophy job, and his letter reads as follows: 'Dear Sir, Mr *X*'s command of English is excellent, and his attendance at tutorials has been regular, yours, etc.'

Gloss: *A* can't be opting out, since if he wished to be uncooperative, why write at all? He can't be unable, through ignorance, to say more, since this man is his pupil, moreover, he knows that more information than this is wanted. He must, therefore, be wishing to impart information which he is reluctant to write down. This supposition is only tenable on the assumption that he thinks that Mr *X* is no good at philosophy. This, then, is what he is implicating. (Grice, II, 16)

b. *A*: Did John go to the partly last night?
   B: He sure did, honey, and don't let anybody tell you any different!

Gloss: *B* has said more than is required. *B* has implicated there is some disagreement about whether John was at the party.

2 Flouting the maxims of Quality

a. (i) *A*: I hate to tell you this, but you flunked the test.
   B: Oh. That's just terrific.

Gloss: It is clear to both *A* and *B* that *B* has said something he does not believe; *A* knows that *B* knows that the violation is obvious to *A*. *A* calculates that *B* is implicating some proposition other than but related to the one he has actually said. The most obvious candidate is the reverse of what *B* said. Therefore *B* implicates that it is disastrous that he flunked the test.

(ii) Metaphor.

(iii) Meiosis. Of a man known to have broken up all the furniture, one says, 'He was a little intoxicated.' (Grice, II, 18)

(iv) Hyperbole. 'Bill hasn't been late in thirty years!'

b. *A* says of *B*'s wife, 'She is probably deceiving him this evening.'

Gloss: In a suitable context, or with a suitable gesture or tone of voice, it may be clear that I have no adequate reason for supposing this to be the case. My partner, to preserve the assumption that the conversational game is still being played, assumes that I am getting at some related proposition for the acceptance of which I *do* have a reasonable basis. The related proposition might well be that she is given to deceiving her husband, or possibly that she is the sort of person who wouldn't stop short of such conduct. (Grice, II, 18)

3 Flouting the maxim of Relation

a. *A* (unaware Bill is in the room): Bill makes me sick.
   B: Heard any good jokes lately?

Gloss: In failing to relate his remark to the preceding discourse, *B* is implicating either that Bill is in the room or at least that *A*'s remark is inappropriate for discussion.

4 Flouting the maxims of Manner

a. Obscurity:
   A: I saw you-know-who yesterday.
   B: You did?
   C: ?????

Gloss: *A*, by being deliberately obscure, implicates to *B* that he does not want *C* to know whom *A* is referring.

b. Failure to be brief or succinct:

Instead of saying 'Miss *X* sang "Home Sweet Home"', a reviewer says 'Miss *X* produced a series of sounds which corresponded closely with the score of "Home Sweet Home"'.

Gloss: Why has he selected that rigmarole in place of the concise and nearly synonymous 'sang'? Presumably to indicate some striking difference between Miss *X*'s performance and those to which the word 'singing' is usually applied. The most obvious supposition is that Miss *X*'s performance suffered from some hideous defect. The reviewer knows that this supposition is what is likely to spring to mind; so that is what he is implicating. (Grice, II, 21)

c. Deliberate ambiguity:

Blake's lines, 'Never seek to tell thy love, Love that never told can be.'

Gloss: Partly because of the sophistication of the poet and partly because of internal evidence (the ambiguity is kept up) there seems to be no alternative to supposing that the ambiguities are deliberate and that the poet is conveying both what he would be saying if one interpretation were intended rather than the other, and vice versa; though no doubt the poet is not explicitly *saying* any one of these things, but only conveying or suggesting them. (Grice, II, 20)

In all these cases of exploitation, 'though some maxim is violated at the level of what is said, the hearer is entitled to assume that that maxim, or at least the overall CP, is observed at the level of what is implicated' (II, 16)[2] I suggested that exploitation is virtually the only kind of intentional non-fulfillment of maxims that the literary speech situation allows, that intentional failure to fulfill a maxim in literature always counts as flouting and is thus always intended to be resolved by implicature.

As an example, consider the third and fourth sentences of Sterne's *Life and Opinions of Tristram Shandy* (1760). Shandy, bemoaning the yet-to-be-revealed circumstances under which he was conceived, writes (emphasis mine):

> Believe me, *good folks*, this is not so inconsiderable a thing as many of you may think it; – you have all, I dare say, heard of the animal spirits, as how they are transfused from father to son, &c., &c. – and a great deal to that purpose: – Well, you may *take my word*, that nine parts in ten of a man's sense or his nonsense, his successes and miscarriages in this world depend on their motions and activity, and the different tracks and trains you put them into, so that when they are once set a-going, whether right or wrong, 'tis not a *halfpenny matter*, – *away they go* cluttering like *hey-go-mad*; and by making a road of it, as plain and as smooth as a garden-walk, which, when they are once used to, the Devil himself sometimes shall not be able to drive them off it.
>
> Pray, my dear, quoth my mother, have you not forgot to wind up the clock?

The reader of this passage (and remember he has just begun that book) already knows by the title that Sterne intends to treat the text as an autobiography or memoir. He knows, in other words, that Sterne intends him to bring to bear on the text his knowledge of, among other things, the rules for narration and the rules for written discourse. In so doing, the reader encounters numerous failures to fulfill the maxims of Manner, Quality, and Relation when he reads this passage. With regard to manner, the text is peppered with colloquialisms and other expressions reserved for spoken discourse (I have emphasized some of them). In addition, there are typographical abuses, notably the use of '&c.' and the dashes, colons, and semicolons which allow a single sentence to run on for half a page. As for quantity, the passage is plagued with repetition. Nouns and adjectives come in redundant, legalistic doublets or quadruplets: 'successes or miscarriages', 'sense or nonsense', 'motions and activity', 'tracks and trains', 'right or wrong', 'plain and smooth'. In addition, given that Shandy is assuming his readers 'have all heard of the animal spirits' it is quite possible that his own reformulation of the doctrine is less relevant here than he thinks. This is the more true given the passage's role in the narrative. Quite clearly, Shandy intends here to give us orientative and evaluative commentary which will permit us to adopt the desired attitude to the circumstances of his conception. But he has not yet told us what the circumstances were, and we thus have no events to which to relate the lengthy evaluation. The first narrative clause in the book does not occur until the end of the chapter, with the sentence 'Pray, quoth my mother ...,' a sentence which itself lacks orientation and relevance. As the reader of *Tristram Shandy* quickly discovers, evaluation often precedes (and engulfs) the event in this book, and Shandy's failure to keep his orientations from blossoming into huge narrative digressions often pushes the event even farther into the offing.

In decoding this passage, the reader does not for a moment think that the failures to fulfill certain maxims that apply to Shandy's utterance are due to ignorance, carelessness, lack of skill, or uncooperativeness on Sterne's part. Rather, he interprets them as being ultimately in accord with the 'accepted purpose of the [literary] exchange'. In other words, Sterne is immediately understood to be *flouting* the rules for narrative and the rules for writing and to be observing the CP at the level of what is implicated. As in the Gricean examples in (4) above, we take it that Sterne here is indicating that the contrast between the manner we expected and the manner we get is related to his own display-producing intent. The violations themselves are amusing, and since amusement is an accepted purpose of display texts, Sterne at least implicates that his intent is to amuse us. He is also calling our attention to the difference between Shandy's way of ordering his experience and our own, to the lack of consensus between us and the fictional speaker. He may also be implicating, for example, a critique of contemporary stylistic norms or orientative information about Shandy's psychological makeup, which we will need to respond as desired to what follows. This opening passage leaves unanswered the question of whether we are to interpret the failures as intentional or unintentional on Tristram Shandy's part. Shandy, the fictional speaker, could be guilty of any or all the kinds of maxim nonfulfillment; Sterne, the real-world author, cannot.

As a second example, reconsider the opening sentence of *Pride and Prejudice* discussed earlier: 'It is a truth universally acknowledged that a single man in possession of a fortune must be in want of a wife.' At the point he encounters this sentence in the text, possibly the only knowledge he reader has about the 'nature of the communication situation', as Fillmore would say, is the fact that he is reading a novel called *Pride and Prejudice* written by someone named Jane Austen. Let us assume that the label 'novel' entitles the reader to assume he is confronting a narrative display text. (I will be supporting this claim a little later on.) Since the sentence in question immediately follows the narrative abstract (the title), contains no narrative clauses and no orientative information about setting and participants, the reader infers that the sentence is relevant either as a continuation of the abstract (the 'brief summary of the point of the story') and/or as an evaluative statement about events to be narrated. On the basis of this information, the reader infers that the sentence is, as Ohmann says, 'a tip-off to the fact that the narrator of the story is being ironic'. I argued earlier that, contrary to Ohmann's claim, the fact that the text is fictional is neither necessary or sufficient grounds on which to justify this inference. Let me attempt a brief Gricean account.

In Grice's view, the words 'true' and 'truth' refer to properties of utterances, not states of affairs. On this account, then, if I say 'it is true that Bill is a miser', I am making a comment not about Bill but about the assertion 'Bill is a miser.' If no such assertion has actually been made, I am implicating that someone might make such an assertion (Grice, III, 21ff). This is the case with Austen's sentence. The speaker of this sentence is making a claim about a hypothetical assertion regarding the interests of moneyed bachelors. Furthermore, the assertion about which the claim is made is one with which the reader is likely to disagree, that is, one he is likely to regard as failing to fulfill one or the other of the maxims of Quality. The speaker of Austen's sentence, however, says he believes this assertion does fulfill the maxims of Quality ('it is a truth') and also that he believes there is no disagreement about this fact (it is 'universally acknowledged'). But there is disagreement – notably the reader's own. Consequently, from the reader's point of view, Austen's sentence itself fails to fulfill the first maxim of Quality, or at least the second.

There are a number of ways the reader could account for the failure. Where p is the assertion 'a single man in possession of a fortune must be in want of a wife' and q is the assertion that p is a 'truth universally acknowledged', he could infer:

1 The speaker actually does believe both p and q and is thus merely ignorant of the ways of bachelors and of what other people think about the ways of bachelors. In this case, the failure is *unintentional*.
2 The speaker believes p but not q. In this case, the speaker in saying q is *flouting* the second maxim of Quality, as in Grice's example 2(b) above, by saying something for which he lacks adequate evidence. He is implicating

that many people besides himself believe *p* and that the reader should believe *p* too.

3 The speaker believes neither *p* nor *q* but is naively trying to get us to think he does. In this case, he is *violating* the maxims of Quality in order to mislead us either about the truth of *p* or about his own beliefs about *q*.

4 The speaker believes neither *p* nor *q* and is being *ironic*. In this case, the speaker is saying *q* is *flouting* the first maxim of Quality and is implicating that his attitude to *p* is something other than that expressed in *q*. As in Grice's example 2(a) above, the speaker is most likely implicating that his attitude is the opposite of that expressed in *q*, i.e., he is implicating that he emphatically disbelieves that *p* and that *q*. But, as Grice points out, irony also involves the expression of an emotive attitude as well as a propositional one. Since the speaker of Austen's sentence is also implicating that *p* is an assertion which might be made, then in implicating that *q* is false, the speaker is also implicating an ironic (contemptuous, mocking) attitude to those who would make the assertion *p*.

The reader of Austen's sentence has no trouble deducing that Austen is saying what is said in (4) and that given the sentence's location in the text, she is further implicating that the ironic attitude to *p* is relevant to our correctly understanding and evaluating what is to follow. This is the 'tip-off' Ohmann refers to. For some reason, we know unequivocally that the author is not trying to communicate (1), (2), or (3). Notice that it does remain possible at this point in the text that interpretations (1) through (3), as well as (4), could apply to the fictional speaker of Austen's novel. That is, the narrator could be someone other than Austen's fictional mouthpiece, someone stupid or naive enough to hold the beliefs and intentions necessary for the first three positions, though if this were the case, Austen would have to immediately and explicitly indicate it or risk a misunderstanding with the reader. Though this case would engender further implicatures, it would not alter the fact that what Austen is saying in the sentence is at least what is said in (4).

Just as it is possible to imagine a naive fictional narrator who, in uttering Austen's sentence, did not intend to be ironic (cf. Richardson's Pamela: 'For what could he get by ruining such a poor young creature as me?' Letter III) so, as I [have] suggested ... one can easily imagine real-life speech contexts in which Austen's sentence could be used in any of the ways outlined in (1) through (3), a letter to or from Ann Landers, for example. How do we know, then, that Austen is implicating disbelief in *p* and *q*? Similarly, how do we know right from the first dash that Sterne is flouting the rules rather than breaking them unintentionally or for some other reason? How do we know that we are smiling with Austen and Sterne and not at them?

Let us begin with the question of how we know the failures are not unintentional ones. In the case of the Sterne passage, one could argue simply that they are so numerous and extreme that no adult speaker of English could have produced them unintentionally. But actually, it is not difficult to imagine an utterance as babbling and incoherent as Tristram Shandy's occurring quite naturally in conversation. The fact that we see the failures in the passage as extreme, then, derives in part from the fact that we assume this utterance to have been composed in writing, subject to deliberation and revision. But even this is not enough. Within the realm of written composition, it is not difficult to imagine the occurrence of utterances as defective as this one. Run-on sentences, overuse of dashes and semicolons, confusion of formal and colloquial registers, failure to stick to the point – these are standard sins of student compositions and even of the drafts of more experienced writers, to say nothing of less monitored forms of written discourse like letters, diaries, suicide notes, or 'writing behavior' in mental institutions. Clearly, it is not the intrinsic properties of the Sterne passage which tell us that in each case of an unfulfilled maxim, the nonfulfillment is intentional. It is the fact that the passage occurs in a work of literature. But what do we know about works of literature which tells us the failures are intentional? We know that had Sterne not intended his text to be this way, his publishers and editors would not have enabled it to appear this way. If the deviance in the passage were there because Sterne was ignorant of the basic rules for written discourse, literary narrative, and fictional autobiography or so unskilled as to be incapable of observing them, his text would never have evolved into a book (at least not in this form) any more than a high school essay with the same sins could appear in a scholarly journal. Similarly, suppose Jane Austen had not intended the opening sentence of her book to be ironic, in which case the sentence is a falsehood. Probably either Austen or her editor would have noticed it and changed it. And even if Austen had been a person whose knowledge of the social world was so limited that she sincerely believed the assertions p and q were true, it is mostly unlikely that her editor would not have anticipated the reader's disagreement and suggested some less polemical way of beginning the book. Indeed, if the entire text were as naive and prescriptive as the first sentence (taken literally), the editor would very likely have returned the manuscript; certainly we would not be reading the book as avidly as we do today.

In short, we know the violations in the Sterne and Austen passages are intentional because of what we know about the circumstances under which literary works are composed, edited, selected, published, and distributed. The literary preparation and preselection processes are designed to eliminate failures which result from carelessness or lack of skill. The more selection and revision processes we know a work has gone through, the less likely we will be to attribute apparent inconsistencies and inappropriatenesses to random and unintentional error. Recall Grice's expanded maxim of Relation: 'An aspect of an utterance which it is within the power of the speaker to eliminate or vary, even if it is introduced unreflectively, will have a purpose connected with what is currently being communicated, unless, of course, its presence can be explained in some other way' (III, 15). The preparation and selection processes are designed to reduce the likelihood of there being any 'other way' in works of literature. Textual criticism is built on this assumption. This is not to say, of course, that we do or should assume all literary works to be somehow perfect. It means only that in literary works, the range of deviations which will be construed as unintentional is smaller than in many other speech contexts. Put the other way around, in literary works the range of deviations which will be construed as intentional is much larger. All works of literature carry the message that there are at least some readers for whom unintentional failure in the text was not sufficient to bring about a breakdown of the CP, namely the readers who approved the text for publication.

It is one thing to know that the failures to fulfill relevant maxims in the Sterne and Austen passages are intentional; it is another to know that, of the four types of intentional nonfulfillment Grice discusses, we are dealing in these passages with cases of flouting, not opting out, clash, or violation. Why couldn't Austen be trying to mislead us (violation)? Why couldn't Sterne be trying to make his text boring and unreadable (opting out)? How do we know that these failures are of the kind that does not endanger the CP? In other words, how do we know that we are to assume the maxims and CP are being observed at the level of what is implicated, and that we are expected to resolve the violations by calculating implicatures? Again, it is our tacit knowledge of the literary speech situation that enables us to make the flouting interpretation, not the intrinsic features of the utterances themselves. The literary speech situation is such that it is virtually impossible for an author to be guilty of any of the other kinds of intentional nonfulfillment Grice mentions.

Consider Grice's cases of *opting out* and *clashes*. In both these cases, the speaker fails to 'cooperate in the way in which the maxim requires', in the first case because he is unwilling to do so and in the second because he is unable to do so without violating another maxim. Neither of these cases can apply to the author in the literary speech situation because literary utterances, like all display texts, are never 'required' at all. They are always volunteered. (Even works produced in response to desperate financial pressures are legitimately read as volunteered material.) It is impossible to imagine a speaker *volunteering* an utterance whose purpose he is unwilling to accomplish or whose purpose he knows in advance he is unable to accomplish. A speaker cannot volunteer the remark 'I don't know what time it is' (except as an oblique way of asking for the time) for the same reason a speaker cannot volunteer the exclamation 'It isn't incredible what big feet he has!' or start telling a story he does not believe to be tellable. As Grice's example 1(a) above suggests, volunteering an utterance is always opting in, and one cannot opt in and out at once. If a writer knows himself to be unwilling or unable to address his audience satisfactorily, then he need not speak at all, and it will be contradictory in the first case and pointless in the second for him to do so. The speaker of a literary work may indeed opt out of the conventional rules for a given genre, as Sterne does, but because the writer is understood to be *seeking out* an audience, this opting out cannot count as a genuine threat to the CP. It counts instead as flouting, and the writer implicates that breaking the rules was in accord with his communicative intent. He is exploiting the rules not to endanger the CP, but to fulfill it. Real opting out, on the other hand, does jeopardize the CP. The speaker who really opts out is genuinely refusing to 'make his utterance adequate to the current purpose of the exchange'. Similarly, it is possible to imagine a *clash* of sorts in the literary speech situation. A writer may want to write, say, about incest, but he knows he would clash with social, linguistic and literary taboos on the subject. If he goes ahead and talks about incest anyway, then willy-nilly he has *flouted* the taboos, for he never was required to talk about incest; and if he doesn't talk about it, the clash he confronted privately never becomes apparent to the reader.

The third type of intentional nonfulfillment Grice mentions is 'quiet and unostentatious' *violation*, the case which produces lies or misrepresentations. This case is certainly possible in nonfictional display texts, though the literary selection process has an obligation to keep falsehoods of any consequence out of print. We have libel laws to cover this possibility. But in the case of fictional display texts, genuine lying is out of the question. Even if it were possible for an author (as opposed to a fictional narrator) to lie about his fictional world, or about his attitude to it, he could not thereby mislead. The reader would be unable to detect the lie unless he were given clues by the author, in which case the author has flouted rather than violated the maxim of Quality. This kind of flouting, as we shall see, does occur in novels.

In sum, the literary speech situation is such that at the level of author/reader interaction, all Grice's types of nonfulfillment except flouting either cannot arise or tend to be eliminated in the process of a text's becoming a work of literature. Given his knowledge of how literary works come into being, the reader is entitled to assume, among other things, that he and the writer are in agreement about the 'purpose of the exchange'; that the writer was aware of the appropriateness conditions for the literary speech situation and for the genre he has selected; that he believes this version of the text successfully accomplishes his purpose and is 'worth it' to us; and that at least some readers agree with him, notably the publishers, and perhaps the professor who assigned the book or the friend who recommended it. From the writer's point of view, these assumptions greatly increase the possibilities for exploiting maxims in his text. By the same token, it is these assumptions which entitle readers to treat an unusually wide range of deviations as floutings in literary works. In contexts where some or all of these assumptions are not in play, as with a teacher reading student term papers, for example, a reader may indeed be unable to decide whether a given deviation was unintentional, or the result of opting out (i.e. not trying), a clash, or flouting.

In distinguishing between the fictional speaker of a work of literature and its real-world speaker, the author, I have tacitly adopted the view that many literary works are, as Ohmann puts it, 'imitation speech acts' (1974, p. 54). Though I disagree with Ohmann on the consequences of that view, I think such an analysis is in itself correct and necessary if we are to describe the reader's role in the literary speech situation. Like Ohmann, I would apply this view only to the traditional category 'imaginative literature'; however, as discussed in chapter three, I would not maintain that this category alone constitutes literature. In a great many cases, then, a literary work may be described as a display text that is composed and addressed to us by an author and in which one or more fictional speakers in a fictional speech situation form a discourse whose intended addressee may or may not include us, the readers of the work. Readers of such literary works are in theory attending to at least two utterances at once – the author's display text and the fictional speaker's discourse, whatever it is. (This duality is not always exploited by the author, as I shall discuss shortly.) At the level of the author's utterance, virtually all failures to fulfill the CP and maxims as they apply to display texts of the genre in question will be interpreted as flouting. Within the fictional speaker's utterance, however, all kinds of nonfulfillment are possible. For example, as I suggested earlier, the reader encountering the Sterne passage might quite legitimately hypothesize that the failure to fulfill the maxims of Relation and Manner are due to naiveté or ignorance on Shandy's part, but this hypothesis in no way alters the fact that Sterne is flouting those maxims. Authors, in others words, can mimetically represent all kinds of nonfulfillment, for what counts as a lie, a clash, an opting out, or an unintentional failure on the part of the fictional speaker (or writer) counts as a flouting on the part of the real-world author and involves an implicature that the nonfulfillment is in accord with the purpose of the exchange in which the reader and author are engaged.

Now there is an important connection to be made between the fact that an author can *mimetically* represent all kinds of nonfulfillment and the fact that he can *really* perform only one. Before making this connection, however, I shall offer a few novelistic examples of the ways in which the fictional speaker of a work of literature can fail to fulfill the CP and maxims as required. Obviously, in order to detect a violated maxim, we must have a predefined idea of how the CP and maxims are defined for the fictional utterance in the first place. For the sake of clarity, I have therefore chosen examples in which the fictional speech act has a definite real-world correlate – letters, memoir, biography, natural narrative, and so on – and will concern myself for the moment only with cases in which the fictional speaker fails to fulfill the CP and maxims as defined for the utterance type *he* is performing, as opposed to violations of purely novelistic norms to which the fictional speaker is not himself subject. In each case, the assumption is that, regardless of what the fictional speaker is doing, the author is producing a display text, and it is this assumption which determines the implicatures by which we resolve the fictional speaker's violations at the level of our dealings with the author.

Opting out

As it turns out, much of the deviance in *Tristram Shandy* actually results not from unintentional failure, but from opting out on Shandy's part. Opting out, you will recall, is the case in which the speaker 'says, indicates or allows it to become plain that he is unwilling to cooperate in the way the maxim requires', and it is one of the cases that, I suggested, places the CP in jeopardy. Consider the following passage from chapter 6 of *Tristram Shandy*, in which Shandy addresses the reader:

> As you proceed further with me, the slight acquaintance which is now beginning betwixt us, will grow into familarity; and that, unless one of us is in fault, will terminate in friendship. – *O diem praeclarum!* – then nothing which has touched me will be thought trifling in its nature or tedious in its telling. Therefore, my dear friend and companion, if you should think me somewhat sparing of my narrative on my first setting out, – bear with me, – and let me go on, and tell my story my own way: – or if I should seem now and then to trifle along the road, – or should sometimes put on a fool's cap with a bell to it, for a moment or two as we pass along, – don't fly off, – but rather courteously give me credit for a little more wisdom than appears upon my outside, – and as we jogg on, either laugh with me, or at me, or in short, do anything, – only keep your temper. (p. 11)

In this passage, Shandy opts out of several of the main obligations of the autobiographer, the obligations precisely *not* to 'trifle along the way' (maxim of Relation), *not* to be 'sparing of his narrative' (maxim of Quantity) and *not* to 'put on a fool's cap with a bell to it' (maxim of Manner). The speaker of an autobiography is by definition engaged in an exchange requiring him to narrate the story of his life and adopt a serious evaluative attitude toward his narrative, or at least some attitude other than just humor. To the extent that the CP and maxims as defined for autobiographies include such requirements, Shandy's utterance, he warns us, will not be 'such as is required for the purposes of the exchange'. And indeed, it is not. The only maxim which Shandy does not fail to fulfill in his book is the maxim of Quality ('Do not say that which you know to be false').

Now this kind of opting out is serious indeed in a speaker/audience situation, given the speaker's position of indebtedness. But in telling his audience to 'bear with him' and 'keep his temper', Shandy opts out of even the indebtedness rule. He merely orders the audience not to let his opting out jeopardize the CP. It is rather like answering an exam question with 'I don't know, but don't hold it against me' or like withholding the punch line of a joke and expecting the audience to laugh anyway. Though he knows he is engaged in a speaker/audience situation, it turns out that for Shandy, what is 'required for the purposes of the exchange' is no more than would be required if he and the reader were engaged in a casual conversation. Shandy's manner is colloquial and conversational, and, as critics have often noted, the rules of Relation and Quantity which Shandy observes are likewise those governing conversation, not autobiographies. Relevance in Shandy's text is not determined by whether a piece of information contributes to our understanding or evaluation of his life. Rather, tellability alone counts as sufficient relevance, just as it does in conversation. And as in conversation, only the most tenuous metaphorical, lexical, or semantic associations are required to motivate a change of subject. Or, if the information is tellable enough, no link to prior discourse is required at all:

> I will not finish that sentence till I have made an observation on the strange state of affairs between the reader and myself ... for the very novelty of it alone, it must be worth your worships attending to. (p. 285)

To say that Shandy structures his utterance according to the rules of conversation is not to say that he is oblivious to his narrative obligations or to the fact that the point of the exchange has been predefined as autobiography. If he were, his violations would be unintentional. Shandy at least in part recognizes his autobiographical obligations, as the passages I have quoted suggest, and at least in part he fulfills them. But he does not consider himself uniquely bound by them. He reserves the right at any time to opt out of the marked speaker/audience situation that autobiography presupposes and instead to treat his relation to the reader as a conversational one. Thus in the passage quoted earlier, he depicts himself and the reader as 'companions' walking a road together; the purpose of the encounter is for them to become friends, for their 'slight acquaintance' to 'grow into familiarity'. Any danger to the CP arising from this arrangement will be due not to Shandy's failure to fulfill the reader's audience expectations (a personal failure), but to a deficiency in the friendship (an interpersonal failure). In sum, the speech situation Shandy recognizes in this passage is not a speaker/audience one at all, but rather the one Grice described for the 'over-the-wall-chat' in which the 'common aim' is 'a second order one, namely that each party should for the time being identify himself with the transitory conversational interests of the other' (II, 11). It is this speech situation – not a speaker/audience one – in which 'nothing which has touched me will be thought trifling in its nature, or tedious in its telling.' Says Shandy himself, 'Writing, when properly managed, (as you may be sure I think mine is) is but a different name for conversation' (109). Throughout his text, the rules for writing and the rules for autobiographical narrative are optional, and may be set aside at any time in favor of the rules for conversation. Obviously, much of the humor of *Tristram Shandy* results from this attempt to import the CP and maxims as defined for conversation into the autobiographical speech situation, a situation which is a priori marked with respect to conversation. The attempt is as hopeless as it is outrageous, since Shandy cannot incorporate into his text the one set of rules which most clearly distinguishes autobiography from conversation, namely the rules for turn-taking. The reader may indeed be walking a road with Tristram, but his mouth has been securely taped shut....

As I mentioned earlier, opting out is one kind of nonfulfillment which puts the CP in jeopardy. Shandy's opting out quite clearly does so. As an autobiography, his text is a disaster. (One need only imagine a historical researcher encountering it in the autobiography section of the library.) But at the highest level of analysis, the level at which the text is defined as a novel by Sterne, Shandy's opting out counts as Sterne's flouting, and rather than jeopardizing the CP, it is understood to be there as a contribution toward fulfilling Sterne's own communicative intent, the intent to produce a display text.[3] The difference between what Shandy says and what a speaker in his position might be expected to say is part of what Sterne is displaying.

Clashes

A clash occurs when a speaker is unable to fulfill one maxim in the way required because doing so would require him to violate another maxim. The fictional speaker of Tommaso Landolfi's short story 'Gogol's Wife' (1963) is faced with several such clashes. He is writing a biography of Gogol, of which the given text purports to be one chapter. The 'chapter' opens thus:

> At this point, confronted with the whole complicated affair of Nikolai Vassilevitch's wife, I am overcome by hesitation. Have I any right to disclose something which is unknown to the whole world, which my unforgettable friend himself kept hidden from the world (and he had his reasons), and which I am sure will give rise to all sorts of malicious and stupid misunderstandings? Something, moreover, which will very probably offend the sensibilities of all sorts of base, hypocritical people, and possibly of some honest people too, if there are any left? And finally, have I any right to disclose something before which my own spirit recoils, and even tends toward a more or less open disapproval?
>
> But the fact remains that, as a biographer, I have certain firm obligations. Believing as I do that every bit of information about so lofty a genius will turn out to be of value to us and to future generations, I cannot conceal something which in any case has no hope of being judged fairly and wisely until the end of time. (p. 298)

The speaker here is faced with a clash between the maxims of Quantity and Manner. As a biographer, he is required by the maxim of Quantity ('Make your contribution as informative as is required') to reveal information which would lead to an increased knowledge and understanding of the subject's life and character; at the same time the maxims of Manner (some subset of the 'be polite' rules) require that he not knowingly cast his subject in a poor light or leave him open to unmerited criticism. Now it is clearly illegitimate to discuss such a clash in a biography. For to say that there is something to reveal and then fail to reveal it is to opt out of the maxim of Quantity and to put the CP in jeopardy. The kind of clash the speaker here faces is the kind writers have to resolve before publishing their texts. The speaker here resolves the clash in favor of Quantity, at the risk of endangering the CP by violating the maxims of Manner. He will, he decides, reveal to us the grim truth about Gogol's wife. Notice, too, that the grounds on which he resolves the clash are logically flawed. According to the last sentence quoted, the upcoming revelation will never be judged fairly but will nevertheless turn out to be of value. Since fair judgment is an important criterion of value in a biography, the speaker's beliefs ought to have led him to resolve his clash in the opposite way, in favor of Manner. The question remains whether this mistake is unintentional or intentional. (The horror to be revealed is that Gogol's wife was an inflatable rubber doll which the dying Gogol eventually exploded and burned along with some of his manuscripts. Gogol, in fact, was never married.)[4]

Pages later, a clash between the maxims of Quantity and Quality emerges:

> Finally, I should speak of her [Gogol's wife's] voice, which it was only once given me to hear. But I cannot do that without going more fully into the relationship between husband and wife, and in this I shall no longer be able to answer to the truth of everything with absolute certitude. On my conscience I could not – so confused, both in itself and in my memory, is that which I now have to tell.
>
> Here, then, as they occur to me, are some of my memories. (p. 302)

As the last line shows, the clash is again resolved in favor of Quantity, at the risk of violating the second maxim of Quality, 'Do not say that for which you lack adequate evidence.'

Finally, at the climax of the story, another clash between Quality and Quantity occurs:

> The true reason why I wished to see [what else Gogol had thrown in the fire besides his wife and his manuscripts] was because I had already glimpsed. But it was only a glimpse, and perhaps I should not allow myself to introduce even the slightest element of uncertainty into this true story. And yet, an eyewitness account is not complete without a mention of that which the witness knows with less than complete certainty. To cut a long story short, that something was a baby. (p. 309)

Again, the clash is resolved in favor of the maxim of Quantity at the expense of the maxim of Quality, and again, the grounds on which the clash is resolved ('an eyewitness account is not complete, etc. . . .') are logically flawed.

The speaker concludes him chapter by assessing the degree to which he has accomplished his communicative purpose:

> I hope I have thrown sufficient light on a most controversial question and that I have unveiled the mystery, if not of Gogol, then at least of his wife. In the course of this I have implicitly given the lie to the insensate accusation that he ill-treated or even beat his wife, as well as other like absurdities. And what else can be the goal of a humble biographer such as the present writer but to serve the memory of that lofty genius who is the object of his study? (p. 309)

What Landolfi is implicating, of course, is that in resolving the clashes the way he did, in favor of Quantity and at the expense of Quality and Manner, the speaker quite undermines his communicative purpose and fails altogether to fulfill the CP and maxims as required for biographies. He has given us a great deal of unreliable information which casts more outrageous

398 *Essays in Modern Stylistics*

aspersions on Gogol's character than the 'absurdities' he intended to refute; furthermore, the clashes are resolved on faulty logical grounds, which themselves are enough to endanger the CP.

Unintentional failure

Unintentional failure on the part of a fictional speaker can result from carelessness or ignorance or from some temporary or permanent perceptual limitation such as psychological trauma, obsession, insanity, or delirium. Unintentional failure is often used in narrative to produce what the Russian Formalists called 'estrangement' or 'deautomatisation of perception'. In all cases of unintentional failure on the part of the fictional speaker, the author implicates the cause of the failure and calls our attention to the contrast between what the speaker said and what we might have expected him to say. One famous example is the opening passage of Faulkner's *The Sound and the Fury* (1929) in which a mentally retarded man, Benjy, describes a golf game:

> Through the fence, between the curling flower spaces, I could see them hitting. They were coming toward where the flag was and I went along the fence. Luster was hunting in the grass by the flower tree. Then they put the flag back and they went to the table, and he hit and the other hit. Then they went on, and I went along the fence. Luster came away from the flower tree and we went along the fence and they stopped and we stopped and I looked through the fence while Luster was hunting in the grass.
> 'Here, caddie.' He hit. They went away across the pasture. I held to the fence and watched them going away.

The passage, you will note, is a narrative, albeit a rudimentary one. It has an orientation (the first three sentences), a sequence of chronologically ordered narrative clauses, a resolution ('they went away') and even a coda of sorts ('I watched them going away'). It is certainly not a felicitous narrative, however. In Gricean terms, its infelicity arises mainly from violations of the maxims of Quantity and Manner. The orientation provides a good deal less information about participants and setting than the maxim of Quantity requires. Within the narrative sequence, causal relations are not indicated and information which has causal relevance is omitted. For example, in the putting sequence – 'They took the flag out, and they were hitting. Then they put the flag back.' – Benjy fails to state or implicate the causal connection among the three clauses. This discontinuity arises obviously from his failure to mention the ball, which he has either failed to see or failed to consider relevant. The maxims of Manner are violated in a way not unlike Grice's example 4(b) on page 162 (the reviewer who says 'Miss *X* produced a series of sounds which closely resembled the score of "Home Sweet Home"'). In both cases, the speaker uses paraphrase where briefer and more accurate terms are available. Benjy, for example, takes six clauses to say what could reduce to 'they putted and then teed off at the next hole.' The essential difference between the two examples, of course, is that Grice's reviewer has intentionally failed to use the word *sing*, whereas terms like *golf*, *putt*, *tee*, and *course* are unavailable to Benjy. By failing to use these terms, then, Benjy is implicating nothing at all, though, again, Faulkner is implicating a great deal. Perhaps the most striking fact about Benjy's narrative is that it is completely lacking in evaluation and in this respect fails in both Quantity and Manner.

With respect to Benjy, the violations in the passage are unintentional, but Faulkner, like Grice's reviewer, is flouting the maxims of Manner and Quantity. Both Faulkner and the reviewer are indicating that part of what they are trying to communicate is implicated by the contrast between what they have said and what they might have been expected to say. Given the context of the reviewer's remark (a review), the reader quickly relates the reviewer's flouting to his evaluative intent. Given the context of the Faulkner passage (the opening of a novel), the floutings are understood to be related to Faulkner's experience-displaying intent. Faulkner is implicating not that golf is a silly waste of time, but that among other things, the speaker of the story has some cognitive or perceptual impediment, that this fact is relevant to our understanding of what follows, and that he intends us to share, contemplate, and evaluate Benjy's view of the world and contrast it with our own.

Benjy's violations, especially his failure to orient, evaluate, and maintain causal sequence, produce a particularly modern form of estrangement to which we often apply terms like 'alienation' or 'the absurd'. The narrative failures we observe in Benjy's passage are the same ones we commonly associate with the novelistic technique of such writers as Camus, Kafka, or Robbe-Grillet. It is probably not an accident that we should apply the term 'alienation' ('making other') to the effect produced in us by disoriented, unevaluated, and causally incoherent narrative. According to Labov, it is exactly these features which, at a certain stage of our linguistic development, distinguish the way we render *vicarious* experience from the way we render *personal* experience. Labov's studies of child narrative showed that by the time children reach preadolescence (9–12 years), they are often able to produce competent and effective narratives of personal experience; however, they are quite unable to reproduce and evaluate vicarious experience. Here, for example, is a preadolescent account of an episode from the TV series *The Man from U.N.C.L.E.*:

> (1) This kid – Napoleon got shot and he had to go on a mission. And so this kid, he went with Solo. So they went and this guy – they went through this window, and they caught him. And then he beat up them other people. And they went and then he said that this old lady was his mother and then he – and at the end he say that he was the guy's friend. (Labov, 1972, p. 367)

Labov comments:

> This is typical of many such narratives of vicarious experience that we collected. We begin in the middle of things without any orientation section; pronominal reference is many ways ambiguous and obscure throughout. But the meaningless and disoriented effect ... has deeper roots. None of the remarkable events that occur is *evaluated*. (Labov, 1972, p. 367)

The similarities between the *Man from U.N.C.L.E.* narrative and the Faulkner text are unmistakable. Labov contrasts the vicarious narrative with the following preadolescent narrative of *personal* experience:

> (2) When I was in fourth grade – no, it was in third grade – this boy he stole my glove. He took my glove and said that his father found it downtown on the ground. (And you fight him?) I told him it was impossible for him to find downtown 'cause all those people were walking by and just his father was the only one that found it? So he got all (mad). Then I fought him. I knocked him all out in the street. So he say he give. And I kept on hitting him. Then he started crying and ran home to his father. And the father told him that he ain't find no glove.

One would need two drastically different grammars to describe narratives (1) and (2). Somewhere in the linguistic (and presumably the cognitive) competence of the ten-year-old, there is a radical distinction between vicarious and personal experience (and thus between first and third person narrative). Benjy, however, lacks this distinction. He uses only one grammar, the grammar of (1), to render all experiences, including personal ones. In fact, Faulkner actually obliterates the vicarious/personal distinction in the opening passage by interspersing the two kinds of experience and using the same language – the language of vicariousness – to render both. Benjy is both a spectator (of the golf game) and an agent in the passage, but his two roles are linguistically undistinguished in his speech. Benjy's speech may not be anything like that of a retarded adult, nor do we need to know anything about retarded speech to respond to Faulkner's style here. All we need to imagine Benjy's world is our own linguistic and cognitive past.

The narrator of Camus' *L'Etranger* (*The Stranger*, 1942) likewise uses the grammar of the various to render his own experience. (Due to the looseness of the standard English translation, this passage is given in French. The English version is given in the Notes.)

> Le concièrge a traversé la cour et m'a dit que le directeur me demandait. Je suis allé dans son bureau. Il m'a fait signer un certain nombre de pièces. J'ai vu qu'il était habillé de noir avec un pantalon rayé. Il a pris le téléphone en main et il m'a interpellé: 'Les employés des pompes funèbres sont là depuis un moment. Je vais leur demander de venir fermer la bière. Voulez-vous auparavant voir votre mère une dernière fois?' J'ai dit non. Il a ordonné dans le téléphone en baissant la voix: 'Figeac, dites aux hommes qu'ils peuvent aller.' (pp. 30–31)[5]

Though we have no reason to think Meursault does not understand the causal relations among the events narrated here, at no time does he assert those relations. As with Benjy's passage, the reader has to establish causality by implicature alone. And as with Benjy's passage, there are unexpected gaps in the sequence. In order to make sense of the passage, for example, we are required to infer that between the time the director picks up the phone and the time he asks Meursault the question, he has called a number and talked with someone else. We need to know this to understand the director's question, and Meursault might certainly have been expected to tell us the full sequence. Meursault's discourse is better oriented than Benjy's, in part because Meursault has an adult's vocabulary. The characters are identified, if only by profession, and the relevant objects are at least mentioned. Meursault knows what game is being played. But he does not provide us with any information about the 'certain nombre' of papers he signs, information which both Meursault and his Audience could be expected to find relevant. He does describe the director's clothing, but the description lacks interest and relevance. In fact, it is scarcely a description at all. It is embedded on the narrative clause '*j'ai vu*' 'I noticed'; that is, it is presented as a mere observation with its orientative and evaluative function quite unclear. The only other even potentially evaluative expression, the phrase '*en baissant la voix*' 'lowering his voice', likewise lacks apparent relevance and thus comes across as a mere observation with no relation to Meursault himself. There is no attempt on Meursault's part to establish a personal evaluative stance with respect to the events. Finally, like Benjy and the narrator of (1) above, Meursault uses, for the most part, the unmarked simple sentence with subject-verb-object word order. And he uses the *passé composé*, the tense of spoken, not written narrative.

These syntactic observations are important, for it is his syntax which most obviously invites us to link Meursault's speech with that of the child, and it is on this link that much of our sympathy for Meursault depends.

Says Sartre, 'The outsider he [Camus] wants to portray is precisely one of those terrible innocents who shock society by not accepting the rules of its game' (Sartre, 1955:28). Meursault's air of innocence, however, may well depend on the fact that he talks not like one who has not accepted the rules of the game but like one who has not yet learned them. Like Faulkner, Camus alienates (makes other) Meursault's personal experience by rendering it through and associating it with the child's grammar of vicarious experience. Readers of *L'Etranger* have, of course, long noted the impression of vicariousness Meursault's narrative gives. Sartre calls *L'Etranger* 'a novel of discrepancy, divorce and disorientation' (p. 33). Camus himself described the 'absurd' state of mind as one in which 'the setting collapses'. In the world of the absurd man, says Sartre, 'one experience is as good as another.... Confronted with this "quantitative ethic" all values collapse; thrown into this world, the absurd man, rebellious and irresponsible, has "nothing to justify". He is innocent' (Sartre, 1955, p. 27). I believe Labov's data provide an insight into the linguistic basis of Meursault's 'innocence' and the sense of 'discrepancy, divorce and disorientation' his narrative gives us. Absence of setting, values, and justification are characteristics not (or not only) of the absurd man's world but also of the absurd man's language. They are the characteristics that cognitively and linguistically distinguish his world from our own adult one while at the same time associating his world with that of our own childhood, or rather with one of the subworlds of our childhood – the world of vicarious experience. This association plays a significant role in Camus's attempt to get us to perceive Meursault as alienated without being alienated by him.[6]

The unintentional failures in the Faulkner and Camus passages are mostly sins of omission. But it is also possible and on the whole perhaps more common for fictional narrators to err not by failing to evaluate, orient, and maintain causality but by failing to do so correctly. Consider, for example, Huckleberry Finn's description of suppertime at the Widow Douglas's house:

> The widow rung a bell for supper, and you had to come to time. When you got to the table you couldn't go right to eating, but you had to wait for the widow to tuck down her head and grumble a little over the victuals, though there warn't really anything the matter with them. (p. 2)

Obviously, the widow is not grumbling but saying grace. In Montesquieu's *Lettres persanes* (*The Persian Letters*, 1721), the Persian traveler Rica makes a similar mistake when he describes in a letter his first trip to the Comédie Française (again, the English translation is in the Notes):

> Je vis hier une chose assez singulière, quoiqu'elle se passe tous les jours à Paris.

> Tout le peuple s'assemble sur la fin de l'après-midi et va jouer une espèce de scène que j'ai entendu appeler comédie. Le grand mouvement est sur une estrade, qu'on nomme le théâtre. Aux deux côtés, on voit, dans de petits réduits, qu'on nomme loges, des hommes et des femmes qui jouent ensemble des scènes muettes, à peu près comme celles qui sont en usage en notre Perse. (p. 75)[7]

Rica has erroneously inferred that the audience members at the Comédie are also actors in the play, and the remainder of his letter continues based on this assumption.

In both these passages, the problem is not a failure to evaluate, orient, or maintain causal sequence. Rather, the fictional speaker maintains, evaluates, and orients the *wrong* causal sequence. In both cases, the speaker says something that he believes to be true but that the audience knows to be false. It is not the case that the Widow Douglas is 'grumbling' and it is not (literally) the case that the public has assembled at the Comédie to 'jouer une espèce de scène' 'to *play* at a kind of dramatic performance.' Grice, you will recall, does not concern himself with unintentional nonfulfillment at all, and it is difficult to see how his model would handle this kind of mistake. Clearly Twain and Montesquieu are flouting the first maxim of Quality in these passages. They are saying what they know to be false. The most we can say of Huck and Rica, however, is that in using the verbs 'grumble' and '*jouer*,' 'play', they are unintentionally failing to fulfill the second maxim of Quality, 'Do not say that for which you lack adequate evidence', and those parts of their subsequent discourse which presuppose the erroneous assertion thereby fail to fulfill the maxim of Relation. This would be the case with Huck's clause 'though there warn't really anything the matter with them' and with much of the rest of Rica's letter on the Comédie. But perhaps such an analysis is not too far from the mark after all. Certainly the humor in both passages derives from the contrast between what the speaker says and what he might have been expected to say had he had adequate evidence. And certainly in both cases the author is calling our attention to the similarity (or even identity) between the evidence which the speaker observed and the kind of evidence on which the use of the words 'grumble' and '*jouer*' is normally based. In both cases, as in the Faulkner passage, the evidence that the speaker is lacking is institutional, not sensory. It is evidence about what the characters observed believe themselves to be doing, evidence that the speaker could not know was lacking. Twain is implicating that the only difference between grumbling and grace is the subject's belief that he is saying grace; grace, then, is as futile as grumbling. Montesquieu is implicating that the only difference between the behavior of the audience and of the actors at the Comédie is the audience's belief that it is not playacting; the audience, then, is as insincere as the players.

Violation

In a violation the speaker 'quietly and unostentatiously violates a maxim' and is 'in some cases ... liable to mislead'. Such cases are not very common in literature for the obvious reason that if the fictional speaker of a work of literature were to successfully violate a maxim in this manner, the reader would necessarily be unable to detect the violation on the basis of the fictional speaker's utterance alone. And if the violation is undetectable, it is, from the author's point of view, pointless. There appear to be two main ways in which authors can make violations on the part of the fictional speaker detectable to the reader, and I shall offer some examples of both, in order of increasing ambiguity.

First, the author can give the reader access to some speech act other than the one in which the violation occurred and can reveal the violation in this second utterance. This is the case, for example, in epistolary novels, where speaker A can write a letter to B in which he tells B a lie, then write to C and tell him the truth. Obviously, the reader needs a way of distinguishing which letter contains the lie. Usually, A will also tell C that he lied to B. Alternatively, the reader will infer from A's letters that A is more likely to lie to B than to C. B, for example, could be A's enemy or a woman A is trying to seduce under false pretenses. It is on the basis of such information that the reader of Laclos's *Dangerous Acquaintances* (1782), for example, distinguishes levels of sincerity between the letters Mme de Mertueil and the Vicomte de Valmont write to each other and the letters they write to others. Eventually, this sincerity judgment gets ironically reversed when Valmont reveals that his love letters to the Présidente de Trouvel were in fact sincere, and he had actually been deceiving Mme de Mertueil.

Alternatively, a violation may become apparent if the speech act in which it occurs is embedded inside the utterance of a second speaker. This is the case of one of Jorge Luís Borges's *ficciones* called 'The Shape of the Sword' (1956). In this story the narrator, an Argentine traveler named Borges, stops overnight at the ranch of an enigmatic Irish immigrant who bears on his cheek a large curving scar, whose history he has never been willing to reveal. He agrees to tell Borges how he got the scar. His story runs thus: while fighting for Irish independence in the 1920s, he risks his life to rescue from the British a comrade named Moon who has become paralyzed by fear. Shortly after, he discovers the same comrade is really a spy and has betrayed him to the British. Just before his capture, he manages to seize the traitor and slash a curving cut in his cheek. The traitor flees to South America. Here the Irishman stops, and we read:

> I [Borges] waited in vain for the rest of the story. Finally I told him to go on.

Literary cooperation and implicature 405

Then a sob went through his body; and with a weak gentleness he pointed to the whitish curved scar.

"You don't believe me?' he stammered. 'Don't you see that I carry written on my face the mark of my infamy? I have told you the story thus so that you would hear me to the end. I denounced the man who protected me; I am Vincent Moon. Now despise me.' (p. 71)

Here the Irishman reveals that in telling his story he has deceived his listener by presenting himself as the betrayed hero instead of as the cowardly traitor Moon. For the duration of his narrative, in other words, the Irishman violates the first maxim of Quality ('Do not say that which you know to be false') with the intention, however, of ultimately revealing and correcting the violation. The case is complicated. At bottom the Irishman's problem is a clash. He believes that unless he violates the maxim of Quality he will be unable to fulfill the CP because his utterance will be intolerably distasteful to his listener. Paradoxically, then, to fulfill the CP, he feels he must place it in jeopardy by misleading the listener. The moment the violation is revealed by the Irishman, of course, it necessarily counts as a flouting on the part not only of the Irishman, but of Borges the narrator and Borges the author as well. Both the violation and the flouting are perceptible only because we have the contextual information that the Irishman has a scar, and we get this information only because we get the story secondhand. On its own, the Irishman's story is a perfectly felicitous narrative of personal experience and bears no sign of the lie.

Secondhandedness also plays an important role in my next example, Defoe's *Moll Flanders* (1722), a novel that, like *Tristram Shandy*, has the form of an autobiography. It is frequently, and I think correctly, argued that Defoe intends us to suspect Moll Flanders of misrepresenting herself and of trying to convince us she is less blameworthy and more penitent than she really is. Those who take this view find support for it in the book's preface, written by a fictional editor figure. Two remarks in particular cast doubt on Moll's penitent attitude. The editor reveals that Moll's original manuscript was 'written in Language, more like one still in *Newgate* than one grown Penitent and Humble, as she afterwards pretends to be' (p. 1) and secondly that in her old age (when she apparently produced the manuscript) Moll 'was not so extraordinary a Penitent, as she was at first' (p. 5). In order to maintain the assumption that in making these remarks the prefacer is fulfilling the maxim of Relation, the reader must infer that the prefacer is implicating that Moll's penitent attitude in the book is insincere and that we need to know this to properly interpret her text. Alternatively, one could infer that the prefacer's intentions are innocent and that the implicatures are Defoe's (the prefacer being Defoe's fictional creation). In any case, the evidence the two remarks provide is evidence that Moll's text itself does not supply. As in the Borges and the epistolary examples, we are given access to the evidence of violation through a speech act other than the one in which the putative violation occurs. Ironically, the prefacer's implicatures cast doubt on his sincerity, too. The communicative purpose he professes is 'to recommend Virtue and generous Principles and to discourage and expose all sorts of Vice and Corruption of Manners' (p. 4). To a great extent, this aim can be achieved only if we believe in Moll's penitence. By suggesting the penitence is insincere, then, the prefacer undermines his own purpose.

I turn now to a second, less straightforward way in which an author can make a violation on the part of the fictional speaker apparent to the reader: the fictional speaker may unintentionally fail to make his violation 'quiet and unostentatious' enough. He may, for example, be inconsistent or even contradict himself. Machado de Assis's novel *Dom Casmurro* (Brazil, 1900) provides an example interesting for its complexity. *Dom Casmurro* is a fictional memoir written by a middle-aged Rio de Janeiran nicknamed Dom Casmurro (the name means something like 'Sir Misanthrope'). The central event in Dom Casmurro's story is the collapse of his marriage caused by his conviction that his wife Capitú has been unfaithful to him. The evidence for this claim is what Dom Casmurro believes to be an exact physical resemblance between his son Ezequiel and his recently deceased friend Escobar, a resemblance which Dom Casmurro takes to be proof that the child is not his own but Escobar's. Now it is clear to the reader that in claiming the child is not his own, Dom Casmurro is failing to fulfill the second maxim of Quality requiring adequate evidence. The question is whether he is doing so knowingly, in which case the failure is a *violation*, or whether he is so blinded by jealousy that he sincerely believes the evidence is adequate, in which case the failure is *unintentional*. The following passage occurs just following the bitter scene in which Dom Casmurro confronts his wife with his suspicions and calls for a separation:

> In the meantime, I had recalled the words of the late Gurgel that time at his house when he showed me the portrait of his wife, which resembled Capitú. You must remember them; if not, reread the chapter. I do not place the number of it here, because I no longer remember which it is, but it cannot be far back. They come down to this: there are these inexplicable resemblances.... (p. 265)

The sentence remains uncompleted. In the chapter whose number he has forgotten, Dom Casmurro recounts an incident in which Gurgel, the father of a friend, points out a coincidental resemblance between Capitú and a photograph of his own deceased wife. Gurgel's words were 'Sometimes, in life, there are these strange resemblances.' The Gurgel incident, in other words, forms an innocent precedent for the resemblance between Ezequiel and Escobar, who is now also dead. It is obvious that Machado de Assis is calling our attention to this precedent here, implicating that we should keep in mind the inadequacy of Dom Casmurro's evidence. It is equally clear that Dom Casmurro is himself thinking of the parallel between the two cases. But in the midst of referring to the Gurgel case, he opts out of the maxim of Quantity as it is defined for written discourse. He fails to put down the relevant reference, on the grounds he has forgotten it, and he fails to complete the sentence paraphrasing Gurgel's words. As always, the reader must treat the opting out as a flouting on Machado de Assis's part and must determine what Machado de Assis is trying to implicate by it. A number of solutions are possible, of which these three are perhaps the most likely:

1. Dom Casmurro really did forget the chapter number. In this case his reason for opting out is sincere, and Machado de Assis is flouting the maxim of Quantity for the sheer fun of it. (Machado was a great fan of Sterne's).

2. In view of the weakness of Dom Casmurro's excuse, Machado de Assis is implicating first that in pleading forgetfulness, Dom Casmurro is lying, and second that the real reason Dom Casmurro is opting out is that he does not want to call attention to evidence that would undermine his case against Capitú.

3. In view of the weakness of Dom Casmurro's excuse, Machado de Assis is implicating that Dom Casmurro is indirectly or even subconsciously trying to call attention to evidence against him in order to confess by implicature what he is too guilt-ridden to confess outright. In this case, in pleading forgetfullness, Dom Casmurro is flouting the maxim of Quality and implicating that he remembers Gurgel's words all too well and wants us to remember them too.

The same three possibilities are raised on another occasion a few pages earlier when, in the middle of a chapter, Dom Casmurro interrupts himself to say:

> Pardon me, but this chapter ought to have been preceded by another, in which I would have told an incident that occurred a few weeks before, two months after Sancha had gone away. I will write it. I could place it ahead of this one before sending the book to the printer, but it is too great a nuisance to have to change the page numbers. Let it go right here; after that the narration will proceed as it should right to the end. Besides, it is short. (p. 251)

Again, Dom Casmurro opts out of the rules for written discourse, and again his excuse is a weak one: the reordered chapter is short and it's too much trouble to change the page numbers. In the 'misplaced' chapter, Dom Casmurro relates an incident in which his wife calls his attention to the 'strange expression in Ezequiel's eyes', an expression which she says she has seen only twice before, in the eyes of a friend of her father's and in the eyes of Escobar. Again, then, the passage which occasions the opting out contains evidence which undermines Dom Casmurro's case against Capitú: if she had reason to believe Escobar was the father of her son, why would she call her husband's attention to any resemblance between them? Again, the three interpretations outlined above are possible.

Depending on which of the three interpretations he adopts for these two cases of opting out, the reader will respond differently to the crucial final passage of the book:

> Well, whatever may be the solution, one thing remains and it is the sum of sums, the rest of the residuum, to wit, that my first love [Capitú] and my greatest friend [Escobar], both so loving me, both so loved, were destined to join together and deceive me.... May the earth rest lightly on them! Let us proceed to the *History of the Suburbs* [the next book Dom Casmurro proposes to write]. (p. 277)

For all readers, the first sentence of this passage fails to fulfill the second maxim of Quality. Hence, for all readers, Machado de Assis is flouting the maxim of Quality here. The question is what Machado de Assis is implicating that Dom Casmurro is doing. For the reader who has adopted interpretation (1) above, the failure is *unintentional*. Machado de Assis is implicating that Dom Casmurro is laboring under a hideous delusion. For the reader adopting interpretation (2), Dom Casmurro here *violates* the maxim of Quality. He knows his evidence is inadequate but is trying to conceal this fact and to mislead the audience into believing Capitú was guilty. For the reader with interpretation (3), Dom Casmurro here *flouts* the maxim of Quality, implicating that he knows he was unjust and that he feels so guilty he cannot talk about it directly. Machado de Assis may be and probably is implicating at least all three interpretations, as in Grice's example of the multiply ambiguous line from Blake.[8]

My purpose in offering these examples is to show that it is possible for the fictional speaker of a work of literature to fail to fulfill the CP and maxims in at least the following ways: opting out, clash, unintentional failure, violation, and flouting. I have also suggested that in all such cases, the fictional speaker's failures count as flouting on the part of the author. In order to cooperate as the literary speech situation requires, the reader confronting a violated maxim in a literary work must interpret the violation as being in accord with the 'accepted purpose or direction of the exchange' in which he and the author are engaged. The reader must assume that regardless of what the fictional speaker is doing, the author is observing the CP as defined for display texts; and he must calculate all the implicatures necessary to maintain this assumption. Consequently, when a fictional speaker fails to fulfill a maxim, it will usually be the case that the author is implicating things in addition to what the fictional speaker is saying or implicating.

In all the examples discussed, the fictional speaker's failures have the same basic effect. In all, it is not only the experiences reported which are unusual and problematic, but the report itself. The verbal version the speaker offers fails to elicit our understanding of events or our agreement with the speaker's interpretation of events. The fictional speaker thus produces a lack of consensus, and the author implicates that this lack of consensus is part of what he is displaying, part of what he wants us to experience, evaluate, and interpret. He may intend us to replace the speaker's version with a better one, question our own interpretive faculties, or simply delight in the imaginative exercise of calculating 'what's really going on'. He may be implicating an ironic or critical comment on literature itself. As I shall be discussing in chapter six, display texts of this type, in which the verbal representation itself is problematic, are also common in nonliterary discourse.

One of the main reasons I chose to focus in this chapter on Grice's account of deviance is the fact that the presence of intentional deviance in works of literature has been one of the arguments most often adduced to support the poetic language doctrine. The fact that literary works tolerate and even relish linguistic deviance is often felt to be the conclusive evidence that the function of language in literary works is indeed not primarily communicative (whereas its function elsewhere is). More often, of course, the explicit or implicit assumptions are somewhat more value-laden: ordinary language will do well enough for the ordinary verbal activities of ordinary people, but as a vehicle for aesthetic expression it is so inadequate that no one could blame the poet for escaping the confines of its rules. In its extreme form, the argument views the rules governing ordinary language as incompatible with aesthetic creation and makes deviance the essence of poetry (cf. Mukařovský: 'the violation of the norm of the standard, its systematic violation, is what makes possible the poetic utilization of language' [1932, p. 20]). As support for a linguistically autonomous literature, the argument depends of course on the assumption that intentional deviance does not occur outside literature or does not occur in the same way it does in literature. Grice's account of rule-breaking in conversation clearly shows that intentional deviance does occur routinely outside literature. And the fact that Grice's account seems perfectly able to handle deviance within literature as well shows that there are no clear grounds for distinguishing the way deviance occurs in the two supposedly opposed realms of discourse. In this regard, it is perhaps worth reiterating that fictivity cannot be viewed as a form of 'poetic deviance' either. As I discussed earlier, fictive or 'imitation' speech acts are readily found in almost any realm of discourse, and our ability to produce and interpret them must be viewed as part of our normal linguistic and cognitive competence, not as some special by-product of it.

Notes

1 If I am not mistaken, any rule of asymmetric conjunction needs to distinguish between narrative clauses as defined by Labov, that is, simple past tense clauses, and other kinds of clauses which less readily implicate temporal sequence. The algorithm will vary, I think, according to whether the first conjunct does or does not denote an event. A number of Schmerling's counterexamples to analyses like Ruhl's and Grice's could be better understood if the difference between event and nonevent clauses were recognized, e.g. Schmerling's 'be nice and kiss your granny' could not imply temporal sequence because the first clause is not an event.
2 'Violate' is used here in the general sense of 'fail to fulfill' as opposed to the special sense of 'quiet and unostentatious violation' (or lying) which Grice gives it above (p. 382). Like Grice, I have also found it necessary upon occasion to use 'violate' in these two senses, but I believe it is clear from the context which sense is intended in a given case.
3 It could be argued that Shandy is producing a display text, too, and intends to. This does not alter the fact that he has opted out of the rules for autobiography.
4 Landolfi's parodic intent will perhaps be better understood in the light of the following passage from a real biography of Gogol. The reader will not fail to appreciate the similarities between this passage and those I have quoted from Landolfi's story, particularly as regards clashes:

It is striking that Gogol appears to have had no relationships with women, either in his free and easy St Petersburg years or later. This circumstance has provided psychoanalysts with a great deal of material for strange hypotheses, but it would hardly pay to go into them. As always in such cases, a grain of truth is present, but the attempt to explain the whole body of Gogol's works, his religious upheaval, his illnesses on the basis of sexual inhibitions, is certainly farfetched. His sexual attitudes are usually explained by excessive onanism during his school days; and this is also said to have led to severe psychic depressions, since Gogol saw in it a grievous sin. Gogol himself emphatically denied this assertion at the end of his life. The alleged evidence for it lacks plausibility. It may be that there is something to these claims, but one should guard against exaggerations (Vsevolod Setchkarev, *Gogol: His Life and Works*, trans. Robert Kramer [New York University Press, 1965], pp. 38–9).
5 'The keeper came across the yard and said the warden wished to see me. I went to his office and he got me to sign some document. I noticed that he was in black, with pin-stripe trousers. He picked up the telephone receiver and looked at me.

'The undertaker's men arrived some moments ago, and they will be going to the mortuary to screw down the coffin. Shall I tell them to wait, for you to have a last glimpse of your mother?'

'No,' I said.

He spoke into the receiver, lowering his voice.

'That's all right, Figeac, Figeac. Tell the men to go there now.'

6 Morally and critically speaking, Camus's attempt has been more successful than we might wish it to be. Meursault's linguistic detachment and his rhetorical innocence have helped foster the conventional view of Meursault as a victim of social oppression and a man who 'accepts death for the sake of truth', as Camus himself put it. As Conor Cruise O'Brien (1970) points out, it is rather startling that several generations of readers should have adopted this view of a man who, besides committing a murder, collaborates in an acquaintance's sordid plot to deceive and humiliate his mistress, stands by while the mistress gets beaten up rather than calling the police, and lies in court to save the friend from punishment for the beating. As O'Brien observes, the myth of Meursault's innocence and martyrdom is partly the result of the power of critics to overshadow the book. But the kind of stylistic mechanisms I have been discussing contribute as well. Meursault's detachment from his actions deadens their moral impact, dehumanizes his victims, and helps the reader forget them, as everyone else in the book does, when Meursault is brought to trial.

7 Yesterday I saw a strange thing, though it happens every day in Paris.

All the people gather together after dinner, and play at a kind of dramatic performance which I have heard called a comedy. The main action occurs on a platform that is called the stage. On each side of it there are small recesses called boxes, and here men and women play together at a dumb show, rather like those to which we are accustomed in Persia.

8 Historically speaking, there does exist a fourth option for the reader of *Dom Casmurro*. For several decades after the novel appeared, the possibilities of the narrator's unreliability and the wife's innocence were not recognized. Dom Casmurro was viewed as the unfortunate victim of betrayal he claims to be, and Capitú was viewed as the beautiful, calculating social climber he says she was. This view of the novel still has credence in some quarters today. If this view is adopted, neither Machado de Assis nor Dom Casmurro has failed to fulfill either of the maxims of Quality, and Dom Casmurro's habit of opting out must be explained in some other way not directly connected with the subject of his narrative. This interpretation must be rejected, however, because it lacks explanatory power and because it requires the reader to make an unsupported assumption, namely the assumption that there is adequate evidence of adultery. Nevertheless, the fact that disagreement over narrator reliability can arise both in the case of *Moll Flanders* and *Dom Casmurro* demonstrates that toying with the maxims of Quality is a risky business indeed within literature as well as outside it. Unless an author makes very clear who is lying and who is not, be a liable to create misunderstandings himself.

References

Fillmore, Charles (1974). 'The future of semantics'. In Fillmore, Lakoff, and Lakoff, *Berkeley Studies in Syntax and Semantics*, 1974, IV, 1–38.

Grice, H. Paul. *Logic and Conversation*. 1967 William James Lectures, Harvard University. Unpublished manuscript, 1967. Excerpt in Cole and Morgan, *Syntax and Semantics, Vol. III: Speech Acts*, 1975.

Labov, William. *Language in the Inner City*. Philadelphia: University of Pennsylvania Press, 1972.

Mukařovský, Jan (1932). 'Standard language and poetic language.' In Garvin, *A Prague School Reader on Esthetics, Literary Structure, and Style*, 1955, pp. 19–35.

O'Brien, Conor Cruise. *Albert Camus of Europe and Africa*. New York: Viking, 1970.

Ohmann, Richard. 'Speech acts and the definition of literature.' *Philosophy and Rhetoric* 4 (1971): 1–19.

——. 'Speech, literature and the space between'. *New Literary History* 5 (1974): 37–63.

Ong, Walter. 'The writer's audience is always a fiction.' *PMLA* 90 (1974): 9–21.

Sartre, Jean Paul (1943). 'Camus's *The Outsider*.' In *Literary and Philosophical Essays*. Translated by Annette Michelson. New York: Criterion Press, 1955.

Schmerling, Susan F. 'Asymmetric conjunction and rules of conversation.' In Cole and Morgan, *Syntax and Semantics, Vol. III: Speech Acts*, 1975, pp. 211–232.

Suggestions for further reading

No attempt at a comprehensive bibliography of stylistics is made in the listings which follow. Complete bibliographical references in stylistics are available in the following works:
Bailey, Richard, and Dolores Burton (eds.). *English Stylistics: A Bibliography.* Cambridge, Mass.: The MIT Press, 1968.
Enkvist, Nils Erik. *Linguistic Stylistics.* The Hague and Paris: Mouton, 1973.
Milic, Louis T. (ed.) *Style and Stylistics: An Analytical Bibliography.* New York: The Free Press, 1967.

The Bailey-Burton bibliography has been updated annually in *Style* since its publication.

General theory

Chatman, Seymour (ed.). *Literary Style: A Symposium.* New York and London: Oxford University Press, 1971.
—— and Samuel R. Levin (eds.). *Essays on the Language of Literature.* Boston: Houghton Mifflin, 1967.
Enkvist, Nils Erik, John Spencer, and Michael J. Gregory. *Linguistics and Style.* Oxford: Oxford University Press, 1964.
Fowler, Roger. *Essays on Style and Language.* London: Routledge & Kegan Paul, 1966.
——. 'On the interpretation of "nonsense strings"'. *Journal of Linguistics*, 5 (1969), 75–83.
——. *The Languages of Literature.* London: Routledge & Kegan Paul, 1971.

—— (ed.). *Style and Structure in Literature: Essays in the New Stylistics*. Oxford: Blackwell, 1975.
Freeman, Donald C. 'Literature', in *A Survey of Applied Linguistics*, ed. H. Douglas Brown and Ronald Wardhaugh. Ann Arbor: University of Michigan Press, 1976. Pp. 229–49.
Hendricks, William O. *Essay in Semiolinguistics and Verbal Art*. The Hague and Paris: Mouton, 1973.
——. *Grammars of Style and Styles of Grammar*. Amsterdam: North-Holland, 1976.
Jacobs, Roderick A., and Peter S. Rosenbaum. *Transformations, Style, and Meaning*. Waltham, Mass.: Xerox College Publishing, 1971.
Jakobson, Roman. 'Linguistics and poetics', in *Style in Language*, ed. Thomas A. Sebeok. Cambridge, Mass.: The MIT Press, 1960. Pp. 350–8.
Kachru, Braj B., and H. W. Stahlke (eds.). *Current Trends in Stylistics*. Champaign, Ill. and Edmonton, Alberta: Linguistics Research, Inc., 1972.
Sebeok, Thomas A. (ed.) *Style in Language*. Cambridge, Mass., 1960.
Smith, Barbara Herrnstein. *On the Margins of Discourse*. Chicago: University of Chicago Press, 1978.
Uitti, Karl. *Linguistics and Literary Theory*. Englewood Cliffs, NJ: Prentice-Hall, 1969.
van Dijk, Teun A. *Pragmatics of Language and Literature*. Amsterdam: North-Holland, 1976.

Approaches to poetics

Austin, Timothy. *A Linguistic Approach to the Style of the Early English Romantic Poets*. University of Massachusetts unpub. diss., 1977.
Banfield, Ann M. *Stylistic Transformations: A Study Based on the Syntax of Paradise Lost*. University of Wisconsin unpub. diss., 1973.
Burton, Dolores M. *Shakespeare's Grammatical Style*. Austin: University of Texas Press, 1973.
Chatman, Seymour. 'Milton's participial style'. *PMLA*, 83 (1968), 1386–99.
—— (ed.). *Approaches to Poetics*. New York: Columbia University Press, 1973.
Culler, Jonathan. *Structuralist Poetics*. Ithaca: Cornell University Press, 1975.
Dillon, G. L. 'Inversions and deletions in English poetry'. *Language and Style*, 8 (1975), 220–37.
Fairley, Irene. *E. E. Cummings and Ungrammar*. Searingtown, NY: Watermill Press, 1975.
Freeman, Donald C. 'Iconic syntax in poetry: a note on Blake's "Ah! Sun-Flower!"', in *University of Massachusetts Occasional Papers in Linguistics*, 2 (1976), ed. Justine T. Stillings, pp. 51–7.
——. 'Syntax and romantic poetics', in *Proceedings of the XII. International Congress of Linguists*, ed. Wolfgang Dressler and Volker Meid. Innsbruck: Innsbrucker Beiträge zur Sprachwissenschaft, 1978, pp. 654–7.
——. 'The grammar of ungrammar'. *Semiotica*, 22 (1978), 369–85.
Jakobson, Roman. 'Poetry of grammar and grammar of poetry'. *Lingua*, 21 (1968), 597–609.
—— and L. G. Jones. *Shakespeare's Verbal Art in 'Th'expence of Spirit'*. The Hague and Paris: Mouton, 1970.

Leech, Geoffrey N. *A Linguistic Guide to English Poetry*. London: Longmans, 1969.
Levin, Samuel R. *Linguistic Structures in Poetry*. The Hague: Mouton, 1962.
——. *The Semantics of Metaphor*. Baltimore: Johns Hopkins University Press, 1977.

Approaches to metrics

Beaver, Joseph C. 'A grammar of prosody'. *College English*, 29 (1968), 310–21.
——. 'Contrastive stress and metered verse'. *Language and Style*, 2 (1969), 257–71.
——. 'Current metrical issues'. *College English*, 33 (1971), 177–97.
Chatman, Seymour. *A Theory of Meter*. The Hague: Mouton, 1965.
Epstein, E. L., and Terence Hawkes. *Linguistics and English Prosody. Studies in Linguistics*, Occasional Papers, 7, University of Buffalo, 1959.
Freeman, Donald C. 'On the primes of metrical style'. *Language and Style*, 1 (1968), 63–101.
——. 'Metrical position constituency and generative metrics'. *Language and Style*, 2 (1969), 195–206.
——. 'Current trends in metrics', in *Current Trends in Stylistics*, ed. Braj B. Kachru and H. W. Stahlke. Champaign, Ill., and Edmonton, Alberta: Linguistics Research, Inc., 1972. Pp. 69–81.
Halle, Morris. 'On meter and prosody', in *Progress in Linguistics*, ed. Manfred Bierwisch and K. R. Heidolph. The Hague and Paris: Mouton, 1970. Pp. 64–80.
—— and Samuel Jay Keyser. *English Stress: Its Form, Its Growth, and Its Role in Verse*. New York: Harper & Row, 1971.
——. 'Illustration and defense of a theory of the iambic pentameter'. *College English*, 33 (1971), 154–76.
Hascall, Dudley. 'Some contributions to the Hall-Keyser theory of prosody'. *College English*, 30 (1969), 357–65.
Keyser, Samuel Jay. 'Old English prosody'. *College English*, 30 (1968), 331–56.
——. 'The linguistic basis of English prosody', in *Modern Studies in English*, ed. David Reibel and Sanford A. Schane. Englewood Cliffs, NJ: Prentice-Hall, Inc., 1969. Pp. 379–94.
Zhirmunskij, V. *Introduction to Metrics*. The Hague: Mouton, 1966.

Approaches to prose style

Adolph, Robert. *The Rise of Modern Prose Style*. Cambridge, Mass.: The MIT Press, 1968.
Chatman, Seymour. *The Later Style of Henry James*. Oxford: Blackwell, 1972.
Cluett, Robert. *Prose Style and Critical Reading*. New York: Teachers College Press, 1976.
Dillon, George L. *Language Processing and the Reading of Literature*. Bloomington: Indiana University Press, 1978.
Halliday, M. A. K. 'The linguistic study of literary texts', in *Proceedings of the Ninth International Congress of Linguists*, ed. Horace Lunt. The Hague: Mouton, 1964. Pp. 302–7.
Hayes, Curtis W. 'A transformational-generative approach to style: Samuel Johnson and Edward Gibbon'. *Language and Style*, 1 (1968), 39–48.

Jacobs, Roderick A. 'Transformational analysis and the study of style', in Jacobs (ed.), *Studies in Language*. Lexington, Mass.: Xerox College Publishing, 1972. Pp. 87–100.
Kroeber, Karl. *Styles in Fictional Structure*. Princeton: Princeton University Press, 1971.
Lodge, David. *Language of Fiction*. London: Routledge & Kegan Paul, 1966.
Martin, Harold C. (ed.) *Style in Prose Fiction*. New York: Columbia University Press, 1959.
Ohmann, Richard. 'Prolegomena to the analysis of prose style', in *Style in Prose Fiction*, ed. Harold C. Martin. New York: Columbia University Press, 1959. Pp. 1–24.
——. *Shaw: The Style and the Man*. Middletown, Conn.: Wesleyan University Press, 1962.
——. 'Mentalism in the study of literary language', in *Proceedings of the Conference on Language and Language Behavior*, ed. E. M. Zale. New York: Appleton-Century-Crofts, 1968. Pp. 188–212.
——. 'Speech acts and the definition of literature'. *Philosophy and Rhetoric*, 4 (1971), 1–9.
Pratt, Mary Louise. *A Speech Act Theory of Literary Discourse*. Bloomington: Indiana University Press, 1977.